Martin's Hundred

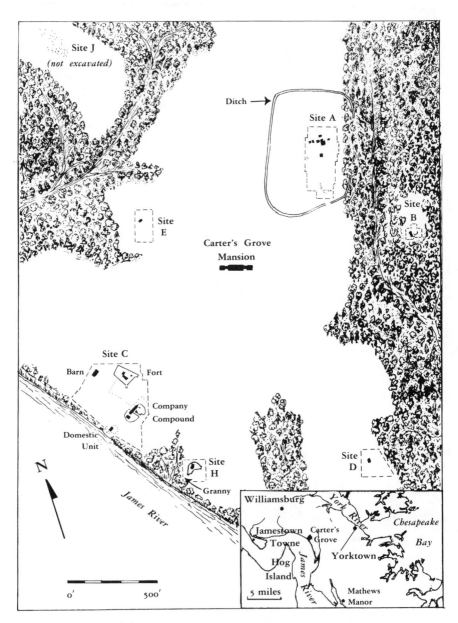

Part of the Carter's Grove tract showing the principal
seventeenth-century settlement sites in the vicinity
of the eighteenth-century Burwell mansion.

Martin's hundred

by

Ivor Noël hume

University Press of Virginia
Charlottesville and London

THE UNIVERSITY PRESS OF VIRGINIA
Copyright © 1979, 1981, 1982 by Ivor Noël Hume

Revised and Expanded Paperback Edition

First University Press of Virginia printing 1991

Copyright © 1991 by the Rector and
Visitors of the University of Virginia
Published by arrangement with Alfred A. Knopf, Inc.

Permission to reproduce photographs
and other illustrations is found after the index.

Library of Congress Cataloging-in-Publication Data
Noël Hume, Ivor.
    Martin's Hundred / by Ivor Noël Hume. — Rev. and expanded pbk.
ed.
        p.   cm.
    Originally published: New York : Knopf, 1982.
    Includes bibliographical references and index.
    ISBN 0-394-50728-2 (cloth). — ISBN 0-8139-1323-3 (pbk.)
    1. Martin's Hundred Site (Va.) 2. Carter's Grove (Va.)
3. Wolstenholme Towne (Va.) 4. Carter, Robert, 1663–1732—Homes and
haunts—Virginia. 5. Noël Hume, Ivor. I. Title.
F234.M378N63   1991
975.5'425—dc20   90-22565
                                                                      CIP

Printed in the United States of America

For Mary and Carl

A Proclamation

By the Governoᵣ and Capᵗ generall of Virginia

In consideration of Gods most mercifull deliverance of so many in this Cuntrie of Virginia from the treachery of the Indians on the 22ᵗʰ day of March last: The Governor wᵗʰ the advice of the Counsell of State hath thought it very fitt, that the 22ᵗʰ day of March both this present yeare and for ever hereafter (in memory of that great preservation) be in this Cuntrie celebrated Holy: And therefore doth straightly charg and Comand [the commander of each plantation], that he, and all other that are in any way undᵣ his charge, do keep that day holy, spending the same in prayer thanksgiveing to God, and other holy exercises; not suffering any of them to worke, as he will answer the contrary at his perill. Given at James Cittie the 4ᵗʰ day of March 1622.

FRANCIS WYATT.[1]

Contents

Illustrations

Foreword

Whentarg hen, on November 26, 1922, Howard Carter knocked a small hole through the blocked doorway leading to Tutankhamen's tomb, his sponsor, Lord Carnarvon, asked: "Can you see anything?" Peering into the shadows beyond the light from his flickering candle, Carter answered: "Yes, wonderful things."

Most Egyptologists would gladly have traded their future careers to have been in Carter's shoes at that moment and to have been the one to utter those words. But just as few authors write a bestseller and few rock groups cut a gold record, so few archaeologists make a discovery that fires the popular imagination or that contributes something to human knowledge that will live on after they are gone. Rarely are we given the opportunity to peer into the past and to see wonderful things that no one has seen before. What keeps us going is the hope that it might happen—and for those of us exploring a seemingly routine eighteenth-century site in Virginia, it did.

On land once known as Martin's Hundred, we were to raise the curtain on one of the most dramatic episodes in early British-American history, events hitherto known only through a few documentary records that were often as confusing as they were enlightening. The international press and television interest generated by our discoveries took most of us by surprise —particularly since the only gold we found was limited to the gilding on a spur and an inlay on a knife handle. As was inevitable, some of the attention proved downright embarrassing; nevertheless, much of it provided a welcome means of introducing our story to a far wider audience than ever would be served through the pages of scholarly journals or in the sleep-provoking gloom of the lecture hall. It is sad that the record of most of the world's archaeological discoveries never reaches the general public, lying instead mummified in the jargon of pseudo-science, languishing unread on library shelves, its pages investigated only by nimble-footed silverfish. But when, like Tut's gold or the *Vasa*'s incredible salvage, the discovery does excite popular interest, there is the need not only to write a scholarly treatise but also to preserve the history of the excavation itelf, for that too is a legitimate part of the record.

Here, then, is the warts-and-all anatomy of an excavation—a project designed to answer what should have been relatively simple questions, but which failed to do so, and instead stumbled into the wrong century. Research originally estimated to take a month or six weeks was still incomplete five years later. Before we were through, our net stretched to ruined forts in Northern Ireland, a mountain pass on the West Indian island of St. Eustatius, through the storerooms of the Tower of London, among crumbling coffins in the vault of an English parish church, past the wreck of a Dutch East Indiaman off the Australian coast, to a typically bizarre British murder investigation, and to a man who escaped from prison hidden in a box of books.

The variety of the studies generated by our digging, and the remarkable coincidences that led us into some of the darker alleys of seventeenth-century life, made the post-excavation hunt for answers to the questions that were raised as stimulating as the uncovering of the archaeological remains themselves. In these chapters I propose to chronicle both, letting them unfold in bits and pieces, a clue here and another there, sometimes fitting quickly and easily together, but just as often sending us out on a limb and leaving us there.

If my use of the personal pronoun gives the impression that the search for Wolstenholme Towne became as solitary and single-minded as Captain Ahab's pursuit of his white whale, nothing could be more misleading. Ahab had a crew; ours was a team.

Through most of the four years' digging, the work was supervised by senior archaeologist Eric Klingelhofer, who, with his assistant Bill Henry, kept the team's spirits up through winter's bitter cold and summer's humid heat. While they endured temperatures that for days hovered around 102 degrees Fahrenheit, and suffered the pain and irritation of poison ivy and chiggers—not to mention the prospect of snakes in a trailer closet, I spent much of my time in an air-conditioned office seven miles away in Williamsburg. When, for hours and sometimes days, the excavators and laborers did nothing but scrape acres of sun-parched clay in search of the faint discoloration that marked the location of a long-gone post, I could be content to watch progress as it developed on the master plan tacked up on the drafting-room wall. Unlike the directors of more far-flung excavations, who have nowhere to go but to their sites, I enjoyed the luxury of being there only when something important turned up. In short, I was given the privilege of skipping most of the "dull" bits.

This is no place to name each of the many team members who worked with us for longer or shorter periods through the four years of digging. They know who they are, and how much both I and the Martin's Hundred discoveries owe to their efforts. Only foreman Nathaniel Smith was with us from beginning to end, an ever-present anchor as reliable as any mariner could hope to find. Ruth Anne Clarke kept our visual record, and in the laboratory, conservator Gary McQuillen wrought enough miracles to run for Messiah, while artifact artist Patricia Kidd restored two-dimensional life to the deadest of shattered objects. All of their talent and labor would have availed us little without an analysis of the equally fragmentary historical evidence by research associate Audrey Noël Hume—whose down-to-document logic was so often aimed and fired with devastating accuracy at the best of my interpretive trial balloons. At the same time, she and the rest of us owed much to the careful preliminary historical studies provided by Colonial Williamsburg historians Kevin Kelly and Harold Gill, as well as to the shared wisdom of curator of textiles Mildred Lanier and curator of metalwork John Davis.

On our finding that we were lunging into the wrong century, the excavations might well have been called off had it not been for the enlightened support of Carlisle H. Humelsine, the president, and later chairman, of Colonial Williamsburg. Even that would not have kept us in the field year after year without the intervention of the National Geographic Society's chairman emeritus, Dr. Melville Bell Grosvenor, who threw the society's financial support behind us at the moment that it was most needed.

Just as large-scale excavations must be fueled with substantial infusions of money, so does the resulting research quickly wither without help from scholars who may have no direct interest in our project, and on whose generosity we trespass when we seek to steal time from their own studies. Howard Blackmore, deputy master of the armouries at the Tower of London, confessed that he shuddered whenever he found a letter of mine in his morning mail. Three in one week, he told me, was almost more than he could bear. Never once, however, did he decline to lead me through the uncertainties of early seventeenth-century arms and armor identification, any more than did the master of the armouries, A. V. B. Norman, and his keeper of armour, Ian D. Eaves, or the always helpful Claude Blair, keeper of the department of metalwork at the Victoria and Albert Museum. Until his untimely death in 1978, I was constantly beholden to America's foremost expert on colonial arms and armor, Harold L. Peterson, senior curator for the United States National Park Service.

At the Museum of London I received frequent and diverse assistance from its keeper of the Tudor and Stuart department, Philippa Glanville, and her successor Rosemary Weinstein, as well as from archaeologist Geoffrey Egan. For help with my pictorial research, and for their hospitality and generosity, I am deeply grateful to Sir Hereward and Lady Wake of Courteenhall, Northamptonshire, and to William Middlebrook, dean of Trent Polytechnic at Clifton Hall in Nottinghamshire. At Stanmore, Mrs. Jean

Crowden gave me access to her late husband's notes on the life of Sir John Wolstenholme, and introduced me to Sir John's puzzling death mask. In Northern Ireland, Dr. Robert J. Hunter, professor of history at the New University of Ulster, joyously led me through the bogs and quicksands of that country's Plantation Period, while archaeologists Brooke Blades and Brian Lacey did their best to provide artifactual answers to my questions about the quality of British colonial life in Ireland. Writing from his great classical site at Aphrodisias in Turkey, the distinguished New York University archaeologist Dr. Kenan Erim offered his thoughts on matters of mortality—and sent pictures to illuminate them.

For help in securing both information and illustrations for the expanded edition, I am much in the debt of archaeologist Dr. Carmel Schrire of Rutgers University who discovered coffin nails where they were supposed to be and chartered surveyor François Jones who found the Exton grave and had the wisdom to photograph it. I owe no less to the Victoria and Albert Museum's funerary pundit, my good friend Julian Litten, and to the Reverend John Flory who allowed us to inject a modicum of chaos into his church at Lydiard Tregoze, as well as to Dr. Margaret Rule whose brilliant excavation of Henry VIIIth's flagship the *Mary Rose* indirectly contributed a postscript to our coffin research.

For a multitude of kindnesses as well as much practical help in Bermuda, I owe more than I can say to Peggy and Allan "Smokey" Wingood, and no less to Edna and Teddy Tucker, also to artist Tracey Eve and wildlife conservator David Wingate. In Sweden, generous and unstinted help was provided by *Vasa* curator Hans Soop and his assistant Ingrid Kaijser, and we could have asked for or received no more from Peter Krenn, curator of the Landeszeughaus at Graz in Austria. To the Earl and Countess De La Warr, who let me disarrange their ancestors and still took us home to lunch, I can say only that their contribution to the history of the English coffin was a pearl of great price.

For medical and pathological advice I am indebted to Dr. D. K. Wiecking, chief medical examiner for the Commonwealth of Virginia, to his ever-helpful deputy Dr. Marcella Fierro, and to Dr. Samuel V. Dunkell, director of the Insomnia Clinic at the New York Hospital's Payne Whitney Clinic. In England, Sir Gordon Wolstenholme, past president of the Royal Society of Medicine and a collateral descendant of "our" Sir John Wolstenholme, generously obtained opinions from colleagues in the forensic and orthopedic branches of his profession, and pathologist Dr. Peter Jerreat reviewed our evidence in the light of his experience as an authority on murder by spade. No one, however, has helped us more than the Smithsonian Institution's curator of physical anthropology, Dr. J. Lawrence Angel, whose on-site study of the close to fifty human burials found at Martin's Hundred provided us with the most authoritative analysis obtainable anywhere in the United States. To Larry, and to Peggy—his wive and scribe—my admiration and gratitude. I have as much difficulty finding sufficient superlatives to properly acknowledge the generosity of medical illustrator and sculptress Betty Pat Gatliff, who volunteered to come to Williamsburg from her home in Oklahoma to reconstruct the features of our first identifiable massacre victim.

For help in testing my belief that much of the pottery unearthed in Martin's Hundred was made in Virginia, I am indebted to Dr. Stephen C. Clement, chairman of the department of geology at the College of William and Mary, whose resulting discoveries may yet provide archaeologists with a new approach to identifying the sources of excavated ceramic bodies. Our research into seventeenth-century coffin characteristics was helped by William and Mary professor of anthropology Dr. Norman Barka, who gave us access to his notes on burials at Flowerdew Hundred. Then, too, I have been similarly aided by my old friend and father of historical archaeology in America, J. C. "Pinky" Harrington, who allowed me to use information about the archaeological history of Jamestown assembled for his own, yet-to-be-published account of work there in the 1930s.

To name all those who have freely given of their wisdom would be akin to identifying each of our crew members; but it would be churlish not to single out Dr. William M. Kelso, who, early in his career, accepted the unenviable task of supervising the preliminary Carter's Grove survey, for it was he who first uncovered evidence there of seventeenth-century occupation. From those small beginnings stemmed the saga of Martin's Hundred—while Bill Kelso went on to become commissioner of archaeology for the Commonwealth of Virginia and one of America's most respected archaeologists.

Because the popular dissemination of our discoveries assumed unexpected and ever-growing importance, I found myself indebted to many people who normally have no place in a strictly archaeological project. Our television film was nursed through weaning and adolescence by the understanding and talented hands of Arthur L. Smith, Colonial Williamsburg's audio-visual department director. At the *National Geographic* offices my constant and long-suffering mentor was Mary Griswold Smith, whose friendship has been among the project's lasting blessings; the same proved true of the National Geographic Society's lecture program chairman, Joanne Hess, who found herself saddled with steering me safely through a Washington press conference and onto the awe-provoking platform of Constitution Hall. Then, too, there were the magazine's able photographers, Ira Block, David Brill, David Arnold, and Jospeh Bailey, who successfully focused their talents on many an unpromising subject, and the Society's curator Peter Purpura, who skillfully conquered similar problems when it came time for us to design and mount the first exhibition of our finds. To those who had to write about them, I offer my felicitude, particularly to National Geographic Society science writer Donald Frederick, who was condemned to compose four press releases about the same subject, and to trying to make his hard-nosed readers believe that they had not heard it all before. That the press coverage was so overwhelming was due in great measure to Don's skill—save on one occasion when it stemmed from the prizeworthy writing of the *Richmond Times Dispatch's* able Williamsburg correspondent, W. Wilford Kale, Jr.

Film, photographs, and word pictures would have been insufficient tools with which to reconstruct the Martin's Hundred story had it not been for the major contributions made by artist Richard Schlecht. He alone could transform images otherwise locked in an archaeologist's mind into a visual recreation of what we believe the Wolstenholme Towne community may have looked like.

I owe more than I can say to my wife, Audrey, for minimizing my literary excesses and for constantly looking stuff up, and to Dr. Thad Tate who very kindly reviewed the manuscript and helped me avoid several slips. I am obliged, too, to Dr. J. Lawrence Angel, David Brill, Dr. Marcella Fierro, Donald Frederick, Betty Pat Gatliff, Dr. Melville Bell Grosvenor, Arthur L. Smith, and Mary Griswold Smith, all of whom read parts of the text and made valuable suggestions for its improvement. No less do I owe to my longtime editor and friend Angus Cameron who cared enough about this manuscript to let it trespass on his retirement.

The resulting account of the 1976 to 1980 excavations, and of the concurrent research, makes no pretense at being the last word on Martin's Hundred. The continuing pursuit of documentary sources and the interpretation of the multitude of artifacts will take several more years. Only then can we publish a final report having any hope of unflinchingly withstanding scholarly scrutiny. Consequently, neither the views nor the interpretations tentatively put forward on these pages are necessarily the enduring opinions of the Colonial Williamsburg Foundation—anymore than they may lastingly remain my own.

To those who expect instant and definitive conclusions placing the archaeology of Martin's Hundred in a broader historical context, I can plead only that we see ourselves as slow and plodding brickmakers. If our bricks prove reliable, that is accomplishment enough. Others may build with them what they wish.

I.N.H.

Preface to the Virginia Edition

As archaeological work of every kind grows more expensive and funding becomes ever harder to corral, such adjectives as *significant* and *first* are writ large on every grant proposal and fall trippingly from directorial lips. In time, of course, the wolf syndrome is recognized for what it is, and new levels of superlatives must be found. The small project that can promise only more of the same, but which if carried through might yield information of undreamed importance, stands little chance of being funded—unless it can be folded into some currently fashionable generic study. Since the days of the lucky yet luckless Belzoni, archaeologists have recognized that their futures can depend on finding something new and preferably revolutionary. Thus in pursuit of recognition we sometimes are guilty of leaping to conclusions with all the agility of kangaroos. What today is dubbed by serious (and usually less successful) colleagues as "courting the media" used to be equally scathingly known as "rushing into print," a charge serious enough to have one blackballed from learned societies—always supposing that the membership could be assembled before you had time to be proved right.

Although historical archaeology in various guises has existed in America for close on a hundred years and acquired a national society as long ago as 1967, the discipline is still a fledgling. Consequently, much that may legitimately be hailed now as a first or as highly significant may find the leaves plucked from its laurels as time and new discoveries broaden the analytical base. In the meantime, however, society has reason to be thankful—and peers cause to be magnanimous—when colleagues risk their reputations on the end of a long limb.

Almost from its outset, the story of the Martin's Hundred project was umbilically linked to the lifeblood of popular acceptance. That it began at all was due to the Colonial Williamsburg Foundation's desire to find historically unimportant space at Carter's Grove that it could put to exhibit use during the 1976 American Bicentennial celebrations. When the chosen site revealed the layout for the *first* early seventeenth-century Virginia plantation to be fully explored, it was of the wrong century to be of interest to the Foundation, and the project would have died at the end of the first season and with only one site revealed had not the National Geographic Society intervened. Without the national and international public interest created by the publication of two articles in the society's magazine, the major site of Wolstenholme Towne would have been backfilled and returned to the plow. Without a nine-month exhibition of the Martin's Hundred artifacts at the society's Washington headquarters where an estimated three quarters of a million people saw them, the collection would have disappeared into stored boxes, perhaps never to be seen again save by a handful of archaeology students. Instead, and thanks to the generosity of the Winthrop Rockefeller Charitable Trust, many now reside in a permanent museum on a site whose partial reconstruction provides knowledge and, equally importantly, pleasure to untold numbers of visitors.

Archaeological purists may dismiss such results as pseudosuccesses pandering to a public equally happy with a trip to Busch Gardens or Wally's World. But if we know what's good for us—and that means project funding—fostering public interest has to be as important an element in archaeological training as a course in surveying or in dating clay pipes. Besides, the historical and prehistoric sites that archaeologists dissect are part of the national heritage. They belong to the People, and we have no business destroying them without giving something in return—something more palatable than an archaeological report intended only for one's peers.

When I began to write this book, that altruistic notion was certainly in my mind, albeit well toward the back. Much more important was my desire to keep the pot of interest boiling long enough to ensure that seventeenth-century Martin's Hundred would not recede from the consciousness and conscience of the organization whose primary mission was, and very properly remains, the preservation and study of eighteenth-century Williamsburg. Written in 1981 while excavations were still in progress, *Martin's Hundred* was essentially a progress report, a warts-and-all journal faithfully chronicling our often faltering steps into a century that remained the Dark Age of Virginia's cultural history.

In bringing the book up to date for this revised edition, I have resisted the temptation to rewrite the bits that turned out to be wrong. To have done so would distort, if not destroy, a page of American archaeological history. I have chosen, instead, to let the warts remain and to summarize the later discoveries and interpretations in two new chapters. In this way, you the reader can see for yourself just how far adrift we were and judge for yourself whether the errors were of such magnitude that the book should have been deferred until we know what we now know—or think we know.

In truth, the story as it can be told thirteen years after the major excavations began is still far from complete. A bewhiskered archaeological adage has it that three months' excavation can be relied on to generate nine of laboratory processing and postdig research and writing. Theoretically, therefore, sixty-six months of digging at Martin's Hundred should generate more than sixteen years of continuous research. That, of course, is nonsense; but it would have been realistic to expect that five or six years of concentrated work would be needed to complete the drafting, artifact conservation, cataloguing, analysis, and publication of the definitive report. Instead, while excavations in Martin's Hundred were still in progress, new projects in eighteenth-century Williamsburg demanded our divided attention and continued to do so through the subsequent years. Consequently, therefore, at the time of its publication, this expanded edition of *Martin's Hundred* continues to stand as the fullest available record of the *first* earliest timber fort to be fully excavated in America, the *first* complete close helmets to be found in the New World, the *first* incontrovertible evidences of the Indians' attempt to oust the English in 1622—in short, a *highly significant* project.

Martin's Hundred

Looking for
the Old Plantation

1

"**B**efore you go back to England, you really should see Carter's Grove. The house has some of the finest paneling in America." It was late in October 1956, and Mario Campiolli, architectural director for the Colonial Williamsburg restoration, was reviewing what I had seen and done during the three months I had spent in Virginia.

On leave from the City of London's Guildhall Museum, I had been invited to Williamsburg to report on eighteenth-century glass recovered in the almost thirty years of archaeological digging since the preservation of Virginia's colonial capital began. The curious train of coincidences which led to that invitation has no relevance here; suffice it to say that word of my research into the dating of seventeenth- and eighteenth-century wine bottles had reached Williamsburg.

Thanks to the generosity of our Colonial Williamsburg hosts, my wife and I had been able to visit many of Virginia's great colonial homes and ruins. Carter's Grove, however, was not one of them. I had been warned that its owner had a reputation for disliking women and might refuse to see me if I had a wife in tow. This apparently formidable person was no male misogynist: Mary Corling Johnson McCrea was a direct descendant of Virginia's colonial governor Alexander Spotswood, and the widow of Archibald McCrea, chairman of Pittsburgh's Union Spring and Manufacturing Company and son of a past president of the Pennsylvania Railroad. After her husband's death in 1937, Mary McCrea lived on in the eighteenth-century mansion that she had saved from ruin in 1928, and that, thanks to the skill and taste of her architect, she had transformed into a home since described as the most beautiful house in America. Mrs. McCrea, too, had her superlatives as one of the beauties of her generation; but to her such accolades meant little; what mattered was that the world should think well of Carter's Grove, and that included visiting British archaeologists—even if one of them was of the wrong sex.

On Saturday, October 27, as we drove the seven miles from Williamsburg, Mario Campiolli explained that in obtaining Mrs. McCrea's permission to visit Carter's Grove, he had only asked that we be allowed to walk through the gardens and to view the mansion's exterior. "She'll be watching us from inside," he said, "and she may or may not be inclined to invite us in." But she did.

Large glasses of bourbon and water quickly dispelled any fears that Mary McCrea's legendary hostility to women would be vented on my wife. Then aged eighty and a ghost of the woman she had been, the mistress of Carter's Grove sat behind the large, horseshoe-shaped table that still dominates the mansion's office room, and for two hours she held court, needing little prompting to tell us about the building's restoration, and recalling details from the 1930s as though they had occurred last week. It was a virtuoso performance that I would always have remembered—even had Carter's Grove not been destined also to become the focus of my life, or at least for five years of it.

Mrs. McCrea showed us the celebrated hall paneling which, in 1881, a vandalously patriotic tenant had painted red, white, and blue to celebrate the centenary of the British capitulation at Yorktown (Fig. 1-1). The great main staircase spoke for itself, though Mrs.

1-1. The paneled hallway at Carter's Grove and the staircase up which Colonel Tarleton is said to have ridden his horse.

McCrea pointed with pride to the small piece of metal driven flush with the wood of the newel post, and told how, in 1781, the British cavalry commander Colonel Banistre Tarleton had ridden his horse up the stairs to waken laggardly troops quartered on the second floor. To emphasize his displeasure, Tarleton had slashed at the banisters with his sabre—and there was the proof, the tip of his blade still impaled in the post. I refrained from asking how a slashing weapon could have been held so that its point could have been thrust straight down, and I ignored what appeared to be the mark of a hammer blow just where the metal had been driven home. It would have been churlish, too, to inquire how the colonel had managed to continue his dramatic ascent after getting his sabre so embarrassingly stuck. Instead, we moved dutifully on to the scene of another Carter's Grove drama, the room where Thomas Jefferson was said to have proposed marriage to Rebecca Burwell and where George Washington had no better luck with Mary Cary.

"It's called the Refusal Room," Mrs. McCrea explained, "and it's haunted." She went on to tell us how, if flowers were left there overnight, their heads would be on the floor by morning. No self-respecting Virginia mansion is without its specters and stray bits of ectoplasm, and Carter's Grove was up there with the best. It even had a dueling legend, a fight between "two hotbloods," one of whom, in the best tradition, "fell mortally wounded"; and if that was not spine-tingling enough, Carter's Grove could also offer a totally undocumented legend that two pirates lie buried in its basement.

Like so much popular history, the best bits are best left unprobed. To Mary McCrea, as the shadows gathered on that October afternoon in 1956, fact and fiction were inextricably entwined; they were part of the magic of the place, and it mattered little that magic and illusion are firmly bonded. Fourteen years later (ten years after Mary McCrea's death), archaeology would give credence to at least one of her stories. Digging in the garden not fifty yards from the house, we discovered a brass harness ornament bearing the crest and motto of the Tarleton family, convincing evidence that the colonel's troops did camp at Carter's Grove in 1781—even if we cannot prove that Banistre bashed the banisters (Fig. 1–2).

In her will, Mrs. McCrea instructed her executors to sell Carter's Grove to a preservationist organization that would undertake to open the house and grounds to the public. Colonial Williamsburg's benefactor, John D. Rockefeller, Jr., had long shared his architects' enthusiasm for acquiring a James River plantation so as to broaden the interpretation of colonial life, only one aspect of which could be presented in the restored eighteenth-century town. It is highly probable, therefore, that he would have purchased Carter's Grove as soon as it came on the market. Unfortunately, Mr. Rockefeller died five months before Mrs. McCrea. He had often expressed admiration for her achievement in preserving the house, although he knew that it lacked most of the eighteenth-century outbuildings so essential to a colonial plantation that was to be exhibited. At Carter's Grove, even those that survived had been drastically altered. Mary McCrea's architect, W. Duncan Lee of Richmond, shrank from claiming that he had "restored" the mansion, preferring to say that he had been instrumental in the "renascence" of Carter's Grove.

1–2. Brass harness or box ornament found in the garden and bearing the crest and motto of the Tarleton family. Ca. 1781.

"An old building can be and should be faithfully restored, and left at that if it is to be used for museum purposes solely," wrote Lee, "but if a person buys an old house, pays a lot of money for it, and intends to use it as a year-round home, he is not going to be satisfied to take his bath in a tin foot-tub and go to bed with a candle in one hand and a warming-pan in the other just for archaeological reasons."[1]

Mary McCrea had no desire to bathe in a bucket; on the contrary, her art deco bathroom was to become one of the mansion's conversation pieces. She and her husband had bought a crumbling pile where chickens roosted in the basement, where dirt and discolored varnish obscured the interior woodwork, and where a stove in the hall had burned a hole through the floor and threatened to set the house ablaze. From such unprepossessing materials, Duncan Lee and his clients created a home fit for the descendant of a royal governor. That the result was not an "archaeologically" correct restoration was beside the point.

Lee had explained his philosophy in the April 1933 issue of *Architecture,* and if his reference to archaeology in relation to architectural preservation seems surprising, I should explain that in those early days in the history of American architectural preservation and reconstruction, architects who believed that everything should be put back precisely as it had been in the eighteenth century were considered to be archaeological architects, even archaeologists. On the other side of the philosophical fence sat the aesthetic restorationists, who believed that they should restore things as they would have been had the colonial builders matched their own skill and good taste. In reality, neither group employed the archaeological techniques which today are recognized as an essential element of any architectural restoration. Consequently, no archaeological search for vanished outbuildings or colonial paths and fencelines had preceded Mary McCrea's renascence at Carter's Grove. She simply preserved, repaired, and to some degree adapted what was there when she bought the property.

Although the plantation would need considerable research and physical effort to restore it to its colonial appearance, Carter's Grove had the advantage of being much closer to Williamsburg than any of the other surviving James River plantations, and it still had more than 500 of the 1,400 acres bought by its first eighteenth-century owner, Robert "King" Carter of Corotoman. So, in November 1963, the Sealantic Fund, a Rockefeller-supported philanthropic organization, bought the plantation for use as a museum to be operated by Colonial Williamsburg. Six years later the Fund deeded Carter's Grove to the Foundation completing the town-and-country interpretive package that Williamsburg educators had long been seeking.

During the time that the Colonial Williamsburg Foundation had served only as the custodian of Carter's Grove, nothing had been done there beyond maintaining the grounds as Mrs. McCrea had left them, and opening the mansion to the public during part of the year. Now, in 1969, it was time to come to grips with Carter's Grove's opportunities and problems; but first the architects needed to know what they had to work with, and that called for an extensive archaeological survey.

Ten days after my meeting with Mary McCrea in 1956, I had returned to my archaeological post in London, assuming that my summer in Virginia had been no more than a pleasant interlude in a career focusing on urban archaeology in Britain. Barely a month later I was invited to return and to steer Williamsburg's archaeological effort toward a fuller interpretation of that town's eighteenth-century past. My experience had hitherto been directed to salvaging fragments from the histories of Roman and medieval London before they were swept away in the rush to rebuild the bomb-torn city. Colleagues considered my interest in later historical periods a harmless if worthless aberration, and even I felt that excavating anything later than the end of the seventeenth century was getting perilously close to absurd-ity. In Williamsburg I quickly learned better. For the next twenty years I was to have little contact with the seventeenth century save for a brief rescue mission to save a bulldozer-threatened plantation fur-ther down the James River.

At some date between 1710 and 1720, Robert Carter added a cluster of James River farms to his already vast estates. The 1,400 acres was an insignificant expansion of holdings that already ap-proached 300,000 acres, and Carter left it in the hands of a manager and gave the income to his daughter Elizabeth, who had married a lesser Virginia planter named Nathaniel Burwell. When Robert Carter died in 1732 he willed to Elizabeth the profits from all the "lands, slaves, stocks of cattle & hoggs, houses, plantations and appurt-[enance]s to the said lands and real estate belonging, lying upon Merchant's hundred In James river," adding that upon her death the property should pass to her son Carter Burwell when he reached the age of twenty-one. His grandfather further enjoined that this James River plantation should henceforth "be called & to go by the name of Carter's Grove."[2]

Carter Burwell's mother died in 1734 and he became master of Carter's Grove three years later. He also got married. On January 6, 1738, the *Virginia Gazette* reported the wedding of Mr. Carter Bur-well and Miss Lucy Grymes, "a very agreeable young Lady, of great Merit & Fortune"—which was a big help. A few years later (nobody quite knows when), Burwell began to build an imposing mansion, a task that took an interminable time to complete. Although the result was worth waiting for, Carter Burwell's time was short; the house was finished in 1755 and he died in 1756. Inherited by his infant son Nathaniel, the Carter's Grove estate was thenceforth managed by his principal guardian, William Nelson of Yorktown, until the boy came of age in 1771.

The house had been completed just as colonial Virginia reached its cultural zenith; but through the ostensibly affluent and elegant 1760s Carter's Grove lacked a master to offer the hospitality charac-teristic of the great Virginia planters of that period. By the time that Nathaniel completed his college education in Williamsburg and was ready to make the most of his inheritance, the clouds of discontent were gathering. Lord Dunmore had been made governor of Virginia; the "Boston Massacre" had stoked extremist fires to the north, and the burning of the British schooner *Gaspee* and the Boston Tea Party were soon to rock everyone's boat. The Revolution saw both friend and foe occupying Carter's Grove lands, and when it was over most people were content to make the best of what they still had. In 1792, Nathaniel Burwell built himself a new house in the summer cool of the Piedmont, and Carter's Grove returned to the status it had endured through much of the eighteenth century, that of a plantation worked on behalf of an absentee or infant owner.

When I was given the task of searching in the vicinity of the mansion for Carter's Grove's "vanished" eighteenth-century buildings, I reviewed the documentary history and was not at all sure that these buildings had been nearly as plentiful as some of my colleagues expected. As I saw it, Carter's Grove was an atypical plantation that would have had relatively few work-related buildings close to the house. Here was a plantation put together by Robert Carter at the beginning of the eighteenth century, and successfully run by managers and overseers, with gangs of slaves operating from the groups of dwellings and work buildings that made up a "quarter." Carter's Grove was divided into several of these.

Thus, at his mother's death in 1734, Carter Burwell inherited a going concern. There was no need for him to follow those planters who had started small and later expanded outward, away from the residential hub, as their fortunes grew and their land tired. Burwell could build himself a fine house at an aesthetically safe distance from tanneries, tobacco barns, blacksmiths' shops, field-slave dwellings, and the like, and restrict his ancillary buildings to those serving only the domestic needs of his family. If my interpretation was correct, we should seek evidence of the plantation's working life not at the mansion's doorstep, but perhaps at a considerable distance from the house. How, then, were we to find the remains of these quarters, which might lie buried almost anywhere across our 500 and more acres?

We had only one eighteenth-century map to guide us; drawn at the end of the Revolution, it showed, in a corner of the sheet, only a small segment of the Carter's Grove tract—not a tremendous help (Fig. 1–3). Most of the plantation's flat land had been farmed for centuries, the plows cutting deep, all the way down to the clay subsoil, and thus churning over the accumulated soil layers that provide an archaeologist with his writing on the wall. Those acres not disturbed by plowing lay in thick woods (and probably always had), the ground beneath them latticed with gullies and ravines (Fig. 1–4).

To dig 500 acres inch by inch, with shovel, trowel, and whisk brush, would take forever. A walk over freshly plowed fields yielded depressingly few artifacts, and hand-dug test holes indicated that little or nothing was to be gained by treating the disturbed plow zone like the Holy Grail. If any traces of buildings had survived, they would have had to have lain deep enough to be bedded in the clay, beyond the reach of vandalous plowshares. The same would be true of post-holes marking the lines of fences, and of silted ditches, well shafts, rubbish pits, and graves. I therefore decided that the only practical course was to take a chance, and bring in a mechanical grader to scrape away the plow zone in strips wide enough for us to examine the clay subsoil for signs of colonial disturbance. I also reasoned that, although the lines of wooden sills and shallow brick foundations might have been totally eradicated by time and the plow, the latter, though it

1-3. The corner of a French military map of 1782. Circled at top right is the approach road to Carter's Grove, flanked by two isolated buildings.

would have shifted brickbats and domestic debris first one way and then another, would have left them in approximately their original locations. Keeping close watch for such artifactual clues, as the topsoil was scraped away, should warn us of the proximity of a site of former human occupation. Once this was located, mechanical digging would halt, and we would revert to conventional hand excavation.

The woods and ravines were a different problem. There was no way in which we could drive a mechanical grader between the trees. Besides, the only justification for such crude digging was that all archaeological stratigraphy had previously been destroyed by the plow, and we had no assurance that land now in woods had ever been plowed. Amid the trees, then, we had no alternative but to dig hundreds, even thousands, of small test holes in rows between the roots, in the hope of finding a nail, a scatter of brick dust, anything that

1–4. Carter's Grove with the James River in the foreground and Grice's Run at the extreme right. The tree-flanked ravine to the left of the plantation closely matches the configuration shown in the 1782 map.

would indicate that someone had once done something nearby. The inhospitable nature of the terrain suggested that even were we to find such evidence, it would lead us to eighteenth- or nineteenth-century garbage dumped down the slopes of ravines, but not to much else. It was true that between the gullies there were small, flat, and inhabitable promontories; but they were so isolated that I thought it doubtful that a highly organized eighteenth-century plantation would have had much domestic use for them.

I estimated that mechanical trenching of the farmed fields, and even selective testing through the woods, would take at least a year —time already allocated to our continuing program of excavation in Williamsburg. We were fortunate, therefore, to be able to contract with Dr. William M. Kelso to head the survey project. He had spent two summers working with us in Williamsburg, had set up a program for historical archaeology in Georgia, and had just completed his doctoral dissertation at Emory University. Also assigned to the project were archaeological assistant David Hazzard, two members of our permanent field crew and, in the summer months, a miscellany of student excavators, most of whom worked on careful, hand-dug testing of the ground in the immediate vicinity of the mansion.

Our belief that occupation sites could be identified by careful scrutiny of the grader-stripped plow zone proved correct. One of two small buildings shown on the Revolutionary War map (see Fig. 1–3) was located in this way—though all that survived in the subsoil were traces of one chimney and eight scaffold-pole holes, four at each end of the building (Fig. 1–5).

Bill Kelso's luck had been much better closer to the mansion, where his hand-dug testing had located the foundations for a dairy and for another colonial outbuilding (Fig. 1–6). Eighteenth-century kitchen debris littered the yard around a well—a shaft which, at a depth of 20 feet, yielded a splendidly preserved shovel identical to those we were using to dig it out. This was hardly surprising, since the shovel had been left there when Mrs. McCrea had the well filled in 1930. More informative was a group of rectangular pits clustered together northwest of the mansion and filled with loam and domestic artifacts of the Revolutionary War period. Although these were first thought to be tanning pits, subsequent excavations by Bill Kelso at nearby Kingsmill plantation left little doubt that they were really storage pits under slave cabins whose last traces had been destroyed by plowing (Fig. 1–7).

By far the most important of Bill Kelso's discoveries was the ground plan of a large, fenced garden, below ornamental terracing on the mansion's river side. Here, rows of post-holes marked the location of two successive fences or palisades designed to keep wild animals away from vegetables and fruit trees growing in what in England would be termed a kitchen garden (Fig. 1–8). It was against the side of the north terrace slope, bedded in silt behind the fenceline, that excavator Daniel Louden found the brass roundel with its clear Tarleton association.

On the high ground immediately north of the terraces, the team found what appeared to be an ice-house pit used in the 1740s while the mansion was still under construction, a clue suggesting that Carter Burwell and his wife may have occupied one of the flanking buildings while awaiting completion of the mansion. The pit yielded some unusual finds—two goose eggs and the skeleton of a chicken. Alas, however, for those of our colleagues who expected us to find rows of slave cabins and plantation workshops; we, too, had laid an egg. They simply weren't there—but something else was.

1–5. Eight scaffold-pole holes and a few brickbats from a chimney were all that survived of one of the eighteenth-century buildings that had stood close to the Carter's Grove approach road.

As the mechanical trenching extended across the fields away from the mansion, occasional dark patches became visible in the subsoil, patches containing small chips of pottery and glass that had nothing to do with the Carters or Burwells. Many of the fragments were unlike anything we had seen from the eighteenth century, but were otherwise undatable; others clearly belonged to the previous century, and probably to the first half of it. But the seventeenth century was not what we were there to find, and so I reluctantly instructed that these anomalous dark patches should not be disturbed. They were to be plotted on our map and covered over again, to be studied at some future time.

Because Bill Kelso was under contract to complete the survey within two years, and because Colonial Williamsburg would have preferred to have had his information yesterday, work went on through the depths of winter, halting only when the ground was too

1–6. Preliminary testing in 1970 uncovered the floor and foundations of a dairy adjacent to the 1755 mansion.

wet or too frozen for the grader to scrape, or the weather too numbingly cold for the crew to hold their shovels. No archaeologist would
pretend that under such conditions he could hope to see every stain
and shadow in the earth. It was astonishing, therefore, that Bill's team
found as much as it did, and even more to its credit that the mapping
was so accurately done.

Supervising an archaeological survey when you know that you
will not go on to fully excavate what you find is certainly one of the
most discouraging of jobs. It would have been small wonder, therefore, if, when the snow blanketed the ground, crewmen had deliberately ignored small marks in the soil that had nothing to do with the
eighteenth-century Carter's Grove, thus minimizing the painful chore
of trying to hold steel measuring tapes between fingers blue with cold.
Enormous credit, therefore, is due to crew leader David Hazzard,
who so carefully plotted the first clues to what would later—much
later—become one of the most important archaeological contributions to America's early colonial history.

To the landward side of the Carter's Grove mansion lay a large,
flat area covering more than eight acres, ground that had been heavily
farmed, but which still seemed a likely spot to have housed eighteenth-century plantation support buildings. Soon after test trenching
began there, four rectangular, clay-filled holes showed up in the subsoil. They looked like—and turned out to be—four graves, their
contents in an advanced stage of decay. There was no sign of datable

I–7. A concentration of rectangular pits discovered north of the mansion
may have been storage places under eighteenth-century slave dwellings.

coffin hardware—nails, screws, or handles, nor any artifacts in the fill over the bones to indicate when they were buried. Remembering that the Burwell family graveyard was located on the far side of the mansion, and knowing that these graves were closer to the kitchen and dairy than to any other building, I guessed that we had found the burial place for slaves owned by the Burwells or their nineteenth-century successors.

These bones were found in the winter of 1970, a time when black people were discovering themselves and their culture in new ways, and a time when news that white archaeologists were digging up the bones of their ancestors would have been greeted with minimal enthusiasm. I told Bill Kelso to quickly cover them over and to cease trenching in that part of the field. I suggested that he should move to the western edge of the field and start working eastward from there; but before he had gone very far, he ran into three more graves. It looked as though we were chopping at the edges of a very large cemetery; so once again I called a halt. We moved the machinery to the north end of the field and began to head southward in a series of

1–8. Rows of post-holes extending southwest from the mansion were revealed in 1970 and identified successive garden fences erected in the second half of the eighteenth century. In the field beyond lay the yet-to-be-discovered fort and compounds of Martin's Hundred.

east-west cuts—until Bill again encountered a series of dirt-filled holes. This time they were not graves, but trash-filled pits dating from the seventeenth century, and we knew that where there was rubbish there had once been people and their homes—though for us they had existed in the wrong century. Once again I called a halt.

We had now attacked this field on three sides; only the fourth remained, and that was flanked by a modern road. One trench alongside the road exposed the top of another large seventeenth-century pit. We had boxed ourselves in on all four sides of a two-acre rectangle: graves on two sides and seventeenth-century remains on both of the others (Fig. 1–9). Had the evidence pointed to eighteenth-century occupation, we ordinarily would have abandoned trenching at this point, and waited for fair weather and a large crew to carefully investigate the area by hand. There was no reason to treat the remains of another century any differently. Like the other, more slender traces of seventeenth-century occupation that Bill Kelso's team had found elsewhere on the plantation, these new finds would have to await study at some future date.

Beyond the road, east of the enigmatic two acres, the ground dipped and rolled through a series of ridges and gullies leading to a creek called Grice's Run. On an 1874 property plan, this territory was marked as a "Cranberry Swamp." Because Colonial Williamsburg historians believed that Robert Carter's early eighteenth-century acreage had stopped short of Grice's Run, our testing did not extend far into the woods in that direction; but we did cross the first ravine, and on the other side our test holes revealed a small area, rich in artifacts, that showed no sign of having been disturbed by later plowing. But again the artifacts dated from the seventeenth, and not the eighteenth century, among them a small brass mathematical counter made by Hanns Krauwinckel of Nuremburg, Germany, between 1580 and 1610 (Fig. 1–10).

Earlier, Bill Kelso's trenching had located yet another potentially rich seventeenth-century site, this one in a field close both to Grice's Run and to the James River. A test cut into a single rubbish pit had yielded some sophisticated examples of English tin-enameled delftware, including part of a purple-stippled salt dish of a type hitherto unrecorded (Fig. 1–11). I knew that if an intact example were to turn up in a New York or London ceramic auction, it would command a nerve-shattering price; thus, finding it at Carter's Grove invited us to believe that someone of wealth and importance had lived there very early in the colonial period. But accepting the invitation could have been dangerous. All too often we mistakenly judge the original worth

1–9. Preliminary trenching northeast of the mansion (top right), showing the unexplored rectangle that proved to conceal most of Site A, a plantation complex a hundred years older than Carter's Grove.

of an object by modern salesroom value, when, in reality, its rarity may stem only from the fact that few such objects were made because nobody liked them. The Edsels of other centuries all too easily become today's treasures.

Even after sidestepping the value trap, we were still left with a luxury object. If all a settler needed or could afford was a simple container for salt, a small turtle shell, nailed to a block of wood, could have done the job and cost no more than the value of the nail. Rightly or wrongly, therefore, we called Bill Kelso's map location the Delft Site, and looked to it as one that might have exciting things to tell us about early colonial life in the Virginia wilderness—but not yet.

By the time Bill's survey was done, his map showed a ring of seventeenth-century occupation spread over about 150 acres all around the eighteenth-century mansion site. For the most part, the clues were limited to very small scraps of pottery, tobacco-pipe fragments, nails, a key, a bead, and small pieces of glass. So few sites from the seven-

1-10. Brass mathematical counter made at Nuremburg by Hanns Krauwinckel between 1580 and 1610, one of the first clues to an early occupation of Site B.

teenth century had been carefully excavated either in America or in England that our dating for their artifacts was far less refined than for the eighteenth century, a period to which I had been devoting myself day in and day out for the past fourteen years. The best I could say of the enigmatic Carter's Grove sites was that I could see no evidence of their having been occupied after about 1650.

The question "When?" was but one of many: Why were there so many sites in so small an area? Who had lived there, and why? What happened to cause them to be abandoned? After Jamestown's shaky start in 1607, the history of Virginia was to be one of endurance and expansion. By the mid-century the worst was long since over—but not, it seemed, at Carter's Grove.

I was well aware that when thinking about these acres in the seventeenth century I had no business referring to them as Carter's Grove. Robert Carter's 1726 will described the property as "lying upon Merchant's hundred in James River."[3] I knew nothing about Merchant's Hundred; indeed I had forgotten so much of my English medieval history that, to me, a "hundred" was a figure slightly larger than ninety-nine. I had much to learn!

Turning to Colonial Williamsburg's history of Carter's Grove (a volume hurriedly prepared for the benefit of the Sealantic Fund), I could find nothing about the property before its purchase by Carter. A footnote rather cryptically referred to "Merchant's Hundred or Martin's Hundred both in James City County," adding that "There is not enough evidence to make any definite statements as to the boundaries of Merchant's Hundred plantation."[4]

Was Merchant's Hundred a private plantation, as Carter's Grove became under Robert Carter's ownership; and was the name synonymous with Martin's Hundred—or were they separate areas of James City County? Records showed that in the second half of the seventeenth century both names were used to define parishes, and the rather vague descriptions of their bounds suggested that they were indeed the same. This was intriguing, but at the time somewhat aca-

1-11. Finding this base from a rare, manganese-stippled delftware salt dish at Site D hinted at more exotic finds to come. Ca. 1620–1640.

demic. Bill Kelso's search for eighteenth-century Carter's Grove was over, and apart from some minor work still to be done close to the mansion, my schedule called for us to turn our attention in quite another direction—to the excavation of Williamsburg's lunatic asylum, which had burned in 1885.

The asylum, built in 1773 as America's first Public Hospital for the Insane, was the only major public building in Williamsburg not yet restored or reconstructed. The Foundation now proposed to remedy the omission and to use it as an archaeological museum. So, in spite of the ribald comments that this decision generated among my colleagues, our return to Williamsburg had its compensations. As for the Foundation's interpretive planners, their disappointment at our finding so little eighteenth-century data at Carter's Grove was by no means offset by their pleasure at our unearthing evidence of earlier occupation. That was of no use to them in developing a plan to convert Mary McCrea's home into an educational tool as a working, eighteenth-century plantation. For the next four years, therefore, no one gave any more thought to Merchant's or Martin's Hundred—except perhaps for the few tourists who took the trouble to stop and read roadside historical markers. About five and a half miles southeast of Williamsburg on the old road to Hampton, and leaning slightly to one side, its base entwined in honeysuckle, there was such a marker. It read:

> On both sides of this road and extending west was the plantation known as Martin's Hundred, originally of 80,000 acres. Settled in 1619, this hundred sent delegates to the first legislative assembly in America, 1619. In the Indian massacre of 1622, seventy-eight persons were slain here.

The Jamestown Perspective

2

If you want to get something accomplished in a hurry, don't give it to a committee—thus sayeth one group of sages. Another says: Do it fast and you'll do it wrong. In the highly complex field of historical preservation, both are right. No one person has enough specialized knowledge to evaluate all the options, let alone carry his plan through once he has decided what it should be. For six years, Williamsburg architects, curators, educators, and purse holders had been unable to agree on what should be done with Carter's Grove. Some insisted that John D. Rockefeller, Jr., would never have wanted his money to be used to buy the plantation unless it was with a view to restoring the house to its eighteenth-century appearance. Others feared that we lacked enough evidence to take the mansion and its environs accurately back to their colonial years, and more questioned whether even if we had the information, we also had the funds to do it. Yet another group argued that Mrs. McCrea's 1928 "renascence" was as much a part of the plantation's history as any other, and that to change what she had left would be to destroy a recent, but nevertheless precious, page of American social history.

These were all classic arguments that had been voiced time and again since the Restoration Movement developed in the 1920s, and they were no more likely to be answered to everyone's satisfaction at Carter's Grove than they had been in countless emotional battles at other times and on other fronts. Nevertheless, something had to be done; the bicentenary of the American Revolution would soon be upon us, and hordes of history-seeking visitors were expected to envelop the Jamestown-Williamsburg-Yorktown area from 1976 to 1981. To help Williamsburg cope with the crowds, something exciting and educational was needed at Carter's Grove to serve as a safety valve. Pessimists contended that the fine house was not attraction enough.

We, the archaeologists, knew that we had let our colleagues down by failing to find all of the ancillary buildings needed to exhibit the myriad crafts and domestic and agricultural activities practiced on a typical eighteenth-century Virginia plantation. But even had we found them, argued one faction, it would not be right to reconstruct some of these workplaces unless the mansion itself were restored to its original form—a project that would take years to complete. An alternative would be to leave the mansion alone and simply use the land to show the *kinds* of activities which we knew from documentary records went on at Carter's Grove, even if we could not say that they did so in the immediate vicinity of the mansion.

That solution, albeit a temporary one, was acceptable to most staff scholars, although there was less unanimity on where to set up the exhibits. They had to be relatively close to the mansion, yet out of sight of it; the ground had to be fairly flat, as well as having been cleared of trees, so that no harm would be done to the existing landscape. One likely area for the exhibits had already been set out as an eighteenth-century apple orchard, and no one was Philistine enough to advocate the slaughter of the saplings. Another good location had been made into a visitors' parking area. That left only one prime candidate—the large field northeast of the house, which had at its center the two-acre rectangle that we had refrained from excavating in 1971.

What were the chances, I was asked, that eighteenth-century building foundations might lie buried in the rectangle—evidence that would make it improper to use the land to demonstrate typical plantation crafts? If, for example, we were to find the remains of another house that coexisted with the Carter's Grove mansion, we would know that it would be wrong to put a tobacco barn at such a location. But if, on the other hand, we could produce no archaeological evidence to define the use of the unexcavated area in the Burwell period, no violation would be done to the plantation's historical integrity by using the land to exhibit some other contemporary activity.

Trenching in other parts of the field had yielded no evidence of its eighteenth-century occupation or use—with the possible exception of the still enigmatic burials. But after twenty-seven years as a professional archaeologist I knew that you can never be sure of anything until the last grains of soil have been examined—and sometimes not even then.

How long would it take to investigate the two acres?

If they held no more than we had already seen, and provided we could get the help of an experienced physical anthropologist to identify the race, age, and sex of the skeletons (dating them would be up to us), we might get the job done in six weeks. If, on the other hand, Bill Kelso's seventeenth-century pits proved to be part of a major domestic settlement, all timing bets would be off. That this might be so had been suggested by Bill's peripheral testing, which had picked up the line of a ditch that created an oval embracing both the graves and the pits, and which disappeared into the woods at both ends, heading in the direction of an easterly ravine.

It must be rare, if not unique in the annals of archaeology, for an excavation to be undertaken in the hope that nothing will be found, yet this was the reasoning behind our return to Carter's Grove in April 1976. The unexcavated area had not been plowed since we had left it five years earlier, its only disturbance the work of groundhogs that we found cavorting in one corner, and that plunged into their burrows at our approach. From the piles of loose dirt at the mouths of their tunnels, protruded chips of brick, and several pieces of seventeenth-century bottle glass, and some nails. Clearly, the groundhogs were living in the past. More important, they had pinpointed yet another sector of our two acres in which early artifacts were to be found.

When the word came to fold our tents in Williamsburg and return to Carter's Grove, I was nearing the end of a two-season dig on the site of the workshops operated by Virginia's Revolutionary War armorer. Having spent the preceding two years on the Public Hospital project, there had been no time to worry any more about the mysteries of Merchant's or Martin's Hundred. Thus, despite having the benefit of Bill Kelso's excellent report on his eighteenth-century discoveries, we were no better prepared to grapple with the seventeenth century than we had been when we left the plantation in the spring of 1972.

I have long argued that before digging up the archaeological remains of any period for which documentary history exists, one should first assemble and review all the available written evidence. I have been equally vociferous in contending that no archaeologist should dig anywhere unless he is thoroughly conversant with the artifacts of the period, and is sure of having marshaled the right team of specialists to answer all his questions. An excavator who is the leading expert on the archaeology of water mills is unlikely to be the best person to interpret the remains of a governor's mansion, just as it is foolish to ask a pottery specialist to interpret the finds from a boatyard. Alas, few archaeologists agree with this view; consequently, there is ample precedent for professional archaeologists going to where the work is, and hoping to learn on the job—invariably at the expense of the site.

We, fortunately, were not that ill-prepared. My wife, Audrey, was a trained excavator who had worked with me on seventeenth-century sites in London, and as archaeological research associate at Colonial Williamsburg for twenty years, she had a vast knowledge of eighteenth-century artifacts—something that cannot be achieved without acquiring a more than passing acquaintanceship with what went before. Our senior archaeologist, Eric Klingelhofer, had also been trained in England, and although his experience had been gained on Saxon and medieval sites, this was training that would stand him in good stead when his Carter's Grove discoveries began to assume "medieval" architectural characteristics.

We were lucky, too, in that in 1964 we had spent several months excavating an extremely rich mid-seventeenth-century site further down the James River, in Warwick County. Described in a 1648 pamphlet as Mathews Manor, the site had been home to Captain Samuel Mathews, a member of the governor's council, and in 1635 a ringleader in the first revolt against the colony's administration. The site, therefore, was of historical importance, as its artifacts testified. Among them were parts of swords and guns, a cheekpiece from a burgonet helmet of the kind that closed around the face, pottery, glass, and agricultural tools including the only intact brass watering-can known to have survived from the seventeenth century (Fig. 2–1).

2–1. Military artifacts from excavations at Mathews Manor on the Warwick River included sword hilts, gun parts, and the cheekpiece from a closed burgonet. Ca. 1625–1650.

Equally important, we uncovered the remains of two large houses, the first with brick foundations and the second built in part from the debris of the first, but constructed on posts seated in holes in the ground.

The dig at Mathews Manor had been thrust upon us when the land developer (who was keenly interested in Virginia history) began to find colonial remains and did not want to be responsible for bulldozing them away unstudied. For us, this was on-the-job training. Never before had I excavated a seventeenth-century house site; all our work in London had been limited to salvaging the contents of rubbish pits, wells, and privies lying deep in the gravel, below houses long since swept away by eighteenth-, nineteenth-, and twentieth-century construction.

In 1964, when the Mathews Manor work was done, no American university offered a degree course in historical archaeology; nor, for that matter, did any British college. The founding of the American Society for Historical Archaeology and its British counterpart, the Society for Post-Medieval Archaeology, were still three years into the future. Even in Williamsburg, the idea that there was more to archaeology than finding architecturally useful building foundations was only beginning to take root. Elsewhere, the excavation of historical sites (when it was done at all) was usually put in the hands of an anthropologist schooled in prehistory. There was, after all, no other available archaeological training that included fieldwork on American sites.

When, in 1956, I first came to the United States, I assumed that Virginia's almost legendary love affair with its past embraced every page of its history, from the first landing in 1607 to Robert E. Lee's gentlemanly surrender at Appomattox in 1865. But that was not entirely true. Virginians were interested enough in the names of families listed among the early Jamestown settlers, and they certainly cared about Lee; but in the intervening two-and-a-half centuries only a couple of events really stood out: Virginians signing the Declaration of Independence, and Virginian George Washington beating the British at Yorktown. Between these historical peaks had stretched the image of verdant plains of gracious living, generations of happy people working on handsome plantations, the gentle rhythm of their lives quickened in the eighteenth century only by visits to Williamsburg in the spring and fall to attend the roistering "public times" when the courts were in session and planters did their business over a bowl of punch or a mug of foaming ale. It was a charming picture somewhat removed from the realities of life as it really had been lived.

The 1960s saw a precipitous change in focus. Social historians became respectable, and so did garbage-happy archaeologists. In Williamsburg, we were glad to take advantage of the growing interest in daily life.

I had previously supposed that the intensive archaeological work at Jamestown that began in the 1930s had brought together a vast corpus of knowledge about the town and the lives of its people. I should have known better. Historical archaeology in the thirties was even less refined than it was in the early sixties. At Jamestown, the artifacts were there, but more often than not their message had been lost.

Because what was not found at Jamestown was to have a direct bearing on the importance of what we were yet to find at Carter's Grove, I must digress long enough to summarize the development of Jamestown and the history of its archaeology.

The Virginia Company of London had been granted a royal charter by James I in 1606, and sent over its first 104 settlers aboard three small ships, the *Susan Constant, Godspeed,* and *Discovery.* On May 13 in the following year they moored at what henceforth would be named Jamestown Island. The settlers first set up a temporary encampment of tents and huts surrounded by a moon-shaped defensework built only of brushwood. This was quickly replaced by a triangular palisade of posts, rails, and pales, with bulwarks at the corners where cannon were mounted. Jamestown thus became a walled community with streets of houses, a church, a military storehouse, and a central square or parade, all within the palisades. It was a defensive concept in town planning whose history went back into remote antiquity, a design to be adopted by any community rich enough, with labor enough, and scared enough to go to all that trouble. By the 1620s, as the Virginia colony took root and expanded, Jamestown had outgrown the palisaded area; streets of houses were laid out beyond it to create what was to be known as New Towne (Fig. 2–2). In that form Jamestown continued as the seat of government for Virginia until 1699, when the legislature moved inland to the new administrative center being built at Williamsburg.

Like most towns made up largely of wooden houses roofed with shingles, bark, or reeds, lit by candles and warmed by wood burning in open hearths, Jamestown suffered several devastating fires. Ironically, however, the one that prompted the move to Williamsburg erupted in the brick-built state house, one of the old capital's least inflammable structures. Although the governor and his government moved away, Jamestown did not entirely disappear; it continued to

27

exist as a port through most of the eighteenth century, and eventually became part of the Ambler plantation, whose colonial brick mansion burned for the third and last time in 1898. During the Revolution, Jamestown was a center of both naval and military activity, and in the Civil War a Confederate earthwork was thrown up within yards of its historic brick church. In short, Jamestown was no Pompeii cut off in its prime, no site left sleeping through the centuries waiting only to be awakened by the archaeologist's magic spade. Instead, it was like most of the world's urban sites, its face ever changing, leaving a cat's cradle of archaeological evidence calling for endless time and superlative field techniques if its overlapping and interlocking strands were to be successfully untangled.

By the end of the nineteenth century nothing of Jamestown survived above ground save for the church tower, which might have been built as early as about 1650. Foundations for the rest of the building were discovered in 1901 by amateur antiquary John Tyler, son of historian and William and Mary College president Lyon G. Tyler. In the same year, the Army Corps of Engineers, under the direction of Colonel Samuel H. Yonge, built a massive sea wall to protect the rapidly eroding Jamestown site. In the course of that digging, Colonel Yonge found the end of a row of brick-foundationed buildings sticking out of the bank, and in 1903 he undertook the archaeological investigation of the complex since identified as the "Country House" (governor's residence), the Ludwell House, and

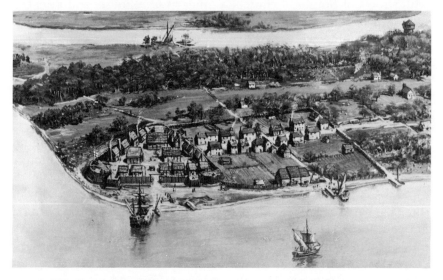

2-2. An artist's impression of Jamestown ca. 1625, after the town had spread beyond the confines of the fort.

the Fourth State House, which burned in 1698, prompting the move to Williamsburg.

When, in 1907, the Tricentenary of the Jamestown Landing came around, considerable interest had been generated in the archaeological discoveries made by Tyler and Yonge. It did not last, and once the flags were hauled down and the trash cleared up, Jamestown was left to itself until 1934, when most of the island was acquired by the United States National Park Service. By that time the country was in the depths of the Great Depression. Even John D. Rockefeller, Jr.'s restoration of Williamsburg had been brought almost to a halt (though it was put about that the project was by then virtually completed), and many of its architectural and archaeological staff members had lost their jobs. Some gravitated to Yorktown, where the Park Service was recruiting for the Civilian Conservation Corps, sending teams out onto the battlefield site to investigate the remains of its complex siege and defense works. The leader of that research, an architecturally trained white Russian who had left Williamsburg before the closure, was transferred to dig at Jamestown. John Zaharov had learned his historical archaeology supervising the hunt for brick foundations in Williamsburg. It was small wonder, therefore, that he could take to Jamestown no knowledge of, or little interest in the potsherds, bits of glass, and countless other small artifacts that had nothing to do with buildings, but which had everything to do with the life of the people who had lived in them.

Through the next two years, extensive digging was done at Jamestown, some of it directed solely by architects looking for foundations, and some by two anthropologists when the wisdom of leaving it to the architects was questioned. Since both anthropologists were trained in different facets of prehistory, their contributions inevitably leaned more toward improved technique than to interpretation. The now distinguished architectural historian Henry Chandlee Forman was to write that he "held responsibility of direct supervision over the excavation, photography and measuring of the Jamestown foundations and their architectural fragments," which, he contended, "more than anything else reflect the culture of the vanished civilization." It was small wonder that the architects and anthropologists did not always see eye to eye. In Forman's view, as soon as a foundation was revealed "there [was] only one person who [could] rightly step forward to take charge—the specialist in colonial construction," and with a deft twist of the knife added that "a Williamsburg Restoration architect would be more proficient in this kind of work than a specialist in Gobi Desert anthropology."[1]

Forman was both right and wrong. Although an expert in colonial brickwork could provide a more reliable interpretation of a structure than could an anthropologist with little knowledge of the period, the latter would almost certainly do a better job of removing and interpreting the soil sequences in, over, and around the foundations. The architects and anthropologists needed each other, but in those days before the value of interdisciplinary research had been recognized, neither side would admit it.

In an effort to find a statesmanlike solution to these increasingly divisive professional and personal differences, the Park Service decreed that henceforth the anthropologists would dig to within three feet of any structure, leaving the foundations and interiors of buildings to be excavated by the architects' men. This bureaucratic wisdom made nonsense of the archaeologists' job, and the three-foot demarcation line between the anthropologists and the architectural engineers proved too narrow to keep them from each other's throats. On at least one occasion, shovels were swung with malice and forethought. By 1936 there was almost open war on the project. This, clearly, was a situation that could not continue.

The Park Service's Washington office did what Washington always does in moments of crisis: It appointed a committee. After reviewing all the evidence, it concluded that nothing could save the Jamestown project but a clean sweep and new leadership, this time with a professional archaeologist in overall charge. Recognizing the importance of the site's architectural remains, the committee decreed that this supervising archaeologist must also have an architectural background. But because archaeology was taught only in schools of anthropology or Old World ancient history, the Park Service committee's requirement seemed impossible to meet. Fortunately, however, a web of circumstances irrelevant to my story did create such a paragon in the person of Jean C. Harrington, possessor of an architectural degree and experience in American prehistory as a student of anthropology at the University of Chicago. Harrington's appointment as Jamestown's supervising archaeologist would prove to be one of the most felicitous in the annals of American archaeology.

When J. C. "Pinky" Harrington arrived at Jamestown in the fall of 1936, only conservator Worth Bailey survived from the old supervisory crew, and it was he, with his growing knowledge of seventeenth-century artifacts, who taught the new Archaeologist-in-Charge the difference between delftware and five-and-dime "china." Harrington was to remain at Jamestown until 1942, when all work there ceased and he was moved to a new administrative job at Yorktown.

He would return after the war to excavate the site of Jamestown's glass factory, and he would continue to maintain advisory supervision of subsequent work on Jamestown Island until his retirement in 1965. Although Harrington is today recognized as the father of professional historical archaeology in America, the sad truth is that most of the digging at Jamestown was done in the two-and-a-half years before he took charge. Much of Harrington's time was spent trying to document what had been done, and to organize the artifact collections. Extracting order from chaos was one thing, recapturing archaeological truth was another. Harrington well knew that once an artifact had been stripped from its context, once a soil stain had been overlooked and shoveled away, no amount of belated care or applied knowledge could give them meaning.

Jamestown's architect excavators had been interested primarily in buildings of the kind that John Zaharov had learned to uncover in Williamsburg: solid courses of laid brick readily identifiable as footings, cellars, and chimney bases. By and large, however, such substantial remains at Jamestown dated from the town's later decades. Most buildings raised in its first years had been slight structures erected on posts seated in the ground, sometimes with wooden sills between, but often without. Such feeble foundations left nothing behind for a laborer-excavator to bang his shovel against, only dirty marks in the subsoil that could be scraped away unnoticed.

Henry Forman, Zaharov, and their architecturally trained colleagues had done their homework; they knew that the earliest Jamestown buildings were constructed almost entirely of wood. Their problem was that digging techniques that had worked well enough in the hunt for eighteenth-century buildings in Williamsburg were simply not refined enough to reveal Jamestown's gossamer threads. Knowing that the earliest settlement was surrounded by a wooden palisade and ditch, serious efforts were made to detect the latter's contours, for once these were found and recorded, the site of the original James Towne would be known—and that, above all else, was what the Park Service and Virginia wanted from the project.

Although the triangular palisade enclosed the entire one-acre township, it had long been described as the "fort"; indeed, it had been called this ever since the settlement expanded beyond it. At one exciting moment in the midst of Forman's excavations, he thought that he had found it. But because a ditch could not be considered an architectural feature, pursuit of the fort had gone to the anthropologists, who reported that "the fill, however, ran out without giving any support to the theory that it was the supposed corner of the fort."[2]

Despite renewed digging in the 1950s, the site of Jamestown's fortified settlement has never been found, and thus all the models and artists' conceptions, and the full-scale reconstruction seen by countless visitors to the Jamestown Festival Park, are based solely on contemporary, documentary descriptions that left much to the imagination. Tourists are told that the site has eroded into the river, though the official Department of the Interior report puts it slightly differently, saying that "the site of the First Fort of 1607 has been completely covered by the James River at a point between the present channel and the seawall opposite the Confederate Fort of 1861."[3] In 1955 Park Service archaeologists attempted to locate traces of it on the river bottom, using a clamshell bucket mounted on a barge. After sixty-five "drops" they gave up, having found nothing that they could associate with the fortified settlement.

To the average visitor, early and late are unimportant: Jamestown is Jamestown, and there must be something warped, even unpatriotic about archaeologists and historians who nitpick over the differences between one period and another. Nevertheless, ninety-seven years as the capital of Britain's Virginia colony was a long time, in which much could, and did happen. Looking back across ninety-seven years of our own era, we have seen the history of flight sweeping upward from Kittyhawk to *Columbia,* weapons of mass destruction march on from the Gatling gun to the neutron bomb and death-ray technology, and Britain's once global empire reduced to wistful memories in the hearts and minds of an obsolete generation. The events of the seventeenth century were as unpredictable and every bit as significant. The flint-lock musket put paid to centuries of military tactics; Englishmen killed their king, toyed with democracy and then crowned his son; the invincible Spaniard found that he wasn't, and the American Indian began the long retreat to the creek called Wounded Knee. New England brahmins notwithstanding, the roots of the United States were planted in Virginia, and our story, the history of Martin's Hundred, began before the *Mayflower* set sail, and was virtually over before the Plymouth colonists were sure of their future. Unlike the Pilgrim Fathers, whose lasting influence on American society was regional at best, the Martin's Hundred settlement (and others like it along the James River) sired the economy that would dominate the South through more than 250 years of American history.

Although more of the nation's colonial history took place in the seventeenth than in the eighteenth century, only a handful of social historians have tried to weave the two together. For most of us, therefore, America's ante-bellum plantation economy is seen as something separated even from the eighteenth century, a gone-with-the-julep culture rooted in Charleston, South Carolina, rather than on the banks of the James River. Thus, in developing Carter's Grove as a re-creation of a working, eighteenth-century plantation, Colonial Williamsburg intended to help set the record straight, and it had looked to archaeology to reveal what should be reconstructed, and where. That our 1970–71 efforts had produced so little pleased no one.

The task given us in the spring of 1976 seemed tailor-made for a team having a track record like ours. All we had to do was to excavate the remaining two acres beside the parking lot, isolate the graves, and prove that there was nothing else there to get in the way of Bicentenary exhibits. The key question being asked was not what we were likely to find, but how soon we expected to be through.

Had we known the answer we might never have begun.

Matters of
Grave Concern
3

$\mathbb{A}$rmchair archaeologists who limit their digging to the pages of the *National Geographic* are accustomed to the vicarious thrill of imagining the voices of pith-helmeted eccentrics crying "Dig here!" to a gang of baffled fellaheen, or following them on the map as they canoe up the Orinoco in search of Eldorado, fleets of piranha playfully snapping at their paddles. By comparison, therefore, the Carter's Grove expedition began as a very low-key affair, the seven-mile journey from Williamsburg to the site offering nothing more hazardous than a truck transmission with suicidal tendencies, and an occasional encounter with a London double-decker bus ferrying tourists in and out of a brewery's "theme park."

Our crew, too, was modest; six people at the outset under the direction of Eric Klingelhofer, plus the prospect of a few summer students should we be so inconsiderate as to prolong the enterprise beyond its projected six weeks' duration. Before taking charge of Colonial Williamsburg's archaeological program, my work in London had relied almost exclusively on volunteer helpers, whose enthusiasm for the past was offset by the unreliability of their presence. In Williamsburg our crew has always been paid, and in the summer months our policy has been to provide temporary employment for local people, particularly the students of the nearby College of William and Mary. Picking the right people for the job is essential to the success of any venture, although my decision to hire football players rather than aspiring archaeologists was not without its critics. What I needed, however, was a work force of healthy and brawny individuals of any background or sex willing to shovel dirt and push wheelbarrows in 100-degree temperatures eight hours a day for three months. This left the trained professional crew members to do both the skilled work and the thinking. It is true that several of our summer workers have been sufficiently inspired to seek careers in historical archaeology; but what we were offering them at the outset was nothing more than temporary employment. We had no time to promise more. A training school is a training school, and a research project is a race against time, weather, and the schedule-busting prospect of finding something "big" too late in the season.

These concerns were not foremost in my mind when we began work on the two Carter's Grove acres we rather unimaginatively named "Site A." My principal concern was the same fear that had sent me into retreat in 1971: What were we to do if the graves we had then found now proved to mark the limits of a large slave cemetery? If its location was to be permanently marked and identified as part of Carter's Grove's eighteenth-century story, we had to establish both the race of the skeletons and the period to which they belonged.

Although none of us could claim formal training in physical anthropology, we did have the promise of a graduate student consultant who could be called on to determine the race, age, and sex of a skeleton even if he could not place the bones in any broad, cultural context. This last job remained our own. Most of us had had previous experience in excavating human remains, and our draftsman was good at skeletal drawing. So, although we were by no means the best-equipped team that ever put trowel to a cemetery, we were confident that we could give Colonial Williamsburg architects the answer to the only question that then mattered to them: Was there or was there not sufficient archaeologically barren land beyond the graves on which exhibit structures could be built?

Any well-planned archaeological project begins with the known and attempts to expand upon it. This does not mean, however, that if we know that a rich and informative cellar, tomb, or whatever, lies at the heart of a site, that we begin by plunging into the middle of it. On the contrary, it is far wiser to creep in from the edges so as first to determine its extent and how best to deal with it. In our case, we knew from the 1971 survey that our enigmatic two acres had rubbish pits on their north and east, and graves on their south and west; but we had no idea whether the graves and pits extended throughout the area or whether they marked the perimeter of something quite different. Then again, although the Kelso survey had shown that the pits contained seventeenth-century artifacts, it had produced no dating evidence for the graves. That both were in the same general area may have been mere chance—or the result of the same controlling factor that made Williamsburg architects want to put exhibits there. It was a flat piece of land in a convenient location.

We began by reexcavating the graves found in the earlier trench-

ing. Because those trenches had been dug 10 feet apart, the space
between them was being examined for the first time. We quickly
discovered that the four graves at the south of the two-acre area were
related to a fifth not previously plotted, all of them lying in a straight
line and set out behind a fence, the latter revealed by the holes for
its posts. So neatly and uniformly were the five graves aligned that I
was convinced that they were all dug at the same time, suggesting that
their occupants were victims of an epidemic (Fig. 3-1).

How does one tell that graves were dug at the same time? The
answer lies in what would happen if they were *not* dug together. Dig
any hole into hitherto compacted ground and shovel the loose dirt
back, and you wind up with more soil than will fill it. So, knowing that
in time the ground will settle, you pile what's left over on top. The
first rain causes some of that mounded dirt to wash sideways, obscur-

ing the original edges of the hole. If you bury a corpse in it (with or without a coffin), the soil displacement will be even greater as, eventually, will be the degree of settling. Thus, a grave 6 feet long and 2 wide will soon be rain-washed into appearing as much as 7 feet long and maybe 3 wide, and a gravedigger returning to cut another hole beside the first will be hard put to know precisely how to line them up—always supposing that he wants to, which is very unlikely. Consequently, graves dug at different times generally exhibit minor irregularities in their head-to-head relationships. These five, however, although several feet apart, differed in their head alignment to only the smallest degree, and so gave every indication of being the product of a single event that took at least five lives.

The three graves previously found at the west of our two acres were more than 50 yards from the other five, and were placed in a

3–1. A row of neatly aligned graves at Site A pointed to more or less simultaneous deaths and to a multiple job for the diggers.

two-and-one configuration, a pair fairly neatly aligned, and one further south, all by itself. All three had one thing in common: each contained the remains of a coffin, whereas the group of five did not. Because wood survives poorly in the clay of Carter's Grove (as, indeed, do bones), all that was left of the coffins were nails and ill-defined dark stains caused by the timber rotting away and converting the clay around it to organic soil. Although archaeologist Eric Klingel-hofer believed he could detect the familiar shouldered outline of conventional eighteenth- and nineteenth-century coffins, I was unconvinced, and became more so when I realized that these remains differed from those of any coffins I had seen before.

I did not pretend to be a coffin connoisseur; but back in London during the postwar years when the City's churches were being dismantled or restored, it had been my job as Corporation archaeologist to be on hand when vaults and tombs were emptied. I was there to keep records of inscribed coffin plates and to salvage anything unusual that might have been buried with the bodies. To that end I examined hundreds of rotting coffins, and without exception they all differed from the three at Carter's Grove in one significant respect: their lids were all made from a single, wide board nailed or screwed to the sides only at its edges. Each of ours, however, had had a row of large nails running down the centerline of the lid, which, when the wood rotted, had dropped and lay in a row along the bones from skull to shin. As the nails were more than 2 inches long and were not bent or clenched at the ends, they had to have been driven straight into the wood and, unless the lids were enormously thick, would have been sticking out on the inside—or so I then thought.

My first explanation was that the lids were made from two narrow boards joined together by a nailed batten running the length of the coffin. It was hardly a very convincing argument; none of the coffins was more than 18 inches wide, and the cutting of boards that wide would have posed no problem to colonial or nineteenth-century sawyers. It was, nevertheless, the only explanation that came to mind, and to test it, I instructed a doubting crew to embark on an equally questionable experiment: We would build a batten-lidded coffin, inserting nails where the archaeological evidence dictated—and bury it. Although the wood was to be cut almost wafer thin to hasten decay, we had no idea how long it would take to rot and to drop the nails into their final resting place; therefore, conservator Gary McQuillen not only built us a coffin, but also two small boxes from the same wood (we called them the coffinettes) which we buried to the same depth. My plan was to dig them up one at a time to check the speed of decay.

When the last of the test boxes had been reduced to stains and nails, we would excavate our coffin and plot where its nails had fallen. If they turned out to lie in the same positions as those in our three graves, then my coffin construction was correct. To test the speed at which a coffin's contents decay in the Carter's Grove clay, we placed inside our coffin, several pieces of meat, and bones, textiles, and leather, to simulate a clothed cadaver. It was all very scientific and might even have been a useful experiment, had I not discovered (long before the wood rotted) that my coffin-construction theory had been hopelessly wrong.

Of our three coffined burials, the two located side by side proved to contain a woman in her late forties and a man in the twenty-five-to thirty-five-year-old bracket (Fig. 3–2). The odd thing about them was not their age difference, but the fact that although the coffins' proximity indicated a family relationship, the man lay with his head to the west—the usual Christian position—while the woman had hers to the east. This was not, I concluded, a particularly cosy relationship, and so was unlikely to have been intentional. On the other hand, if Eric Klingelhofer was right, and the coffins had been angled at their shoulders, no confusion of position during burial would have been possible. I contended, on the contrary, that the widened soil stains that Eric had recorded were occasioned not by the coffins' construction, but by their occupants' shoulders having prevented parts of the coffin walls from crumbling inward. The coffins, I argued, were plain, four-

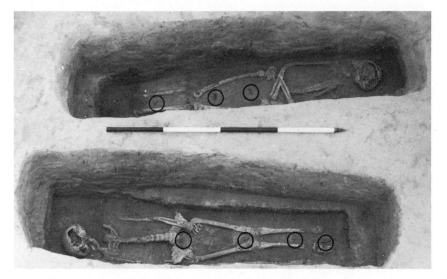

3–2. The coffined remains of a man (top) and a woman at Site A, each with a row of nails (circled) running down the center line of the skeleton.

sided boxes (with or without peculiar lids) and that once closed and moved around a few times, no one could have been quite sure which end was which. Indeed, if both coffins had been carried to the grave-side on a single wagon, and the woman's had been set down while the man's was being interred, by the time her turn had come the gravedig-gers could easily have forgotten at which end lay her head. Further-more, if they were burying both their master and mistress, there may well have been no one in authority around to make sure that the servants concerned themselves with such niceties.

In 1970, when we began our survey of the Carter's Grove planta-tion, we first laid out a grid to provide the necessary mapmaking coordinates and a plan on which all archaeological features could accurately be plotted. That grid was centered on a right-angle pro-jected from the north face of the 1755 mansion, and we soon found that most of the remains of eighteenth-century outbuildings and fence-lines were square to it. Had the house been oriented to the prime compass points (north-south or east-west), the discovery that other contemporary features had the same orientation would have meant only that they, too, were compass oriented. In reality, however, the mansion had been built at an 18-degree skew to compass north—probably because its owner, Carter Burwell, wanted his house to face down the James River and to have a good view of approaching ships. It was therefore reasonable for us to deduce that otherwise undatable archaeological features, such as fences and foundations, exhibiting the same deviation from north were part of the eighteenth-century planta-tion layout. By extension—and more important—we could also con-clude that those features that did not, belonged to some other period. Our eight graves (the group of five and the coffined three) did not, nor did the rows of post-holes, which had clearly dictated where the burials were placed. These holes were becoming ever more plentiful as the clearance of our two acres progressed, and it was evident that they were part of an elaborate system of fences and ditches extending all the way from the five graves at the south to the seventeenth-century trash pits at the north. Logic dictated that, since the Carter's Grove plantation survived through the eighteenth and nineteenth centuries, lines surveyed in the 1750s would continue to be honored—in which case fenced enclosures that did not do so, should be older rather than newer than the mansion. The question was: How much older?

We found no potsherds or other datable artifacts in any of the eight graves; but the nails used in the three coffins were hand wrought (not of machine-cut or round wire types), and therefore conventional thinking put them no later than the first decade or so of the nineteenth century. Even if I were right, and the coffins were plain, four-sided boxes, evidence of their shape would not help us in dating them. Cheap coffins have been made that way in every age since Man first decided that a hole in the ground was not enough. True, our boxes had strangely constructed lids, but I had dismissed them as a single carpenter's idiosyncrasy (we called him the Crazy Coffin-Maker of Carter's Grove) and as of no datable, stylistic significance.

Following the fenceline post-holes northward led us into the midst of an area in which had stood a house and at least eight other buildings and structures. From artifacts scattered around them and protruding from the tops of nearby rubbish pits, it soon became clear that we had stumbled into the remains of a farming settlement that had ceased to exist by about 1650 (Fig. 3–3).

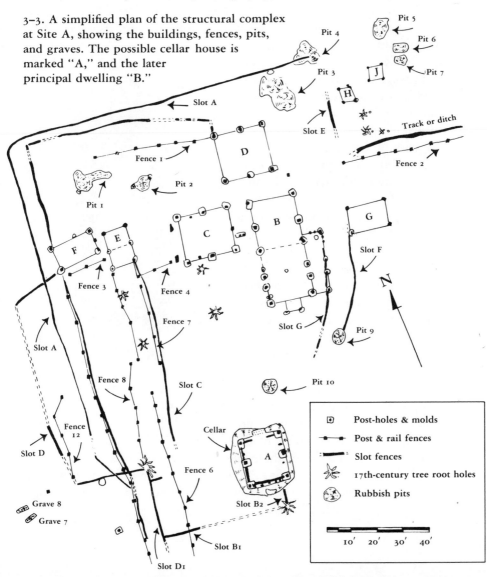

3–3. A simplified plan of the structural complex at Site A, showing the buildings, fences, pits, and graves. The possible cellar house is marked "A," and the later principal dwelling "B."

Every archaeological feature, be it the filling of an abandoned well or a thin layer of garden loam, is dated by the most recent artifact found in it, evidence described in archaeological parlance as a *terminus post quem,* a date *after* which the well was filled or the garden last disturbed. The reverse of that evidence is a *terminus ante quem,* evidence proving that a house was torn down or a grave dug *before* a known date, one usually derived from historical documentation. Thus, for example, our roadside marker (as well as more reliable historical documentation) told us that much of Martin's Hundred was put to the torch in the Indian uprising of 1622. Find the remains of burned houses and the bones of the mutilated dead, and we would have a *terminus ante quem* of March 22, 1622, the day of the massacre.

Our estimate of ca. 1650 as a terminal date for the site came from far less dramatic evidence. The testimony was provided by broken glass bottles unearthed on the site—at least 108 of them. All were of the fragile, four-sided variety generally called case bottles (because they were transported and kept in wooden or wicker cases), a type that continued alongside conventional wine-bottle shapes into the nineteenth century, but that provided Englishmen with their only glass wine-bottle shape in the first years of the seventeenth century (Fig. 3–4). In the mid-1640s a new and stronger bottle shape was created, a globular body below a tall and thick neck. This was not only more durable, it was also easier to make, and once introduced, it swept ceramic wine bottles aside and relegated the case bottle to the housing of spirits. We know from finding fragments of the new bottles at Jamestown that colonist Ralph Wormeley was ordering them from England and instructing that they be made

3–4. A four-sided case bottle, one of more than a hundred represented by fragments found on Site A. Ca. 1620–1645.

with an identifying seal on their side bearing his impressed initials (Fig. 3–5). Wormeley died in 1652. Thus, since custom-made bottles of the new shape were reaching Jamestown by that date, and since our site was

3–5. Made for Ralph Wormeley of Jamestown, who died in 1651, this bottle shape is typical of the 1650 to 1665 period. Significantly, not one fragment of such a bottle was found on Site A.

so rich in the older case-bottle fragments, we could deduce that if life at Site A continued after about 1650, pieces of the new bottles should be among the finds. But they were not.

If our settlement had been gone by the middle of the seventeenth century, and the eight graves belonged to it, it followed that their occupants died before about 1650—making them among the earliest European skeletons to be found and studied on a British-American site.

The results of the skeleton study took our breath away. Our physical anthropologist reported that the five supposed contagion victims comprised two black women and three white men each with some black characteristics; in short, potential mulattoes. The coffined couple fitted the same pattern: a probable black male and a woman who was either black or a mulatto. Strangest of all was the occupant of the isolated coffin, a man aged about sixty whose poorly preserved remains gave the impression of being another white male with black traits. If he, too, was a mulatto, sixty years old, and buried before 1650, it followed that he was born some seventeen years before the first British colonists arrived at Jamestown. Where, we asked, were whites bedding with blacks in 1590?

If our own dating and our consultant's racial information was correct, here was sensational new data on race relations in the early years of American slavery. The first group of blacks sold into servitude in British America had been landed from a Dutch ship calling at Jamestown in 1619. Most historians agree that these were not slaves in the finite sense, but servants bound to colonist masters for a specified number of years before securing their freedom. Whether these blacks were formally indentured nobody knows. Clearly, they were not immediately seen as heaven's answer to the white man's labor problems, for by 1650 there were still only about 300 blacks in Virginia—even though at Carter's Grove we were being told that they and their progeny accounted for eight out of eight.

The distribution of the graves did not bespeak a cemetery in the usual sense, and therefore it was hard to see the eight as segregated black dead. Although the five assumed contagion victims were together, the coffined three were separated from them and close to buildings whose artifactual evidence pointed to a relatively high standard of living. Was this a community of free blacks?

Although we quickly dismissed that explanation, we would later learn that by the 1660s there was at least one free black family living in Martin's Hundred parish. That our three coffined individuals should be identified as black or part black was surprising. The coffin builders had lavished more than fifty nails on each of the boxes, and in the seventeenth century nails were sparingly used. It was, however, the alleged racial mixing that really had us worried, for if four of the eight were mulattoes, we were faced with a hitherto undocumented degree of cohabitation.

An advantage of doing one's archaeology in Patagonia or the Sudan is that the press learns nothing of one's discoveries until there has been time to digest and interpret them. In Williamsburg, it is commonplace to be told about our latest finds by the checkout girl at the grocery store only hours after they are uncovered. Consequently, I was fearful that these racial "findings" would reach local reporters through the grocery vine, and that I would quickly find myself having to comment on the very questions I myself was asking. A second anthropological opinion was needed, and needed quickly.

We were lucky in that Dr. J. Lawrence Angel, world-renowned curator of physical anthropology at the Smithsonian Institution, was in the country and willing to come down to help us. Larry was, and still is, the foremost authority in the United States when it comes to the interpretation of decayed human remains, and because he was already gathering statistics on colonial Americans, he had a personal interest in what we were finding.

When presented with the dating evidence, Larry Angel quickly concluded that we had *not* made a racially sensational discovery. He did agree, however, that several of the skeletons exhibited characteristics which, if the archaeological and historical evidence had pointed to ours being a slave cemetery, would not have been out of place there. But, Larry added—and this was the key to the apparent misinterpretation—a group of 600 skeletons found in London's Farringdon Street in 1925 was recorded as exhibiting mouth characteristics similar to some usually found among blacks. According to the published report,[1] the London bones were thought to represent the twice-shifted contents of a churchyard whose occupants may have dated back to the first half of the seventeenth century. Regardless of the date at which these Londoners had lived, the important thing was that Larry could cite evidence documented prior to 1925 that whites with non-Western mouth traits were buried in England before any significant racial mixing had occurred there. The index of mouth projection exhibited by the Farringdon Street group was 95.5, partway between West Africans at 102.5 and modern United States whites at 92.5.

Had the local newspapers gotten wind of our initial "racial revelations," the timing could not have been worse. We almost certainly would have found ourselves on the Associated Press and United Press wires, not to mention the pages of *Time* and *Newsweek*—nine days of blinding limelight and a lifetime of embarrassed retractions. The lesson in all of this was not new to me. If I seem to make more of it than may be warranted, I do so because the siren call of the superlative— the first this, the oldest that—would be heard time and again before this project was through, and in the end we would have to heed the call of the Lorelei and take our chances.

Larry Angel's reassessment of the Carter's Grove skeletons did not result in the conclusion that they shared a single racial origin; there remained one in the group of five, a woman in her early thirties who exhibited some nonwhite characteristics: a short, wide nose; striking tooth projection, shovel incisors, relatively long shins—leaving the door open to her being an Indian, a black, or an aberrant white. Larry explained that (contrary to popular student belief) the racial identification of skeletons, particularly when they are as decayed as ours were, is no easy task. Broad nasal apertures, mouth projection, long shins, and wrinkled molar crowns are all common, even usual, in groups firmly identified as black; but they also occur in other races and regions, making a firm identification of single individuals something less than an exact science. Thus, for example, shovel-shaped incisors are characteristic of most Indians, but are found among a few blacks and fewer whites. Our first consultant's conclusions were understandable, Larry insisted. Having identified one woman as black, and believing that what we had found was a slave cemetery on an eighteenth-century plantation, where whites and blacks would not ordinarily be mixed, the young anthropologist had put strong emphasis on the nonwhite traits to try to make historical, rather than strictly anthropological, sense of the group as a whole. In reality, of course, the presence of a dead black or Indian servant among an otherwise white group (improbable in the eighteenth century), would not have been impossible or even unlikely in the second quarter of the seventeenth century. Here, then, was a classic example of the malleability of archaeological evidence and of the dangers inherent in trying to equate what we find in the ground with what we *think* we already know.

Although our eight graves were only linked to the seventeenth century by the umbilical cord of fencepost holes connecting them with the artifact-yielding buildings and pits to the north end of the two-acre site, I was as confident as I could ever hope to be that the lives of these people had ended in or near those buildings. The big questions, therefore, were: Who were the people and what were the buildings?

The largest was a house that had begun as one of three measuring 20 by 18 feet and that had been enlarged to 40 by 18 feet, with a lean-to addition at one side projecting 7 feet, 6 inches and 22 feet long. By early Virginia standards this was a sizeable house, though of relatively light construction. All we found of it were the holes where framing posts had stood in the ground, indicating that the walls had rested neither on brick foundations nor even on block- or pier-supported wooden sills, but had risen straight from the earth (Fig. 3–6).

Neither in this large house nor in the smaller ones adjacent to it did Eric Klingelhofer and his crew find even the faintest indications that horizontal pieces of wood (interrupted sills) had stretched from post to post. A small number of bricks were found in pits around the site, but if bricks were used anywhere, they would have been for chimneys. Sixteenth- and seventeenth-century Dutch and Flemish paintings sometimes show post-constructed houses with panels of brickwork between the uprights, a technique called brick nog-

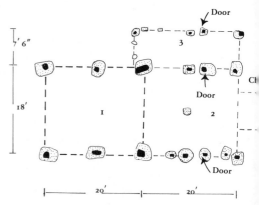

3–6. Plan of the principal dwelling at Site A, showing how the original unit (1) was later doubled in size (2), and then provided with a lean-to addition (3).

ging. We thought it more likely, however, that as bricks were so scarce on the site, our house walls were made with clay plastered over vertical and horizontally woven sticks, the same kind of wattle-and-daub construction common in Europe since prehistoric times.

Understanding what post-holes have to say carries us more than halfway toward grasping the fundamentals of all archaeological reasoning, and since such holes were to be the warp, if not the weft of our story, it is important to know what they can tell us.

Before the invention of the double-bladed post-hole digger or the mechanical post-hole auger (both of which cut round holes not much bigger than the diameter of the post), relatively large holes were cut with a spade. The displaced soil was stacked to one side, to be shoveled and tamped back once the post was installed. The post would later rot away, be pulled out, or be burned out, leaving behind another hole of approximately the post's diameter. These we call post molds. Very rarely would they deliberately be filled in; instead, nature would do the job, washing soil from the sides and from the existing land surface—including whatever small artifacts might happen to be scattered nearby (Fig. 3–7). If, for example, an 1856 penny finds its way into that mold-filling silt, it follows that the post must have gone and the mold have been lying open at a date after the coin was minted. Since the lifetime of a wooden post in Virginia can be gauged in decades rather than centuries, finding the penny would indicate that the post (and probably the entire fence) was of nineteenth-century date.

That piece of rudimentary logic is only part of what the holes and molds for posts can tell us. Equally important is what they have to say about the site both at the time the posts were erected and when they disappeared. Just as our 1856 penny tells us that someone was doing

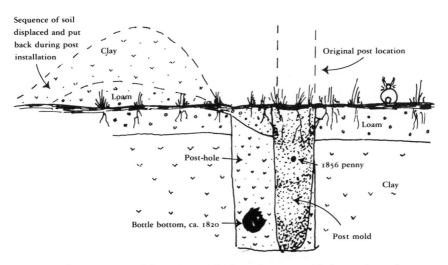

Sequence of soil displaced and put back during post installation

Clay

Loam

Original post location

Loam

Post-hole

1856 penny

Clay

Bottle bottom, ca. 1820

Post mold

3–7. Artifacts recovered from a post-hole and post mold determine when the post was installed (after ca. 1820), and when it was removed or rotted out (after 1856).

something on our site as recently as 1856 or later, so do artifacts found in the back-filling of any hole in which a new post was bedded give us clues about what was going on there at that time. If we find potsherds in the fill, we can conclude that someone was already living nearby; otherwise there would be no reason for a pot to get broken and its pieces to be lying on the land surface where the post-hole was being dug. If, on the other hand, the posts were being erected on land that was about to be inhabited for the first time, there should be little or no domestic refuse to be shoveled into the holes. Consequently, the almost total absence of artifacts from our Site A post-holes (there were plenty from the molds) was strong evidence that no one had built there before.

Archaeological relationships are established through both horizontal and vertical associations, the latter being by far the most reliable and informative. Thus, for example, if a row of post-holes is dug through clay layer B into subsoil C, and later is covered by loam layer A, it follows that the post was installed and removed *after* stratum B was laid down but *before* layer A covered over its mold. If, subsequently, other holes are cut, through layer A, an archaeologist will find those holes before seeing any sign of the previous "B" holes and so will know that although the two sets of holes occupy the same horizontal location, they cannot otherwise be related (Fig. 3–8).

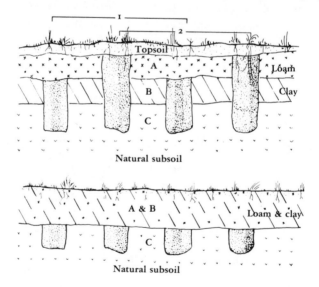

3–8. The sequential relationship of two pairs of post-holes and their molds can be determined by the strata through which they were cut or by which they were covered. Once those layers are plowed (below), all such evidence is destroyed.

Once a farmer puts his plow to our hypothetical site and churns layers A and B into one, he destroys all evidence of which post-holes cut through what stratum. The archaeologist has no alternative but to strip aside this ruined evidence and get down to the undisturbed subsoil. When he gets there he finds the bottoms of the post-holes; but now their patterns are confused; the A level and B level holes go into the same ground with nothing to show which are which, unless the two sets are of uniformly different depths or shapes, or one hole cuts through another. All too often, we find no such distinctions, just a mass of holes dotted over the site, and which we must try to interpret on the basis of past experience and guesswork. With the holes marked as dots on our site plan, we play the old childhood game of connecting them to create a picture of a clown or a jackass, or, in our case, of fences and buildings.

Playing this game is easy; the tough part is knowing whether you have won or lost. If, for example, you have two parallel rows of holes 18 feet apart, four to the row and 10 feet from post to post, you have the option of interpreting that as a single building measuring 30 by 18 feet, or as two structures measuring 10 by 18 feet, with a 10-foot gap between them (Fig. 3–9). We were to be faced with just this kind of problem at Carter's Grove's Site A and on every site where plowing had destroyed the soil stratigraphy.

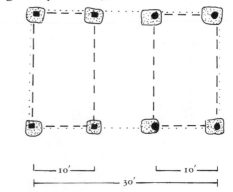

Although the largest of our Site A buildings had been built on posts in the same manner as every lesser structure from servants' quarters to corn cribs, the house probably looked a lot better inside than out. Fragments of window glass and the lead strips used to secure it in casement frames left no doubt that at least one of our buildings had some-

3–9. Two rows of post-holes, of similar size and depth, set on 10-foot centers might be interpreted either as one building 30-feet long or as two structures 10-feet wide.

thing better than shutters or oiled paper to cover its window openings. More surprising was the finding of a fragment of a tin-glazed delftware fireplace or wall tile, decorated with a standing figure painted in blue, a design to be seen on comparable tiles in paintings of the 1660s by the Dutch artist Pieter de Hooch (Fig. 3–10). Our tile, too, was likely to be of Dutch rather than English manufacture, and it immediately raised the question: Under what circumstances would delft tiles have been imported into Virginia in the second quarter of the seventeenth century?

Decorative tiles served a functional purpose when used as wall skirting—they prevented water used in mopping the floor from soaking into the wall-plaster. They were, however, by no means essential to the survival of Virginia colonists or of their homes. Such tiles were luxury items, and apparently imported before Jamestown had retail stores to which a homebuilder could go to purchase whatever he could afford. Indeed, there is no evidence that Jamestown ever aspired to the shopping-mall convenience that we now take for granted. In all probability, therefore, the individual who wanted to embellish his Site A house with Dutch tiles would have had to

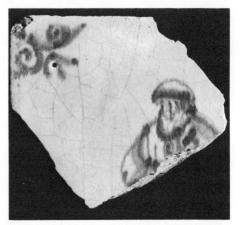

3–10. Fragment from a delftware tile found on Site A (above). A detail from a 1660 Dutch painting by Pieter de Hooch shows matching tiles around the fireplace.

order them from London, and that points to a degree of confidence and stability not found in Virginia much before the 1630s.

Many more artifacts attested to the affluence of the Site A household. The previously mentioned bottles—more than 108 of them—indicate much more glass-bottle usage than was common in the 1630s and 1640s. No surviving Virginia probate inventory prior to 1650 shows any household having more than five. Why so many? It was a question that was to remain without an answer for three more years. Equally enigmatic, at least at the outset, was half an elaborately decorated pair of fireplace tongs, its iron shaft enriched with a brass element resembling a furniture finial (Fig.3–11). So unusual was this embellishment that I supposed it to have been added to cover a repaired break, for I knew of no such iron and brass combination in any tongs of the period. This time, the correct explanation was more quickly forthcoming. In a 1644 painting by the Dutch artist Jan Olis I found just such a pair.

Riches on the hearth extended to the table. We found a knife whose haft was encrusted with silver, as well as fragments of Venetian-style drinking glasses, the latter apparently rare enough in Virginia that when the Dutch traveler David de Vries visited Jamestown in 1633, he noted in his journal that Governor Harvey received him "with a Venice glass of sack."[2] Although glasses were represented at Site A only by a few very small fragments, European pottery was more plentiful and in larger pieces. There were tin-glazed wares from the Netherlands as well as sherds which I first thought might be Portuguese. Pieces of slipware dishes decorated to rep-

3–11. Part of a pair of ornamental iron fireplace tongs embellished with a brass collar from Site A. Ca. 1620–1645.

resent the veining of marble left no doubt as to their origin: they had come from northern Italy. Then, too, there were double-handled earthenware flasks from Spain (Fig. 3–12) and more durable, stone-ware, bottles and jugs from the Rhineland, as well as several pieces of a fine, green-glazed earthenware which some authorities attributed to France but which I believed were more likely to be Dutch.

One of these green vessels was shaped like a medieval bell-metal cooking pot: three legs, a buff-colored body, green glaze, and a highly unusual handle, flattened and pinched at the top. I had seen nothing like it until, in the National Gallery in London, I came face to canvas with Jan Steen's 1660 painting known as *The Poultry Yard* (Fig. 3–13). There, in the hand of an egg-harvester, was our pot, pinched handle and all. Jan Steen's version was somewhat taller and a little less medieval in character than ours, suggesting that his was somewhat later in date; but there

3–12. An Iberian earthenware flask, or costrel, from Site A. The upper body is coated with a thin tin glaze and decorated with a crudely painted blue star. Ca. 1620–1645.

could be no doubting that both had a common source. Jan Steen being a Dutch and not a Flemish or French painter seemed to give support to my belief that the green pots were of Dutch manufacture.

Few of these European artifacts came from the immediate vicinity of the house and its adjacent buildings, for once the seventeenth-century land surface had been plowed and finally scraped away by our mechanical grader, there was nowhere for artifacts to hide but in post-holes and pits. The largest of the pits was a full 30 feet in diameter, an enormous hole in the ground which we first thought to be the eroded top of a well shaft. We had high hopes of it, for as every archaeologist knows, the best-preserved information invariably lurks in the waterlogged depths of silted wells. Wood, leather, textiles, indeed all organic materials can last almost indefinitely in the air-excluding moisture of wells. In London I had even found thin strips of wood covered with ink writing and dating from the first century A.D.

Although we dared not hope for so literal a message from the past to emerge from Site A's well, we firmly believed that we were in reach of something important.

The earth-filled hole was so large that its excavation called for specialized treatment. I elected to divide the fill into four pie-shaped units, and began by digging down through two diagonally opposite segments, thus leaving standing sections (often called profiles) bisecting the hole. This was not a new technique; known as the quadrant method, it had been developed in the nineteenth century for excavating European burial mounds.

We soon realized that we were not going down into a well, but rather into what looked like an abandoned, silted, and then deliberately filled cellar (Fig. 3–14). The round hole had become rectangular, and soon a flight of clay steps appeared at the north end. But if this was a cellar hole, where were the remains of the building that had stood over it?

3–13. An unusual green-and-yellow-glazed kitchen pot from Site A (above). The pot's distinctive pinched handle suggests that it is Dutch, and this detail from Jan Steen's *The Poultry Yard* (1660) provides supporting evidence.

We stopped digging and began to reexamine the clay surface all around, searching for evidence of post-holes, foundation trenches, or even the footing for a chimney. But we found nothing; yet there was no doubt that the cellar was indeed a cellar. Baffled, Eric Klingelhofer and his crew returned to clearing it out, carefully removing the remaining two quadrants down to a layer of yellow clay that had silted into the hole after its building ceased to exist.

Out of the overlying mixed loam and clay fill had come most of the artifacts, including the "Jan Steen" pot and the fireplace tile fragment, clear evidence that neither could have belonged to this cellared structure and that life went on at Site A after the building had gone. The silted clay beneath the loam fill had washed into the hole over a period of time—but "a period of time" can mean anything from several hours to many years. When heavy rains hit the site soon after the clay had been removed, nature graphically demonstrated that it could put it all back in the space of a single weekend.

Below the silt we came to a flat, clay floor with slots around its edges interrupted by small post-holes, indicating that the rectangular cellar hole-in-the-ground had been walled with vertical studs covered with boards, the lowest of which had been set in the slots. Few artifacts had been left behind on the clay floor to hint at the building's purpose,

3–14. The Site A cellar pit at an early stage of excavation by the quadrant method.

but it may have been no coincidence that both a broadax and a double-handled drawknife found there related to the carpenter's trade (Fig. 3–15).

Clearing the floor and emptying the wall slots still did not tell us what kind of building this had been. The stud holes were far too small to carry timbers bearing the weight of a house. For days we seemed to have nothing but a 20-by-19-foot packing crate set in the clay—until we scraped away a little of the floor's surface and found six massive post-holes, three along each of the 20-foot sides, creating a two-bay structure. The holes were larger and deeper than any we had hitherto found on the site, being more than 3 feet square and sunk 1 foot, 10 inches into natural clay below the floor (Fig. 3–16). Seated in each hole was a clearly defined post mold left by timbers measuring up to 8 inches square. Finding the exact positions of the corner posts enabled us more accurately to define the building's size (18 feet by 16 feet, 6 inches), but we still had little concept of its above-ground appearance. That a wood-framed house should be standing entirely within a cellar hole, rather than covering it, made little sense. The slope of the site was such that rainwater shedding into the adjacent ravine would first have been interrupted by the wall of the building and would have seeped with ever-increasing ease down the outside

3–15. A carpenter's drawknife and an ax were found on the floor of the Site A cellar pit. Ca. 1620–1630.

and into the basement. But we knew that it had not done so.

A single storm put 2 feet of water into our excavated cellar and cut numerous gullies into the west, or uphill, clay wall. Here was graphic evidence of what the rain could do, given half a chance. That it had been prevented from doing so during the life of the building was proved by the fact that the lower clay sides had remained straight and clean prior to the seventeenth-century silting that had occurred once the structure was gone. If the structure had stood entirely within the cellar hole, the only way that seepage could have been avoided would have been for some kind of flood-diverting ditch or wall to have been built sufficiently far from the building for the water to be channeled around it—and we found no evidence of that.

Once we began to find buildings and realized that Site A was turning out to be early, extensive, and important, light bulbs burned late as we struggled to do our literary homework. My wife Audrey concentrated on the history of Martin's Hundred and Carter's Grove, while Eric Klingelhofer searched more widely for documentary references to building construction details in seventeenth-century America. It was he who found the most logical explanation for our strangely framed cellar hole. It came, not from Virginia records, but from New

3–16. The Site A cellar pit after excavation. The large post-holes extending below the clay floor had once carried the weight of the roof.

York or what was then New Amsterdam, and from the pen of that colony's secretary, Van Tienhoven, who in 1650 wrote the following:

> Those in New Netherlands and in New England who have no means to build farm-houses at first according to their wishes, dig a square pit in the ground, cellar fashion, six or seven feet deep, as long and as broad as they think proper, case the earth inside all around the wall with timber, which they line with the bark of trees or something else to prevent the caving in of the earth, floor this cellar with plank and wainscott it overhead for a ceiling, raise a roof of spars clear up and cover the spars with bark or green sods, so that they can live dry and warm in these houses with their entire families for two, three, and four years . . .[3]

Here was a thoroughly reasonable answer. With the eaves of the roof extending far beyond the walls and resting on the ground, any water approaching the building would thus be channeled around it before it could reach the hole in which the subterranean home was seated (Fig. 3–17). That we failed to find any trace of such channeling is readily explained: All evidence of it had long since been eradicated by plowing. Recalling Dutch colonial secretary Van Tienhoven's statement that these cavernous structures were occupied until such times as the farmers could afford something better, we deduced that ours, too, marked the first phase in the evolution of Site A. Remembering, too, the woodworking tools found on the floor, we conjectured that it may have been the temporary home of carpenters sent to construct other, more conventional buildings. But sent by whom and for whom?

Back we came to the fundamental questions upon whose correct answers all our archaeological interpretations depended: Who owned this property; what did he do there, and for how long? Was he perhaps the sixty-year-old occupant of the isolated coffin, or the much younger man who lay beside an older woman closer to the house? I doubted whether we could ever be sure, but we had been left a few tantalizing hints, some almost microscopically small but one as large and as solid as a cannonball—all pointing to an unmarried man, one who managed to survive longer than virtually all his contemporaries who knew him as the "Governor" of Martin's Hundred.

From the upper filling of the cellar hole had come two short strands of silver wire and another of gold, each about as thick as sewing thread, the kind of wire used in the early seventeenth century to decorate better-quality clothing. More revealing was the discovery of a short length of woven gold twisted and glued into a point, a sartorial embellishment which was called just that—a point. They hung from the ends of shoulder laces and in rows dangling from men's garters. Here, therefore, were the remains of once elegant clothing such as the Dutch artist Thomas de Keyser depicted in his famous 1627 portrait of the diplomat and poet Constantijn Huygens

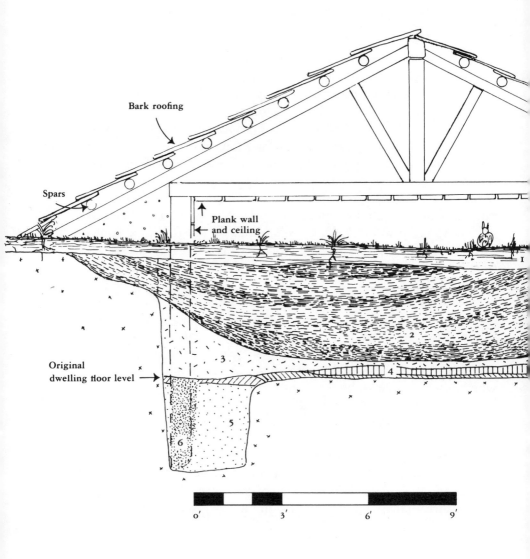

(Fig. 3–18). He is shown seated with gold woven in patterns through his coat and breeches, and with gold points hanging from his garters. Beside Huygens stands his clerk, his clothes bordered with silver— gold for the master and silver for the clerk.

Englishmen, too, dressed according to the dictates of fashion and wealth. Thus, in 1621, several military captains leaving for service in Europe had themselves immortalized by the celebrated court painter

3–17. A section through the Site A cellar house, coupled with a conjectural reconstruction. Layer 1 represents the modern, plow-disturbed topsoil; 2, the earth and garbage filling of the living space after the building was destroyed; 3, silted clay that washed into the hole after the roof had gone; 4, layers deposited during the building's lifetime; 5 and 6, post-holes and molds for the main roof supports.

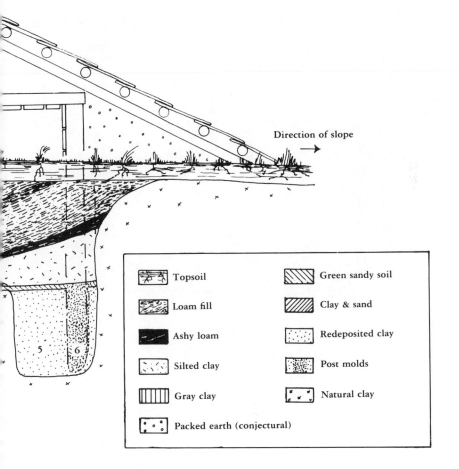

Direction of slope →

Topsoil		Green sandy soil	
Loam fill		Clay & sand	
Ashy loam		Redeposited clay	
Silted clay		Post molds	
Gray clay		Natural clay	
Packed earth (conjectural)			

Daniel Mytens, each veritably ablaze with gold threads and dangling points. We are safe in assuming that plantation "governors" and military lieutenants heading for America would have appeared similarly resplendent as they boarded their ships at Deptford or Portsmouth. How they looked when they disembarked after weeks of insanitary confinement aboard small and uncomfortable ships may have been somewhat different. It is clear, nonetheless, that clothing continued to define social stratification just as it had done through the Middle Ages. Although in England the last of the medieval sumptuary laws was repealed by order of James I, in Virginia, in 1621, the governor received instructions from London to "Suppress drunkenness gameing & excess in cloaths [and] not to permit any but ye Council & heads of hundreds to wear gold in their cloaths."[4] One of the council members unaffected by the order was the head of Martin's Hundred, and therefore the only man there legally permitted to wear gold in his clothes. His name was William Hardwood.

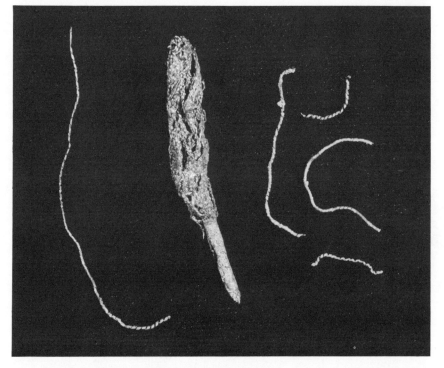

3–18. Threads of silver once woven into clothing fabric and woven gold twisted and glued into a point (enlarged, above). In the portrait by Thomas de Keyser, opposite, the Dutch diplomat Constantijn Huygens wears golden threads in his clothes and gold points to his garters, while his clerk's clothing is ornamented with threads of silver.

Putting the Governor in his Place

4

No document survives to tell us when the Society of Martin's Hundred was founded, but it probably received its patent in 1618, when the Virginia Company of London was struggling to expand and reinforce its shaky financial base by selling land to subsidiary companies and individuals. Although the first Martin's Hundred settlers reached Virginia in 1619, their leader William Harwood did not join them until more than a year later. He may have been an afterthought, a new company man sent over to direct the already resident directors, or a replacement for one who died.

Most of what we know about the history of Virginia in this period stems from the work of a barely remembered lady, Susan Myra Kingsbury, who, at the turn of the present century, transcribed and edited the surviving Court Book of the Virginia Company of London. When it was published by the Library of Congress in 1906, Miss Kingsbury's professor at Columbia University, Herbert L. Osgood, described the Court Book as being "among the most precious manuscript treasures which have found a lodgment within the United States."[1] Then a graduate student at Columbia, Myra Kingsbury subsequently became professor of social economy in Bryn Mawr College, and in 1933 and 1935 she published two more volumes of records relating to Virginia Company affairs, some (like the Court Book) from the archives at the Library of Congress, but others from private and university collections in England.

Almost as valuable a contribution was made by H. L. McIlwaine, who transcribed, edited, and in 1924 published the "Courte Booke" of the colony itself. Under the title *Minutes of the Council and General Court of Virginia,* these records cover the decade 1623 to 1633 and, like court transcripts the world over, they provide insights into the mores and peccadilloes of the populace not to be found in statutory and other legislative annals. What people actually did is always more revealing than the wording of what lawmakers wanted them to do or not do.

In addition to Kingsbury's and McIlwaine's cornerstone resources, two more scholarly editors have placed us in their debt: John Camden Hotten, whose *The Original Lists of Persons of Quality 1600–1700* includes the names of those alive in Virginia in 1624 and of those who died in the previous year, and Annie L. Jester, whose *Adventurers of Purse and Person* contains the census or muster of 1625, which shows who was then living in Martin's Hundred and throughout Virginia, and lists some of their material assets. From these sources we know that William Harwood was living in the Hundred between 1623 and 1625, a fact of no little importance to us, since his name was absent from the Virginia Company records in 1622, when the plantation faced its greatest challenge.

Linking Harwood to our Site A by means of a few gold and silver threads was tenuous at best. One garter does not a governor make. Indeed, we could (and did) argue that because Virginia's legislative council found it necessary to enact its own sumptuary law, people other than councillors and heads of hundreds were wearing gold in their clothing. Then, too, with most clothes being imported, and their owners dying with alarming rapidity, hand-me-downs must have been commonplace. An old pair of breeches with gold threads at the thigh and a hole at the seat was still an old pair of breeches, and no archaeologist studying a few threads can be sure whether he is looking at the remains of rags or riches. Fortunately, William Harwood's immortality does not hang solely by a thread. We found another, more substantial link in the form of an iron cannonball, 3 3/4 inches in diameter and weighing 6 3/4 pounds—a relatively big ball, for a large gun. In the 1625 census, Harwood was the only person in Martin's Hundred listed as possessing a "peece of Ordnance, 1 wth all things thereto belonging",[2] and nothing belonged more than a cannonball. On the other hand, does one ball make a cannon? Who can say that someone did not borrow the ball from Harwood's magazine and use it to grind wheat into flour?

In archaeology so much is built on foundations of conjecture that invariably there are alternative scenarios for just about everything. The best we can do is to attack them all and endorse only those that most stoutly withstand the buffeting of cynical colleagues. William Harwood is one such survivor. For about nine years he was the dominant figure in Martin's Hundred, although we have no evidence that he was ever given the official title of "Governor" by the London-based society. He is so described only in Virginia, where the title may have been no more than a synonym for leader. Another unofficial source reveals that Harwood came from Barnstaple in North Devon, but attempts to locate him there led only to the baptism of a William Harwood on July 11, 1565—which would have made him fifty-four when Martin's Hundred was settled, too old, perhaps, for so taxing a command. The problem proved to be irrelevant. We learned later that this Barnstaple William Harwood had died where he was born —three years later.

Our Mr. Harwood remains a gray figure in a company of shadows. On occasion we find him referred to as William Horwood, and are reminded that Sir Edward Horwood was one of four knights heading the list of Martin's Hundred shareholders. No Horwoods are listed in Britain's genealogical bible, the *Dictionary of National Biography,* but there is a Sir Edward Harwood who was shot at the siege of Maestricht in 1632 and who had a brother George, a London merchant. Did either of them have a son named William? We still don't know; any more than we can identify the Martin who gave his name to the Society. Low down on the list of shareholders we find a Christopher Martin who may have been the heir of Richard Martin, who became Recorder of the City of London on October 1, 1618, and died on the 31st of the same month. If the Society of Martin's Hundred was indeed granted its patent no later than 1618, Richard Martin could very well have been its figurehead, leaving his three shares to Christopher at his death. Richard Martin was a Devon man, and in 1601 had been Member of Parliament for Barnstaple—which brings us back to William Harwood.

He arrived in Virginia in August 1620, aboard the *Francis Bonaventure,* and was promptly appointed to the colony's governing council. The following year he asked to be relieved of that duty on the grounds that his presence at Jamestown took him away from more pressing concerns in the Hundred. Hard though it is to imagine what weighty problems could have prevented Harwood from serving on the council, the Virginia Company announced that minister Robert Paulett would replace him because the Society's business was "requiring his presence continually."[3]

That was on June 10, 1622, when the Virginia Company's council was still congratulating itself on having successfully settled so many people in the previous year that it "hath bredd such abundance of ioy as could not be contained amongst o'r selves, but hath declared it self by publique thanksgiveinge unto God Allmightie."[4] A little less than three months earlier (although they were as yet unaware of it) the Company's bubble had burst. On March 22, the Indians of Tidewater Virginia had risen against the English, killing the settlers, burning their houses, slaughtering their cattle, and destroying their crops and the will of the survivors to endure. In Martin's Hundred, one of the hardest hit of all the private settlements, 78 were reported killed, the highest death toll anywhere.

Although William Harwood's lieutenant, Richard Kean, headed the list of the dead in Martin's Hundred, the "Governor" is strangely absent from the records in the post-massacre months. By order of Virginia's Governor Wyatt, responsibility for the safety of who and whatever was left in Martin's Hundred was shifted to a blustering hothead from across the James River at Hog Island, bestowing on Captain Ralph Hamor "absolute power, and comand in all matters of warr over all the people in Martins hundred, and to charge and comand all the said people in the said Hundred, uppon paine of death to obey him uppon all such occacons, and to suffer themselves to be ordered and directed by him."[5] Why Harwood could not be his own commander or why he could not make the appointment remains a mystery; but the record is clear in showing that henceforth Harwood and Hamor were to be in frequent litigious combat.

It was in court that Harwood was last heard from. He had entered into a contract with a new minister for Martin's Hundred Parish, agreeing to an annual salary of 2,000 pounds of tobacco and a now-unknown quantity of corn to be paid the minister by the parishioners. In April 1629, the latter went to court, claiming that the plantation was by then very small, and that Harwood had saddled them with an unfair burden. The court agreed, making Harwood personally responsible for paying the minister a third of both the tobacco and the corn, and leaving the parishioners to provide the rest. Clearly, therefore, as late as the spring of 1629, William Harwood was still in control—if not satisfactorily in control—of the affairs and fate of Martin's Hundred.

Once we turned to documentary evidence to interpret what we were finding in the ground, we were asking far more fundamental questions than the whereabouts of Harwood when the Indians attacked. We needed to get a handle on the entire history of the settlement if we were correctly to interpret where our site fitted into the Martin's Hundred puzzle. The key facts were these:

According to the Martin's Hundred Society's own record, its ship the *Guift of God* left England in 1618 carrying 220 settlers to populate a 20,000-acre tract, a hundred acres for each share purchased by the London investors. Following the latter's instructions, the new Virginians began to build themselves an administrative center to be named Wolstenholme Towne, after the Society's most prominent shareholder, Sir John Wolstenholme (Fig. 4–1). A backer of Henry Hudson's ill-fated voyage of 1610 in search of a Northwest Passage, and of William Baffin's attempt in 1615, Wolstenholme's name had been given to three locations on the Arctic's frosted rim: a cape, a sound, and an island—none of them high on anyone's "I wish I could go there" list. Although he also got a bay in Bermuda, Wolstenholme Towne in Virginia seemed to offer Sir John his best chance for cartographic immortality. But few things turn out as we expect them to; the cape, sound, and island kept his name—the town lasted only three years.

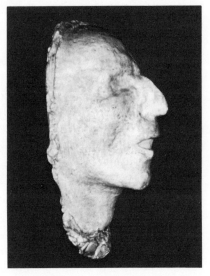

4–1. The reputed death mask of Sir John Wolstenholme, who died in 1639. Taken when his coffin was opened in the 1870s and his body found to be remarkably well preserved, the mask bears disturbingly little resemblance to his tomb effigy in St John's Church, Stanmore, where the mask is also to be seen.

The Indian uprising of March 1622 destroyed everything but two houses and "a peece of a church,"[6] and reduced the population of Martin's Hundred from about 140 to around 62 who may have temporarily abandoned the plantation and sought shelter at Jamestown. Later, about 20 returned to try again; but despite shipments of replacement people, by 1625 the residents in all of Martin's Hundred numbered a meager thirty. In May of the previous year, a decision made in London abruptly changed the flow of Virginia history and had a devastating effect on the future of privately patented plantations such as Martin's Hundred: James I, tired of wrangling, backbiting factions within the Virginia Company, and angry both over its failure to make the American foothold militarily secure and at its reliance on a one-crop economy—the tobacco which he was on record as detesting—withdrew the Company's charter and declared Virginia a royal colony. Henceforth its affairs would be administered by the Crown and no longer by committees of stockholders.

The step made sense. Although assigning national goals to joint-stock companies may have had the initial advantage of getting the private sector to underwrite development costs, the investors' subsequent pursuit of profit could set them at odds with national policies based solely on political or territorial considerations. Even though the Virginia Company's sister firm, the Bermuda or Summer Isles Company, was to keep its charter for many more years, and Britain let the East India Company run its own show (complete with fleets and private armies) until 1773, there was little future for an American company that could neither handle the natives nor return a profit.

Although the transference of authority to the Crown was clear and clean enough at the Virginia Company level, the legal status of secondary patent holders like the Martin's Hundred Society was more murky. London stockholders, and private "adventurers" who actually moved to Virginia, found their land rights in doubt. For several years after the transfer of power from Corporation to Crown, the governor of Virginia was reluctant to take control of the private or "particular" plantations or to grant land patents to property already purchased but undeveloped by London investors. By the same token, once the king had dissolved the parent company, Martin's Hundred shareholders were not about to send more people or pour more money down their Virginia drain.

Reporting to London in 1624 on the status of the private plantations, Virginia's Governor Wyatt listed Martin's Hundred as comprising 800,000 acres "as is alledged,"[7] suggesting that he had only the vaguest notion of the extent of the Society's holdings. Its original patent does not survive, but we know from the revised charter of 1622 that 1,500 acres intended for public use were then added to the first grant of 20,000 acres. Yet regardless of whether, in 1625, the Hundred embraced 21,500 or 800,000 or 80,000 acres, its recorded population of no more than thirty must have left much desirable real estate undeveloped, and controlled by a "governor" appointed (and presumably paid) by a corporation no longer in business. Just how William Harwood handled this difficult situation is a question crucial to our interpretation of the archaeological chronology at Martin's Hundred.

At this early stage in the digging we knew nothing about the Society's core settlement at Wolstenholme Towne—beyond the fact that little of it survived the 1622 Indian attack. Our Site A structures showed no evidence of destruction by fire; its pottery seemed to date from the 1630s and 1640s rather than the 1620s, and although we had found graves, we had seen no post-hole patterns resembling the plan of a church. In short, Site A could not be the remains of Wolstenholme Towne. How, then, could it relate to Harwood, who had vanished from the records before 1629 had ended?

Because the documents raise this question but not its answer, we must fall back on "What would I do?" reasoning. William Harwood's name was not among the shareholders when the Society of Martin's Hundred got its new patent in 1622, and he therefore owned no land of his own within the Hundred. At the same time, though a servant of London masters, Harwood was himself the master in Virginia. Assuming that he first lived in the company town and that eventually he found this too confining, he might well have moved to a new homesite elsewhere on the 1,500 acres of public land—the only real estate that did not legally belong to one of the London investors. Alternatively, Harwood may have stayed in town until the Indians destroyed it, or until the dissolution of the Virginia Company, and then moved out, taking part or all of the Society's public land for himself. There being no more company employees to house and feed, and with all the returned settlers located on acres previously assigned to them, who was to say that the "governor" should not take the land for which no public now existed?

Assuming that we were right in seeing no evidence of pre-1622 occupation at Site A, we could argue that Harwood moved there after the massacre and built a house in which he lived for the last few years of his life. Even if he was absent when the Indians attacked and in the period when his people fled to Jamestown, Harwood certainly was back by the end of the year, and with a staff of sufficient size that in the first three months of 1623 nineteen people belonging to it died of contagious disease. He was there, too, in August 1626, when Robert Adams of Martin's Hundred was in Harwood's house and heard a man named Richard Crocker accuse Ralph Hamor of profiteering and being unfit to serve on the council. For this and similar slanders repeated some time later in the woods at Martin's Hundred, Crocker was condemned to a month in jail, to a seat in the pillory with his ears nailed to a board, and thereafter to providing a bond of 300 pounds of tobacco as security for his subsequent good behavior.[8]

Life was tough and justice rough in Virginia in the colony's spawning days, but no tougher or rougher than in England in the same period. Scant record of the good times has survived, and most of what we know stems from transcripts of disputes and narratives of disasters. Thus, Richard Crocker's indiscretion gives us our only reference to Harwood's house.

If Site A was indeed William Harwood's plantation, which, after his death or departure, existed for another twenty years, we have no way of knowing which fences and buildings were his, and which belonged to later owners. That the settlement grew in four or more steps is fairly certain. Thus, for example, the lean-to extension to the large house overlay the silting of a shallow ditch or well-worn track, indicating that the house had co-existed with the ditch or track before the extension was added. Then, too, varying spacing of fenceposts pointed to different enclosures built by different people at different times. In some instances the fences were associated with ditches, and when the silting of one was cut by the digging of another, it was easy to see which came first.

Knowing from the spacing of the posts that fences differed in their size and construction is one thing; interpreting what these fences looked like is quite another. Posts set more than 9 feet apart suggest a rail rather than a paled fence, the greater weight of the latter calling for relatively close spacing. Then, too, the higher (and therefore the heavier) the fence, the deeper should be the post-holes; but because at Site A we were dealing with land that had been plowed for centuries, we could not be sure how much of the tops of the post-holes had been destroyed and therefore how deep they had been dug.

Some fences had no pre-dug post-holes, those made of wattles being woven around slender stakes that were simply pounded into the earth. If we are lucky, and the stakes were driven deep enough to reach the subsoil, they may show up as dark molds no more than an inch or two in diameter. All too often these tiny pockets of loam attracted the roots of grasses and other plants, causing their outlines to become blurred and their significance to be overlooked. For this reason the archaeologist not only records the location of every bona fide post-hole and mold, but also of each root hole. Only when these are plotted on the plan can we see whether they make recognizable patterns or exhibit a uniformity of spacing that betrays the hand of man.

No archaeologist feels comfortable with totally negative evidence. Contending that something did not exist because we have failed to find it is bad enough, but arguing that it *did,* even though we haven't found it, is infinitely worse. There was, nevertheless, one type of colonial fence that left no marks in the subsoil but whose presence can be deduced by the very fact that no trace is found. Called a snake or worm fence, it was built from split rails laid horizontally in zigzag lines, the rails stacked one upon another and held in place by their own weight (Fig. 4-2). When we find an area of intense occupation (pits in the subsoil, garbage in the overlying soil layers) concentrated within clearly delineated edges, but having no post-holes at its perimeter, we must suppose that some kind of enclosing barrier had existed: perhaps a snake fence.

We were scarcely more comfortable with another, thoroughly tangible kind of fencing evidence: a rectangular-sectioned slot averaging 9 inches wide and 10 deep, which embraced the main area of Site A's occupation at north and west. Running a total distance of 265 feet, the slot was interrupted by not a single post-hole. Expecting to find evidence of posts, we at first thought that the narrow trench was dug to seat the bottom few inches of the palings of a palisade-type fence to keep small animals from squeezing underneath to chew on the vegetables. But without supporting posts and rails, this could have been no ordinary paled structure.

The term "palisado" was widely interpreted in the seventeenth century; it could mean anything from a massive fortification of vertical planks (like the walls of Jamestown) or split trees, to an elaborately ornamental garden fence. What we had found was neither. Careful scraping of the soil filling the slot at Site A revealed a series of dark triangles packed around with redeposited clay (Fig. 4–3). The triangu-

4–2. Snake fences, like this one at Williamsburg, Virginia, around the restored magazine, were built on the land surface and left no lasting traces in the earth.

4–3. A narrow trench partially enclosed the buildings of Site A. The triangular dark stains in the unexcavated section are believed to be ghost images of split-log palings.

lar patches had been left by decayed pieces of split wood set vertically
in the ground. Averaging 4 inches in thickness and 18 in width, the
wood had been set with its broadest face flush against one side of the
slot, and held in place by ramming clay down around it. The wood
was thick enough and the slot deep enough for the timbers to stand
to a height of 3 feet or more, and stout enough to take several years
to rot. In short, it was a primitive kind of barrier calling for few tools
and little construction skill, yet strong enough to keep small animals
out of produce gardens and tall enough to be an adequate delineator
of property.

That interpretation fitted the archaeological evidence well
enough, but we lacked documentary support for it. Furthermore, the
miles of carefully researched and reconstructed fences in nearby Williamsburg included not a single foot of such fencing. But why should
it, we argued? Williamsburg's fences belonged to the eighteenth and
not to the seventeenth century.

For the past thirty years Audrey and I have been collecting copies
of sixteenth- to nineteenth-century genre art (pictures of paintings
clipped from magazines; postcards, slides, sales catalogues) and we
have assembled a fairly catholic library of picture books that run a
gamut from European museum catalogues to a pictorial history of
ladies' underwear. Thus our approach to most archaeological problems is to turn to the pictures. This time, my first clue came from a
series of postcards illustrating details from an elaborate piece of late
sixteenth-century needlework called the Bradford Table Carpet.
Created in England (and now in London's Victoria and Albert Museum) the carpet's Elizabethan designer had depicted a manor house
surrounded by a low fence of wide, vertical boards, each apparently
touching the ground, if not set in it, yet unsupported by posts save at
the gate.

Colleagues were quick to attack my evidence. "You can't believe
a needleworker!" they insisted.

Next I found a picture of a surveyor's plat for a piece of property in Tothill Fields, London. Dating from about 1612, the plat
showed five houses each with its garden either wholly or partially
enclosed with fences identified as "pales," and drawn as wide boards
rounded at the top (like those in the Bradford Table Carpet), and
with no visible means of support. "A stylized rendering," said my
rather unfriendly friends. "You can't put much store by a surveyor's
plat."

I knew that they could be right. But with the bit now firmly between my teeth, I plowed on. Soon my usually helpful sources began to dry up. I could find plenty of Dutch and Flemish paintings that showed paled fences whose boards touched the ground, but whether they went into it or were supported behind by posts and rails, one could not tell. Having exhausted my seventeenth-century avenues, I turned as a last resort to the eighteenth century, and as has happened so often in the Martin's Hundred saga, the gods smiled. A 1750 engraving illustrating *The Country Housewife's Family Companion* included a carefully delineated rendering of our fence. This time there could be no doubting the artist's skill or that the pales were actually seated in the ground. Enclosing a yard wherein a milkmaid is shown servicing a cow, the fence's pales have slipped sideways in their slot, and the illus-

tration depicts no back-supporting rails bridging the gap (Fig. 4-4). Later, I found several more eighteenth-century prints showing wide-boarded fences seated in trenches, but with a single rail nailed close to the top to prevent the pales from slipping. There is nothing to say that ours had not been similarly secured. Finally, Eric Klingelhofer came up with proof that fences built in trenches and unsupported by posts were known in Europe long before the Martin's Hundred settlers erected theirs; he produced a fifteenth-century German wood-cut showing such a fence under construction and the trench open to receive it (Fig. 4-5).

4-4. An English farmstead within a slot fence which, lacking a stretcher, allowed its pales to slip sideways. From *The Country Housewife's Family Companion*, 1750.

Learning that I was right produced singularly little satisfaction. It is the thrill of the chase that excites an archaeological historian, pursuing the proof with all the intensity of a hunter, the adrenalin flowing until the moment of the kill; then an instant of high elation—and it's done. The excitement drains away. Later, the mantle of scholarship envelops the new piece of knowledge; we fit it dispassionately into place, all that it took to gain it forgotten, the thrill denied. This is but one of several reasons why few of us read archaeological reports for pleasure, and why so many archaeologists, knowing it, do not bother to write them to be read.

Although the satisfaction of capturing and impaling a new piece of evidence fades swiftly, finding two conflicting documentary answers to a single archaeological question is just plain frustrating. This was the case when we found shallow depressions running alongside some of our post-supported fences, and identified them as the remains of ditches. Remembering that in England hedges often grow up to take the place of fences, and that roadside hedges are usually flanked by ditches, I deduced that fences beside a trackway running the length of Site A were part of a ditch, hedge, and fence combination. To prove this, we needed the testimony of some colonist or visitor that he had grown, trimmed, repaired, removed, or seen hedges in Virginia. With so much else to write home about, our chances of finding such a reference seemed remote. Yet find it we did—from the poisoned pen of one of the least attractive individuals to grace the pages of Virginia history: Captain Nathaniel Butler.

Recalled from the governorship of Bermuda in the fall of 1622,

4–5. A fifteenth-century European illustration of a slot fence under construction. The drilled holes in the yet unused palings indicate that the stretcher was secured with wooden pins (treenails).

Butler made a side trip to Virginia on his way home, spending six weeks there, two of them as the honored guest of Governor Wyatt. In reality Butler was in Virginia as a spy sent by his patron Sir Nathaniel Rich and others of a dissident group within the Virginia Company who were intent on the ouster of its management. Butler's purpose was to write a "true" report on the parlous condition of the colony in the aftermath of the Indian uprising. Describing conditions facing new arrivals, he stated that so little provision was made for their reception that they "are not onely seen dyinge under hedges & in the woods but being dead ly some of them for many dayes Unregarded & Unburied."[9] Here, then, was confirmation that hedges were used as a means of creating enclosures in Virginia. Captain Butler, for all his faults, should be accepted as a reliable witness on so uncontroversial a matter as hedges, or so one might think.

By the time he reached England, Butler had drafted a devastating document titled *The Unmasked face of our Colony in Virginia as it was in yᵉ yeare—1622.* Company officials hastened to prepare a rebuttal, drawing on the testimony of "divers Planters that have long lived in Virginia as alsoe of sundry Marriners and other persons yᵗ have bene often at Virginia." The hedgerow objectivity of such a blue-ribbon group should, in theory, be as dependable as Captain Butler's. Countering him point by point, witnesses for the defense answered the charge that newly arrived settlers were left to die under hedges, saying:

And for any dyinge in the feilds . . . & lyinge unburied, wee are altogether ignorant, yett yᵗ many dy suddenly by yᵉ hand of God, wee often see itt to fall out even in this flourishinge & plentifull Citty [of London] in yᵉ middest of our streets, as for dyinge under hedges theris noe hedge in all Virginia.[10]

We paid our money and took our choice, and wishy-washily identified our ditch-hedge combinations as *possible* ditch-hedge combinations.

Of our post-supported fences, the longest extended 300 feet from the structural complex at the north, southward past the graves that had brought us back to Carter's Grove, and headed in the direction of a break in a ditch that enclosed most of the site and that had first been identified by Bill Kelso in 1971. Just 100 feet short of that apparent entrance, the post-holes stopped. Another shorter, parallel row of post-holes 18 feet to the east died on us at approximately the same point. Together they defined the southern extremity of the trackway or avenue that provided the approach to the house and its outbuildings. Our problem now was to determine why it stopped short of the perimeter ditch.

We never did find the answer; instead, we discovered fifteen more graves, most of them in the path of the avenue had it extended the last 100 feet to the outer ditch (Fig. 4–6). Four of them had been dug on the same north-south axis, but the rest followed the usual Christian practice of lying with their heads to the west. Of the four north-southers, two skeletons had their heads at the north and two at the south. One of the latter had had her grave disturbed by the digging of another, clear evidence that not all the interments occurred at the same time.

Larry Angel identified five of the skeletons as male and five as female; the other graves were smaller, and almost certainly contained the remains of children, of whose slender traces little could be said. Four of the adults (two women and two men) had been buried in shrouds or garments secured with brass pins. Each woman had a pin resting on her skull, and one of the men had two by his head and two more at the torso, one of them resting on the right arm. This male, aged about twenty-seven, had been buried in a coffin whose wood had vanished, leaving only its nails—including the now familiar yet still unexplained row of large nails from head to foot along the body's center line. Five feet to the south, and parallel to it, lay another coffin, this one containing a woman in her mid-twenties—perhaps the twenty-seven-year-old man's wife. She, too, had had the central row of lid nails running the length of her coffin.

By this time, although we had yet to learn the true meaning of the center-line nails, we had torpedoed our original conclusion that our Carter's Grove (Martin's Hundred) coffins were the work of a single eccentric craftsman. About thirty miles further up the James River at Flowerdew Hundred—another early seventeenth-century private plantation—archaeologists under the direction of Dr. Norman Barka had found two coffined burials. When Dr. Barka showed me his drawings of the skeletons, there were our telltale nails. If this was still evidence of eccentricity, it had to be contagious.

A lecturing trip to Brown University led me to the answer, for in my audience was an archivist for Plimouth Plantation who subsequently sent me a 1651 engraving of English gravediggers with coffins on the ground beside them—coffins having A-shaped lids (Fig. 4–7). Looking again at the drawings of our burials, I noticed something that previously had escaped me: nearly all the centerline nails lay with their heads to the right, as they would if the lid had been made from two, butting boards, the right overlapping the left (Fig. 4–8). Here was the answer, a solution incredibly simple once one surmounted the barrier of belief that all coffin lids were flat.

4–6. Two burial complexes at the southern extremity of Site A, one adjacent to the fenced approach road to the plantation buildings (1–5), the other straddling it (9–23) and of later date. Grave 17 is cut by 18, and 19 by 22, proof that unlike graves 1–5, the later group was not interred at one time.

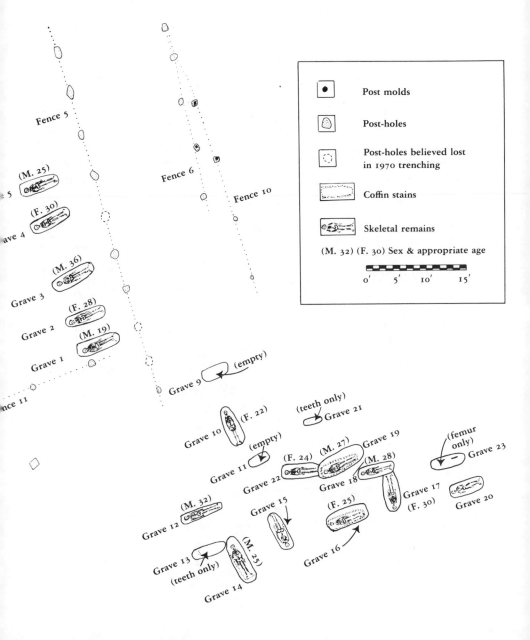

The 1651 engraving had appeared in a tract prophecying the Great Plague that would rage through London and the adjacent counties fourteen years later. Two more plague-related illustrations, one printed in 1625 and the other in 1665, made us wonder whether the A- or gable-lidded coffins were specially designed to contain distended corpses that would not fit into the conventional, flat-lidded variety. It was a short-lived theory, for I soon found a ca. 1680 engraving of the gibbet at Tyburn, and beside it a cart carrying two A-lidded coffins to receive the miscreants once they were cut down (Fig. 4–9). A-lidded coffins were becoming more common by the minute; but we were still asking why they were made in that way.

I found the answer in the collected writings of a late eighteenth-century folklore enthusiast, John Brand, who had devoted much of his life to collecting documents and oral descriptions of the origins and practices of all manner of rural activity—from celebrating New Year's Eve to how to play Tappie-toussie. Brand's notes titled "Pall and Under Bearers" described how, in the seventeenth century, each English parish possessed three or four mortuary cloths of differing materials and qualities, to be rented by mourning families to cover the coffin on the way to its grave. These palls could be of velvet or cloth

4–7. Gable-lidded coffins awaiting burial in an English churchyard. From *Monarchy or No Monarchy,* London, 1651.

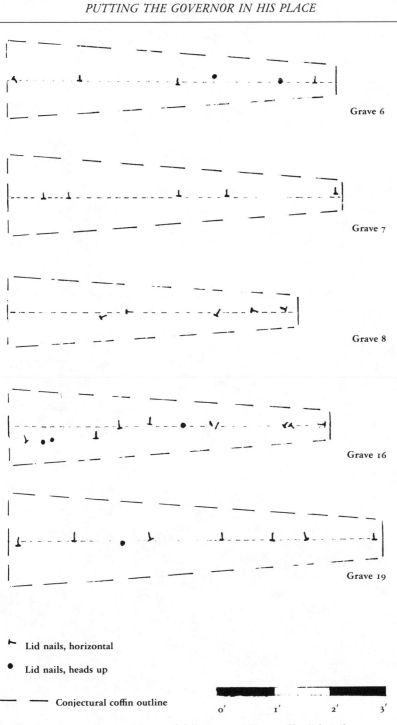

4–8. The head to point positions of fallen centerline coffin lid nails found in graves at Site A.

edged with linen or silk (Fig. 4–10). For the unmarried dead, and for women dying in childbirth, the pall was white. "This," wrote Brand,

> is spread over the coffin, and is so broad that six or eight men in black clothes that carry the body (upon their shoulders) are quite hid beneath it to their waist; and the corners and sides of it hang down low enough to be borne by those (six friends, men or women, according to the occasion) who, according to custom, are invited for that purpose.[11]

Thus modern pallbearers who carry coffins are doing the work of the seventeenth century's under bearers, for in those days gentlemen pallbearers did no more than lightly grip its edges as they walked in the funeral procession. It is not the bearers who matter to us, however, but the pall itself.

Turning to paintings and engravings of funerals in the sixteenth and seventeenth centuries, I found that palls were often far more elaborate than those rented from the parish. Families of quality had

4–9. An engraving ca. 1680 showing gable-lidded coffins awaiting occupants at London's Tyburn Tree. These coffins are likely to have been used to carry the corpses only as far as Surgeons' Hall for dissection.

4–10. Bearers carrying a pall-draped and gable-liddled coffin (1678).

their own, usually decorated with their heraldic arms or striped in the colors of their medieval tabards. A pall was meant to be seen, a dramatic element in the pomp of passing. If it was to be seen to maximum advantage by the crowds of dutifully mourning tenants lining the route, the coffin lid should not be flat. It should rise to a ridge over which the cloth would be draped, its embellishments repeated on both sides so that nothing would be missed.

I had yet to find any document or literary source to confirm this interpretation, but logic and the pictorial evidence fitted snugly enough together. Did that mean that the ceremony of the pall was part of the social ritual that attended our Martin's Hundred dead to their gravesides? I doubt it. As the Tyburn engraving demonstrates, an A-lidded coffin served as well to box the least missed as it did the most revered. I was convinced that this was simply the way coffins were built in Europe in the seventeenth century. One important piece of evidence was still wanting, however: I needed to find an intact example of a seventeenth-century coffin surviving in the vault of an English church, where I could study its construction and draw the positions of its nails.

With so many ancient churches still in use in England, finding one with seventeenth-century coffins in its vault should not be too difficult —or so I thought. A letter to the Bishop of London explaining my quest and seeking his help drew a list of clergymen and ecclesiastical archivists who might be of assistance. My next inquiry elicited a response from the librarian at Westminster Abbey saying that I could not have access to the vaults unless I already knew that an A-lidded coffin was housed there. Furthermore, he very much doubted that there were any. "One would expect the coffin of a member of the Royal Family or of one of the grander members of the nobility to have a flat top in the 16th, 17th and early 18th centuries since it was the habit at that period to place over the coffin a pall on which was placed the recumbent funeral effigy of the deceased."[12] Back to square one.

Following a hot tip that a vault under the village church at Clifton, Nottinghamshire, contained members of the Clifton family going back to the fifteenth century, I sought the vicar's permission to have it opened. On the train journey from London I felt certain that confirmation was at hand. I could see the rows of Clifton coffins sitting A-lidded in their niches, waiting only to have the cobwebs pulled aside to reveal their slightly rusted, rose-headed nails. I had seen too many Vincent Price movies. The reality was very different. A narrow flight of steps led down to a vault so stuffed with rotting coffins that one could barely squeeze through the entrance—as the bearers of the last of the Clifton dead had discovered. His coffin had been shoved in through the doorway, roughly pushing its predecessors aside (Fig. 4–11). There was no hope that the vault contained the evidence I was seeking, for if there is one thing you cannot do with an A-lidded coffin, it is to stack others on top of it. Nevertheless, I did not come away entirely emptyhanded. Among several handsome memorial effigies in the church was one to Sir Gervaise Clifton, who died in 1669, its central element a full-sized marble sculpture of an A-lidded coffin (Fig. 4–12). The carver, however, had thoughtlessly omitted the marble nail heads.

There, for the time being at least, the trail turned cold.

4–11. The passage to a burial vault at Clifton Church, Nottingham. Flat-lidded coffins block the doorway at left.

4–12. A gable-lidded coffin or mortuary chest rendered in marble as part of the tomb of Sir Gervaise Clifton, who was buried in Clifton Church, Nottingham, in 1666.

Painters and Potters

5

Peering into the face of a skeleton while picking dirt from around its teeth with all the care of a dentist, an archaeologist cannot help but be aware that he is eyeball to eyesocket with someone who knew the answers to many, if not all the questions he is asking. For my part, I know that although the bones may be those of a person whose culture rendered him superficially different from me, a cold wind still made him shiver, liquor fuddled his senses, and in the night a woman's arms made yesterday and tomorrow unimportant. In these, and in virtually every other human emotion, we are alike. Our hands touch, but the silence of eternity holds us apart. And that's what is so damned frustrating!

In all, Site A yielded twenty-three graves in four groups: fifteen straddling the roadway; the five supposed contagion victims behind its west fence 8 feet away; the single coffined man off by himself a further 100 feet to the north, and finally the coffined couple another 75 feet closer to the plantation complex. If the single man (who was in his sixties) was William Harwood, who we think died around 1629, we might also suppose that the man and woman lying closer to the house succeeded him as owners of the plantation—but not if, as seems likely, Harwood's successor was one Thomas Kingston, who served as burgess for Martin's Hundred Parish in 1629 and acquired at least 2,000 acres of its land. Mrs. Kingston did not lie beside him; instead she got herself a new Thomas, marrying Thomas Loving in 1639. He, too, had property in Martin's Hundred, at least 2,700 acres. It is unlikely, however, that our coffins contained the Loving couple, for he did not die until 1665, fifteen or more years after we think Site A was abandoned.

Because we cannot identify the occupants of our coffins, it by no means follows that Thomas Kingston did not succeed William Harwood, or that after Kingston's death in 1636, his holdings were not acquired by Thomas Loving. The case simply is not proven. The archaeological evidence certainly points to occupancy by a relatively prosperous household throughout the life of the site. In addition to the already mentioned gold and silver threads, we found near the large dwelling three tinned-brass hooks and an eye of a type used to anchor men's breeches to their doublets in days when a belt held up a gentleman's sword and not his trousers (Fig. 5-1). One hook had its matching eye attached, indicating that they were a spare pair rather than having been discarded while attached to clothing, since getting out of one's breeches without first unhooking the doublet would have been distinctly difficult. Nevertheless, the hooks and eye did point to *matching* clothing. I am well aware that trying to see a seventeenth-century man through his hooks and eyes is no more convincing or conclusive than trying to anatomize President Harding on the evidence of a cuff link. An archaeologist's job, nevertheless, is to make the most of what he finds—while trying to avoid the trap of making too much.

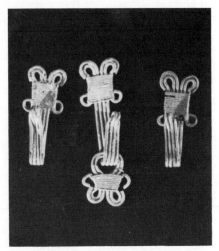

5-1. Tinned-brass hooks and an eye made to anchor a man's doublet to his breeches, a style fashionable in the 1630 to 1650 period. Found on Site A.

Fortunately for us, Man (or more probably, Woman) has always had a talent for breaking crockery, and on its evidence we have learned to know the Greeks, the Romans, the Saxons and, for that matter, all of the other pot-smashing cultures and empires that have preceded us. The trick with pottery—like properly interpreting breeches hooks—is to tell the expensive from the cheap, and thus to determine the owner's social status. That, at least, is the theory. In practice such differentiation can be well nigh impossible, unless you are sure that a site was occupied only by the landowner and his immediate family—no servants or slaves with their cheaper tablewares to get dropped and thrown into the master's trash pit. Then again, we must be sure that what we find is truly representative of the household. The rich man whose cook breaks only the common kitchen wares may end up being judged—or misjudged—by those alone. At Site A the range of ceramic wares was in line with what we would expect of a relatively large and wealthy household—plenty of broken cooking and chamber pots, and a small but significant assortment of imported European pieces of good quality.

Most of the pottery was smashed into very small sherds and, as always seems to be the case, not enough survived from any one pot to enable us to reconstruct more than a low percentage of the vessels. Although frustrating, this is always more distressing to the curator than to the archaeologist, who needs only a single fragment to know that a vessel of its type once was used on his site. On the other hand, opportunities to join fragments together can have a strictly archaeological application when the matching sherds are recovered from different layers or locations.

The laboratory staff's morning ritual is to wash, dry, and then number every artifact from the previous day's digging. The numbers identify the artifacts' locations on the site, both horizontally and vertically. Thus, for example, sherds marked C.G. 1736A come from a layer of sandy brown loam in the top of a polygonal-shaped refuse pit, while those marked C.G.1736B are from a stratum of gray loam under, and covered by, 1736A. If joining fragments from the same pot are found in both layers, we can conclude that no appreciable time elapsed between the deposition of B and A.

Once an excavation ends and we are sure that no more artifacts will be coming from the site, the lab staff begins the enormously time-consuming exercise called cross-mending. Taking all the pottery from everywhere on the site, we lay it out on long tables, dividing it up first by the type of ware (stoneware, delftware, slipware, and so forth), then by shape (bowls, mugs, pans, and the like), next by elements such as rims, bases, and handles, and finally by whatever other subdivisions we can detect, such as color, thickness, glaze variations, potting marks, and abrasions caused by use. When no more subdividing is possible, we should find ourselves with the sherds grouped as parts of individual pots. From this we get two things. The first is a vessel count.

Knowing that fifty-four fragments of Rhenish stoneware bottles were found on a site tells us very little. They could represent fifty-one pieces from one bottle and three from another, or they might be fifty-four sherds from as many vessels. Not until we can determine, say for instance, that we have fragments from nine Bellarmine bottles (the number of pieces from each being immaterial) can we learn anything useful about the people who lived on the site where they were found.

The second function served by cross-mending is less obvious but no less important: It may bring together sherds not only from different layers but from disparate parts of the site. Thus, on Site A, sherds from the upper filling of the cellar hole mended to other sherds from two rubbish-filled pits, one south of the house and the other northwest of it (Fig. 5–2). This juxtaposition told us that when the cellar hole lay open and abandoned, the two pits were also in existence and being

5–2. Site A's principal structures and pits, showing how joining (cross-mending) potsherds linked fill over the abandoned cellar house (A) to that of adjacent rubbish pits, and how they in turn were linked to one another. Matching pairs of initials are those of tobacco-pipe makers whose marked products provided further evidence of comparable dates for the filling of holes. Although only one line links the main dwelling to any of the deposits, there is reason to believe that, in reality, all the linkage radiated from that central source.

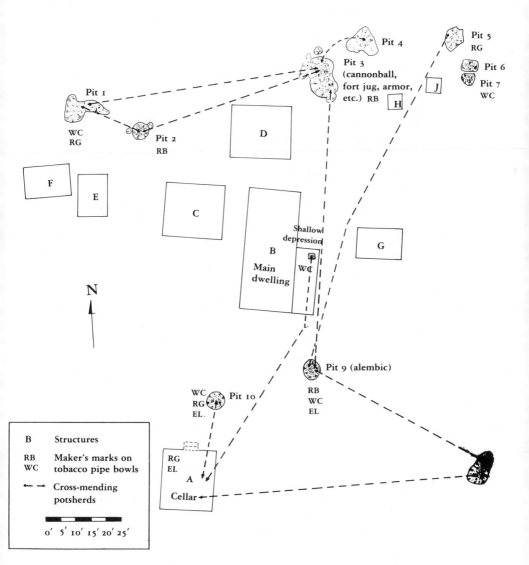

filled at much the same time—otherwise fragments of a single vessel could not have been thrown into all three. If, as we suspected, the cellared structure was the first building erected on site A, the pits were of a later date. Thus, the cross-mending of the pottery gave us what we needed most—a hint of chronology on a site otherwise singularly short of recognizable time sequences.

I cannot deny that when we reduce our site's buildings to letters (Structures A, B, and C), our sequences to Roman numerals (Period IV, V, and VI), and our artifacts to Arabic catalogue numbers, we have gone a long way toward the one thing we are trying to avoid: wringing the last ounce of life and humanity out of everything we have found. That cannot be helped, for order is the essence of analysis. What can be helped, and cannot be condoned, is leaving it at that once our counting and comparing are done. Many archaeologists feel that tables of numbers and scientific-looking bar graphs are the measure of scholarship—which is why the products of many an important excavation never fire the popular imagination. Instead they end their days as a collection of boxed fragments, or at best are arrayed in museum cases as examples of things that have been found. Because incomplete pots and fragments from rusted swords rarely can compete with the whole vessels and shining weapons one sees in art museums, excavated artifacts fail to do a good job of telling their tale at any level. What, then, is the alternative?

We have to put them in their historical place, graphically demonstrating where they fit into the jigsaw puzzle of the past. We have to find a way to exhibit the whole picture. At Martin's Hundred, as I noted in the previous chapter, we have spent long hours trying to find parallels for our artifacts in the genre paintings of Dutch and Flemish artists. From the late sixteenth century until the 1670s, scores of painters fed an art market drawn from farmers and shopkeepers whose taste ran less to great religious and allegorical canvases than to simple tavern scenes—drunks fighting, soldiers playing cards, peasants dancing, and old men making the most of young milkmaids. The drunks have pots in their hands, the soldiers carry weapons, the peasants have laid aside their tools, and the milkmaids have jugs (Fig. 5-3). Thus do we see our artifacts in contemporary settings, playing a part in the life of their time.

People who have given little thought to seventeenth-century art history immediately question whether we can legitimately look at paintings of European people, European pots, and European architecture, and expect them to resemble English blokes, bowls, and buildings—and, more importantly, whether we can stretch the linkage from

Land's End to Virginia. So reasonable is the question, and so vital the viability of the answer, that our Martin's Hundred's artifacts must briefly be set aside in its favor.

That there could indeed be a close visual relationship in the seventeenth century between what one saw on both sides of the North Sea dawned on me while crossing it on the Harwich-to-Rotterdam ferry—an experience otherwise devoid of merit. I realized that today's Common Market has created a bland sameness about both towns; European-style road signs are to be seen in Harwich, as is the uni-world architecture of apartment buildings; German cars park in the streets; milk comes in liters and cheese in grams—gone are the Urban District Council signs of yesteryear, going the Victorian terraced houses and the Austin and Morris cars; gone the pint, and gone the pound. I remembered early eighteenth-century English building directories that spoke of Dutch brick and Flemish tile; I recalled that the English glass industry had been built by emigrant Lorrainers and the English delftware industry by Flemings from Antwerp, and that for thousands of years English life had been influenced by refugees fleeing across the Channel from political and religious oppressors.

Off the boat and back in the library, I looked for evidence of Tudor and Stuart common marketry. It began in 1496 with the *Inter-*

5–3. A typical tavern scene by the Haarlem artist Adriaen Brower (d. 1638) showing peasants at play and their pots in disarray.

cursus magnus, Henry VII's commercial treaty with the Netherlands, whereby mutual privileges and fixed duties were granted to English and Flemish merchants. The relationship languished during the reign of Mary, suffered during the Spanish war with France that led to Britain's loss of Calais, but assumed new importance under Elizabeth, who spent more in support of the Protestant Netherlanders than on any other military commitment save for that in Ireland. When, in 1567, Philip of Spain sent the Duke of Alva north to impose a final solution on the Netherlandish problem, Protestant Flemings fled across the English Channel in unprecedented numbers. They settled in East Anglia and in Kent, bringing with them their taste and their talents, setting both to work in parts of England still living in an essentially medieval world, little touched by the gilded hand of the European Renaissance. It was small wonder, therefore, that fifty years later towns in southeast England were looking, for instance, as much like Egmond-aan-Zee as today flats in Harwich look for all the world like apartments in Rotterdam.

Egmond-aan-Zee is not a name on the tip of every tongue, but it found a place in our puzzle by virtue of having been painted from behind. I came upon it in Manchester's City Art Gallery, a small panel painting less than 11 inches in height, and executed around 1630. Regardless of its diminutive size, the picture shows this Dutch fishing village in astonishing detail—every house, every fence, well, and hitching post (Fig. 5–4). Unlike most paintings of Dutch towns, which concentrate on the best of their architecture, this one sees Egmond-aan-Zee from the seamy side, putting the less substantial buildings in the foreground, the ones whose post-holes we are most likely to find paralleled on early colonial sites in Virginia. The key question was whether or not the artist had been accurate in what he drew.

Beyond the buildings and close to the sea, the land swept up into strangely undulating headlands, and atop one of them was a navigational beacon. A quick look at a modern Dutch road map showed dunes where the painter had his lumps, and just off-shore a lighthouse. I had little doubt that he had painted the truth. Doubting colleagues continued to question to what degree Egmond-aan-Zee could be assumed to resemble, say, the back of seventeenth-century Harwich, much less Jamestown in Virginia. There is, however, a geological relationship between all three. The Netherlandish coast, and that of both England's Thames estuary and of Tidewater Virginia, are composed of clay and sand—not quarriable rock. Lacking building stone, the architecture of all three relied on bricks made from the clay and wood from the trees that grew on it. Tiles and shingles, not slate, covered most roofs, and board or rail fences substituted for dry stone walls. Thus, remembering that the southeastern English and the English Virginians were a polyglot lot, architectural similarities in the two regions are easier to assume than to question. As for the ceramics, glass, weapons, and other common possessions of the two, archaeology leaves no doubt that many, if not most of them were identical, although the flow of these items was westward from continental Europe, rather than the other way around.

The Dutch and Flemish painters of the seventeenth century were trying to make a living. Although landscapes (unless they were of famous places) only needed to be pretty, towns had to be recognizable. Scenes of contemporary life, on the other hand, had only to include the kinds of people the buyer knew and liked, doing things in settings that were familiar—a kitchen, a barn, a tavern. Only when the picture was painted as a portrait to be sold to the sitter did the setting have to be as real as the face. Consequently, we have to exercise caution in accepting paintings as photographically accurate evidence; some can be, others definitely cannot. The trick is learning which is which.

When, in 1655, the Dutch artist Nicholas Maes painted the pic-

5–4. The simple houses at the outskirts of the Dutch town of Egmond-aan-Zee. Formerly attributed to Adam Willaerts, the painting suggests the kinds of dwellings erected in early English Virginia. Ca. 1630.

ture known as *The Idle Servant,* he showed an admonishing
housekeeper in the center with a German stoneware jug in her
hand. The following year he painted *The Listening Housewife* (Fig.
5–5), facing left and holding what appears to be the same jug. It is true
that two households could easily have possessed identical jugs; they
were made by the thousand, and several of their type reached Martin's

5–5. The almost identical jugs in these details from paintings by Nicholas
Maes, *The Idle Servant* (above) and *The Listening Housewife* (opposite), were
painted in 1655 and 1656.

Hundred. But the jug is not the only link between Maes's two pictures. In both we can see into a back room where a man and a woman are seated at a table drinking; and in both, the woman wears a similar black cap and holds a comparable tall glass of red wine. Like the stoneware jug, these people are the artist's props, details drawn from memory that he can handle dextrously and quickly.

The only way to determine which artists are working from memory and which from life is to study their pictures in such detail that you get to know their work by the back of a chair, the placement of a candlestick, or the color of a cap. Sometimes they blatantly gave away the tricks of their trade. When other inspiration failed, they painted themselves in their studios. A landscape painter is revealed briskly at work on a country scene with nothing more inspiring in front of him than a blank studio wall. Immediately he is struck from our list of depictors of barns and fences, for even if he is masterful in his rendering of them, we can never be sure that this barn went with that fence, or that a window really would have been in precisely the relationship to that artist's door. Relying less on memory, but no less suspect, are Maes-style artists like Joos van Craesbeeck, who showed himself in his studio painting as rigid a group of models in the role of revelers as you can expect to find in a department store window. Common to this picture and to several others by better-known artists is a flagon set in the foreground, beside a seated toper, but with its handle pointing *away* from him and in the direction of the artist, who put it there after his models had taken their positions.

I began the archaeological anatomizing of paintings early in the 1960s, when I found myself questioning the often heard claim that England's superb genre painter, William Hogarth, was a reliable source for virtually every aspect of English life in the second quarter of the eighteenth century. The more I studied his pictures (and the engravings copied from them), the most distrustful I became. The bonding of his brick walls was often architecturally incorrect; a table knife looked more like a miniature scimitar (his eighteenth-century biographer and pictorial analyst, John Ireland, took it for a razor), and wine bottles Hogarth put on his tables in the 1750s were the same as he had drawn decades earlier. Clearly, in later life, Hogarth was drawing from memory, ignoring the fact that objects he had learned to paint in the 1720s had changed their shapes during the ensuing years.

Having learned to treat Hogarth's visual statements with caution, I came to the Netherlandish artists more wanting than willing to believe them, and as it turned out, with good reason. Perhaps most prolific of the Flemings was David Teniers the Younger (1610–1690), who began painting in his twenties and lived to be eighty. Specializing in scenes set in taverns, military guardrooms, and apothecaries' and alchemists' shops, he preserved for us an endless array of scruffy people in less than elegant surroundings. In many of these pictures we find a shelf anchored to a back wall, and on it a pot closely resembling one found at our Site A, and considered by us to be a chamber pot (Fig. 5–6). Teniers's version, however, invariably has what may be either a spoon or a pestle protruding from it—raising fair questions about the validity of our chamberpot interpretation. At the same time, we have good reason to doubt whether Teniers's pot ever stood on that shelf. Not only does it turn up in several pictures, it is usually accompanied by a glass flask having a twist of paper stuffed in

its mouth. Peering about in these same paintings we find other similarities: a split wooden block used as a seat or footstool, a split-ended bench (often with a broom leaning against it), a colander-shaped, earthenware dish being used as a brazier from which to light a pipe or warm an old man's hands. Then there are Teniers's people: a man with his back to us whose posture leaves no doubt about what he is doing (some-

5–6. A Virginia-made earthenware chamber pot (above) from Site A. Ca. 1630–1645. A typical David Teniers the Younger shelf (below) and on it a vessel very similar to the Martin's Hundred pot. Detail from *A Gambling Scene at an Inn,* undated.

times into a tub or simply against a wall), a red-capped fellow in a window or peering out of a crowd, and someone entering or leaving a room, a stock trick to create a sense of movement and to suggest that more is going on just beyond the frame.

In the foreground of one of his tavern scenes, this Flemish Hogarth shows a blue and gray stoneware bottle decorated on its sides with three medallions (Fig. 5–7). This is no fictional pot; on the contrary, it is of a distinctive type whose medallion fragments have been unearthed at Jamestown, on another Virginia site in northern Tidewater, on a fort site in the Virgin Islands, and from a dirt pile flanking a roadside utility trench in Frankfurt, Germany. In each case the medallion bore the date 1632 or 1634. Recalling, therefore, that Teniers's earliest paintings date from around 1635, we had grounds to argue that this was one of them. The date was important to us, because on a bench to the left of the picture stands a delicate drinking glass whose stem elements resembled some very small fragments we had found on Site A. Taking the picture at its face value, our critics might argue that the artist was showing us that we were wrong in concluding that the presence of delicate drinking glasses pointed to an affluent household (as the previously quoted comment by David DeVries, about being received by the Governor with a Venice glass of sack, seemed to suggest), for in Teniers's painting the glass is precariously perched on a bench in the tackiest of taverns.

I concluded that Teniers had drawn the glass from his stock of real or imaginary props, and had put it on his bench without giving any thought to its cultural implications 350 years later. A glass was synonymous with drinking, and it made a pleasant change from painting earthen beer-pots and stoneware bottles. Nevertheless, David Teniers's picture did have something to tell us; it said that this type of glass was in use as late as the 1630s, otherwise he would not have learned to paint it with such fidelity. Furthermore, even if the picture had been painted several years later than the dates suggested by the stoneware bottle, its evidence still fitted well alongside our persisting sense that Site A was occupied in the 1630s and 1640s, thus placing most of its life in the post-Harwood period.

The fragility of glass was such in the seventeenth century that although it was not costly to make, and when broken had no value at all, it may well have had a far higher value in Virginia than it would where the factories producing drinking glasses were within easy reach. Goblets of silver or silver-gilt had greater intrinsic worth, and while it is quite likely that Harwood and his successors owned such things, their value as bullion made sure that they were not left behind to fall into the hands of archaeologists. We must therefore seek evidence of status, if not in the glass, in the top-of-the-line imported

5–7. Detail from David Teniers the Younger's painting of a lute player in a tavern, showing a Rhenish stoneware bottle (foreground) of a type common in the 1630s, above it a drinking glass whose stem includes elements paralleled by fragments from Site A.

ceramics. Immediately, however, we find ourselves in danger of confusing the desirability and price of today's antiques with their original worth.

That problem was brought home to me after we found fragments of a large, brown stoneware Bellarmine bottle in the rubbish-filled cellar. Decorated with three medallions and of pleasing shape, it would, intact, have been a highly desirable antique. Later I learned just how desirable; in London's Chelsea Antiques Fair I found a very close parallel for our three-medallion bottle, the first of its kind I had seen in thirty years of collecting German stonewares. It cost us more than $1,200, and today the price would be higher still. With that in mind, it was easy to see our sherds as evidence of wealth. I was able to put this discovery in a more sober perspective when, in the Brussels Royal Museum of Fine Arts, I found a small panel painting by the Dutch genre painter Adriaen van Ostade (he was born in the same year as David Teniers, lived almost as long, and painted as much), and in it an even closer parallel for our bottle than I had bought at the Chelsea fair (Fig. 5–8). Van Ostade's setting for the bottle was not the home of men with golden garters, but a beat-up table outside a rural

5–8. An intact Rhenish stoneware Bellarmine bottle purchased to parallel another whose fragments (above) were found at Site A.
Opposite: A painting by Haarlem artist Adriean van Ostade (1610–1684), showing a Bellarmine bottle closely matching the Site A fragments.

tavern, where two rustic musicians were playing while a third sang, the bottle aspiring only to keep him in voice. Like wine bottles today, the Rhenish stoneware bottles of the sixteenth and seventeenth centuries were valued for their contents, not for themselves.

Unquestionably of greater original worth than the stoneware bottles were the delftwares produced in Flanders, Holland, England, and to a lesser extent in other European countries. Delftware was not common on our site, and most of the fragments we did find belonged to two plates of the same type, both decorated with radiating blue stripes. Although I knew that a bowl painted in the same pattern had been found in Bristol, England, and that no one there had doubted its English origin, the more I looked at our plates, the less English I thought they looked.

In the fields of antiques and archaeology there is an ever-fashionable tendency to keep in shape by jumping on every passing bandwagon. A new ceramics factory is discovered, and at once vessels long labeled as something else are claimed to be products of it. In 1976, when our broken plates were found, we were entering our Portuguese phase—following the publication of some allegedly Por-

tuguese sherds dug up in Northern Ireland. I had taken one of our fragments to London, to a ceramics expert who had studied the Ulster pieces, and who agreed that ours might indeed be related to those. Two years later, while looking through our collection of fragments from the West Indies for something entirely different, I came upon a little box containing several sherds and a few tobacco pipe-stem fragments that I had picked up on a mountain trail on the island of St. Eustatius. Among the fragments was a blue-striped sherd from a plate so like ours that when they are placed together, no delftware expert has yet been able to tell them apart (Fig. 5–9).

Although St. Eustatius (known there as Statia) passed in and out of many hands in the seventeenth and eighteenth centuries, it was never under Portuguese control. First settled by the Dutch in 1636 (some historians put it earlier), the island remained Dutch until the English took it in 1665 and lost it to the French a year later. Thus, in the period we were assigning to the occupation of Site A (ca. 1625 to 1645), Statia was solely Dutch, making it almost certain that the striped plates are Dutch and not Portuguese.

The testimony of imported European pottery frequently relies on widely scattered evidence: a Flemish painting, an inventory descrip-

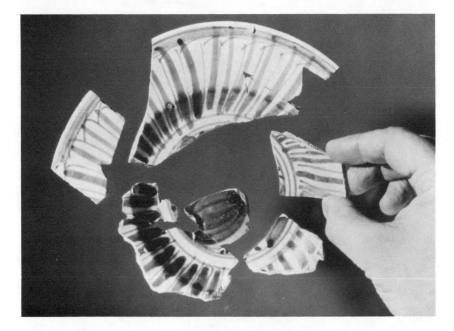

5–9. A fragmentary blue-striped delftware plate from Site A and, in the hand, an almost identical sherd found on the West Indian island of St. Eustatius, settled by the Dutch in 1636.

tion, an intact example in a museum collection; but given time and the wisdom of experience it can be assembled. When dealing with pottery made locally, however, we are in far deeper water. Rarely do pictures, inventories, or conveniently dated examples survive to guide us. We are strictly on our own, piecing our conclusions together on circumstantial evidence.

The first hint of our finding what might be earthenwares made in Martin's Hundred, and within hailing distance of Site A, came when Eric Klingelhofer called me at my office to report that excavator Richard M. Veditz was in the process of uncovering a very strange vessel. Rick was working in one of the site's several rubbish pits, and lying in the middle of it there was indeed a very odd pot. With what we took to be its conical base sticking up, it was thought by the crew to look more like a space-age nose cone than any seventeenth-century object (Fig. 5–10). Turned the other way up, it reminded me of the base of a Roman amphora, a storage jar designed to rest in an iron stand or to be thrust into a hole in a rack. Unlike amphorae, our vessel seemed to have a hollow handle projecting from one side. That was broken, but otherwise the pot was intact. I remember commenting that with its spike sticking up, the thing looked a bit like a pottery version of a Saracen's helmet.

5–10. The locally made alembic *in situ* on Site A. To the right lies a handle from an Iberian flask (Fig. 3–12), and at the extreme right, a broken clay roofing tile believed to have been used in the kiln wherein the alembic was fired.

That facetious identification was closer to the mark than any of us realized. The vessel proved to be one referred to by seventeenth- and eighteenth-century chemists as a helm, being "the head of a Still or Alembick, so called, because it is something like an Helmet."[1] It was, as my 1749 dictionary stated, the top element of a distilling appa- ratus—the oldest piece of chemical equipment yet discovered in Amer- ica. Stills were used to brew medici- nal curatives and essences as well as liquor, and they came in three parts: at the bottom some kind of fire box to heat the contents of the straight-sided pot that sat on top of it—a container called a cucurbit— which could be filled either with the material from which the distil- late was to be extracted, or with sand in which sat a glass flask hold- ing whatever liquid had to be con- verted to steam (Fig. 5–11). That steam rose into the still's third sec- tion, the alembic or helm, where it condensed on the inside and ran down into a narrow trough within the rim and out through the spout which I had taken to be a handle.

Many seventeenth-century al- embics were made of copper, and so looked more helm-like than did ours; nevertheless it was a splendid object, one of the finest pieces of earthenware potting in this period that I have ever seen. Its maker must have thought so too, for when he was through glazing the inside, he dabbed a totally unnecessary blob of green glaze to the top of the finial as a crowning touch. Once in the kiln, his creation was to suffer a minor blemish; its interior glaze ran down and caused the rim to stick to whatever it rested on, and

5–11. A sketch from Randle Holme's *The Academy of Armory* (1682) illustrating the three parts of a common still.

consequently the glaze became chipped and the rim scarred when the potter freed it. The damage was of no practical concern as far as the alembic's distilling capabilities went; but it was of great significance to us.

Lying in the pit beside the upturned alembic was part of a clay roofing tile, its underside unevenly spread with a greenish-yellow glaze identical to that inside the helm. Even in Europe, roofing tiles rarely were glazed, and never on the underside. That only occurred when tiles were used as flooring or as supports in potters' kilns. Across our fragment's glaze stretched a curving scar where the rim or foot-ring of a pot had stood, the arc closely matching the curve of the alembic's scarred rim. We had good reason to conclude that our helm (or another like it) had stood on this tile in the kiln. It followed as surely as fleas do dogs that the kiln could not be very far away. Nobody, we argued, would carry a piece of junk kiln "furniture" any distance—yet no kiln had we found.

With the site stripped of its plow zone and scraped down to barren clay to a distance of fifty feet beyond the complex of archaeological features, we were as sure as we could be that nothing had escaped us. Where, then, was the kiln?

Few traces of seventeenth-century pottery kilns have been revealed in Virginia. A curious, brick-walled structure was found in 1955 at Green Spring plantation—the home of colonial governor Sir William Berkeley—and was identified as a kiln by archaeologist Louis R. Caywood. Large quantities of spoiled pots and tile fragments coated with glaze were found in and around the structure. Although the kiln's firing system was never fully explained, it had every appearance of being part of an ambitious and sophisticated pottery-making effort. A much more conventional kiln was discovered in 1973 and excavated by Dr. William Kelso—the same Bill Kelso who had supervised our preliminary efforts at Carter's Grove. His kiln was located in Westmoreland County, and according to documentary evidence was operated for only one year (1677) by a potter named Morgan Jones. Having flues cut into the natural clay and radiating from a central firing area, the Morgan Jones kiln belonged to a type that in England can be traced back at least into the pre-Roman Iron Age (Fig. 5–12). In short, had Site A been home to either the Green Spring or Morgan Jones style kilns, we would have seen evidence of it. Instead, we found nothing but a strange, straight-sided and heavily burned pit cut into the south edge of our cellar hole. Being only 3 feet long and with no flue channels running in or out of it, the pit was incapable of being fed below ground, and far too small to bake more than a couple of alembics at a time. Wood ashes on the pit's scorched clay floor spilled into the partially filled cellar hole, and among them we found a small iron shovel that looked more "industrial" than domestic.

Having at first assured admiring colleagues that the marvelous alembic was made in Martin's Hundred—if not actually on Site A, we were under increasing pressure to find the kiln in which it was made. When we failed to do so, admiration began to turn to scorn. I, too, was beginning to doubt. I remembered finding a later seventeenth-century kiln site perched on an eroding cliff edge three miles upriver from Jamestown, a site that although it yielded no kiln (it had fallen into the James) did give up more than 20,000 fragments of spoiled pottery and other kiln waste. That 1963 discovery was a far cry from the single scarred tile fragment that I was now claiming as evidence of local pottery manufacturing in Martin's Hundred.

There is an old potter's adage which says that you can distinguish between the work of one craftsman and another by the style of his handles and his rims. When shaped by hand, these details identify a potter as distinctly as do his fingerprints. That may be a bit too sweeping, yet to an archaeologist (as to a potter), differing techniques of pottery manufacture do spotlight the products of different craftsmen

5–12. The foundations of Morgan Jones's 1677 earthenware kiln excavated in Westmoreland County, Virginia.

and different workshops. Two fragments from the handle of a vessel called a bucket-pot were found in the same pit as the alembic—a handle ornamented with thumb and finger impressions pinching it up into a series of crests (see Fig. 10–6). Similar finger impressions were used to decorate and secure the alembic's spout, convincing me that both vessels were made by the same potter.

One of the things you learn from studying the waste from a pottery kiln is that the clay bodies of the pieces do not all look alike. Variations in temperature and atmosphere (oxidizing or reducing) affect hardness and color, causing an underfired pot to emerge friable and pale pink, and an overfired vessel to come out stoneware-hard and a purplish black. Nevertheless, in more than twenty years of examining Virginia-made pottery, I had developed a fair nose for Tidewater clay, and I was convinced that most of the lead-glazed kitchen wares from Site A were Virginia made, although I could not say where. At the same time, the color and character of the wares seemed to set them apart from the alembic and the bucket-pot handle. On the other hand, if these were made on or close to Site A, it was reasonable to expect the same potter to have served all the earthenware needs of Martin's Hundred.

The first step toward resolving this question was to determine whether or not the clay used to make the supposedly local pottery was geologically similar to that of the Martin's Hundred subsoil. If so, we could say that our pots were made there—or somewhere else in Virginia or Europe that offered comparable clay. It would be supportive evidence, but not positive proof. If, on the other hand, the clays were *not* alike, the "No" would be loud and unequivocal.

I took our problem to Dr. Stephen Clement, Professor of Geology at Williamsburg's College of William and Mary, and asked whether he would be willing to run a series of spectrographic tests on allegedly local potsherds and on clay samples dug from our site at different points and different depths. Steve agreed, and found that although many of the mineral elements differed from sample to sample, one pattern did emerge. The potassium-to-titanium ratio remained approximately the same. Building on this clue, Steve accepted scores of samples: Martin's Hundred clays fired at different temperatures (to see whether elements burned away), specimens from undisputed Tidewater kiln sites, samples from English kiln sites ranging from Staffordshire in the north to Bideford in the southwest and London in the southeast, and others from sites in Holland and Germany, as well as fragments from France, Spain, and northern Italy.

International patterns based on potassium:titanium ratios began to show up. Samples from Staffordshire differed markedly from others from a kiln site north of London; a fragment from Martin's Hundred which we thought either to be French or a misleadingly overfired product from the West of England turned out to match the latter, and not the French sample. A butter-pot fragment visually belonging to a type usually attributed to Staffordshire, but which we thought was of too early a date to have been exported from that source, did turn out to match butter-pot samples from Burslem in Staffordshire. On the other hand, several more fragments that looked much the same, yielded markedly different potassium:titanium ratios.

All of this seemed to hold great promise for the comparative study of ceramic bodies far removed from our immediate problem. Much more significant to us was the discovery that while the ratios remained much the same throughout the eastern Tidewater area, samples from Long Island, New York, and from Maine were distinctly different.

Although the spectrographic evidence gave credence to my argument in favor of many of our earthenware pots being of local manufacture, it could not say *how* local. The alembic was to offer us another piece of localizing evidence. Indigenous to its clay and imbedded in its wall were small, reddish tubes which, when in contact with the alembic's interior glaze, had caused brown streaks of iron oxide to discolor it. Steve Clement identified the tubes as semi-fossilized root casts which are present in clay known as the Norfolk Beds, and which have been found in clay samples studied from Kingsmill, immediately upstream from Martin's Hundred, and downriver at nearby Mulberry Island. He explained that the Norfolk Beds also underlie the Carter's Grove lands.

After we had determined that most of our kitchen wares from Site A fitted the Tidewater clay pattern, it was natural that we should turn our attention to the origins of the potter—or potters. Where did he—they—serve their apprenticeship and learn their art? In England certain regions are known for individual potting shapes and styles. The factories of North Devon (Bideford, Fremington, and Barnstaple) and those in and around the neighboring Somerset village of Donyatt are famous for slip-covered wares decorated with incised ornament, a technique known as sgraffito. Black-glazed pans and jars with distinctive rims came from Buckley in Flintshire; bright yellow and apple-green glazes on thin, buff-walled pots were made in Surrey and Hampshire, and red wares decorated with lines and dots of trailed white slip were made in Kent and Essex. A potter who learned his business in any of those centers could be relied on to try to emulate their styles and techniques wherever he went—at least until he found that the clay or his new customers did not respond to them.

Turning again to our library of comparative fragments, I recognized a rim fragment from a three-legged cooking pot called a pipkin as being visually almost identical to another, nearly complete pot from one of our Site A pits. I had found the sherd more than twenty years earlier on the tidal foreshore of the Thames at London (Fig. 5–13). So alike were the rims that even the way in which the potter's fingers had smeared the clay while shaping the spout matched exactly. Recalling the saying about individuality of rims and handles, I was tempted to say that both sherds were the work of the same man, and therefore that the Site A pipkin was imported from London. But Steve Clement proved that even if the same hands made both pots, they did so in different places. His analysis of the clay showed that the Site A pot fitted the Tidewater Virginia clay group, while the Thames sherd matched others from a kiln site in the English county of Essex.

Among the several thousand earthenware sherds from Site A were a few decorated with trailed whitish slip in the style of the Essex kilns (a ware called Metropolitan slipware because it was marketed in the London metropolis), and others with sgraffito decoration reminiscent of Somerset and North Devon. At first I assumed them to be imports, there being no evidence that such sophisticated wares were

5–13. A locally made cooking pot from Site A and an almost identical spout fragment found in the Thames at London, ca. 1630–1645.

produced in Virginia in the seventeenth century. Pioneers, we mistakenly thought, would be concerned only with utility, thus discouraging a potter from lavishing any more work on his pots than was necessary. We had misjudged both the aspirations of the settlers and a potter's artistic integrity. Before we were through, we were to learn that both they and he put much store by the maintenance of their English standards. These people had not crossed the Atlantic to become Virginians but to make Virginia English. The slipware and sgraffito-decorated sherds turned out to match the Tidewater clay. Their rim shapes were the same, and in several instances the same design elements appeared in both the applied and incised motifs; clearly, therefore, regardless of the fact that one technique was primarily attributable to the southeast of England and the other to the southwest, both were here the products of the same decorator. If we could prove that they were made by a Martin's Hundred settler, Carter's Grove would be able to claim the distinction of being not only the site of the earliest British-American potting manufacture yet discovered, but also the source of wares as competently made as their British parallels. But still we had no kiln, and now there was nowhere else on the site to look for it.

Knowing that kilns rely on draft and that they have sometimes been found cut into the crest of a hill, I reasoned that, since our prevailing wind came from the southwest, the potter might have built his kiln on a promontory about a hundred yards to the east of Site A, on the far side of a ravine. We were aware that someone had lived or worked over there in the second quarter of the seventeenth century, for Bill Kelso's 1971 survey had turned up artifacts that included sherds of Virginia-made pottery.

I knew very well that our mandate did not extend to opening up a new seventeenth-century site. It was too late in the year to begin. More importantly, the primary function of Colonial Williamsburg's department of archaeology is to excavate eighteenth-century sites in town—not to chase real or imaginary seventeenth-century pottery kilns through the woods of Carter's Grove. We had spent an entire summer and most of the fall demonstrating to our architect colleagues that they should *not* erect eighteenth-century exhibits on Site A. In sum, we had done enough—perhaps more than enough!

Unlike the archaeological dilettante who finances his own excavations, or the college anthropologist who may enjoy the luxury of "pure research," most digging on American historical sites is motivated by something besides scholarly curiosity. The archaeologist provides a service to (and thus is the servant of) architects restoring colonial houses, landscape architects intent on reconstructing lost gardens, museum directors wanting something for the public to look at, and government contractors working on state or federal lands and desirous of fulfilling their legal obligations to the past as quickly as possible. In Williamsburg we serve both architects and the past, and try to maintain a pragmatic balance; but like the historian whose documents tempt him into so many fascinating byways that he is in constant danger of forgetting where his research is supposed to be leading, the archaeologist, too, is prone to give chase to whatever he thinks he may be finding. Consequently, his planning and his goals gyrate as wildly as a compass needle in a box of magnets. It is thus beholden upon an archaeological director to be ever mindful of the breadth of his mandate and the length of his budget. He must be prepared to tell his assistants: "Thus far, and not a foot more."

I assured Eric Klingelhofer that he and the crew had made a major contribution to our scant knowledge of early plantation life in colonial America, and that we would have to be content with that. "If the potter's kiln is in the woods beyond the ravine," I said, "it's not going anywhere. It's in no danger of being plowed out or being built over."

"That's true," Eric answered. "But how do we write a final report on the pottery from Site A if we haven't found the kiln?"

"Through a liberal use of qualifiers," I told him. "Plenty of 'maybes,' 'perhapses,' 'it is possible thats,' and a sprinkling of 'further-digging-may-show' conjectures."

Eric was no more satisfied with that answer than I would have been. But the decision had been made, and there it stood—until Friday, September 24, when I received a call from Colonial Williamsburg's president, Carlisle H. Humelsine. "I need your help," he told me. "Melville Bell Grosvenor, chairman emeritus of the National Geographic Society, is in town earlier than expected. Are you people doing anything that might interest him?"

I answered that although work at Carter's Grove was winding down and bad weather had made the site unfit for visitors, I had put together a slide summary of what we had found.

"Why don't you show him that."

Thus did I stumble into one of the most influential encounters of my archaeological career, a meeting destined to leave an indelible mark both on Carter's Grove and on the pages of colonial Virginia history. Though in his mid-seventies, the kindly and patrician Melville Grosvenor still exercised an alert and vigorous watching brief over the activities of both the Society and its world-renowned *National*

Geographic magazine. The son of its pioneering editor, Gilbert H. Grosvenor, he had spent a lifetime in love with America, and he understood as well as anyone in the nation how much the preservation of its heritage contributes to the well-being of the American people. More importantly, Mel Grosvenor possessed the wisdom to put his still boyish enthusiasm for everything American into a global perspective. The *National Geographic* had taken its armchair adventurers everywhere and shown them everything, from sailing a felucca on the Nile to walking on the moon, and for decades he had been in the thick of it. Now Mel Grosvenor listened with equal attention to the woefully incomplete story of our discoveries at Martin's Hundred.

Although he was hearing the name Wolstenholme Towne for the first time, he stopped me now and again to ask pertinent questions that made me feel that he had been involved with the project at least as long as I had. But when I was through, he said nothing. The silence stretched out.

"Well, er . . . that's really about it," I muttered lamely. "It's been a er, um . . . an interesting summer." Still silence, but as I passed him to turn up the lights, the old man put out his hand to stop me.

"You ought to find that kiln, you know."

"I wish we could."

"It wouldn't be right to stop now."

I agreed. Then he asked me the size of our current budget, and when I told him, he smiled. "We'd contribute part of next year's costs, if that's what you need to keep going. You shouldn't give up until you've found your kiln."

And that was how the National Geographic Society became our partner, and how we were able to cross the ravine and begin the search for whatever might lie on the other side.

Pipe Dreams

6

The difficulty of building a strong archaeological team is matched only by the task of keeping it functioning when snow dapples the fields and the ground below lies frozen.

Thanks to the National Geographic Society's support, we were back in business, but I knew that we could not open the new site until the winter of 1976–77 was behind us. So, to keep the crew usefully employed, we extended the 1971 survey through 150 acres of woodland east of the ravine beside Site A, and beyond the proposed new area of excavation—which we unimaginatively identified as Site B.

For three months the crew, led by assistant archaeologist William Henry and foreman Nathaniel Smith, scoured the woods in search of more areas of colonial occupation. Woodland that in summer becomes a jungle of honeysuckle, Virginia creeper, poison ivy, and struggling new trees wears a very different face in winter. Partially melted snow lingers in the shallow concavities of silt-filled ditches and in the tracks of old logging trails, white ribbons across the brown blanket of last year's leaves. Posts from long-forgotten fences stand in silhouette against the afternoon sun, freed of the weeds and vine foliage that hid them through the spring and summer. Here and there, even though the posts may have gone, bits of their wire protrude from the bark of trees that have grown around them. Then, too, there are the trees themselves, creating patterns both of age and species, indicative of Man's creativity or of his forbearance, some left to grow, others thinned or eliminated.

Lying across a stream bed we came upon a fallen white oak on whose trunk were carved a set of initials and a date—nineteen hundred and something, the last digits mutilated by flaking bark. The tree had almost certainly been a surveyor's boundary mark, a reminder that the earliest of Martin's Hundred's property descriptions relied on landmarks long since lost. Thus, for example, the badly damaged

1638 patent for Thomas Loving's 1,500 acres (which may have in-cluded the Harwood and later the Carter's Grove plantations) reads in part as follows:

> Beginning at a deep . . . the upper part of Martins Hundred at the land of Wm. Geofer . . . and so runneth down the River unto the land of Wm Barke . . . down by the North East side of Wm Barkers land until . . . amount in all unto seven hundred & fifty poles . . . thence North East by North three hundred & twe . . . thence of a right line unto the End of Bedfords Land . . . the river & down by Bedrods marked trees . . . place where it begun . . .[1]

That description may have been perfectly clear on the day that it was recorded—provided one had a map showing the locations of the adjoining properties. But once the landmark trees began to fall, and neighboring tracts changed hands and were subdivided, reconstruct-ing a plat to show who owned what became difficult. At a distance of more than three centuries it can be almost impossible.

We have problems enough at a distance of a single century, as was graphically demonstrated when Bill Henry's explorers came upon the grave of Matilda Jones. Her headstone still stood, its inscription bold and clear:

The Grave
of
Matilda
Wife of
Thos. Jones
Born 25 Feb. 1808
Died 27 March 1849
A Fond and Faithful Wife
possessing a noble nature
and a strong hope in Christ
has thus fulfilled her mission.

We could find no other gravestones nor any sign of a house; Matilda Jones seemed to be alone in the woods, out of sight of family and home; yet her stone was no hastily chipped marker. On the contrary, it was as well and as expensively carved as any that one sees in Virginia churchyards or in the private cemeteries of relatively wealthy families. I told Bill Henry that although she might seem to be out in the cold with the rest of us, county or census records would quickly establish who Matilda was and how she related to the land where she lies.

Wrong again. Our research department historians were unable to answer either question, and she remains today, as she was when we found her, a name carved in stone, as enigmatic as an Easter Island statue. Although Matilda Jones had nothing to do with our research, our inability to solve her puzzle cast an added chill over the winter's work. Having failed to make the most of a name and a date handed to us from the well-documented nineteenth century, searching for seventeenth-century questions to answer seemed about as worthwhile a longshot as entering the *Reader's Digest*'s innumerable sweepstakes. But still the testing went on, the crew digging holes down to the natural clay every 10 feet on traverses extending out onto each of the tongues of land that sloped down to the swamp of Grice's Run (see Fig. 1–4). We all knew that short of total stripping, we could never be sure that sites had not escaped us. Nevertheless, the crew kept digging, sifting through the soil for a nail, a potsherd, even a speck of brickdust, anything that would say: Somebody did something here!

Now and then we got help from nature. Fallen trees lay with their roots in the air after having torn massive holes in the ground, giving us a free look into the subsoil beneath them. Then, too, there were the groundhog burrows through whose excavated spoil we sifted with as much care as we did the dirt from our own test holes. A moment of excitement followed news that a team member had discovered oystershells spilling from an eroding bank—usually evidence of domestic occupation either Indian or European. This lot was European; associated bottles, crockery, and tin cans put it no earlier than about 1930.

We suffered many such disappointments, but Bill kept his crew's enthusiasm warm through frequent assurances that the earliest sites ought to lie closest to Grice's Run and to its confluence with the James River. This was true. On two promontories that we had marked on our map as the most likely locations for colonial homesites, the test holes yielded shells, fragments of seventeenth-century tobacco pipes, and a few small sherds of pottery. Enlarging one of the test holes revealed a shallow, seventeenth-century trash pit from which foreman Nate Smith recovered two hoe blades, both better preserved than any we had found on Site A. The name Wolstenholme began to be bandied about.

By this time, however, spring was approaching, and it was time to focus on Site B and its hoped-for pottery kiln. The Grice's Run sites' locations were recorded, and the test holes back-filled. If they marked the remains of Wolstenholme Towne, its revelations would have to wait until another year—and perhaps another team. Our mandate from Colonial Williamsburg and from the National Geographic Society was limited to finding the source of the Martin's Hundred pottery and, if time permitted, to testing another site in an open field beside the river and closer to the eighteenth-century mansion.

In compiling the 1977 budget, I had added an item whose only reason for inclusion stemmed from Mel Grosvenor's insistence that it be there. "Have you been shooting movie footage?" he had asked. "You should, you know."

I confessed that we had not. The project had begun with no expectation of making a filmworthy discovery. In any case, we had never filmed our archaeological work in Williamsburg purely for archival purposes, and so the thought would not have occurred to me. Besides, past experiences with films and television had taught me that neither is successfully served by merely pointing a camera and pressing its button.

Most archaeological films are shot after a discovery has been made, and therefore are to some extent faked. Artifacts are reburied and discovered again to the reenacted amazement of the archaeologists. Consultants are seen arriving on the site and never noticing that their hearty greetings are being recorded. A tomb is opened on camera, and inside it we find a 4,000-year-old film crew waiting to pick up the reverse shots as Professor Pontefract approaches the burial chamber and the TV audience. If, as it so often seems, the post-discovery reenactment is unacceptably phony, the only alternative is to film the project every step of the way in the hope that there will be a sufficiently dramatic payoff to justify writing a film around it.

In the mid-1960s I had been involved in making a film about the architectural and archaeological investigation of Williamsburg's historic Wetherburn's Tavern. It had taught me that even filming something as simple as the excavation of a trash pit could become a vastly time-consuming business. A feature that would normally take twenty minutes to excavate could stretch sevenfold when film with synchronized sound was being shot.

It had become my conviction, therefore, that either we make a film about a project, on the understanding that the archaeology will progress only as rapidly as the film-makers' needs permit, or we concentrate on the archaeology and don't make a film at all. Hurried film-making leads only to poor footage, too few editorial options, and less than perfect sound. On the other hand, unexpected delays imposed on a strictly archaeological project by unscheduled filming can end a season with its goals unfulfilled, and bitter resentment on the part of a field crew that came to dig and not to wait in silent inactivity while a camera rolls on some other part of the site.

National Geographic Society encouragement to apply for funds to shoot motion-picture footage was probably more instinctive than calculated, just as recipients of the Society's grants are considered to be mounting an *expedition* even if, like us, they only planned to trek seven miles or so down the road. So used to global travel is the Society, and so dependent had it been in earlier years upon film documentation to prove tales told by returning explorers, that a motion-picture camera has become as necessary a part of their kit as mosquito netting and a Winchester rifle.

Unlike most archaeological ventures, our expedition in search of seventeenth-century America could call on the services of an experienced, professional in-house film crew. Colonial Williamsburg's educational film unit (known affectionately as Eighteenth-Century Fox) had been in existence for more than thirty years. Both its producer and director well understood the problems inherent in archaeological filming, and, just as important, they were sympathetic to our needs and limitations. Consequently, the prospect of filming the 1977 season's work was far less disturbing than it would have been had we been forced to cooperate with a film crew brought in from Hollywood or New York. That, of course, had not been the National Geographic Society's intention. All it proposed was that while keeping our conventional photographic record of black-and-white prints and color slides, we also should take some pictures that moved.

But what, I asked myself, would or could we do with such movie footage? Site A was behind us; parts of it were already back-filled, and those areas still exposed had suffered severely from rain and frost. We could not now go back and re-create anything—even if we wanted to do so. Site B occupied so small a piece of high ground that even if it did conceal the remains of the pottery kiln, it was unlikely to offer anything of sufficient visual impact to stand alone as the subject of a film. Furthermore, the budget allocation for motion-picture film was just that—the price of film and its processing. A fifty-eight-minute production designed for public television might cost twenty times more once one added crew salaries, editing costs, music scoring, and all the steps leading to final-release prints.

Had I not been interested in film and its value as a means of providing relatively painless education, I might well have been content to have shot several thousand feet just to be able to report that we had it in the can. Instead, I proposed that we should make a properly scripted film that would retrospectively examine what we had found at Site A (mainly through its artifacts in the laboratory) and use that to set the historical scene. We would then film our progress on Site B, starting with the winter's woodland survey and going on to the end—what and wherever that might be. If we found nothing, that would be the payoff. We would say simply that this is how the majority of archaeological projects end. I would serve as on-screen narrator (because I came free and could be relied on to be available), and would give day-by-day commentaries on the digging as it progressed. We would be seen interpreting our discoveries, and probably reinterpreting them again and again as each new find changed our perspective on the last.

In short, the audience would become part of the expedition; it would share our excitement and, where necessary, our disappointment. Such a concept would be ludicrously expensive were we forced to hire an independent film-producing company to be on hourly standby for a full year; but with our own professional unit only seven miles away, that problem was eliminated, and we instead had a unique opportunity to make an archaeological film that would be totally honest and truly different—or so I believed.

A preliminary treatment proved sufficiently intriguing to the National Endowment for the Humanities to secure us a grant covering half the production costs for the film, which I had tentatively decided to call *Search for a Century.* By late March, Bill Henry's men had stripped away the last of Site B's dormant underbrush; the survey stakes were set, and our grid of 10-foot squares was laid out. The film unit was on hand as foreman Nate Smith began to scrape the ground surface in one corner of the first square, and I told our imaginary audience that with all the preliminaries behind us, we were at last ready to dig.

Even as the crew scraped away what was left of the ground's dead leaf cover, small fragments of pottery began to show up, and once the digging began we realized that artifacts, predominantly potsherds, were scattered all through the soil. This was in marked contrast to Site A, where we had found virtually nothing in the oft-disturbed plow zone. Here on Site B, history reached right to the surface. There could be no shortcuts, no bulldozing or even shoveling away of the topsoil to help us more quickly reach the good stuff deeper down. Every inch of the site had something to say.

Bill Kelso's 1971 survey had told us where the artifacts seemed most plentiful, the greatest concentration coming from a series of test cuts on the crest of the ridge. Other exploratory holes extending away from that central area had yielded appreciably fewer artifacts, and finally none. When I speak of the "greatest concentration" of artifacts, the term is relative. Used in Egypt or Mesopotamia it might apply to several feet of accumulated domestic debris and countless thousands of sherds. On our Site B, the most prolific "Kelso hole" yielded four sherds, nine pipe-stem fragments, and a brass mathematical counter.

When an archaeologist starts work on a site whose potential is still unknown, several red-caped devils perching on his shoulders urge him to go for the gold, to start digging where he knows that something is to be found—in our case, the area where the test holes had given up the most sherds. Start in the middle and work away from it, whisper the demons, in that way you'll get quick answers. Uncovering something dramatic right at the start will inspire the crew and show your sponsors that their faith and money are not misplaced. Besides, the site's original occupants almost certainly began at a central hub and gradually spread out. It's only right and logical, therefore, that the archaeologist should do the same. Once you find the hub, you'll know how to trace the wheel.

These are all tempting arguments and, like Beelzebub's best, there is enough truth in each to command serious attention. But they were not for me. I argued that because all excavation is destructive and because the remains of seventeenth-century buildings are often so fragile that they can be severely damaged by a single misdirected swipe from a shovel, we should begin where Bill Kelso's test holes had shown nothing and work slowly toward those that held promise. We would otherwise be in danger of plucking the heart out of the site and wondering later why we could not bring it to life. Several months would elapse before I was to learn that the heart of this site lay not where the artifacts were most plentiful, but in an area where they were scarce—and it was there, unwittingly, that I directed Bill Henry to begin.

We actually began in four parts of that area simultaneously, dividing the crew into two-man teams per 10-foot square, taking off the root-disturbed topsoil and then moving on to another square. In this way we could take most of the site down a layer at a time, mindful always of the dictum that the last thing to go into the ground must be the first to come out. It was a slow process, and as more and more squares were opened, we became less and less sure of ourselves. Apart from a patch of burned clay and a scattering of brick chips to the southwest, there was virtually nothing to indicate how the site had been used. In the absence of any laid-brick foundations or of any discernible post-holes, we could only hope that the burned clay patch related to the kiln. Certainly there was no shortage of potsherds, and most of them appeared to be of local manufacture—but not all.

We were finding fragments from several dishes of North Devon sgraffito-decorated ware (Fig. 6–1). What, we asked ourselves, were these imported wares doing here if Site B was the site of a kiln? Particularly puzzling was the fact that not a single fragment of a Devon dish had been found on Site A, where we believed William Harwood had lived—Harwood who came from Barnstaple, where the dishes may have been made. In archaeology, speculations burgeon as constantly as mud bubbles in a soufrière, and just as quickly burst. The possibility that Harwood might have lived on Site B rather than on Site A surfaced, was kicked around, and rejected. The site was too small and too isolated to have been the seat of the governor. At the same time, however, we were finding clues that pointed to an affluent household rather than a humble potter's kiln: table knives encrusted with silver, and one inlaid with gold; part of a gilded spur; and the firing mechanism from a snaphaunce musket, a gun of better quality than the period's standard matchlock. Then, too, we found the basket hilt from a broad or back sword (the former double-edged and

6–1. A fragmentary yellow-glazed dish imported from North Devon, sgraffito-decorated with a standing-bird design akin to motifs found on dishes made from local Virginia clay.

the latter single), a weapon of lesser quality than a rapier whose guard had been found on Site A, but still no potter's tool (Fig. 6–2).

In addition to the rapidly growing collection of seemingly contradictory metal artifacts on Site B, we were finding many fragments from tobacco-pipe stems, an artifact class long hailed by historical archaeologists as a fount of incredible knowledge (Fig. 6–3). As early as 1936 anthropologist J. Summerfield Day, working at Jamestown, expressed his belief that the wide range of pipe-bowl shapes unearthed there might provide an evolutionary series that could be used to distinguish different depositional dates—very small pipe bowls being the oldest, and progressively larger ones indicating an increasing availability of tobacco at affordable prices, and thus later dates.

There was truth in Day's theory, and the idea was picked up by his successor at Jamestown, J. C. "Pinky" Harrington. Meanwhile, in England, the keeper of London's Guildhall Museum, Adrian Oswald, was working along the same lines, but drawing his datable specimens from the City's medieval ditch and from building sites across the Thames River in Southwark—where I first worked as a professional archaeologist. Oswald published his bowl chronology in the British

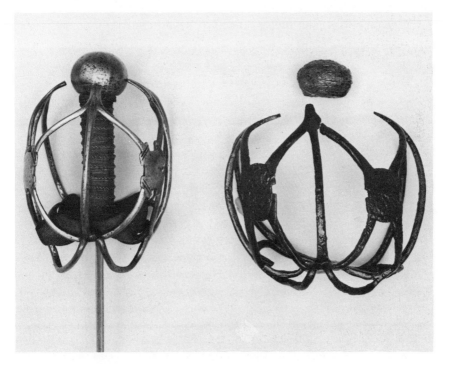

6–2. Basket guard and pommel from Site B (right), shown beside the hilt of an antique sword of similar type. Ca. 1630.

Archaeological News Letter in April 1951, and two months later, Harrington came out with his study of Jamestown's pipes in the *Quarterly Bulletin* of the Archeological Society of Virginia. Although both men subsequently continued their pipe research, it was Harrington who, in 1954, went on to propose what seemed to be the answer to every ignorant archaeologist's prayer—a purely mathematical method of dating pipes that called for no ability to distinguish one bowl shape from another. All we had to do was to measure the diameter of the holes through the stems by thrusting up them a drill bit of matching diameter, gauged in sixty-fourths of an inch. One simply determined the size of the appropriate bit and compared its number of sixty-fourths to those on Harrington's chart, which broke his pipe-hole evolution down into five groups, beginning with 1620 to 1650 and ending with 1750 to 1800.

At first blush this may sound like the kind of idiot research beloved only of English eccentrics, but in reality it was founded on an immutable fact: Between the time that pipe smoking was introduced into Europe in the late sixteenth century and the end of the eighteenth century, pipe-stems were made progressively longer. They also became thinner, and thin stems meant smaller holes, decreasing in size from 9/64 of an inch in the early seventeenth century to 4/64

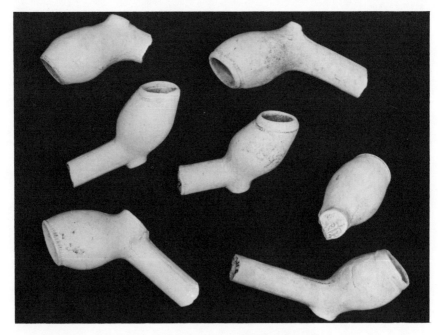

6–3. Tobacco-pipe bowls from the pit at Site B, discarded no earlier than 1631.

in the days of the elongated "church wardens" in the late eighteenth century.

Harrington was careful to offer his chart as a trial balloon, but despite a few efforts by English pundits of the pipe to shoot it down, his basic premise was enthusiastically seized upon by most American historical archaeologists—who at that time were still thin on the ground. In 1962 anthropologist Lewis R. Binford took the Harrington Theory and converted it into the Binford Formula ($Y = 1931.85 - 38.26X$), a straight-line regression with which to arrive at a mean date for any assemblage of pipe-stem fragments, regardless of their number.

I found the casting into mathematical concrete of Harrington's tentative proposition a little disconcerting; yet if he had been unduly cautious and his date brackets were more accurate than he claimed, the Binford Formula might indeed do all that it promised. Nevertheless, I still had difficulty believing that pipemakers the length and breadth of Britain stretched their stems and narrowed their holes at a given signal. Furthermore, I knew of documentation showing that in the eighteenth century, English pipes came in three sizes: short, medium, and long. I felt that these, and perhaps other factors that had not occurred to me, might seriously distort the Binford Formula's dating. Then again, I was not convinced that I needed a *median* date for a site's occupation, the filling of a trash pit, or whatever the pipe-bearing feature might be. What most archaeologists want are *terminal* dates before or after which this, that, or the other event occurred.

Lack of faith in mathematical formulae or in computer analysis is today akin to having denied the Pope in England in 1555, and I had no desire to smolder at the stake. Besides, I had found that applying the formula to groups of pipes dating between the years 1680 and 1760 tended to provide median dates that corresponded fairly well with dating arrived at by other, more conventional means. On either side of the 1680 to 1760 brackets the results were less impressive. Samples from seventeenth-century sites that we had explored prior to the Martin's Hundred project offered results such as these:

NUMBER OF FRAGMENTS	FORMULA DATE	DATING ARRIVED AT BY OTHER MEANS
90	1631	1645–1653
924	1636	1645–1660
300	1622	1650–1660
648	1698	1690–1700

Thus, by the time one reached 1700, the Binford Formula was doing so well that it was hard to doubt its validity, and hard, too, to dismiss critics who argued that perhaps in the early seventeenth century it was our "dating arrived at by other means" that was in error. Nevertheless, applying the formula to pipes from several deposits on our Site A produced some dubious answers. Thus, for example, the formula dating for pipe-stems failed to support the dates for related artifacts from the filling of the cellar and from two trash pits which indicated that all three were being filled at much the same time (see Fig. 5–2). The date for each deposit was different: 1647, 1629, and 1626—a spread of more than twenty years. By putting all the pipe-stem fragments from Site A together, however, we got a median date of 1631 —within the site's estimated lifespan (ca.1625 to 1645), but not quite in the middle. If, instead, we had never found the cellar that gave the 1647 reading, and had had to date the entire site on the evidence of the two "early" pits, their 1626 and 1629 formula dates would have been converted into a combined Binford mean date of 1622—which seemed absurd. The trick was in providing this.

As work on Site B progressed, it became increasingly clear that close parallels existed between it and Site A; some of the pottery was identical. On the other hand, we were finding much less bottle glass, and more and more of the North Devon sgraffito-decorated slipware that was absent from Site A. All in all, it looked as though Site B's most intensive and artifact-yielding occupation was the earlier of the two, perhaps within the brackets 1625 to 1640. But then we found our only rubbish pit, and I quickly began to push my dating even earlier.

In the top of the pit's brown loam fill we found both a European iron ax and an Indian stone ax from the Late Woodland Period (ca. A.D. 1000 to 1600)—a weapon that might have been used as recently as the massacre of 1622. Here, perhaps, was our first evidence of the great uprising that had left Martin's Hundred in ruins—just what we most wanted to find. Our eagerness to find the site of a home ravaged in the massacre and razed in its aftermath was not prompted by a sensation-seeking desire to be present at the scene of a disaster, but rather by a very practical need to distinguish between artifacts in use prior to 1622 and those made in the following decades. Site B could become our Rosetta Stone for reading the artifacts of British America in the early seventeenth century.

In addition to "ours" and "theirs" axes, the pit began to yield more evidence of military preparedness—and perhaps even of conflict. Several pieces of mail came to light, in one instance the links so well preserved that they were still freely interlocked and their tiny rivits still visible. We knew from the 1625 muster that the post-massacre settlers in Martin's Hundred had as many as thirteen coats of mail; so there must have been many more in previous years, when the population was so much larger.

Site B's armor supply went beyond a few coats of mail. We were finding small rectangular iron plates from a vest or jacket called a brigandine. The plates had once been riveted to a fabric base, each row overlapping like scales on a fish, creating something akin to a bullet-proof vest—except that it was not bullet-proof, the plates being liable to buckle and part like louvers on a Venetian blind (Fig. 6–4). That may have been why, when the Tower of London released a hundred brigandines to replace armor lost in the uprising, they were described as "old and much decayed but with their age growne also altogether unfit and of no use for moderne service."[2]

Brigandines and coats of mail were relatively light armor (a mail coat weighs about fourteen pounds) and were generally worn by the military rank and file—and in Martin's Hundred, presumably by servants and artisans. Masters would have worn more elaborate armor, both for greater protection and to inspire confidence in their leader-

6–4. Riveted iron scales from brigandine vests found at Site B (left). The exterior of a velvet-covered brigandine (right), showing the rows of rivets securing the plates to the fabric. This example is believed to be Italian.

ship. We were reminded of this distinction when, in our pit, Nate
Smith began to uncover the end of what looked like an old stovepipe.
It proved to be a cop or couter, an elbow section from a suit of armor
(Fig. 6–5). Like the links of mail, the earth had treated it so kindly
that much of the original bluing was still visible on the surface. Incuse
panels and "rope" decoration along the edges marked this as an
element from armor of relatively good quality, coming at least from
a corselet or half suit, and perhaps even from a three-quarter suit that
covered the wearer from head to knees. Either way, this was a remarkable discovery to make on a small woodland site. Indeed, only one
other example has been unearthed in Virginia, and that was found
during the Civil War when Confederate engineers were building an
earth fort near the old church at Jamestown.

A couter was anchored to the lower and upper arm elements of
a suit of armor with riveted, leather straps, and was not easily separated from them. "So where's the rest of the arm?" we asked. No
answer was forthcoming, and we speculated that the suit had been in
a house burned after the massacre, that the straps had parted in the
fire, and that the bigger pieces had been carried off by Indians who
returned to pick over the debris. Later still, when the Martin's Hun-

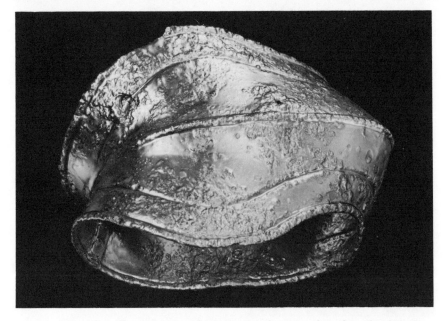

6–5. A couter, or elbow section, from a suit of armor; found in the Site B
pit, the metal was so well preserved that even its surface bluing survived.
Opposite: Sir Anthony van Dyck's 1641 portrait of Charles II, at age eleven,
wearing armor having similar couters.

dred survivors returned, a clean-up squad swept the remaining elbow into the pit. Right or wrong, this scenario kept spirits high as we dug deeper and uncovered a truly marvelous diversity of artifacts: scissors, table knives, two small brass boxes, a piece of linen fabric woven with copper and gold threads, a still-working lock from a large trunk, and much local pottery that included the central design element, in the form of a bird, from one of our decorative slipware dishes. Then, too, there was most of a splendid, blue-and-gray stoneware jug from the Rhineland, one of the largest and most complete of its period known to me from any American site (see Fig. 7–4).

With the movie crew peering over my shoulder, I tried to explain how it feels to peel away the dirt from an attractive artifact, each pass of the trowel and flick of the brush revealing a little more, and increasing the odds that the next will expose a broken edge and the realization that the object is not complete. "Some archaeologists will tell you," I said, "that they don't care if they find an intact pot or just one fragment. Well, I do!"

From a purely archaeological viewpoint, a single sherd is enough. That is all we need to prove that such a vessel once graced our site —always supposing that we have the knowledge to correctly interpret the fragment, and that we intend only to tell about, and never to show it. Once we try to interest the public in what we have found, we need intact or at least restorable artifacts, preferably with visual appeal. I could see that our blue-and-gray jug, even though broken into many pieces, had what in England we used to call "coo-worthiness," the kind of thing that made kids smear their sweaty little fingers all over the exhibit case and say "Coo, look at that, will yer!"

Turning to the camera as I worked, I did my best to heighten the drama. "I think the big question in everybody's mind is whether we're looking at relics of the massacre. It was one of the most dramatic events in the whole of Virginia history, but up to this point," I said, "no archaeologist has found evidence of that 1622 attack on a colonial homesite." I knew that I was getting far out on a limb. But I had insurance.

Back in the lab Audrey was working with each group of tobacco-pipe fragments as they came in. Despite our reservations about the validity of the Binford Formula, she was busily measuring every stem hole, and the answers she was getting were telling us what we wanted to hear. The pipes from the pit were all providing dates earlier than 1622. Only those from the topsoil (and thus divorced from the pit) gave a formula date of 1630, and there were only seventeen fragments from that upper layer, far too few in our opinion to constitute a valid sample. Below, the readings from each stratum were coming out like this:

LAYER NUMBER	NUMBER OF FRAGMENTS	FORMULA DATE
2076A	27	1616
2076B	66	1619
2115A–B	60	1621
2115C	22	1617
2115D	7	1616
2115E	23	1616

Knowing that Martin's Hundred was not settled before 1619, the 1616 dates had to be taken with several grains of salt. In each case, the sample was very small. Knowing from the way the layers overlapped that the pit had been filled within a very short space of time, I could see no reason why we should not group all 205 pipe-stem fragments together to give us one, potentially more accurate sampling. When Audrey did that, their median date came out at 1619. In short, everything fitted—with the exception of one pipe bowl that looked suspiciously large. On camera, I tried to leave the door open for a later, hasty retreat. "I may be wrong," I hedged, "but that pipe doesn't look as early as the Indian massacre." Then quickly back to a positive note: "But this delftware dish could be."

The pit took two days to clear, and as Nate Smith and I approached the bottom, we could see that the shape was becoming singularly like the ashpit and stokehole for a small furnace or kiln. But the clay sides were not reddened by burning, and I could only conclude that if that was what it was, the kiln over the pit had never been used—and that made little sense.

Because the site lay deep in the woods, the morning sun was slow to reach us. Not until close on midday did it lift high enough for its rays to shaft down through the trees, mottling the pit with leaf shadow and making the film crew less than happy. I was working alone in the hole, facing east and clearing out the last of the primary fill. Still in place against the west edge I had left a rim fragment of the slipware dish. It was an attractive artifact with a good many yellow dots and squiggles on it, and after a cursory wipe of its surface I planned to leave it *in situ* (archaeological parlance for letting it stay where it was) until the sun cleared the trees and the film crew could get an evenly lit shot of it.

Still clinging to our pre-massacre thesis, I brushed away the last of the loose dirt at the pit's east end and turned my attention to the west. As I did so, a shaft of sunlight as tight and bright as a theater spot lanced through the foliage and shone right on the slipware fragment. Instantly my jumble of dots and squiggles became the four digits of a date. Clearly, unequivocally, and in figures an inch high, the dish read—1631.

The camera was not running when I saw it; more important, the microphone was dead—along with my massacre theory and the credibility of the pipe-stem dating formula. I had committed us to filming the story as it happened, and so, after a brief pause to wipe metaphorical egg off my face, on we went. Carefully I pried the tell-tale sherd out of the clay and held it to the camera. "It isn't very often that an archaeologist gets his answer handed to him on a plate," I told the audience, "but that's what's happened here. We were looking for the Indian massacre of 1622, but the plate says 'Sorry, you're in 1631— or later.'"

Being in error is part of the archaeologist's interpretive process. What is not to be expected is that he should remain permanently wrong. When one is fool enough to let one's thought processes be recorded on film, however, the mistakes are liable to be better remembered than last-reel corrections. The 1631 dish debacle was a classic of the genre, yet at the same time it was a great moment in American ceramic history. Steve Clement's earlier spectrographic testing of comparable fragments from Site A left no doubt that we had found the earliest dated piece of American pottery; proof that early colonial craftsmen could match almost anything that contemporary earthenware potters were producing in England and in Europe (Fig. 6–6).

Assuming that the Martin's Hundred potter worked in England before seeking a better life in Virginia, we can see his 1631 dish not only in the context of American craftsmanship, but also in that öf British slipware production, where it most closely parallels the so-called Metropolitan ware from Essex. The earliest dated example of that pottery known to me is marked 1630, while the next date on any kind of English slipware is 1638—which puts the Site B dish in very distinguished company.

Vastly outweighing the archaeological discomfiture the dish caused me were the benefits of finding a dated object at the bottom of our pit. The odds against doing so were astronomical, for the number of dated ceramics found on seventeenth- or eighteenth-century archaeological sites is minuscule; indeed, more than half a century of digging and the recovery of hundreds of thousands of broken ceramic objects from the soil of Williamsburg has given us just one dated specimen. Because our dish exhibited severe glaze discoloration, apparently acquired in manufacture, it almost certainly could be classified as a waste product (called a waster by both potters and archaeologists), and would therefore have been discarded in the same year that it was made. If that was so, it followed that everything we found in the Site B pit had been thrown there in or after 1631. Thus, although we had been denied our 1622 Rosetta Stone, we at least had a chip from another, of 1631.

The damage that this discovery did to the Binford pipe-stem dating crutch can, or should, be seen as a cautionary lesson rather than as an exercise in bashing a sacred cow. Besides, those colleagues who are still reluctant to let go of the teats can cling to the intriguing coincidence that regardless of the pit's pipe testimony, the little group of seventeen fragments from the disturbed topsoil came within one year of the dish date.

6–6. The bird-decorated slipware dish dated 1631 from the Site B pit.

hallmarks of Failure

7

$\mathcal{S}$everal weeks after we found the 1631 dish, and while we were still cleaning, repairing, and studying the wealth of artifacts from Site B's pit, an old colleague stopped by to see us. Frank "Pete" Macdonald had worked on our crew for a couple of summers, and his hobby was collecting German stonewares of the sixteenth and seventeenth centuries. Knowing that I, too, collected them, he had brought a newly acquired catalogue to show me. Published by the Western Australian Museum, it contained numerous drawings of artifacts recovered by divers from a Dutch ship wrecked on a coral reef off the Wallabi Islands. Pete thumbed through the pages, pointing out the numerous fragments of German stoneware bottles. "So many different types all lost together at one time. An amazing find!"

It was indeed. I asked if I might look through the pages more carefully in case the drawings showed other objects that would ring bells for us. No sooner had I taken the catalogue from him than it fell open at a page of brass objects that included three small boxes, one of them identical to the largest of those we had found in our pit (Fig. 7–1). The parallel was so exact that not only was the punched, rosette decoration on the lid the same, but so also was the maker's mark— a hand with a pointing finger.

I had thought our box to be Dutch, for the rather simplistic reason that the Dutch specialized in the manufacture of brass domestic objects. As for its purpose, a coating of lead on the inside of its bottom suggested that it might have been intended to house tobacco or spices. The Australian examples also had lead on their bottoms; but the catalogue, without further explanation, called them "patch boxes."[1] Of much more immediate importance to us, however, was their date. Never having seen such boxes before, I had no idea of their age, beyond an opinion that the decoration was consistent with what one expects to see on ornamented metalwork from the seventeenth century. Having found our box in a pit filled no earlier than 1631, we could say that it was of a type still in use, but not necessarily new, in the 1630s. For all I knew, it might have been twenty or thirty years old at the time of its burial—until Pete Macdonald walked in with his Australian catalogue. The artifacts illustrated in it came from the *Batavia,* a Dutch East Indiaman wrecked on the Wallabi Islands' Morning Reef in 1629—only two years removed from the date on our dish.

That three of the boxes had been recovered from a Dutch ship was gratifying support for my Netherlandish attribution for our specimen. It also indicated that the boxes were relatively new in 1629. On the other hand, my tobacco-box identification did not gibe with that of Myra Stanbury, who compiled the *Batavia Catalogue* and who called hers patch boxes. Because the catalogue claimed to be no more than a preliminary listing of what had been found, it offered no documentation for its statements, leaving us to guess at Miss Stanbury's reasoning, and also at what she meant by a patch box. What kind of patches?

The obvious next step was to write and ask—which I did. In the meantime, I turned to that fount of all etymological knowledge, *The Oxford English Dictionary.* It offered only one interpretation: "A box for holding patches for the face," citing as its earliest reference a 1674 edition of the *London Gazette* wherein an advertiser reported the loss of "two silver powder Boxes, and a patch Box." Taking the dictionary at its word, we could deduce that if the brass boxes were indeed made to contain patches, they were the kinds of patches used as facial adorn-

7–1. Lid from a small brass box found in the ca. 1631 pit at Site B (left) and an almost identical box lid (right) from the Dutch East Indiaman *Batavia* wrecked off the coast of Western Australia in 1629.

ment. Another plunge into the *O.E.D.* revealed that such patches were in vogue by 1592. Beaumont and Fletcher's 1625 play *The Elder Brother* gave us that memorable line: "Your black patches you wear variously, some cut like stars, some in half moons, some lozenges." Costume historians C. Willet and Phillis Cunnington have pointed out that facial patches were worn both by women and men. Thus, in 1640, Henry Glapthorne's play *Ladies Priviledge* had one of its male characters being advised that "If it be a lover's part you are to act, take a black spot or two . . . 'twill make your face more amorous and appear more gracious in your mistress' eyes."[2] Glapthorne would not have thought it either necessary or polite to add that the patches served as much to cover the ravages of pox and suchlike scarring diseases as to gild otherwise pristine lilies.

With one's choice of companionship as narrow as it was in Virginia in the 1630s, it seemed unlikely that stick-on beauty was a must for either sex. In hot weather patches could be expected to peel off and even be disconcertingly transferred from one amorous face to another. What, too, were they doing aboard the *Batavia?* They could, perhaps, have been shipped as amusing Western novelties for sale to inscrutable oriental traders; but for a little woodland site on the edge of civilization in Virginia, no simple explanation leapt to mind. Were they to be traded to the Indians? If not, were the patches worn by women or men on Site B? Our only clue to the presence of a woman was a single glass bead, and that, too, could have been intended for trade. All the other artifacts were masculine: armor, weapon parts, agricultural tools. It was true that women smoked tobacco and that we found plenty of tobacco pipes, and true also that women rather than men are most often associated with pottery and kitchen utensils. In Martin's Hundred, however, we knew that in the post-massacre period there were several solely male households. Then again, how male was male?

Although the ills of the early Jamestown venture had been blamed on there being too many among the settlers who considered themselves gentry and too precious to get down to hard work, by the 1630s everyone sailing to Virginia must have known that you worked or died. I found it hard to believe, therefore, that any of our Martin's Hundred men would have been seen mincing through the mud in fancy frills, or even that the women would have had the time or inclination to wipe away the flies and sweat and to substitute cloth patches. Nevertheless, long before psychologists and sociologists began to take all the fun out of our peccadilloes, there were those who shook their heads and muttered "It takes all sorts. . . ." Deftly flipping through her growing files of documentary sources, Audrey reminded me that this could fairly be said even of Virginia's tiny, 1630s population.

"What about Nathaniel Moore of Accomack who had an affair with a calf."

"What, indeed!"

"Or Thomas Hall; remember him?" she asked. "The lad who couldn't make up his mind?"

One of the reasons (as I have previously observed) why many historians never finish what they begin is because they are too easily tempted into time-consuming byways. For us, patch-wearing in Virginia suborned us into joining the long line of curiosity-seekers who had peered up the skirts of Mr. Hall. Though not a resident of Martin's Hundred, his case went to trial on March 25, 1629, which, after all, was right in our period.

Hall was born in the north of England, at Newcastle-on-Tyne, where he claimed to have been christened Thomasine, not Thomas, and to have been dressed as a female by his parents. He had continued thus for another ten years while living with his aunt in London. Then, in the summer of 1627, he cut his hair, put on male clothes, and enlisted as a soldier to join the Duke of Buckingham's ill-fated expedition against the French on the Isle of Rhé. On November 8, all that was left of the Duke's army returned to England, Hall disembarking at Plymouth, where he again put on female clothes and took a job as a lacemaker. At the age of twenty-four, changing yet again, he elected to take his chances as a servant settler on a ship bound for Virginia. Presumably he took his female clothes with him in case he should have further second thoughts, for in 1629 he was again beskirted, and passing as a woman on a plantation across the river from Martin's Hundred—until someone blew his cover and spread the word that "the said *Hall* did ly wth a maid of Mr *Richard Bennetts* called *greate Besse.*"[3] Two local men heard the rumor and took it upon themselves to grab Hall and see what was up. They concluded that Thomasine was a man. John Tyros, however, in whose household Hall worked as a female servant, remained convinced that he was Thomasine and not Thomas, a conclusion later supported by testimony from one of three women who made a similar inspection. Hall was taken before the local magistrate where he claimed to be both man and woman. When asked why he chose to wear women's clothes, he gave the surprising and rather unsatisfactory answer that *"I goe in weomans aparell to gett a bitt for my Catt."*[4]

Although the magistrate ruled that Hall should continue to dress as a woman, this did not satisfy his neighbors. One Sunday a group of both sexes grabbed him again. Satisfied that he was male, they sent him back to the magistrate, who referred the matter to the acting governor of Virginia, John Pott, who should have been particularly well equipped to arbitrate such knotty issues, having for years been the colony's physician. Pott's court concluded that Hall was a true hermaphrodite and, in a Solomon-like decision, ruled that he/she should "goe Clothed in mans apparell, only his head to bee attired in a Coyfe and Croscloth wth an Apron before him And that hee shall finde suerties for his good behavio^r."[5] Thus was the confused and probably deeply unhappy Thomas Hall condemned to endure the daily derision of his countrymen—and women.

This, as I noted, had nothing to do with patch boxes, there being no evidence that in either male or female guise Hall wore patches. What matters, however, is the warning inherent in this sad little tale, namely that even among the small population of Virginia in 1629 there were some whom fate had made different and who did not fit into our stereotyped vision of the Nation's First Families and Founding Fathers. History, like telephoto lenses, tends to draw people together into groups, eliminating the differences that made them individuals. An army becomes a rectangle to be moved about on military maps, no longer an assemblage of people from widely differing backgrounds and with equally differing hopes and fears. Who, for example, would suppose that the flamboyant Duke of Buckingham's invasion force might have included someone like Hall, whose presence on the Isle of Rhé probably had less to do with patriotism, hatred of the French, or the hope of booty than with the chance to prove to himself whether his God had intended him to wield a sword or a lacemaker's needle.

Had the catalogue of the *Batavia*'s artifacts been more specific, I am sure I would never have taken the time to learn the lesson of Thomas Hall. When, eventually, I received an answer from Australia, I discovered that Myra Stanbury had not been referring to facial patches at all, but to the small pieces of cloth used to wedge bullets in place when loading rifles. Several greased squares of fabric had been found in one of her brass boxes; but for us they raised new questions. Although the art of cutting spiraling grooves on the insides of gun barrels to make the bullets rotate had been developed in the fifteenth century, four hundred years later it remained a difficult and therefore costly technique. Thus, even into the nineteenth century, the rifle was a weapon still not in general military use. Why, we wanted to know, were there three patch boxes aboard the *Batavia* in as many sizes, all by the same maker? The presence of the cloth squares in one of the boxes suggested that they were for use and not for trade, yet it seemed unlikely that ship's officers would have been equipped with rifles. Even supposing that the *Batavia*'s boxes did contain rifle patches, it still did not prove that they were made for that purpose. We, therefore, would be unwise to conclude that because we have an identical box from Site B, the site necessarily was home to someone who owned a rare and costly gun with a rifled barrel.

Equally worrying was our inability to be sure that the site had been home to anyone. Apart from the single, rich pit and another smaller hole containing a broken pair of scissors and a sword guard, we still had found no really definable archaeological features. There were a few post-holes, but they refused to combine to create any sensible pattern on our plan. Pottery continued to be plentifully scattered through the two soil layers that covered the natural clay across most of the site, and although the majority of the sherds were of local manufacture, we were finding enough that were not so as to raise real doubts about this being the site of a pottery kiln—unless the potter had a taste for wares other than his own.

Helping to support our original kiln-site theory were fragments from two more of the bird-decorated 1631 dishes, both bearing the glaze discoloration that I believed identified the first dish as a potter's waster. Then, too, there were many pieces from at least two sgraffito-decorated dishes ornamented with the same bird. Both the slipware and incised dishes seemed to be the work of the same potter, a man technically competent, if somewhat bird-bound when it came to thinking up designs. Most of the local pottery was undecorated and ran a gamut from vessels wretchedly pale and soft as the result of firing at too low a temperature to others blackened by overfiring. Both extremes are to be expected on a kiln site, but in far greater numbers than we were finding them.

In March, just before we began the Site B excavation, Audrey and I had taken a busman's archaeological holiday to tour Mexico's Yucatan Peninsula to look at Mayan architecture. While visiting the ruins of Uxmal we stayed at a hotel in whose exotic grounds worked a potter who made reproductions of ancient and traditional Mayan pottery. His kiln was dome-shaped, about eight feet in diameter, was loaded and fueled through a single doorway, and its draft was controlled by means of a hole in the roof capped by an ashcan lid (Fig. 7-2). The walls were of rocks bonded with clay, and inside the kiln the pots stood on a rickety platform made from bits of bent iron strap, one end stuck in the ground and the other into the wall. Fueled by bundles of billets merely thrown on the floor, this kiln was so simple that it neither had nor needed any subterranean ashpit or flue channels, yet it evidently was capable of firing its pottery to a hardness comparable to most of the fragments being found on our Martin's Hundred sites. Once it was dismantled and the ground under it plowed, nothing would be left of that Mexican kiln for an archaeologist to identify.

7–2. A peasant's pottery kiln at Uxmal in Mexico. The dome is built on the land surface with no below-ground flues like those shown in Fig. 5–12. *Opposite:* A potter at work in Johann Comenius's *Orbis Sensualium Pictus* (London, 1685); his kiln is strikingly similar to the Uxmal structure.

Those of us who have excavated or just read about ancient kiln structures are inclined to assume that all pottery kilns leave channels and pits indelibly cut into the subsoil (see Fig. 5–12). We do so because that is what we and other archaeologists find. But what we have not found we do not think about. Thus it was possible, or so I reasoned, that many a potter built kilns no more elaborate or enduring than the Uxmal example, and so left no traces for us to find. That thesis offered a convenient excuse for our not having found our Martin's Hundred kiln—perhaps too convenient.

Not only were we without our kiln, for whose search the National Geographic Society was paying, we also were shooting a good deal of grant-purchased film, footage that showed little but people scraping and a narrator-archaeologist exhibiting all the symptoms of a conjurer about to drop his balls.

"And there's another problem," I told the camera. "All the artifacts are saying that people lived here, but so far the evidence of their food is limited to two fragments of bone and eight oystershells —not even dinner for one." Walking to the edge of the gully that divided Sites B and A, I continued: "Maybe they threw the bones and shells down into the ravine. But if they did, why didn't they throw the broken pottery and the rest of the artifacts after them?"

Rhetorical questions, fortunately, are quickly forgotten. Mine had no answers. Test cuts down the slope revealed nothing. Eric Klingelhofer, who had been supervising and interpreting a survey of

the soil's chemical content, suggested that the bones had been broken down by acidity, and that the shells of oysters eaten by Site B's inhabitants had been reduced to invisible traces of calcium. In support of his theory, Eric could point to a major calcium concentration extending over most of the western half of the excavated area. Although it is true that some soils are far kinder to bones than are others, the fact that two bone fragments and eight oyster shells had survived posed the question of why these should endure if all the rest had been absorbed into the ground. As if to show that not all of Site B's soil was hostile, the delicate and slender bones of a female sharp-shinned hawk were found at the bottom of our artifact-rich pit.

Although the vanishing bone theory failed to attract many true believers, Eric's soil analyses did indicate quite convincingly that the site had been put to two different uses, the division between them marked by a north-to-south ditch that passed through the middle but whose age was uncertain. While Eric was charting calcium and phosphate concentrations, Audrey was plotting the distributions of artifacts and finding that all but a few came from soil layers east of the ditch (Fig. 7–3). Both the artifact charts and the soil analyses pointed to a

7–3. Plan showing the principal features at Site B.

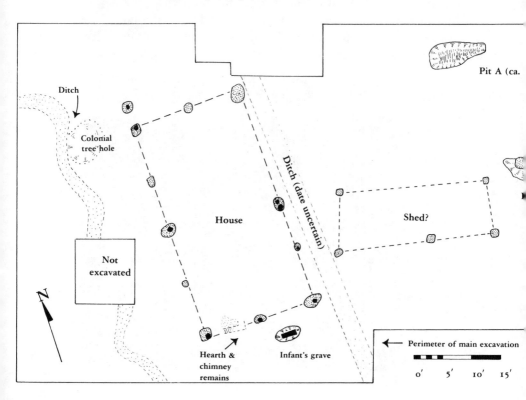

vaguely rectangular patch occupying most of the site west of the ditch, indicating an almost complete absence of artifacts but high levels of calcium.

The cross-mending of artifacts (to determine whether fragments from the same object have been found on different parts of a site) is a tedious job, but in this instance it provided a classic demonstration of its value. A fingernail-sized fragment of a blue-and-gray German jug found at the lowest level within the artifact-barren rectangle proved to be one of the missing pieces from the handsome jug we had found in the pit (Fig. 7–4). Then, too, a delftware sherd from the bottom silt of the ditch mended to another piece from the same pit. Clearly there had been a close relationship between seventeenth-century happenings on both sides of the ditch. We could deduce, therefore, that our stoneware jug had been dropped and broken to the west of it, and that most of the pieces had been picked up and carried east across the site to be dumped into the pit. That seemed to put living to the west and trash dumping to the east.

The testimony of the charts proved correct. On scraping down to the natural clay west of the ditch we found the post-holes for a house measuring approximately 37 by 19 feet (Fig. 7–5). Here was the heart of

7–4. The restored Westerwald blue-and-gray stoneware jug; from the ca. 1631 pit at Site B.

our site, and it was here (carefully avoiding the artifact-rich area to the east) that I had begun our excavation—though mercifully stopping short of the subsoil while we waited for other parts of the site to be dug down to the same level. The burned patch that we had thought might have been part of the potter's kiln turned out to be a hearth for the house.

Recalling that one of Audrey's documents gave the measurements for a house to be provided for a servant in Martin's Hundred to be only 14 feet long and 12 wide, what we had found could be construed as a large house. It was, after all, as wide as, and only 3 feet shorter than the master dwelling on Site A, and we thought that that had belonged to Harwood, the settlement leader. The quality of our Site B artifacts continued to have a "big house" look to them. People who used decorative stoneware jugs, ate with silver-decorated knives, and wore gilded spurs and half suits of armor had to be of some substance. Unfortunately, our only tabulation of Martin's Hundred's residents and their strategic possessions comes from the census or muster of 1625, leaving much quitting and dying to change the cast before the 1631 dish was discarded. If, however, the pipe bowl in the hearth can be taken at face value, it is just possible that the 1625 census contains the name of Site B's master.

That census listed seven households in the Hundred. William Harwood's was the largest; he had three houses and six servants. Then there were the Emersons, Ellis and his wife Ann, and a son aged eleven. A daughter had died since their arrival in 1623. They had two servants and lived in one house. Next there was the team of Robert Adams and Augustine Leak. They had two houses, the second probably built when Leak's wife Winifred came over to join him. Between

7–5. Final post-hole evidence at Site B house.

them they had one servant. There was another male unit, that of Stephen Baker and Humphrey Walden, who apparently owned neither house nor servants. Much better off were the Jacksons, John and Ann, and their child of twenty weeks; they had a house and two servants. Samuel March and his wife Colice, and a man named Samuel Culley seem to have lived together but owned no house, though they had guns for all three and armor for one.

Finally, the muster noted the presence of "Robert Scotchmore and his Company now planted heare and reconned before in the Maine."[6] Like most of these people, Scotchmore had come over in 1623, but he and several others had remained on the Governor's Land at Pasbehaighs near Jamestown. With Scotchmore was Thomas Kniston, who may later have been the Thomas Kingston who we believe succeeded to William Harwood's plantation—our Site A. There is no telling how large Scotchmore's company was or why he moved it to Martin's Hundred, but it almost certainly included at least one servant, a man named Roger Kidd.

This, then, was the Martin's Hundred group at the beginning of 1625. Only Harwood and the Adams and Leak team had more than one house, and only Harwood's household amounted to more than four adults. By seventeenth-century standards, four people could easily have lived in comparative comfort in a house measuring 36 by 19 feet. An analysis of the armor possessed by all the households (with and without houses), compared to the evidence for a plate corselet, mail shirt, and brigandine found on Site B, first leads us to rule out Baker and Walden, who had no armor of any kind. The Jacksons had no brigandines, Adams and Leak had no mail, and the March-Culley group had neither mail nor brigandines. By this process of elimination we are left with Harwood, the Emersons, and the enigmatic Scotchmore and company, whose house and arms in Martin's Hundred were not listed, but who had possessed three armors and as many guns before they left Pasbehaighs.

We have no way of knowing whether every structure was listed in the 1624–25 muster. Much depended on the whim of the census taker. In some areas, store buildings and palisaded enclosures were specified, but in others they were not. To conclude that such features existed only in certain concentrated areas makes far less sense than deducing that one tabulator always put them down and that another left them out. Unhappily for archaeologists and historians, Martin's Hundred almost certainly was one plantation where the inventory-taking was less than thorough. Furthermore, regardless of the early pipe-bowl in the hearth, Site B may have first been occupied by people who reached Martin's Hundred after the muster was completed.

Armchair archaeologists and readers of the *National Geographic*'s sunny accounts of excavations are rarely aware of the strain under which an archaeological director works. Everything he does is destructive. Once he has given the word to strip off a soil layer or shift a stone, he can never put it back exactly as it was. Because his reasoning, and therefore his planning, is based on the premise that the ground's most recent disturbance must be the first to be removed, he is forever worrying about whether or not layer D in square 10 is older than stratum C in square 12, and which should be removed first. A wrong decision may leave not only an embarrassing hole when the site's key features are photographed, it can result in the loss of crucial evidence linking one area to another. When the site is extensive and the crew large and none-too-well-trained, the director and his supervisors spend as much time averting disasters as they do making progress. Fortunately for us, both site and crew were small, offsetting in some measure the ground's persistent reluctance to tell us what it knew.

More test squares and trenches cut outward from the main area of excavation (like spokes from a wheel's hub) made certain what we already suspected: the artifacts were thinning out. Cuts down the slopes on all three sides of the promontory yielded nothing. Overall, the artifact distribution seemed limited to a patch of ground measuring no more than 50 by 38 feet, confined within apparently invisible barriers. Finding no holes for an enclosing fence or palisade, we once again fell back onto that thinnest of archaeological ice—the gone-without-a-trace feature. A fence of wattles woven around light stakes driven into the ground might not have penetrated to the clay subsoil and could easily have rotted away, leaving no marks in the upper loam layers. Alternatively, a worm or snake fence would leave no lasting impression in the ground. Either explanation made sense, but sense and evidence are horses of very different colors.

Just to turn the screws on our dilemma, the absence of post-holes where we needed them was offset by the enigmatic presence of five east of the house. If these formed any valid pattern, it was of a shed measuring about 28 by 10 feet, but having no central post on one side, and thus creating a disconcertingly long span for a single roof beam. As if to defy archaeological interpretation, one end of this frail and skinny structure was only 4 feet, 6 inches from the house, yet not at right angles to it. Having no evidence for the date of these post-holes, we took the coward's way out, marking them on the plan but failing to identify them as a structure.

One way and another, inspiration was in short supply. Expecting a productive and busy season's digging, and in fulfillment of our agreement with the National Geographic Society, we had hired eight extra crew members early in June. Now the site was dying on us. We sensed that we had found just about all we were going to, and the morale of the crew declined as the weather got hotter and each trench more barren than the last. The film crew was still on hand to record both our good times and our bad, but even at the best of times the excavators felt put upon by the needs of film-making, which seemed only to hinder archaeological progress. In the hot and damp Virginia spring, weeds pop up almost overnight, and although from an archaeological viewpoint they do little harm in areas not being worked, the camera's roving lens can be relied on to find them and give a TV audience the impression of an ill-kempt site. Consequently, our crew spent vastly more time cleaning and scraping for photography than would have been necessary for our own, more tightly framed still pictures. Then came the flies.

Local Virginians call them mayflies; but these have nothing to do with the harmless insects of the order *Ephemeroptera.* They are really deer flies which come out in May and June and whose females bite like bitches. We had been spared them on the open and windy Site A, but here in the hot stillness of the woods they attacked every available inch of exposed flesh. So, with a dispirited and increasingly irritated crew doing more slapping than digging, I admitted defeat. We would abandon the site until the autumn.

I tried to see the flies as a skillfully disguised blessing. Were we to continue on Site B until we were certain that not a root stain remained to be scraped clean, we would find ourselves halfway through the summer with a large crew on our hands but not enough time to accomplish anything useful elsewhere. Because it is the preliminary work on a site that calls for the most manpower, I usually try to get most of the season's heavy labor behind us in the summer months, leaving the more critical work to the permanent crew, which works on through the milder autumn weeks. If we delayed our move as late as July, we would in all probability find ourselves having started something we could not finish, particularly when we knew that we had to return to dot "i's" and cross "t's" at Site B.

Eric Klingelhofer had finished the draft of his report on Site A, and was working with a skeleton crew testing an area southwest of the Carter's Grove mansion, one close to the river and relatively fly free. Bill Henry and his Site B stalwarts were happy to join him. For them, getting out of the woods made splendid sense; but it left me with the problem of what to do about the film that was hanging around my neck like an increasingly putrescent albatross. Through no fault of its producer, director, and camera team (which had suffered along with the rest of us), we had a film that was going nowhere. I had warned the National Endowment for the Humanities, whose grant we were spending, that taking archaeology as one finds it might compel us to end on a note of failure; but I had felt so sure that the site of the pottery kiln was within our reach that I had never taken such a prospect seriously. Now failure was looking me in the eye with a basilisk's stare. It was true that we planned to return in the autumn and might yet find something pictorially dramatic (though I doubted it); but by then the tree foliage would have changed, and so would have several members of the crew. Furthermore, there could be no hiding or adequately explaining that we had abandoned the site for several months and now were back to find nothing more. The only sensible course seemed to be to accept defeat and wrap up the film on a "You can't win 'em all" note.

Once committed to that downbeat ending, I could at least assure the field crew that it would be able to get through the rest of the summer without filmic interruptions. The show was about sites A and B, and no matter what we might find elsewhere, there was no way we could write it into the script without wrecking the structure of what we had already shot.

Eric Klingelhofer's new site was another of those found in the 1971 survey, at which time several post-holes, ditch lines, and a large, black soil patch about 30 feet in diameter had shown up. When these scattered features were discovered, we knew nothing about the history of Martin's Hundred and could not even offer an intelligent guess at their meaning; but thanks to my wife's dogged research, by winter's end of 1977 finding the site of Wolstenholme Towne was becoming as exciting and as considered a prospect as our quest for the kiln. The evidence that Bill Henry's crew had unearthed at the head of Grice's Run augured extremely well, and we even went to the expense of building a road through the woods to enable our vehicles to reach those sites, believing that they might mark the location of Martin's Hundred's administrative center. Had it not been for the flies, I would have been tempted to change our priorities, substituting the Grice's Run sites for the one by the river where Eric was already at work. Instead, we went where the flies were not.

Peeces, Pallisadoes, and Problems

8

To borrow from a pair of hoary clichés: moving to the new site by the river brought us out of the woods and into the fire. In the midst of an open field with not a single tree for shade, the temperature shimmered in the high nineties, and for ten July days vied with itself to top 105 degrees. One expects higher temperatures while digging in Egypt, but there the air is dry. Here, on a narrow peninsula between two large rivers, the James and the York, the humidity rises to keep pace with the temperature. Before long, the crew was debating whether it might be happier back amid the woodland flies.

The new excavation, in the indeterminate area designated as Site C, was limited to opening a strip measuring approximately 100 by 200 feet, its location chosen to embrace the large patch of dark soil that the Kelso survey had located in 1971, as well as a few of the post-holes and ditch lines plotted at that time. Knowing that summer crews begin to fall by the wayside in the second week of August, leaving a diminished permanent team to finish what the temporary people have started, we considered this to be no more than another, more thorough testing of Site C's potential. At the start, it promised little. Across two-thirds of the opened area, not so much as a post-hole hinted at good things to come. Only the dark stain of a silt-filled ditch scarred the drab, yellow expanse of the clay subsoil, a ditch that we assumed to be of relatively recent date.

Site B had lain undisturbed since it was abandoned in the seventeenth century, but Site C (like Site A) had been plowed for generations, leaving us nothing above the subsoil. I knew, therefore, that stripping away the artifact-barren plow zone could do no harm—except among fellow archaeologists, for whom the very thought of mechanical equipment brings on hot flushes. For us, it provided the only practical means of getting the job done before time and the budget ran out. As the stripping and scraping reached the test area's western extremity, the grader hit the corner of a protruding piece of iron. Careful hand work showed it to be part of a spade blade apparently discarded into the back-filling of a post-hole.

Although there are some tool shapes that have changed little in a thousand years, the spade is not one of them. By the eighteenth century, most garden spades had an entirely iron blade with a socket divided into two flanges nailed to a wooden haft; but in the seventeenth century most spade blades were partly of wood, with only the cutting edge shod with iron. Flanges extended upward from it and were nailed to the sides of the wood, thus securing the iron shoe and reinforcing the wooden part of the blade (Fig. 8–1). The first artifact from Site C belonged to this seventeenth-century type.

Our second artifact turned up while excavating the first—several badly decayed links of mail. They differed from those found on Site B not only in their inferior preservation but in their superior quality. Several of the links were of brass, a feature often encountered at the edges of better-than-average mail garments. Though not much to look at—indeed, unrecognizable to anyone unacquainted with armor construction—these few brown-and-green (iron and brass) links gave us much-needed encouragement. Any site that had been home to tools and armor had to have something to tell us.

As the scraping extended northward, the edge of Bill Kelso's big black patch began to show up, as did a row of large post-holes. Soon post-holes were turning up in profusion, but all limited to the southwest corner of the exposed area and west of a clearly defined line of holes spaced about 9 feet apart. I assumed that we had run into the edge of some kind of fenced yard, perhaps with post-built sheds inside it, and that the big black patch was a silt-filled cattle pond.

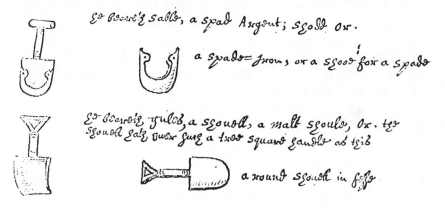

8–1. Wooden spades and an iron shoe or blade edge as drawn by Randle Holme in the mid-seventeenth century.

When faced with deciding which of several contemporary fea-tures to excavate first, logic leads us to the largest—not because we expect it will be the most interesting, but because rain will do it the least damage. At Site C, I knew that erosion from one storm could double the diameter of excavated post-holes, but it would take a flood to drastically change the appearance of a pond's perimeter. So, al-though the post-holes would ultimately be the key to our interpreta-tion of the site, I elected to dig the large features first: the big black patch, and a much smaller, rectangular area of similarly dark soil a few feet to the south of it. Both immediately began to yield military and domestic artifacts, all apparently thrown away at a time when fire had generated a considerable amount of ash. The ash was scattered along, and mixed with the gray soil outlining the western edges of both the pond and the rectangular area which was proving to be a pit. Whence came the ash? That was a question whose answer was of paramount importance to us. Was it merely the residue from domestic or indus-trial hearths, or did it come from burning buildings?

The presence of many nails, and part of a brick with a potsherd stuck to it where the glaze had melted, pointed to the destruction of a building by fire; so, too, did a mud-dauber's clay nest burned bright red and brick hard. Under normal circumstances such nests dissolve into fine clay particles if exposed even to prolonged rain—which is why they are usually built under the eaves of buildings or in the corners of window frames. If the host building burned, the clay nests would be converted to baked pottery, and that is what had happened here. Cynics could argue (and they did) that mud-daubers build nests not only on buildings—the inside of an old crate would serve as well, and burn as briskly. That debate was still going on when, several feet to the north of the pit, Eric Klingelhofer's scrapers came upon the post-holes, molds, and sill-slots for a small shed, the molds and slots filled with ashes, leaving no doubt that at least one structure had been consumed by fire.

Artifacts from the pit included part of a musket barrel, a well-preserved butcher's cleaver, and a stirrup, this last find of importance in that it pointed to someone's intention to ride a horse (Fig. 8–2). The question, therefore, was: Did he have a horse to ride? We had found two small horseshoes at Site A, and where there were shoes there almost certainly had to be a horse. Not so a stirrup, which could have been attached to a saddle brought over by a colonist whose mount died on the way. The question was important, because the documentary evidence is conflicting. In 1616 there were said to be only six horses in all of Virginia; twenty mares were requested in

1620, but there is no proof that they thrived or even arrived, and in the 1625 muster not one horse is listed in Martin's Hundred—or anywhere else, for that matter. In June 1620, however, the Council for Virginia had issued a glowing report on the state of the colony that gives no hint of equine shortage, instead declaring that "The Horses also [are] more beautifull, and fuller of courage" than those of the breeds from which they came.[1] After the 1622 massacre that had resulted in heavy losses among the livestock, and before the 1625 muster, Governor Wyatt had issued a proclamation promising death to anyone convicted of stealing "beasts & Birds of Domesticall & tame nature,"[2] putting horses, mares, and colts at the top of the list (with peacocks and turkeys at the bottom), indicating that in September

8–2. An iron stirrup from Site C. Discarded ca. 1620–1622.

1623, when the word went out, there were horses, mares, and colts to steal. We had hoped that evidence for the presence or absence of horses on these Martin's Hundred sites would be a clue to their date, but the documentary contradictions put paid to that reasoning.

Nothing is more frustrating than digging a site whose date is uncertain, whose ownership you do not know, and whose purpose remains glumly obscure. The more hard-to-date artifacts one finds on such a site the greater the frustration—and the greater one's obligation to answer those questions. A small site that yields no more than a scattering of patternless post-holes and a handful of nondescript potsherds can be written off as of no importance, now or then—whenever *then* was. Not so a site where structural remains are plentiful and where quality artifacts abound. Clearly, at our Site C, somebody of consequence did something that posterity should know about.

From the ash-strewn edge of the large, pondlike depression came the firing mechanisms for no fewer than five matchlock muskets, one with its retaining bolts still in position and meaning either that the gun's stock had burned away or that the mechanism was a spare

(Fig. 8–3). Going back to the 1625 muster we found that although the Adams-Leak household had six muskets referred to as "Peeces fixt," their inventory listed no spare parts. William Harwood's, on the other hand, read "Peeces fixt, 10; Matchcocks, 25 and 10 lb of Match,"[3] indicating that in addition to ten guns in working order, he had twenty-five replacement mechanisms. That what we were finding were indeed spare or discarded parts was evident, because none was found alongside a musket barrel or other metal parts, thus precluding the possibility that whole guns had been thrown away. It was significant, too, that all but one of the "matchcocks" were either broken or incomplete, suggesting that arms repairing had been practiced nearby —something that Governor Harwood's men would have done, as it was he who was in titular if not practical charge of the Hundred's defenses.

Hitching the guns to Harwood seemed logical enough in the context of Site C, until we recalled that we had already used the cannonball and the golden clothing threads to put him on Site A. Just to add another "X" to the equation, between the pit and the pond we came upon fragments from the rim of a North Devonshire, sgraffito-decorated dish like those we had been finding on Site B. We had remembered then that Harwood came from Barnstaple in North Devon, and that the fragments could have, too. Was there a significant connection, we now asked, between the dishes from Sites B and C, and was Harwood the source of it? If so, why was there not a single sherd of this ware from his supposed home on Site A?

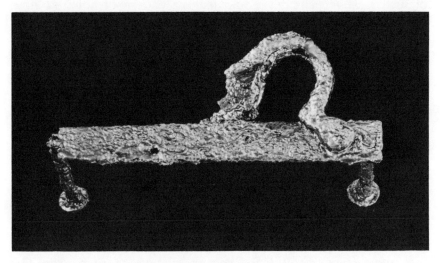

8–3. The iron firing mechanism for a matchlock musket, found with its retaining bolts in position. Discarded ca. 1622.

Keep digging, we told ourselves, it'll come clear soon enough. Archaeologists, by and large, are an optimistic breed.

In tandem with work on the pit and pond areas, other crew members were scraping along the line of post-holes that seemed to limit occupation on the landward side. To the north the holes extended beyond our cleared area, but to the south the line ended in a cluster that at first made little sense, some obviously being the holes for posts, but others irregular and probably created naturally by the roots of trees. Although we could see no obvious corner, the north-south line evidently turned west and headed off beyond the area of excavation, the holes keeping the same 9-foot spacing that characterized the landward line (Fig. 8–4). The key to the relationship between these two fences lay in the confused cluster, which covered an area measuring about 8 feet square and from which the fencelines extended not at a right angle (as property fences could be expected to do), but at an angle of 73 degrees.

I do not recall whether it was Eric or I who first noted that the strange angle and the cluster of holes looked like the corner of a triangular fort. Certainly neither of us took the idea very seriously. The 9-foot spacing of our posts bore no resemblance to the construction of the reproduced fort at Jamestown's Festival Park. There the palisades were built with posts the size of telegraph poles set side by side in the ground; in short, the kind of palisaded fort one associates with nineteenth-century American cavalry outposts, and particularly with their Western movie reconstructions. The below-ground remains of such massive palisades would leave a pattern of holes so close together that most of them would merge, creating an irregular trench. Ours did nothing like that.

It was Audrey who pointed out that no matter how the U.S. Army built its forts at Cheyenne or Laramie, the documentary evidence for Jamestown's fort described something quite different. She was referring to Samuel Purchas's ponderously titled *Hakluytus Postumus, or Purchas His Pilgrimes,* first published in 1625. Purchas was rector of St. Martin's, Ludgate, and a puller together of other people's manuscripts. The *Dictionary of National Biography* considers him to have been "neither a faithful editor nor a judicious compiler," and charges him with having lost many of the documents entrusted to his care, thus making his book the only extant version of writings that would have been far better preserved in their original forms. Purchas's description of Jamestown and its fortifications was borrowed for the most part from the narrative of William Strachey, who was there in 1610. The fort, wrote Strachey, was built "with a Pallizado of Planckes and

strong Posts, foure foote deepe in the ground, of yong Oakes, Wal-
nuts, &c."[4] A palisade so constructed could easily be built with its
main supporting posts set on nine-foot centers, the spaces between
them spanned by two or more horizontal rails or stretchers to which
the vertical pales were nailed.

More careful scraping of our corner cluster enabled us to sort out
which of the subsoil scars were tree holes and which were seatings for
posts. The latter proved to create an almost square unit projecting
beyond the lines of our two fences or palisades. Turning again to
Purchas (and Strachey), Audrey reminded me that the triangular
fortification at Jamestown had "At every Angle or corner, where the

8–4. The southeast corner of the Site C fort as revealed at the end of the
1977 season. The watchtower is in the right foreground, and to the left of
it, the scar of a track passes into the compound between posts five feet
apart. Slots running parallel to the palisade post-holes are interpreted as a
parapet step (see Fig. 11–4). The deep hole in the middle distance is the
well. To the left of it extends the shallower concavity of the livestock pond,
which may have been used after the fort's buildings were destroyed.

lines meete, a Bulwarke or Watchtower."[5] Clearly, therefore, we had found our watchtower—and a fort. Beside the tower, Eric's continued scraping revealed a shallow scar in the subsoil, beginning at a point about 10 feet outside the palisade and extending 17 feet inside it before disappearing beside our pit. Where the scar passed through the palisade, the space between the tower and the first of the south wall's posts measured only 5 feet instead of 9, an anomaly that had contributed to our earlier confusion. Now, however, Eric deduced that the narrower post-hole spacing indicated a gate, and that the scar in the ground was the result of people and livestock tracking through it. I agreed that the dark line looked like a path, but putting a gate so close to the tower seemed to me to be militarily unsound. It offered an enemy an unnecessary degree of shelter. But I was wrong again, as Strachey pointed out. At each of Jamestown's watchtowers, he told us, "there is a Gate likewise to goe forth, and at every Gate a Demi-Culverin."[6] We had no evidence of a cannon, but we most assuredly had a gate.

Convinced that we were finding military fortifications, I reported to the National Geographic Society that "by the time these excavations are completed American historians will have the first physical evidence of the way in which the Jamestown fort was constructed."[7] If that claim sounds a mite pretentious, one has to remember that we were trying hard to make up for having failed to find the potter's kiln at Site B.

To describe the defenses at Jamestown as a fort can be misleading, at least in the early days of the settlement's existence. The first protection, hastily thrown up after the three ships decanted their passengers, was of brushwood and designed to keep wolves and Indians from interfering with colonists sleeping in tents and under light wooden shelters. That frail barrier was soon replaced by the first palisades, which also created a wall around the entire settlement, enclosing an area of about an acre (Fig. 8–5). The result was a miniature version of the medieval walled city, the kind of protected community that London "undertakers" were to develop in Northern Ireland at Londonderry and Coleraine. At Jamestown, as early as 1612, houses were being erected outside the palisaded nucleus, and by 1619 the need for more space, coupled with a fading fear of the Indians, promoted the development of a more open community that came to be known as New Towne (see Fig. 2–2). By then it would have been fair to say that Jamestown had a fort, whereas previously it would have been more correct to term it a fortified settlement. The distinction was one of long standing, and could be compared to the contrast between

England's walled cities and its rural castles with their tenant-housing villages nestling for protection about their gates.

Into which category our Martin's Hundred fortification would fit we could not tell. It could encompass the whole of Wolstenholme Towne (if that was where we were), or it might be no more than a defensework around a single farmstead. Interpretation would have been easier had our documentary sources so much as hinted at there being a fort or even a palisaded house somewhere in the Hundred. No such items were listed in its contribution to the 1625 census, and so one might be tempted to conclude that none existed. But careful reading of the "muster" in its entirety suggests otherwise. Although the census-takers were provided with a list of questions, thought up by the King's Privy Councillors in London, that specifically asked "What fortifications, or what place is best to be fortifyed?",[8] answers depended on the priorities of the man working the district. Thus, for example, the census-taker for the Lower James River's Elizabeth City area recorded twenty "pallizadoes" among a total of seventy properties, whereas elsewhere in the colony only one inventory lists a palisade, and spells it "pallisado." Thus, both spelling consistency and geographical grouping can help determine the range of a census-taker's beat. At Martin's Hundred, as I have noted, the job seems to

8–5. An artist's interpretation of the first palisaded fort at Jamestown, under construction in 1607. Pointed tree trunks are shown being attached to a single rail, rather than the riven or sawn palings believed to have been used in the Site C fort.

have been rather cursorily done, even to omitting any details of the newly arrived "Robert Scotchmore and his Company." Even so, to leave out a well-built fort would be carrying laxity to the level of treasonable slothfulness—always supposing, of course, that the fort still existed in the winter of 1624–25.

In trying to correctly interpret the muster, we must not only distinguish between one scribe and another, but also interpret what they meant. What, we wanted to know, did the Elizabeth City census-taker mean by a "Pallizado"? Our research into fence styles at Site A had shown that to English lexicographers, a palisade could mean anything from "a slight sort of Fence set up to beautify a Place or Wall," to "strong sharp-pointed Stakes set up in the Ground to keep off an Enemy."[9] In short, the word had a wide range of meanings and could be applied to something as light as a flower-garden's picket fence to a Fort Laramie–style wall of pointed tree trunks. Most of Virginia's palisades must have fitted somewhere in between, many defending planted land from animals, and others protecting buildings from all comers. Thus, for example, plantation owner Edward Bennett of Warisoyack (in what would later become Isle of Wight County) was listed as possessing "Dwelling houses, 2 in severall Pallisadoes; Store, 1 wthin one of ye Pallisadoes."[10]

Bennett was not alone in having his houses and store within a pale-constructed defensework. The colony's treasurer, George Sandys, had three defined as forts. One was at Jamestown (and may have referred to Sandys's official responsibility for the Virginia Company's old town fortification), and was listed simply as "a Large Forte"; but on property vaguely defined as "his other Plantacon" he had "a Large forte Palled in" apparently containing a "Peece of Ordnance mounted, 1; Dwelling house, 1; other houses, 4." Sandys's third fort was again described as paled in, and was located on yet another tract, where he housed five men in a single dwelling house and kept their supplies in one storehouse.[11]

To discourage us from jumping to premature conclusions, Audrey served not only as our pursuer of historical truth but also as our professional devil's advocate. Suppose, she argued, that we were wrong in believing that we were digging in Martin's Hundred, and that in reality it lay further down the James River. Knowing that George Sandys had one of his plantations somewhere between Jamestown and Martin's Hundred, was it not conceivable that ours could have been the Sandys tract, and that what we were finding might be his fort? After all, she persisted, no other forts are listed in the muster, and we know that the Martin's Hundred Society's claim to ten miles of river frontage extending from "Wolstenholme Towne five miles upward towards James Cittie and five miles Downeward towards Newport News"[12] cannot be fitted into the available space between Mulberry Island on the one hand and Archer's Hope on the other.

This was true; but trying to push Martin's Hundred further downstream only made matters worse. Audrey's affection for George Sandys was not shared by the rest of us; but being a person of sometimes tiresome tenacity, she would make sure that we had not heard the last of him.

Fortunately for the budget and the excavation's progress, the debating went on in the office while the digging continued in the fort. Although most of the domestic artifacts found on the edge of the supposed pond had been broken into small pieces before they got there, some objects survived intact, among them the shell of a turtle (Carolina Box Tortoise), which had burned through at its crown, perhaps as the result of being used as a cooking vessel thrust into the ashes of a fire, or alternatively, when its turtle occupant was cooked. Then again, the shell might have been used as a cup or dipper, and have become charred when the building over it burned down. Equally enigmatic was an iron shackle of the kind that had a barrel-style padlock built into it (Fig. 8–6).

This is one of the oldest types of padlocks, was known in Europe at least as early as the ninth century A.D., and was still being made for police use in the nineteenth century. Our question was: Who or what was being shackled in the fort at Martin's Hundred?

I think it was Eric Klingel-hofer whose reading of the early Virginia records turned up an order requiring that the head of every household should possess a ferrular for the punishment of servants

8–6. Shackle padlock found in the Site C fort. Discarded ca. 1620–1622.

heard swearing. Our Latin being as rusty as the shackle, there seemed logic in deducing that *ferrular* came from the Latin word *ferrum* (hence, ferrous) meaning iron, and, by extension, that putting someone in irons meant securing them with shackles. Unfortunately, we had the wrong root. The word did come from the Latin, but from the

Latin for the giant fennel, a plant whose stems were used to make canes—to beat boys who made mistakes in their Latin.

I had elected to excavate our pondlike black patch by the same quadrant method we had used to explore the cellar on Site A (Fig. 8–7). It has both advantages and drawbacks, the most serious of the latter being that you can never see any layer fully exposed. You see half now, and half later. For a mound built at one time and for one purpose, this slicing technique loses no data; but when a large hole has been filled over a long time, and when erosion and stomping around by animals have tied the stratigraphy in knots, interpretation and planning based on half the evidence can get you into trouble.

We soon found that our first pair of quadrants were giving us entirely different information. At the southwest we had ashes, many broken artifacts, and much irregularity at the edge, suggesting that animals had come there to drink; but at the northeast there were few artifacts, and heavily compacted silt. Probing could not find its bottom, whereas at the southwest we came to natural clay after going down only a few inches. Clearly the hole was sloping toward the northeast and giving credence to the pond theory. At a depth of 4 feet

8–7. A pond inside the fort being excavated by means of the quadrant method.

into the silt we found half an earthenware chamber pot, and a foot lower an intact, two-handled cooking pot. Uncracked and with only a chip at its rim, the vessel could only have been thrown into the "pond" when it contained enough water to break the fall (Fig. 8–8). Why, we asked, would anybody throw away a still useful pot—unless overcome by a mischievous urge to see how big a splash it would make.

The Great Cooking-Pot Mystery did not long hold our attention, in part because we had no solution, but mainly because we soon had something more important to ponder. On the afternoon of August 4, Eric reported that a convex iron object was showing up in the deep hole at the pond's northeast side, a hole whose steeply sloping sides made us believe it to be a well shaft. The iron object looked as though it could be a helmet, he said.

"What's its condition?" I asked.

"Not good."

By the time I reached the site, excavator John Quarles had exposed more of the iron, and at once I could see that Eric was right. At least three helmets had previously been unearthed in Virginia, all of them of the simple "pot" type formally called a cabasset, though that is a relatively modern term derived from the Spanish *cabeza,* meaning the head. In addition to these three, part of a more elaborate type that offered both neck and ear protection (a burgonet) had been found in excavations at Flower-dew Hundred and, in 1964, downriver at Mathews Manor, I had found the cheek and chin element from a heavier variety known as a

8–8. An intact earthenware cooking pot found in the silted fort well. Though made from Virginia clay, the pot is not thought to be a Martin's Hundred product. Discarded ca. 1622.

closed burgonet (see Fig. 2–1). None of these helmets were as elaborate as the one being revealed in the well at Martin's Hundred, which closed entirely over the wearer's face leaving only a slot through which to inspect the enemy.

The well shaft had tapered to a diameter of little more than four feet, and the helmet lay squarely in the middle, partly in the familiar clay silt and partly beneath it in a stratum of gray mud. As iron decays in a wet environment, rust becomes bonded to the dirt around it, iron oxide slowly leaching out to create a film of increasing thickness but decreasing strength. Judicious paring with a spatula enabled me to thin the skin of rust-bonded clay down to a point where it was more rust than clay. There I stopped, hoping that a millimeter or two further down lay solid iron. Using a dissecting needle I probed for it, but found nothing. Fearing the worst, I sent for conservator Gary McQuillen and asked him to bring a magnet.

The magnet exerted no pull at all, and I had to admit to a tensely waiting crew that I rated our chances of successfully lifting the helmet intact at no better than one in five. Gary was more optimistic; he put it at fifty-fifty. My scraping had revealed more details: The face elements were unhooked (as they had to be to take the helmet off), but the visor and chin section, called the bevor, remained closed so that the wearer's face would have been concealed. I could see traces of the eye slot in the visor and part of a peak or bill bent down over it. I knew this projection to be a characteristic of close helmets (those that closed over the face) in the early seventeenth century, but I could not recall that such a helmet had ever been found intact on a British colonial site (Fig. 8–9). A phone call to our military historian consultant, Harold L. Peterson in Washington, confirmed my view of the discovery's importance. Harold went further, saying that if we could get it out in

8–9. A cavalry officer's close helmet as first revealed in the fort well.

one piece, it would be the earliest complete close helmet unearthed in the New World.

The rarity of Johnny Quarles's discovery was exhilarating—until we remembered that it was still in the ground and about as stable as wet cardboard. Rather than enjoying the satisfaction of a unique discovery, we stood an excellent chance of going down in the annals of historical archaeology as those idiots who failed to save America's first close helmet. To add to our problems, we were now in the summer storm season, and the shaft was in daily danger of flooding.

Had the rust had time to dry thoroughly, we might have been able to impregnate it with sufficient glue to hold it together. But it never did. Moisture rising from below ensured that water-soluble glues would not set, while cellulose varieties sat in a useless white film on top of the rust. I guessed that the helmet's interior was filled with silted clay, which, although it had helped to prevent crushing under the weight of the overlying silt, added its weight to our problems. I was certain that if we continued to dig down around the helmet and then tried to lift it out unsupported, it would collapse like a shattered egg. Our best hope lay in lifting it out still bedded in the clay around it. To that end, I designed a square steel box comprising two L-shaped sides that could be bolted together around the block of silt and mud in which the helmet rested, and a separate base plate that could be slid under the sides like a cookie cutter, slicing through the mud about 9 inches below the helmet's still buried right side (Fig. 8–10). Then, with the base secured with machine screws, and with cables fastened through the box's rim, we would hook it to the hawser of a winch truck—and pull.

Having already exposed the helmet's left side, we had robbed that side of the protection that the clay still gave to the right. In case something went wrong, therefore, we decided to use the steel box as a frame that would let us make a mold of the exposed side. Thanks to the generosity of the General Electric Corporation, which donated the necessarily large supply of its RTV 88 molding compound (which was not to be found in Virginia or its neighboring states), Gary McQuillen successfully covered the surface of the helmet with an inch-thick coating of this flexible rubber. The next step was to fill up the rest of the box with plaster of Paris, thus creating one half of a block mold. On reaching the laboratory, we planned to turn the box over, unscrew the bottom (which would by then have become the lid), and proceed to excavate the helmet's right side. That done, we would repeat the RTV 88 and plaster of Paris steps to create the other half of our mold, and once the plaster set we could unbolt the sides of the steel box to expose the junction of the two-part mold. With the two halves of the mold securely tied together, Gary would next extract the silt from within the helmet, dry the interior thoroughly, and reinforce

8–10. Originally drawn in advance of the event, this sketch of the procedure to be used to lift the helmet from the well was made for the benefit of the press. It did not take into account the problems that would be presented when other artifacts lying beneath the helmet, got in the way.

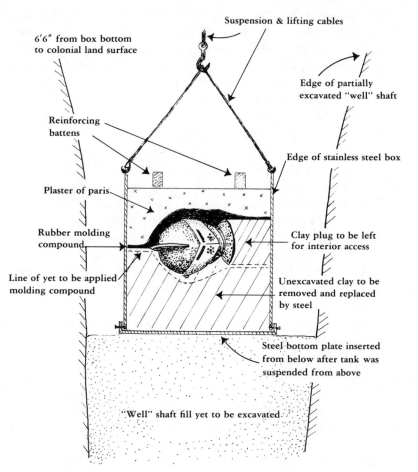

Suspension & lifting cables

6'6" from box bottom to colonial land surface

Edge of partially excavated "well" shaft

Reinforcing battens

Edge of stainless steel box

Plaster of paris

Rubber molding compound

Clay plug to be left for interior access

Line of yet to be applied molding compound

Unexcavated clay to be removed and replaced by steel

Steel bottom plate inserted from below after tank was suspended from above

"Well" shaft fill yet to be excavated.

The Method Employed in Raising and Preserving the Carter's Grove Helmet
August 17, 1977

Sketch not to scale

Unexcavated clay

Plan view from above showing left side of helmet as lifted within box it with fiberglass. Only then would he open the mold and start the delicate job of cleaning the helmet's outside down to the layer of rust that most closely corresponded with the original iron surface.

This was the theory; but practice and untested theories often have little in common. No sooner did we begin to cut down around the helmet than we were in trouble. Resting against one side of the well shaft and sloping under the helmet was a backplate from a suit of armor. Its condition seemed no better than the helmet's, and there was no way to get the steel box into position while it remained there— short of cutting straight through it. At any other time, finding an apparently complete armor backplate would have been cause for jubilation, but now I was prepared to sacrifice it rather than threaten the helmet's safety.

Groping in the mud I began to change my mind. I could feel the backplate getting less fragile the deeper I got, indicating that part of it had been less subject to the damaging effects of moisture fluctuation that had done such damage to the helmet. If we could reinforce the part we could see, perhaps the still buried end (it actually was the neck and shoulders) would be strong enough for us to pull the plate free without seriously undermining the block of clay and mud in which the helmet rested. It was worth a try.

After scraping the soft rust away from the plate's waist, Gary glued strips of fiberglass screen over the exposed interior surface, and with that set, he applied a thick layer of plaster. We knew that we might never get it off again, but we had agreed to settling for preserving the armor's outer surface, at the expense, if necessary, of its inner face. Moisture problems plagued the operation, and three days elapsed before we were ready to try to pull the plate free, three days of agonizing over the rightness of my decision to let Gary try to save it. Suppose I had fallen into Aesop's classic dog-with-a-bone trap, and in greedily reaching for the backplate I was about to lose both it and the helmet?

Progress on the site was always controlled by the approach of Friday. With long-range weather forecasts notoriously unreliable, and fearing that vandals might damage unfinished work over the weekend, we tried to complete each phase by late Thursday, saving Friday as insurance. This time we needed it. On Thursday afternoon Gary and Eric were still reinforcing the backplate, and Friday's forecast was for late afternoon and evening thundershowers—and 2 or 3 feet of water in the well.

It was 2:30 on Friday afternoon before we were ready to attempt to ease the plate from under the helmet's supporting block. Inch by inch Gary and I undercut the clay, groping in the mud for the back-plate's neck edge, and hoping all the time that it was not attached to something else that extended even further beneath the helmet. A glance at the sky was enough to tell us that the late afternoon thunder-storm would be early. I decided to wait no longer and undercut no further. It was time to cross our fingers and pull.

Nothing happened; then, an inch at a time, the plate began to shift. But when we tried to lift it upwards to clear the side of the well shaft, lumps of clay attached to the armor's outer face began to yawn and fall away. I saw one large piece drop off taking a smooth layer of rust with it, and I was certain that the decayed metal was breaking up, leaving us holding nothing but the fiberglass and plaster reinforce-ment. There was no time to stop; we were committed, and for better or worse we kept on lifting.

With a final heave and a relatively dextrous movement (consider-ing the plaster's weight), we turned the slab over onto a waiting tray, and there, to our silent astonishment, we saw a virtually complete cavalry armor backplate, its surface glistening with the moisture that clung to it (Fig. 8–11). All the outer rust had dropped away with the clay, leaving the metal so clean that brass rivets and the remains of leather straps were still visible. It seemed too good to be true, and in a way it was. The originally thin plate's inner surface had corroded so deeply that the protected outside was now like paper, barely more than a ghost image. But we had it, and in one piece. More important, we had extracted it without dislodging the helmet.

Eric's day book entry read: "Gary & INH in well—In p.m. removed backplate almost entire! Rain hit site at 3:05."

The weather was getting to everyone. Day after day, the journal read "Very hot and humid," "Hot," "Hot & humid," and that, cou-pled with the physical strain on the excavators and the mental tension of the supervisors stemming from our fear of making a mistake, made a difficult situation worse. On August 16, Eric's entry noted "Pump broke! Good God, can anything else go wrong?" and then "Bill sick today. I have backache and headache all day." But in the well (which was several degrees cooler than the flat, shadeless expanse above) good progress was being made. The steel frame for the helmet was securely in place, and Gary applied his molding compound without any difficulty. The next morning we poured plaster on top, and by early afternoon the winch truck was in position. Getting the box's bottom in place had been the hardest part. There was too little room in the shaft to slide it horizontally, and instead, it went under at an angle, preventing its bolt holes from lining up. To add to our problems, pieces of wood were preserved in the mud, and in two instances I had no alternative but to slice right through them.

We overcame the fastening difficulty by strapping cables under the base plate and around the sides of the box, a move that gave it greater strength—which was just as well. When we devised this lifting technique, it never occurred to us that by the time we were ready to pull, the box and its contents would weigh more than 200 pounds.

The film crew had been on the site throughout our lifting preparations, frying along with the rest of us, and doing the best it could to

8–11. An iron backplate from the fort well, after laboratory treatment. Discarded ca. 1622.

capture the action without, I must confess, much cooperation on our part. Fearing that the filming would get in our way, I had told the producer that our mission was to get the helmet secured and up as quickly as we could. There would be no time for "Take Two's!" As it turned out, the film crew's presence was no hindrance, and in the final moments it was worth its weight in celluloid. I had been so busy worrying about getting the box safely out of the well that I had given little thought to what we then would do with it. Manhandling the plaster-reinforced backplate into our own small truck had been easy enough, but a 200-pound block whose bottom stayed in place only as long as tension remained on the lifting cables was a very different problem. It was film unit electrician Bill McAllister who came up with the answer. His equipment truck had a hydraulic tailgate. The winch truck could lower the box onto that, and then Bill could raise it up to the level of his truck's floor, and we could push it aboard.

With the entire archaeological crew assembled around the hole, our own photographer Ruth Anne Clarke poised, and movie cameraman ready to roll, nothing was left for me to do but pray and surrender control to the photographers.

The winch truck's engine roared; the hawser drum began to turn; the cables on the box stretched as taut as piano wires, and for an interminable moment—nothing. Too late I realized that if the toggle bolts on the cables slipped, the lines would come flying out of the hole like a steel bolas, cutting a bloody swath through the audience. But that didn't happen; instead, the box began to move, first lurching a few inches sideways, and then up it came, clods of mud falling off into the water below.

"The bottom's not holding!"

It had yawned a couple of inches, but the falling mud came from the outside and not from within the box. Slowly, the box continued up. As it cleared the edge of the shaft I could see that the bottom was bulging badly in the middle and that water and mud were dripping from it; but by then we knew we were safe. A few moments more, and Bill McAllister had his truck's tailgate under the box. The return to Williamsburg in the film unit's truck was uneventful. We could relax. All that remained was to get the helmet into the lab and let Gary McQuillen do the rest.

Gary and several staff members were on hand at our loading dock as the truck backed as close to the doors as it could reach. We had only to push the box out onto the tailgate for it to be gently lowered onto a waiting trolley. Perhaps in relaxing, our strength had ebbed, but the box seemed even heavier than before; its mud-caked dead weight, encumbered by its slack cables, did not slide gracefully onto the hydraulic tailgate; every inch was grudgingly yielded. Those of us who had been lovingly nursing it all day were hot, tired, mud-caked, and cursing it as we levered and pushed the box out onto the platform.

"Look out!" somebody yelled.

Too late. The hydraulic system failed under the weight, sending tailgate and box crashing to the ground. At such moments no suitable expletives come to mind. We could only be thankful that the box had not broken open, scattering helmet fragments across the parking lot. If damage had been done, we would find out soon enough.

It had taken us from August 4 to August 17 to get our helmet out of the ground and into the laboratory, thirteen days of knotted emotions: hope, exhilaration, and excitement vying with bouts of fear and desperation—fear that the weather would defeat us, that the box would not fit, that plaster would not set, that cables would break, and that together the helmet and our reputations would be ruined. Then, too, we faced the ever-nagging prospect that time and fluctuating water levels might have dealt even more unkindly with the helmet's right side than the left, and that we had gone to all this trouble to save something that no longer existed.

I realize that a reader who has never been involved in making a unique archaeological discovery might have difficulty understanding how totally wrapped up in it one can become. If the safe salvage of America's first close helmet had not become an obsession on a par with Captain Ahab's white whale, it was only because our quarry was smaller.

With the box safely in the lab, I listened to the rain rattling against my windows in the night and muttered "Go ahead, rain! You can't hurt us now!"—which was a singularly myopic and selfish point of view. The helmet was but one artifact; the site was still out there —flooding. Eric's day book entry for August 18 began: "Rain all last night and part of morning! Spent till 1:00 pumping out Site C— partially done—well emptied."

That afternoon, back in the lab, we were ready to turn the helmet box over and remove the base plate, an operation performed in the glare of the film unit's lights and watched by reporters and photographers from the local press. We had become a media event.

The clay revealed in the box was a bluish gray, interrupted by two black and fibrous patches—all that remained of the tops of pieces of wood sliced off by our cookie-cutter base plate. Working with the box raised on a platform between us, Gary and I could scrape and pare away the clay with all the care and precision denied us in the close confines of the well. Slowly the center of the square of clay began to turn brown as we approached the rusted metal; then the stain became a convex shape, growing larger and more contoured as the side of the helmet emerged. Faint green stains at the collar soon became the heads of brass-capped rivets, and a strange, twiglike projection became a pivoting prop to hold the visor open. The helmet was all there and had suffered no ill effects from its precipitous descent aboard the non-hydraulic tailgate. Time and the ground had been less kind, however; they had attacked the right side with as much vigor as they had the left, and Gary's magnet indicated that little or no metal survived. He would have to settle for cleaning and reinforcing the rust.

That disappointment aside, we could rejoice in having successfully brought this infinitely fragile object out of the ground and into the lab without inflicting the slightest damage. Tomorrow's newspaper would report the surgery step by step under a three-column headline: ARCHAEOLOGIST DIGS INTO UNEARTHED HELMET—which, of course, was not yet true.

Back to B
9

As Virginia summers progress, outsmarting the weather becomes a major preoccupation, and in August 1977, with the helmet out of the way, our prime concern was to complete the fort well's excavation before storm water caused its side to collapse. We had no idea how far we might have to dig to reach bottom. An eighteenth-century, brick-lined shaft, revealed in an eroding cliff a mile downriver, had been more than 30 feet deep. Our well shaft had no evidence of any lining. At a depth of 5 feet we had hit a layer of fossil shell, and it was through this unstable marl stratum that water was running in. Although I knew from examining the cliff face at the river's edge that we could expect to find more clay below the marl, an unlined well cut through such material could be dangerous to excavate.

I had directed the exploration of several wells in Williamsburg, and for those whose brick walls had been dismantled when they were abandoned, I had devised a technique of lowering a new liner made up of steel cylinders bolted together. Installing them one upon another, and getting them to slide down the enlarged shaft under their own weight was always difficult, and sometimes hazardous when cylinders became wedged and popped their bolts. Nevertheless, the technique worked, although we had never had to take it to a depth of 30 feet.

Experience in excavating Roman wells in London had taught me that there were more ways than one to dig a hole. There, builders using drag-lines to dig vast basements would slice through the ancient shafts. When the building foremen were in a cooperative mood, they would let their operators work elsewhere while I dug down into the wells to a depth of 4 or 5 feet. Then they would bring the machine back and go down around and through the shaft to the point where I had stopped, whereupon I would come back and continue digging. By going down in these leapfrogging stages, I was never more than shoulder deep in the wells, and the holes around them were wide enough for there to be nothing to fall from the sides onto my head. I had twice used this method to excavate unlined well shafts in Williamsburg, and although it had proved quick and safe, the hole it made in the surrounding subsoil was enormous. I thought it possible, nevertheless, that when we had finished with the rest of our Site C, even quite extensive damage to the ground beneath it could be repaired without lasting damage to the terrain. Eric was by no means convinced, and although he winced when I suggested so Draconian a solution, he said nothing. Later, in his day book, he wrote: "INH says that the best way to dig it [the well] will be to bring in a drag line *across* it?"

That was an oversimplification. I was by no means wedded to the idea, but two things were certain: We were not going to risk crew lives in an unstable shaft, and we were not going to leave unexcavated a well which, deeper down, might hold more and better-preserved armor. In the end the problem solved itself.

On Monday, August 22, I went back into the well to start work on extracting the wood exposed when we had removed the helmet, and almost immediately I discovered that the hole was shrinking into a small, rectangular pit or sump that bottomed out at a depth of only 7 feet, 4 inches below the land surface. Our well had been dug just deep enough to draw rainwater percolating through the clay into the first marl stratum. The sump was less easily explained. The end of a wooden post stood in one corner, a post too slender to have been part of any bucket-hauling rig, and the entire boxlike hole was filled with bits of grass, twigs, bark, seeds, and sandy mud. It hardly seemed necessary to dig a sump to catch material that would otherwise have settled harmlessly to the bottom of the well—particularly if its primary function had been to replenish a cattle pond. More logical than the catchbasin theory was the possibility that a workman was sent down during a summer drought with orders to keep digging into the marl until he found water, and that he reached it very quickly. Whatever its intent, the "sump" provided archaeological preservation for organic remains that otherwise would not have survived. Among the largest pieces of wood recovered was part of an oak post 4 1/2 inches in diameter, the ax marks at its pointed end as fresh as the day the blows fell.

With this post found only 8 feet from the line of our fort's palisade, we asked ourselves whether it could have been part of the latter. It was too slender to have been one of the main supports; but was it possible that its well-preserved point had stuck up, and not down into the ground, where it inevitably would have suffered some surface decay, and that it had been one of the fort's vertical palings? If so, it would mean that Strachey's Jamestown description of a palisade built with posts and *planks* would not parallel ours. In the end, I decided that our post tapered too quickly (more than an inch in less than 2 1/2 feet) to have made an adequate pale. Nevertheless, finding this pointed stake made us stop, think, and worry.

Archaeologists venturing into unknown worlds do a lot of that —particularly when their employers are asking for prompt interpretations of what is being found, and when interest generated by one season's digging can determine whether or not there will be funds for another. Having failed to find a kiln on Site B, we badly needed the fort as a superior substitute if we were to hope for another National Geographic Society grant to help us through 1978. Consequently, even the bubbles from a potentially torpedoing piece of evidence could lead to sleepless nights and falling hair. The well's enigmatic stake therefore belonged in the same league with Audrey's specter of George Sandys and his "Large forte Palled in."

Of all the well's artifacts, one ceramic fragment was potentially the most informative—as far as the site's evolution was concerned. It was the neck from a jug of German blue-and-gray stoneware, an object of some elegance and impressed on the handle with the potter's initials, a ligatured WM. In more than thirty years of studying and collecting Rhenish stonewares, I never before had seen or heard of an example marked in this way, and subsequent inquiries among curators and collectors have produced no parallels. The neck was not the first fragment of such a jug to come our way, however; on the contrary, its size, decoration, and even its interior character and color were identical to a base found in one of the rubbish pits on Site A. I was convinced that both fragments came from the same kiln—if not from the same jug (Fig. 9–1).

It seemed unlikely that someone had broken the jug on one site and had then carried a piece of it to another site a third of a mile away, just to confuse future archaeologists. More plausible was a scenario wherein a Martin's Hundred settler about to sail for America bought several identical jugs from the same English supplier. That dealer would have purchased his stock from a shipper or a Netherlandish exporter who, in turn, would have bought his jugs from a factory in the Rhineland. There they would have been sold by the dozen and drawn from stock taken off shelves housing identical products from a single kiln batch. Because these jugs were of the same type and size, they would in all probability have been the work of the same potter and decorator. It is quite reasonable to suppose, therefore, that jugs that began as clay in the hands of a single German potter remained together until they finally wound up in a home half the world away.

The key factor in all this is that there be only one ultimate purchaser and owner. That pot buyers for two unrelated Martin's Hundred households should go to the same London middleman and buy identical jugs is somewhat harder to swallow. Assuming, therefore, that the "one man, two jugs" theory is correct, a crucial link is forged between Sites A and C; yet at this stage in our reasoning, "A" was thought to date in the 1630s and 1640s—a time when fort building in Martin's Hundred was considered unnecessary.

In 1634 a palisade had been built across the peninsula between the James and York rivers, and thereafter, the settlements east of it (and Martin's Hundred was one of them) ceased to be troubled by Indians. Logic dictates that our Site C fort had to be earlier, built either when the first Martin's

9–1. The neck and base from similar if not identical Westerwald stoneware jugs. Decorated in blue and stamped with the maker's initials WM on the handle. The neck fragment was found in the fort well. The base came from a pit on Site A. Jug date ca. 1600–1625.

Hundred settlers arrived, or amid the slamming of stable doors after the massacre of 1622. As the originally shipped population numbered about 220 in 1618 and barely 30 in the two years following the attack, it seemed fair to deduce that the effort involved in building a fort of any size would have been expended when the manpower was greatest.

The German jug fragments were not our only potential link between Sites A and C—there was also Governor Harwood. If any fort-building was to be done, either he or his predecessor would have directed it and been responsible for the structure's maintenance. Indeed, he might have lived within it before establishing a farm of his own. Harwood's conjectured association with Site A hitherto had hung on the slender evidence of that cannonball and the few strands of gold and silver clothing threads that we had found there. The jug fragments now offered a connection between the person in authority at the fort (Harwood?) and a resident of Site A. To establish that the latter was indeed William Harwood we would have to prove that my original commencement date for Site A, in the 1630s, was wrong, for he disappeared from the records in 1629.

Just as our film of the excavations on Site B had been shot without knowing how the plot would develop, so the first draft of these chapters was being written before the Martin's Hundred digging ended and all the evidence was in. Consequently, a weekend at the typewriter generated new Monday morning debates. One of them stemmed from my musings over the relationship between the fort on Site C and the dwelling on Site A. If the German jug pieces were a legitimate link between the two sites, and if the cannonball really identified Governor Harwood as one—if not the first—occupant of Site A, was there any archaeological association between the latter's German jug bottom and the cannonball? Could they have been thrown away at much the same time, and therefore have been the property of the same person?

Checking with Eric Klingelhofer and his excavation register (known as the E.R. Book), I found that the jug base came from layer "L," close to the bottom of a rubbish pit numbered 1737. Our previously described fencing slot passed across and through the top of this pit, clearly demonstrating that if the pit was not the earliest feature on the site, it also was not the latest. So far, so good. "But what about the cannonball?" I asked.

Collections supervisor William Pittman brought us the answer. "It's 1737L," he said.

So the jug base and cannonball not only came from the same area of the site, they had been thrown into the same layer of the same pit, unquestionably at much the same time. The news sent us hurrying to reexamine the rest of the pit's artifacts. Among them were more military objects than had been found in any other single deposit on Site A—the point from a halberd or from what may have been a rare type of spear called a brandistock, parts of an armor backplate identical to the one from the fort well, and a sword pommel that may well have come from a rapier whose guard we had found in a small hole immediately to the north of Pit 1737. Here, it seemed, we had almost as much evidence of a military presence as we had from the fort. But dating was still the problem. Nothing from the pit could make us certain that it dated to the immediate post-massacre period—except perhaps the pipe-

stem fragments, and we all knew that we had destroyed the credibility of their testimony when we found the 1631 dish on Site B.

"Why not give the Binford formula another try," I suggested to
Audrey, "just to see how it comes out."

"It's a waste of time," she replied.

"Try it just for fun."

A few minutes later she was back with her answer. "What sort
of date did you say you'd like it to be?"

"Sometime between 1623 and 1629."

"Well you've got 1623.09." While we stood stunned, Audrey
hastened to insist that it was sheer coincidence. There were only
fifteen fragments, she said, far too small a sampling to be statistically
valid—even if the formula was right, and we knew it wasn't. Furthermore, Audrey went on, the sample was very uneven, comprising one
fragment with a bore measuring 7/64 of an inch, twelve at 8/64, and
two at 9/64. Taking either of those flanking fragments away, we
would get a very different figure.

"How different?" I persisted. Reluctantly, Audrey went back to
her calculator; but try as she would, the results steadfastly refused to
stray far from my estimated Harwood occupancy brackets of 1623 to
1629. Omitting the single 7/64-inch fragment gave us 1620.41, and
taking away the 9/64-inch pieces only carried us forward to 1628.83.

"It still has to be a coincidence," said Eric. And I had to agree.

Even if we continued to reject the favorable pipe-stem dating, the
exercise had made us look again at the pipe bowls from Pit 1737, and
they, too, had a surprise for us. One bore the maker's mark R.B., a
mark identical to that on another pipe bowl found in the pond beside
the fort well. To argue that unrelated occupants of Site C and A would
have bought their pipes from the same English source (when there
were literally dozens to choose from in the London area alone)
seemed to be raising coincidence to a new level of improbability. It
was far easier to believe that the artifactual evidence pointed unwaver-
ingly toward the presence of William Harwood on both sites.

That someone of social prominence had lived inside the fort was
suggested by a small fragment of cast iron that turned up in the top
silting of the pond. Molded in relief on one face were the letters L:Y,
which I interpreted as being part of the motto of the British Order
of the Garter: HONI:SOIT:QUI:MAL:Y:PENSE—"Evil to him who
thinks evil." My republican colleagues, who since 1783 have been
denied the privilege of growing up under the Crown, were reluctant
to believe that so much could safely be read from two letters. They
abandoned their skepticism, however, when Gary McQuillen cleaned

another cast-iron fragment recovered from Site C's plow zone, revealing three more letters of the same size—PEN. Put together, the pieces now gave us the L:Y:PEN of "mal y pense" (Fig. 9–2).

The lettered fragments came from a cast-iron plate used to prevent fire from damaging the back of a chimney's hearth and to project heat into the room. Made largely in the Weald of southeast England, these firebacks usually were decorated, often with the arms and supporters of the reigning monarch: Elizabeth I (1558 to 1603), James I (1603 to 1625), or Charles I (1625 to 1649). I could recall none with the arms of Charles II. Knowing that Martin's Hundred did not exist before 1619, the crucial question was whether the fragments came from the arms of James I or Charles I. If they were the latter's we would have firm evidence that our fort was lived in after 1625—after the Indians' destruction of Wolstenholme Towne. Since the arms of both kings included the garter motto, it looked as though we would have to find much more of the fireback if we were to have any hope of dating it before or after 1625.

On the basis of information available to us at the end of August

9–2. Fragments from a cast-iron plate intended to protect the back of a fireplace. Those at left, representing the plate's lower left corner, are cast in relief with the right back foot of a lion and, within a ribbon, the inscription **DIEVET**. The other fragments come from a circular ribbon embossed L:Y:PEN (See Fig. 11–6).

1977, the historical sequence at Martin's Hundred might have gone something like this: The fort either enclosed Wolstenholme Towne, the Hundred's core settlement, or stood adjacent to it, and was built in 1619 or 1620. After the 1622 uprising, when everything except two houses and part of the church was destroyed, Harwood returned and lived among the handful of survivors close to the safety of the river and the fort's palisades. After Virginia became a Crown colony in 1624 and the Virginia Company's charter was revoked, he took for himself the land that had hitherto been under his control as the chief officer in Virginia of the London-based Society of Martin's Hundred. This was the 1,500 acres set aside in the repatent of 1622 as being for public use, and which we can assume to have been cleared and cultivated by Harwood and the Society's servants. Leaving the poorly drained and Indian-ravaged site of Wolstenholme Towne, Harwood moved to the more desirable Site A at some time between 1623 and 1625.

All this was no more than educated guesswork. I well knew that we still had no firm dating for Site A's artifacts, and colleagues frequently reminded me that I had previously estimated their date range between about 1635 and 1645 to 1650. I countered that so little is known about early seventeenth-century ceramics that one could easily be off by ten or even twenty years.

"But you weren't off by ten or twenty years when you bracketed Site B," Eric reminded me. "You told us 1630 to 1640 and then found the 1631 dish to prove it."

"A lucky guess," I told him. And it probably was. It also reminded me that in addition to our apparent Sites A and C connection, we also had the North Devonshire sgraffito pottery link between the fort and Site B. There comes a time, usually at the end of a long, hot summer, when an archaeologist finds his reasoning spinning, getting him nowhere. We had reached that point. Until we could open up more of Site C, all we could say of it was that we had found what we believed to be part of a palisaded enclosure—and what we *knew* to be a helmet.

It was absurd to settle for that. One way or another we would have to raise the money to continue through another summer, if only to determine the size of the fort and how or if it related to Wolstenholme Towne. The still unexcavated field extended another 400 feet to the river's edge, a distance that should give us the rest of any reasonably sized fort, if not of a fortified town. Determining the size of Site C was essential not only for planning how to tackle it, but also for estimating how much and how long it would take to dig it. With only one 73-degree-angle corner exposed, no such projections were possible. It was imperative for planning purposes, therefore, that we should determine the length of one palisade wall and find another corner angle. With that information in hand, I could accurately project the third corner of our apparently triangular fort, and thus determine its size and the magnitude of the work still to be done.

On September 6, the last day of the 1977 excavation, and while most of the crew was busily covering the excavated post-holes with plastic sheeting prior to back-filling for the winter, I instructed the grader operator to strip away the plow zone in a northerly direction, extending the line of our east palisade. As crew members shaved the clay subsoil, new post-holes began to show up—four of them, still on nine-foot centers and extending the wall line to a total length of 130 feet. There it stopped. Our search for the four posts for another watchtower proved futile; worse, the line of post-holes turned west, not at the expected 73-degree angle for an isosceles triangle, but at an angle close to 90 degrees. Patches of burned clay were showing up within the enclosure, as was a loam-filled slot running parallel to the wall line at a distance about 2 feet, 9 inches from it. We had found similar slots (interrupted here and there by plow damage) along the entire length of the east wall, as well as paralleling what little we had of the south palisade. Evidently, this often faint scar had been an important element of the fort on all three sides.

To expose any more on the last day of the dig would have been folly. We had wanted to find the length of one wall and to locate another corner. Now we had both—and little good did they do us! Projecting our 73-degree and 9-degree angles in an attempt to complete a triangle led to extension of the palisade lines about 400 feet, to a sharp point close to the existing river's edge (Fig. 9–3). There was room, therefore, to find all of the fort on the surviving land surface, but militarily and architecturally such an enclosure made little sense. The fort could not be triangular; but whether it was four-, five-, or even more sided, we could not say. So we were back to first base, with no concept of the size or shape of our fort, and therefore no way to plan an economical, archaeological assault on it. Ahead lay six months of waiting for the winter rainwater to drain away and permit the subsoil to dry sufficiently to once again bear the weight of our grader—six months of nail-chewing frustration.

With back-filling complete and the tents struck, our remaining troops returned to Site B, where Bill Henry had been continuing low-keyed exploration whenever the flies permitted and we had men to spare. No potter's kiln had shown up, and there was now no doubt in anyone's mind that Site B, regardless of its wealth of artifacts, was of secondary importance in the history of Martin's Hundred. Rarely does an excavation turn out exactly as one may have hoped at the outset, and it should thus come as no surprise that values change as the jigsaw puzzle takes shape. Archaeologically, therefore, the downgrading of Site B was no cause for dismay. Whether or not the National Geographic Society's research committee would be as sanguine was quite another question. It might well say "No kiln, no money for 1978." Of more immediate concern was the embarrassing question of what to do with a film half of which was devoted to raising hopes for Site B, only to end on a "You can't win 'em all" note as the crew packed up and walked away. We might have gotten away with that, had it really been the end of our endeavor. But of course it was not.

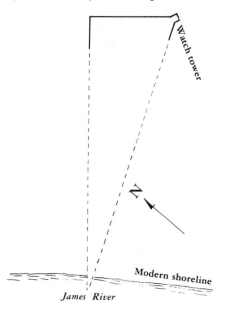

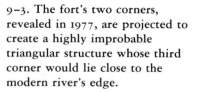

9–3. The fort's two corners, revealed in 1977, are projected to create a highly improbable triangular structure whose third corner would lie close to the modern river's edge.

Not realizing how important Site C was to become, and being distracted by the speed with which it began to unfold, I had given little thought to any need for more filming. Too late, I realized that we had no footage showing the excavation of the palisade postholes or even of the well in its early stages. The simplest solution was to omit Site C and end on Site B, as we had planned. The trouble with that, however, was that the *National Geographic* intended to publish an article on the excavations, and we could hardly expect it to ignore the fort or the discovery of the helmet, whose picture had already appeared in several dozen newspapers across the country. The film's audiences would expect to see at least as much as the magazine had to tell; besides, we had all that dramatic footage showing the helmet emerging from the well—and there was more to come.

In the laboratory, work on the helmet was going according to plan. With the two halves of the plaster mold firmly strapped together, conservator McQuillen had turned it over so that the helmet's still clay-filled neck was uppermost, enabling him to excavate within it using a spoon and a spatula. As we expected, the helmet's interior was largely filled with clay—36 pounds of it. With that extracted and the scale rust removed from inside, the next step was to line the helmet with fiberglass resin and narrow strips of fiberglass screenwire. With that set, we knew that the rust base that substituted for iron was strong enough for Gary to use his Airbrasive treatment on the helmet's exterior without fear of its collapsing. The trick now was to open the rubber-lined plaster mold.

We knew that the mold was too heavy to be lifted apart by hand, and that any lateral movement of the upper half would almost certainly snap off the frail visor prop that projected from one side of the helmet. We agreed, therefore, that half the mold would have to be raised vertically upward by means of a geared-and-ratcheted fence tightener. To that end, Gary set four projecting bolts into the sides of the mold's upper half to which lifting cables would be attached. The success of the operation depended on the one factor over which we had no control—whether or not the rubber casting material would peel away from the helmet, allowing the two halves of the mold to part.

Once again the film crew and still photographers assembled, and standing beside the white plaster block with its wire-linked bolts projecting like terminals from the neck of Frankenstein's monster, I explained what we were about to do and what might go wrong. There was only one right way and four wrong ones, I said. The mold might not part, in which case the whole thing would go up as one. If the suspension was not exactly centered, movement would be lateral as well as vertical, and the helmet might crack like an egg. It was possible, too, that the helmet would come away from the bottom half of the mold but be left hanging from the top. Finally, there was the unthinkable alternative: the helmet would come free from neither half and would be torn apart as the mold opened.

With the fence tightener lashed to an overhead beam, an assistant took the first pulls on the lever, while below Gary and I crouched beside the mold ready to react to whatever might happen. Every click of the ratchet rang like a pistol shot as the cables became taut. I had visions of the bolts ripping out of the plaster and the freed cables lashing out at the dangerously close audience. But just as I was about to tell everyone to retreat to a safe distance, Gary saw movement. A thin, dark line was growing between the upper and lower layers of the bright red rubber. Then it stopped. Something was hung up inside. We tried to push screwdrivers into the gap and to use them to lever the two halves of the mold apart, but it was too heavy. Besides, levering one edge meant exerting downward pressure on another, and that was the last thing we wanted. Our only hope was to keep pulling from above.

The click, click, click of the ratchet came faster. Something had to give, and logic dictated that it should be the greased faces of the two rubber layers. As a close helmet forever closed in the mold was of no use to anyone, we had no choice but to keep pulling.

Again the upper plaster block began to move, going up at a rate of about an eighth of an inch with each click of the ratchet. From Gary's and my positions it was impossible to see what was going on inside the mold. Only the cameraman had a clear view into the helmet itself. Electrician Bill McCallister was the first to realize what was happening.

"The whole thing's going up!" he shouted.

It was true. Instead of remaining cradled in the lower half of the mold, the helmet was stuck to the top and was going up suspended beneath it like the gondola under a blimp (Fig. 9–4). If we lowered it down again the helmet would be crushed, but if we went on up it might drop out and shatter. Our best bet was to keep going and try to catch the helmet if it fell. Although the cameraman kept shooting, the rest of the film crew rushed to assist. Shoulders and heads got between the lens and the action, and the microphone was swamped by voices all talking at once—*cinéma vérité* in its rawest form. But we were grateful for every helping hand. Some were outstretched to catch the helmet; others hauled away the now empty lower half of the mold and substituted a box onto which I proposed to set the upper half once we had lifted it high enough to turn it over, helmet side up.

Again the film crew had saved the day. The difficult maneuver was completed without further mishap. Half the helmet lay revealed in all its rusty splendor. Now it was up to Gary to find a way to free it from the other side of the mold. As for the film sequence, the chaos at the end only heightened the drama, and made the "helmet bit" strong enough to stand as a short film in its own right.

For several more weeks interest remained focused on the laboratory as Gary McQuillen worked to restore Site C's helmet to its final, spectacular appearance (Fig. 9–5); meanwhile, Bill Henry and the field crew were busy with the far from spectacular but no less important task of restoring Site B to the orderly state wherein we had left it in July. Since then, summer rains had eroded trench edges, silt had accumulated in post-holes, weeds had sprouted, flourished, and died, and under the plastic sheets put down to protect the scraped clay subsoil, a rich green mold had grown. Over it all, the autumn's leaves drifted down like big brown snowflakes. In short, Site B was in one hell of a mess, and persistent bad weather helped not at all. By November 2, the gods notwithstanding, it had to be immaculate, for on that day the National Geographic Society's Research Committee was coming to inspect the work and to decide whether or not its funds had been well spent.

The Society's grants go to worthwhile projects in many exploratory fields from anthropology to zoology, projects watched over by a committee of respected scholars drawn from government agencies, universities, and the Smithsonian Institution. No committee of man-

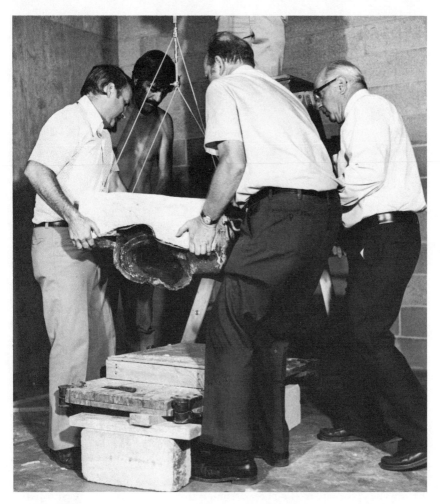

9–4. The helmet at the brink of disaster, still gripped in the upper half of the plaster mold after the lower half had been moved away.

ageable size could include a member fully versed in every discipline supported by the Society, and I knew that although it included two distinguished anthropologists, neither was trained in the very specialized field of historical archaeology, or even, for that matter, in European classical archaeology, from which our techniques are derived. Since this was to be my first meeting with the committee, I had no way of knowing whether the lack of a member skilled in our discipline

9-5. The helmet after laboratory treatment. The iron strip projecting beside the right cheek is a prop designed to hold the visor up. Discarded ca. 1622.

would help or hinder our chances for further financial support. If Site B could be presented in an awesome degree of cleanliness, everyone might be so impressed by all the obviously hard and careful work expended on it that they would be reluctant to question whether the site was really worth it. Alternatively, they might look at us through the other end of the telescope and focus only on that question. Might it not "prove" me incapable of telling woods from trees? But then again, wouldn't they surely concede that archaeological ethics demand that a site once opened cannot be abandoned until one is sure that it has nothing to say?

No matter what the committee might think, our "fort" had been back-filled and was now under water. So, like it or not, Site B was all we had to show. We would have to hope that the wealth of artifacts laid out in the lab would make up for the absence of anything spectacular in the field. I clung to that thought, and to the knowledge that the celebrated historian of colonial America, Louis B. Wright, was a member of the committee. Though not an archaeologist, he had been one of the first American scholars to recognize that the ground is capable of contributing records worthy of analysis by traditionally document-oriented historians. In Louis Wright I was sure we had at least one friend at court. At the Weather Bureau, we had none.

For most people, waking up to the radio's revelation that we face a day partly cloudy with an 80 percent chance of rain by late afternoon means not forgetting the umbrella, and remembering to tell one's withering tomato plants that help is at hand. To an archaeologist, such a forecast can be a knife in the ribs. Faint traces of past human life can have miraculously survived the centuries only to be washed away in a matter of minutes; post-holes cleaned for photography change their shapes as their edges dissolve, while the morale of a crew faced with yet another clean-up job goes with them. After a fair day on October 31, November dawned gray and forbidding. By the time Bill Henry got his troops to the site, a light drizzle was falling, dampening spirits and boding ill for the rest of the day. Under normal circumstances he would have abandoned any attempt to clean anything. But tomorrow was to be inspection day. Bill's day book entry told the tale: "Started cleaning site in light drizzle that turned to heavy rain. Crew sent home at 2:00 p.m."

The National Geographic Society's committee reached Williamsburg on a chartered bus late in the morning of November 2, and after lunch I summarized the year's discoveries—one eye on the rain trickling down the window panes. If only it would come on harder, I thought, maybe chairman Melvin Payne would call off the site visit. But the committee was made of the stern stuff one should expect of a society devoted to exploration and the great outdoors. No one was in the least daunted by the weather; each member had brought appropriate attire. They had come to see the excavations, and see them they would.

Our normal route to Site B had been on foot, down a path cut into the face of the ravine that divided it from Site A. The track was steep but short. Now, however, it had become a mudslide, impassible to all but goats wearing alpine boots. The alternative route was over a mile-long track through the woods, one pitted and rutted by our vehicle's wheels and ridged with exposed tree roots. Over this obstacle course we proposed to transport the committee seated in vans and an open-backed truck. I had not bargained for members bringing their wives, yet all but two of the latter insisted on leaving the bus and piling aboard.

When wives are bored and unhappy, husbands' opinions are likely to be discolored, their enthusiasm tempered, and their attention-span shortened. I recall whispering to Eric that I wished to God the wives had stayed on the bus! Bringing up the rear, I watched the truck ahead of me pitching and bouncing, its damp passengers rising and sinking not quite in synchronization with the vehicle. When it was coming down, the committee was still going up.

My apologies for the roughness of the ride were laughingly brushed aside. Later the wife of one member confided that she thought the truck ride through the woods was the best part. She had a point. The site had become a treacherous sea of mud. Previously back-filled test trenches hidden under a blanket of freshly fallen leaves had become traps into which committee members sank and had to be rescued clinging to the handles of shovels. Under a plastic tent four "specimen" archaeologists were exhibited digging in an area whose only virtue was that the ground around it was firm enough to support spectators. The crew looked sodden, and its welcoming smiles won more marks for stoicism than for sincerity. But the committee members understood, and no one asked why we were risking damage to the soil layers by digging in such weather.

Six weeks later I got word that our request for the Society's continuing support through 1978 had been approved.

Although Site B had not lived up to our expectations, it was, judged by any other standards, a major discovery, being one of the very few pre-1650 house sites yet excavated in America (see Fig. 7-3).

The problem was how to interpret its evidence. In addition to its 37-by-19-foot dwelling, the site yielded only one more building, that ridiculously narrow shed with barely enough posts to hold it up. We had found one rubbish pit which we could prove had not been filled before 1631, and although large quantities of local pottery were scattered about the site—some of it apparently kiln waste—the number of weapon and armor fragments that we had found pointed as strongly to a military presence as it did to a potter. If the still enigmatic Dutch "patch box" really was intended to hold rifle patches, that otherwise potentially distaff object took its place on the spear side. All in all, with males outnumbering females by twenty to seven at Martin's Hundred in the post-massacre years, we could fairly deduce that Site B had been home to a male household.

One key task had yet to be completed. The dwelling's clay hearth had to be dismantled, something we could not do until the site's final, master photographs had been shot and printed. For months we had kept this important feature under protective plastic sheeting. Residents of the forest, however, failed to appreciate our concern, and instead saw in the plastic cover a warm and inviting subterranean playground. When we took up the plastic to shoot the final photographs we found that a mole had tunneled about in the hearth, turning the surface of the red-baked clay into a miniature Mars-scape. Cosmetic damage was considerable, but the archaeological loss was small; enough of the hearth and chimney survived for its construction to be determined, and for us to recover a vitally important tobacco-pipe bowl that had been lost into the clay when the hearth was first laid. Because the bowl shape could date as early as 1620, we now had evidence indicating that the house might have been built several years before the 1631 dish was discarded.

Site B still held one more surprise, and true to form, it once again demontrated how fragile were our conclusions. Cleaning up 5 feet southeast of the chimney, artifact officer John Hamant came upon a rectangular, clay-filled hole partly hidden under the roots of a tree we had hitherto avoided removing. On December 29, a numbingly cold day, John and Eric Klingelhofer completed excavation of the hole, revealing the fifty-eight nails and a dark stain in the ground which were all that was left of an infant's coffin—a coffin with the now familiar line of nails down the middle. Of the bones, no traces survived—neither did our thesis that Site B had been inhabited solely by men. Only then did I remember the glass bead that we had found earlier in the year, which may have belonged to this child's mother.

Squatting beside the grave and carefully plotting the position of each nail, we were thinking more about coffin construction than the centuries-old circumstances that had brought us to this spot on a bitter December afternoon. It was artist-photographer Ruth Anne Clarke who put the slender traces in focus. "I can see those poor people coming out of the house to bury their baby," she said. "Can you imagine how they felt—so far from home?"

Suddenly the wind seemed colder. I was glad we were about ready to shovel the dirt back and move out. Ruth Anne had conjured up the ghosts of Site B, and it was time to be gone.

Murder in the Company Compound

10

Organizing an archaeological excavation is like planning a military campaign. You know how many people you have and, if your supply corps has done its job, you have the right quality and quantity of equipment. You also (you hope) have sufficient funds in hand to pay the troops and keep the equipment moving even if progress turns out to be slower than expected. Always your principal enemy remains the weather. It can be too wet for mechanical equipment to operate, so windy that tents are ripped to shreds, or so hot that the ground bakes too hard to dig and the crew falls sick with heat stroke and fatigue. As we began our third season in Martin's Hundred, I thought we had enough experience to estimate the price the weather would extort. What we did not know was the size of the site.

For efficient planning purposes, returning to the fort and continuing where we had left off had a mesmeric appeal. I knew in which directions to head, and I knew that something spectacular could quickly be accomplished. The enemy, however, had other ideas. The site was a perennial catchbasin for rainwater shedding from the high ground behind it. This spring it was worse. Dirt pushed back into the excavation at the end of 1977 had not bonded into the clay subsoil. Much of it had been spread over plastic sheets to protect the archaeological features below, and so, instead of draining away, the water concentrated in the area of the old excavation and became a quagmire in the midst of which—adding insult to injury—marsh grasses began to sprout. I knew that it would take weeks of drought and summer sun before we could send machinery in to remove last year's back-filled dirt.

The winter of 1978 took its time, and not until March 20 could the crew return to Site C. With a direct assault on the fort out of the question, our best ploy was to begin closer to the river and to work inland toward it. Rows of test holes dug in a strip parallel to the river and about 30 feet back from the cliff edge proved disappointing. The long-plowed field yielded few artifacts. When you heard a crewman's jubilant shout at finding half a rusted nail, you suspected that this was not one of Martin's Hundred's richest areas. In reality, however, relying on the negative testimony of test holes is about as assured of success as trying to come out ahead in Las Vegas.

Although the test holes were unrewarding, the ground closest to the cliff was drying fastest, and so I instructed Eric Klingelhofer to bring back the mechanical grader and to begin stripping away the plow zone along a line parallel to the river. We would keep moving inland until something showed up.

If the fort was related to Wolstenholme Towne—and we had no evidence that it was—it should have served one of two purposes. As I have noted earlier, the entire town could have been contained within the palisades, or the fort could have been set apart, the settlement's stores and dwellings outside it, like English medieval villages that grew up under the protecting walls of castles. Assuming that 300 to 400 feet of cliff erosion had occurred since the early seventeenth century, and knowing that the landward wall of the fort stood a good 500 feet back from the present cliff edge, there once should have been about 800 feet between it and the shore, enough room for a palisaded village or for a settlement with a fort at its rear. Either way, our decision to begin beside the river and to creep up on the fort from the outside made historical as well as archaeological sense.

Ten days after returning to the site, things began to happen. A line of five large, loam-filled holes appeared in the subsoil, not irregular patches of the "maybe-it's-a-roothole" variety, but square-cut holes, two with clear traces of inner post molds. The spacing between them was similar to that of the fort's posts, but they were running in quite the wrong direction. At this early stage in an excavation, particularly when the ground is wet and the weather uncertain, one simply plots the holes on the site plan and marks them on the ground with colored surveyors' tape: red for certain post-holes, blue for "possibles," and green for those that probably are tree-root holes.

Landward of our new line of holes, more soon appeared, and these left little doubt as to their purpose. They created a rectangle for a building measuring 15 by 25 feet, with slots at each end representing the remains of partial sills. Having no traces of a chimney, but with doors at both ends, the structure looked most like a storehouse. As work progressed within the building, more post-holes were being uncovered to extend our first five holes into a fence or palisade creating an arc around it.

By mid-April we had found not only our "store," but, running east from it, a much larger building, the same 15 feet wide, but 60 feet long and with an exterior chimney at its east end. We called it the "Long House" for obvious reasons, although we were not sure that it had been a single family dwelling or even that it had served but one purpose. On the contrary, construction at the west end of the south wall differed from the rest, in that there were no sill-slots between the post-holes, suggesting that the wall, rather than being solid, had two large doors closing against a central post. The west wall, too, lacked sill-slots. As if to emphasize the difference between this end of the building and the rest of the Long House, the palisade line swung around and butted against it, thus isolating the separate store and the double-doored end (Fig. 10–1).

The obvious explanation was that something went on within that encircling palisade that had to be kept protected or apart. Lacking any of the parallel slots that we had found to be characteristic of the fort (and which I was tentatively identifying as the foundation for a parapet step), the newly found palisade, we concluded, was intended to confine rather than to defend; in short, a compound for livestock. The supposed pair of doors at the west end of the Long House might well

10–1. The post-hole pattern of the Company Compound as seen from the west. The Carter's Grove mansion and its fenced garden are visible in the center background.

have matched those shown with great clarity by the Flemish artist Jan Siberecht in a painting now in the Brussels Museum of Fine Arts. Most Dutch and Flemish paintings of rural scenes are quite small, but Siberecht's is a massive work measuring almost 6 by 3 feet, and showing with almost photographic fidelity every detail from the nails in the doors to the dirt on a servant's bare foot. Siberecht's double doors close on a central post set in the ground and, leaving no doubt about what went on inside, he shows the head of a horse peering out (Fig. 10–2). Although *The Farmyard* was painted in 1660, the concept of peasants sharing opposite ends of a dwelling with their livestock was common in medieval England, and continued in Ireland into the nineteenth century. But how should we interpret it in Martin's Hundred? It was all very well to find parallels in other places and at other times; but what level of society occupied such buildings in Virginia in the 1620s?

That question was to plague us for many more months. At the outset, finding and recording whatever it was, offered enough problems to keep us fully occupied, particularly when, to the east of the Long House, we came upon a massive clay- and loam-filled hole in a relationship to the house that closely matched the shape and location of the store to the west. This new feature was as large as the "big black patch" discovered in 1971 which first led us to the fort

10–2. Jan Siberecht's 1660 painting of a Flemish farm shows the house with a stable at one end, as seems to have been the case at the west end of the long house.

(see Fig. 8–7). There were other similarities, too, for at the new feature's edges were flecks of wood ash, burned clay, and many nails. If the hole really was a duplication of what we had found in the fort, we might have another well shaft to explore and the prospect of more important artifacts to find. My own assessment was more conservative. The new dark area's generally rectangular shape and its placement in relation to the adjacent structures made me think that it was a back-filled cellar under a companion building to the store. I saw the ashes and nails as evidence of its destruction by fire. Furthermore, like the store, this feature was enclosed by a looping row of post-holes beginning at the Long House's chimney and ending against its south wall.

Preliminary scraping around the edge of the big black patch yielded an unexpected find—one-third of a silver coin. Nothing makes an archaeologist happier than "coin evidence"—something with a date on it that leaves no doubt that the site was occupied at least as late as the year of the artifact's manufacture. Our excitement quickly evaporated, however, when laboratory cleaning showed that the coin bore no date. It would have made little difference if it had, for it was a coin of Charles I (the Holy Roman Empire's Charles V), and therefore dated anywhere between 1519 and 1558. It only reminded us of something we already knew: once minted, silver coins were worth their weight—and ever more would be so. As a rule, therefore, a coin is only emphatically helpful if its date of minting is *later* than the one the archaeologist has assigned to the layer in which it was found—thus proving him wrong. The chance of finding a coin issued at one date and then deliberately withdrawn at another (thus giving a date after which it could not have been in circulation) is so small as to be ignored. Indeed, I knew of only one such English coin, a tiny copper farthing issued in the reign of James I and withdrawn a couple of months later as being too small.

Only paper money can become totally worthless overnight. Even coins whose face value was more than their weight in gold, silver, or copper would continue to circulate, devalued to their current metallic worth. That is not true of modern America's bogus "silver" coinage, whose laminated composition makes it hard to retrieve the base copper within its less valuable nickel-alloyed cover. In the seventeenth and eighteenth centuries, however, forgers found it worthwhile to make copies of even the lowest denominations, each slightly smaller or thinner than the official issues so that, in quantity, the "saved" copper could be used to mint even more forgeries. Considered an act of treason against the Crown (to which all British coins theoretically belonged), the counterfeiting of even halfpennies and farthings could cost the forger his life. As late as 1794, diarist John Stedman, then living in London, noted how much more humane the English had recently become. "Our civil laws are altered for the better of late," he wrote. "No malefactors to be crushed to death for want of pleading, and no more women to be burned for coining as formerly, but to be hang'd to the gallows as men."[1]

This numismatic digression serves as a reminder that archaeologists and historians studying other times—even quite recent other times—must never forget that the game of life may then have been played by quite different rules from our own, and that it is in their context that we must attempt to interpret the good and bad of it.

The divided coin of Spain's Charles I had been part of the business of life in Martin's Hundred. Intact, it had a Spanish face value of two escudos; cut into pieces, the latter passed for whatever that amount was considered to be worth in any country in the European world. No one would have tossed silver away as valueless, and finding it at the edge of our new "cellar" raised questions allied to others generated by two more discoveries from the same location. These were lead seals used to identify the origin and quantity of merchandise, usually bales of cloth. Embossed on one side was a Germanic letter "A," and on the other what I first took to be a teasel head, an heraldic device associated with the Fullers' Guild of London (Fig. 10–3).

Thousands of so-called cloth seals have been found on the fore-

10–3. Lead bale seals with the pine cone emblem and initial letter of the city of Augsburg. Found in the Company Compound. Discarded ca. 1619–1622.

shore of the River Thames at London, where they had been discarded from adjacent warehouses. I had picked up several hundred myself, among them another example of the "A" and "teasel" variety. Recalling that Geoffrey Egan, an archaeologist on the staff of the Museum of London, was the reigning expert on these seals, I sent him drawings of our new-found examples. He replied that although there is half a seal with the "A" on it in the collection of London's Clothworkers' Company, he believed that the seals really came from Augsburg in Germany—hence the "A." He later proved himself right by discovering that what we had both taken to be a teasel brush was really a pine cone, Augsburg's principal heraldic device. Egan knew of no seals of this type being found there, but cited two from Amsterdam, and four from Denmark at Vordingborg, Elsinor, Copenhagen, and Kalø. The Danes, Egan wrote, attributed their examples to the first quarter of the seventeenth century, though on what evidence he could not say. Our correspondence stretched over several months, during which time both he and we were finding more examples. By the time we were through, our big, black patch was to give up fragments of five "A" seals. A year later, Egan came upon conclusive evidence of his Augsburg identification. In the collection of the Bury St. Edmunds museum he found a seal bearing on one side the pine cone and on the other the "A" above an ox, along whose body stretched the letters AVGSB. . . .

Neither Egan nor I are convinced that all lead seals were used to certify bales of cloth—although Augsburg was well-known for its fustian and its linen. When seals are hammered over fabric, the impression of the weave tends to be captured in the lead. This was not so of any of our Site C examples. Nevertheless, regardless of the nature of the merchandise, the fact remains that five units of an Augsburg export were among supplies sent to Martin's Hundred. To us, that suggested bulk importing greater than one would expect of an individual family setting up a home in Virginia. I read it, therefore, as evidence of supplies shipped by the Society of Martin's Hundred to be housed in and issued from the company store—where money like the Spanish silver coin changed hands. Thus, if the store was a store and the Long House was embraced in part by the same palisade that surrounded it, both had to be related. When we remembered their proximity to the fort, logic dictated that they were owned and operated by the Martin's Hundred management, in short, the two buildings (and other structures still being uncovered) were elements in a fenced area best described as the "Company Compound" (Fig. 10-4). The Long House was too large to have been a single family unit, and if I was right, and the large earth-filled area to the east represented the cellar hole under a building paralleling the "store" to the west, we not only had multiple structures, but evidence of careful, even formal settlement planning.

Progress in the large hole was slow, and not helped by the unexpected onslaught of appallingly bad weather. The day book for April 26 read: "Rain. Site ruined! Gale Warning." It came too late. The plastic over the thirty-foot aluminum-framed tent we had set up

10-4. The impaled area dubbed the Company Compound and, above, part of the fenced corral linking it to the fort.

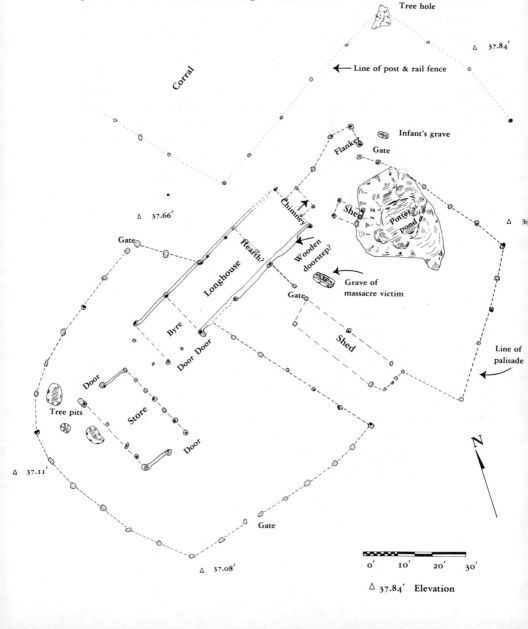

to protect the "cellar" was ripped to shreds, and the excavation quickly became a lake. This was the day that David Brill, the *National Geographic*'s assigned photographer, first visited us. Recently returned from spectacular archaeological projects in the Middle East and South America—where ruins rise like ghosts, changing shape and color as the sun works its creeping wizardry—Dave clearly was dismayed to be shown a flat field of mud, interrupted here and there by patches of black plastic held down by old automobile tires. Underneath, I assured him, lay pages of Man's history every bit as interesting and worthy of our attention as Aphrodisias or Chichen Itza. Dave graciously said that he would take my word for it. He'd come back when we had something worth photographing.

As work progressed under the repaired tent, I realized that my "cellar" was misbehaving. What had looked on the surface like straight sides with a projection at one end for an expected flight of steps, now became far less regular. There were no steps to the "steps," only a gentle slope, and the walls turned into an unpredictable variety of shallow depressions and sudden drops that looked nothing like a cellar, nor even a carefully dug cattle pond. Only one thing was certain: We could not dig out the fill with shovels, for wherever we moved there were artifacts.

At the north edge of the hole lay a scattering of small, rectangular iron plates from a brigandine vest, most of them so fragile that they had to be reinforced in the ground, walled around with plaster, and lifted in blocks. It takes several hundred plates to make one of these armored waistcoats, and there were not enough for that. Nevertheless, it was evident that part of such a garment had been dropped here. As the fabric rotted, the plates were freed to wash down into the hole as seventeenth-century rains eroded the edges and the bottom silted up. The distribution of the brigandine plates made it clear that after Man had done with this large hole, Nature was left to tidy it up.

Most of the artifacts lay toward the center of the hole, whose generally oval shape measured approximately 21 by 25 feet. Potsherds of locally made earthenware were the most plentiful artifacts, and as we dug deeper, thumbnail-sized fragments gave way to almost complete pots (Fig. 10–5), some badly underfired and others twisted and blackened by overbaking in the kiln. Once again we were finding a potter's waste, his range of shapes including virtually every type that a colonist (or even a home-hugging Englishman) might need—with the exception of candlesticks and money boxes, the latter not much in demand when hard cash was in short supply. We found none of the decorated slipwares in the hole that had so excited us at Sites A and

B, but their rim shapes were paralleled by that of a badly underfired dish. We also retrieved a bucket-shaped pot with a thumb-and-finger-decorated handle identical to another found in the same Site A pit as the magnificent alembic (Fig. 10–6). I knew of no such pinched-handled pots from sites in England (although I was aware that bucket pots with plain handles had been unearthed on kiln sites in the West of England), and therefore finding two of these decorated handles of what in any case was a rare ceramic shape, had to be more than coincidence—particularly when both were found in conjunction with kiln waste. There had to be a connection between the Company Compound and the more sophisticated plantation at Site A.

Although the potter's fingerwork on both pot-handles seemed the same, the hardness and color of the wares were not. I was reminded of an old, rural Virginia potter who once told me that it takes long experience (which "foreigners from out-o'-State" sometimes never master) to tell good Virginia clay from bad. They may look the same, but they fire differently. Only endless experimentation, he told me,

10–5. Mary Ryder excavating one quadrant of the pond in the Company Compound. A musket barrel and other iron artifacts are visible at left; kiln-spoiled pots lie in the foreground.

can lead you to the good stuff. Perhaps we were seeing the seventeenth-century truth of that wisdom in the quality differences between the products of Site A and those from Site C's Company Compound. If so, we should also be seeing evidence of a pair of time brackets—the aging and maturing of a single potter who survived both the 1622 massacre and the sickness and privation that had carried colonists off by the score. That our potter was mindful of the latter prospect was demonstrated by his making (and our finding) at least two bulbous-shaped vessels in which one burned aromatic herbs to fight both the smell and contagion in sickrooms. They were called fuming (short for perfuming) pots, and were of such a specialized nature that no examples had hitherto been recorded from an American colonial site. Indeed, I had seen nothing like them in English collections. But no matter where our potter learned to make them, he was evidently responding to the needs of his neighbors, who may have suffered a 50 percent mortality rate in the years before the 1622 attack.

Liberally scattered through the clay silt, pieces of burned wood were emerging that we at first suspected came from the destruction of nearby buildings. More careful examination suggested otherwise. When we came upon pieces large enough to reveal their original shape, we found them to come from relatively light tree limbs, with no evidence of adze or saw work. Burned in an open hearth, they quickly would have been reduced to white ash; instead, they had turned to charcoal as they would in a closed furnace from which oxygen was excluded—thus, perhaps, in a potter's kiln. This explanation could also justify the presence of many flat slabs of heavily burned clay which might have come from a kiln's floor and of other shaped pieces that looked like parts of its doorway. Then, too, the extraordinary irregularity of the pit itself could result from clay digging, either for potting or for use in constructing wattle and daubed clay walls and chimneys for buildings in the compound.

Not all the pottery found in the pit was of local manufacture. There was a London-style delftware pharmacist's pot and most of a tall, earthenware jar of a type we attribute to a factory in the West of England, although we are not sure which one. Fragments of several of these balustroidal jars had turned up on the Martin's Hundred sites, and we were convinced that they had been in use as late as the 1630s. The big question was: How much earlier could they date? The remains of two burned posts and ashes in many of the post molds for the store and Long House tempted us to believe that the buildings had been destroyed in the 1622 uprising. Since we could as yet find nothing to suggest that anyone came back to rebuild after the fire, I assumed that everything we were finding got there before March, 1622. If, however, the West-of-England jars were introduced later, then I was wrong.

The evidence we needed was slow in coming, and when it did, it arrived from a most unexpected quarter. William Shakespeare described it thus: "On a ship at sea. A tempestuous noise of thunder and lightning heard"—his opening stage direction for *The Tempest,* the play he wrote in 1611 reputedly inspired by accounts of the wreck of Sir George Somers's flagship *Sea Venture.* Bound for Virginia with a fresh supply of colonists, the *Sea Venture* was lost after a hurricane, having been driven onto a reef off the southeast coast of Bermuda in 1609. In November 1979, a director of the Bermuda Maritime Museum, Allan "Smokey" Wingood, sent me a collection of potsherds that he had recovered from a wreck he believed to be that of the *Sea Venture.* Most of the sherds came from West-of-England jars like ours. Could his fragments date early enough to have come from that ship, Wingood wanted to know. Yes, was my answer—if our pots were broken before the 1622 massacre. If Wingood's jars did come from the *Sea Venture,* then his would be the corroborating evidence we needed to date ours to the 1619 to 1622 period (Fig. 10–7). If one or the other of us was right, then both were right—an archaeological variation on the chicken-or-egg enigma.

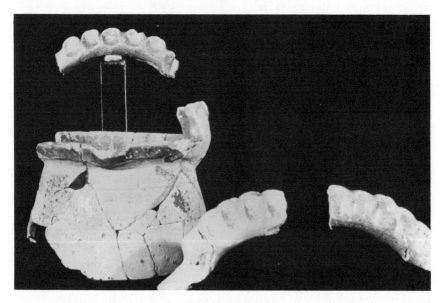

10–6. Part of a bucket-pot found in the Company Compound; in the foreground, a similar handle, also made from local clay, found with the alembic on Site A.

10–7. Project historian Audrey Noël Hume and Allan Wingood, director of excavations on the 1609 wreck of the *Sea Venture,* compare a West-of-England jar fragment from Site C with almost identical earthenware jars from the ship.

If the *Sea Venture* sailed from London without stopping at a West-of-England port, it seemed very unlikely that our jar type would have been represented in her cargo—in which case, no matter what her date, Wingood's wreck was of some other ship. A quick checking of the records eliminated that problem. The *Sea Venture* had put in at Plymouth, where she had remained for several days. But Plymouth is on the south coast of Devonshire, whereas the potting industry was located on the north coast between Barnstaple and Bideford. We next had to prove that our jar type did find its way to Plymouth. That proof came from another 1979 piece of evidence, the published report of pottery found in excavations in Plymouth's Castle Street, which included our balustroidal jars, there attributed to North Devon but vaguely dated to the "seventeenth century or later."[2] Subsequently, in Bermuda, I examined all the artifacts from Allan Wingood's wreck, and had no reason to doubt that it could date from the first decade of the seventeenth century. The circle was complete: If the Bermuda jars came from the *Sea Venture,* they gave us the proof we needed to date ours from the Company Compound prior to 1622, and together the Bermudian and Virginia jars provided documentation to help archaeologists in Plymouth more accurately date theirs.

In addition to the earthenwares, our Company Compound pit contained several metal objects, two of which could relate to potting, though the rest clearly did not. A long-handled, spatula-bladed iron tool looked to me like an ice chopper—until it was cleaned in the lab and found to be pierced by rows of circular holes. Too heavy for kitchen use, and once attached to a substantial wooden handle, it proved to be a blunger, a tool used by potters for mixing clay in water-filled pits (Fig. 10–8).

The second iron object that may have related to potting certainly did not begin life as a ceramic tool. It was the breech and broken barrel from a matchlock musket. That it had indeed been put to some secondary use was suggested by its extraordinary weight, which was far too great for a gun of its size. X-ray photography told us why: The barrel was filled with pellets of lead shot. The X-ray pictures also showed that that the gun had no breechblock and so must have been plugged with a piece of wood to prevent the shot from falling out. We could see, too, that the barrel had been heated to such a temperature that shot closest to the walls had melted to form a thin, interior skin.

When a summary of our discoveries appeared in the *National Geographic* magazine in June 1979, readers' letters "explaining" this phenomenon outnumbered all others. Each reminded me that several guns unearthed on American Civil War battlefield sites have been found to contain multiple charges packed one upon another. In the heat of battle a nervous soldier who shut his eyes as he pulled the trigger could be unaware that the guns firing all around him did not include his. He therefore would reload on top of the first charge, and if the problem was in the chan-nel from the percussion cap, or the first charge was wet, the gun still would not fire, no matter how many times the soldier re-loaded. I was well aware of that explanation, but it was not the right one for us. First, our gun lacked its threaded breechblock and was in no condition to be fired, let alone reloaded; sec-ond, there was far too much shot in the barrel for even several re-loadings. Third, had there been gunpowder in the gun along with the shot, it certainly would have ignited and blown the shot out, when the barrel got hot enough to melt lead.

My explanation was less dramatic and stemmed from a discovery I had made in Lon-don nearly thirty years earlier. In a trash pit of the first half of the seventeenth century I had found a fragment of an earthen-ware pot with an overabun-dance of glaze piled up at the junction of the side and bot-tom. Trapped in that glaze was a small pellet of lead. I had as-sumed that the potter's source of lead for his glaze was shot, remelted, and mixed with frit. That, however, was not the way the process usually was de-scribed. The 1738 edition of Chambers's *Cyclopaedia* tells us

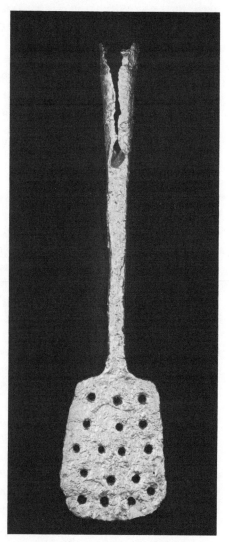

10–8. An iron blunger. Once fitted with a long wooden handle, this tool is believed to have been used by the Company Compound potter to chop and stir while mixing his clay in water. Discarded ca. 1619–1622.

199

that glazing was "usually done with mineral lead; i.e. lead pulverized by throwing charcoal into the melted lead, and the ashes of lead; which, in effect, are only its scum and scoria." But Chambers's notwithstanding, a small ball of lead shot had become trapped in the glaze of the London pot. Was it possible, therefore, that in Virginia, where a potter had no natural source of lead, he made use of small-gauge gunshot?

Of all their supplies, lead and gunpowder were the most carefully hoarded by the Virginia colonists—even to the point of enacting legislation prohibiting anyone from discharging guns for practice or amusement. In the post-massacre inventory of the colony's assets, some Martin's Hundred families had as little as five or six pounds of shot, and even Governor Harwood, in charge of the settlement's arsenal, had only 300 pounds. Might it be, I wondered, that with lead in such short supply even before the massacre, our potter hid his small stock in an old gun barrel, perhaps even having stolen it from the Company's store?

None of my colleagues rushed to embrace my glazing-lead theory, and the question would have remained posed but unanswered had it not been for our 1979 excavation of another, small site two fields downriver from the Company Compound, where a pit apparently dug for watering livestock yielded a broken earthenware mug. It was of local manufacture and of a type well represented from other Martin's Hundred sites, but with one small difference—trapped in piled-up glaze at the bottom were three pellets of lead shot of the same size as those we had extracted from the gun barrel.

What we came to call the "potter's pond" contained a second gun barrel, this one empty and making no pretense at being a ceramicist's tool, any more than did an agricultural bill-hook, which survived in almost mint condition and made us wonder why anyone would have thrown it away. There was also a small, sheet-brass cooking pot that had started life with an iron handle and legs; we wondered why they had been broken off and taken elsewhere when so many other iron objects were lost into the pond. Most of them were in very thin pieces and badly corroded, but thanks to experience gained in raising the helmet from the fort well, salvaging even the most fragile objects had become routine. Recognizing what we were lifting sometimes was more difficult. With depressing ease a crushed iron frying pan could take on the appearance of plate armor. In the space of two days we found both, first the pan and then an armor backplate broken into several pieces before it was thrown away. Only three of them had reached the pond, and again we asked why? Why would anyone discard so basic a piece of armor? Why would they first deliberately break it up, and then not throw all the pieces away together?

As I scraped the silt from around two of the backplate fragments, a lump of clay dropped away to reveal a patch of convex-shaped iron about two inches in diameter. Being busy with the armor, I at first ignored the new find, assuming it to be another pan or, at best, part of a cauldron or flesh pot. Then the backplate fragments reminded me that in the fort well a backplate lay with a helmet, and that the small patch of iron showing through the gap in the clay could as easily be the side of a helmet as of a cooking pot. At least two colleagues were working within six feet of me, but I said nothing, fearing that I would get everyone excited over nothing. The odds against our finding two helmets on one site were astronomically long.

Using a thin spatula and a paintbrush I slowly enlarged the window in the clay wall to reveal more of the convex shape behind it. Inch by inch it got bigger; then the metal took a 60-degree turn and stopped in a rolled ridge. I knew then that I was looking at part of the crest of another helmet, and it took only a few minutes more to ascertain that it was of the same, face-covering type that we had found in the fort. But unlike the tight confines and constant water problems that beset us in the well, here we could work all around the helmet, using a refined and streamlined version of our original lifting technique—which we now called the "plaster mushroom method."

We continued to reinforce the rusted metal with a 50 percent solution of cellulose glue, just as we had done for the first helmet, and again we exposed only one side, leaving the rest bedded in the clay. I could see that despite some crushing as a result of ground pressure, this helmet was in better condition, and unlike its predecessor, whose recovery had been hampered by its proximity to the backplate, this one's only problem was a small earthenware pot whose projecting handle was stuck up the nose of the visor (Fig. 10-9). With the first coating of glue set, our next step was to cut narrow strips of fiberglass screenwire which, when dunked in the acetone-diluted glue, became supple and sticky. Strip by strip we covered the rusted metal with the wire mesh which, when the glue dried, left the helmet's exposed side wrapped like an Egyptian mummy. Next we cut a trench all around to a depth several inches below the helmet's estimated maximum width, thus leaving it standing on a slightly undercut clay pedestal. We then covered both helmet and pedestal with generous layers of wet paper towels, building up a cushioning surface devoid of any pronounced bumps and lumps. With that done, we coated the whole thing with plaster of Paris, the mixture stiff enough to be smeared and shaped to grip the undercut sides of the clay pedestal.

Plaster sets up at different speeds depending on its ratio to water; too much water and it has no strength, too little and you cannot work it. Like so much in archaeology, getting it right is learned by experience. While setting, plaster becomes very hot, and not until it cools does it acquire sufficient strength for us to take the next step—undercutting the pedestal until it teeters like a mushroom on a damaged stalk. Then slicing the clay stalk right through, we turn the plaster mushroom over, converting it into a bowl filled with the clay in which the artifact lies buried, not to be removed until it reaches the laboratory.

Getting the first helmet out of the well and into the lab had taken two weeks; the second took six hours and a fraction of the labor and equipment. Once there, however, we had no shortcuts. The transition from eggshell-thin rust to a helmet that could be X-rayed, drawn, photographed, and finally exhibited, would still take several weeks.

On the site we were left with some new questions and a lot of old ones, the most persistent being whether or not the juxtaposition of a backplate and a close helmet, first in the well and now in the potter's pond, was telling us something, or whether both were mere coincidences. For my part, I have long argued that it takes three such findings, not two, to turn coincidence into a possibly significant pattern—an extension of the old archaeological adage that any two holes make a straight line, but we need at least three to make a row. Regardless of any yet unrecognized relationship be-

10–9. The second close helmet *in situ* in the Potter's Pond, a small example of the potter's handiwork beside it. Both discarded ca. 1622.

tween the discarding into water of identical pieces of armor on two sites, there was no denying that in the Company Compound pond, a potter's garbage and a close helmet made strange pitfellows.

We had been willing to dismiss the first close helmet as an eccentric and unique find into which we should not try to read too much. Finding another quickly made us change our minds and look again at information provided by the Tower of London, whose experts had told us that the fort's helmet, with its one-piece visor, could be considered unrepresentative of the period. The second helmet also had a one-piece visor, though with a larger bill or peak above the eyes to shade and protect them (Fig. 10–10). The Tower of London collections contained no exact parallel for either helmet. Indeed, very little of what we were finding could be precisely matched there. A small, triangular piece of iron from the fort (which I had mistakenly supposed to be part of a couter or elbow cop) was identified by Master of the Tower Armouries A. V. B. Norman as coming from the cheekpiece of a burgonet of a fairly common type. Much later, when I asked

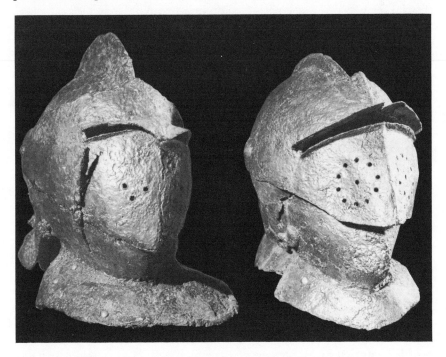

10–10. The fort and Company Compound close helmets. The former has a much more pronounced crest, an indication that the skull is older than its one-piece visor. The second helmet has a similar visor, but the construction overall is lighter.

to borrow a parallel for that helmet for inclusion in a National Geographic Society exhibition, Keeper of Armour Ian D. Eaves confessed that the Tower collection possessed no example that was a sufficiently close match. "If I were to stick my neck out," he wrote, "I would guess that your [helmet] might be Italian."[3]

Our problems of identification were not limited to the armor. No one knew more about early firearms than the Tower of London's Deputy Master, Howard L. Blackmore, and no one was more anxious to help; yet it was discouraging to open the first chapter of his standard work *British Military Firearms 1650–1850* and read in the first sentence that "The middle of the seventeenth century may be taken as a convenient period at which to commence the study of British military firearms, as only a few guns made before then have survived."[4] Alas, the plain and simple versions of anything have rarely excited curators and collectors, and just as we can see Chippendale chairs any day of the week but may wait a lifetime to find a genuine, documented, seventeenth-century kitchen table, so it is the costly and ornate early guns that have survived—not the musketeers' ordinary matchlocks.

Beginning in the second half of the sixteenth century, the musket in one form or another became the battle-winning weapon of every European army, and so it was for the British, as long as the enemy played by the rules. In 1607 a Fleming, Jacob de Gheyn, published a manual of military instruction, illustrating in a series of fine engravings each step in loading and firing a matchlock musket, and for a while it became the drill sergeants' bible.[5] De Gheyn was followed in 1622 by Francis Markham's *The English Military Discipline,* which was easier to read, but still listed nineteen commands for loading and presenting the gun and fourteen more for firing it. In battle, parade-ground orders were cut to three: Make ready. Present. Give fire! Even so, a nimble Indian with a good eye could get off half a dozen well-aimed arrows while a musketeer was getting himself ready to fire one reasonably well-aimed ball a distance of about 30 yards.

A matchlock musket was not only slow to load, it weighed 10 or 12 pounds, so that it had to be supported on a U-topped staff—which the musketeer had to carry around with him. If he inadvertently tipped the gun's barrel below the horizontal, the ball was liable to roll out, there being no wads or cartridges to hold it in place. Priming powder was placed in a covered pan which had to be opened by hand before a lever-controlled length of smoldering match was thrust down into it. Several things could go wrong. The pan cover was prone to swing open before you were ready, in which case the priming powder could (1) blow away, or (2) be rained on. Worse still, a little too much saltpeter in the match could make it spark as well as smolder, and an errant spark could fire the gun before you were ready. The manual required that musketeers should stand guard or move in battle array with both ends of a three-foot length of match smoldering. Lack of attention to the "other" end could ignite your own powder supply. While demonstrating in our film how to fire a matchlock, the fuse burned three holes in my shirt and one in my thumb. At night, the glowing match ends provided excellent targets for a waiting enemy —provided you had not spotted his glows first. There were other surprises, too, as a marksman aboard the *Mayflower* discovered off Cape Cod in November 1620. In an effort to irritate a whale "to see whether she would stir or no; he that gave fire first, his Musket flew in peeces, both stocke and barrel, yet thanks be to God, neither he nor any man els was hurt with it."[6]

For all their faults, muskets were among the most important pieces of equipment owned by Martin's Hundred colonists. Although we have no inventory of the supplies brought over in 1619 aboard the *Gift of God,* we do have a copy of a list that John Smith published in 1623 to help would-be settlers pack their bags. Under "Armes for a man" he advised taking the following:

1 Armor compleat, light	17s.
1 long peece five foot and a half, neere Musket bore.	1£. 2s.
1 Sword	5s.
1 Belt	1s.
1 Bandilier	1s. 6d.
20 pound of powder	18s.
60 pound of shot or Lead Pistoll and Goose shot.	5s.
	3£. 9s. 6d.

Smith added that "if halfe your men be armed it is well, so all have swords and peeces."[7] Unclear though this is, we may perhaps assume that at least half of one's servants should be provided with some kind of body armor. Although Smith's list includes everything from augers to waistcoats, no single item approached the value of the musket, an item more costly than a "compleat" suit of armor; as he included no match, he may have been thinking of the more sophisticated snaphaunce rather than a matchlock musket. The list ends with the note that "this is the usuall proportion the *Virginia* Company doe bestow upon their Tenents they send."[8] The same may reasonably be assumed of the Martin's Hundred Society, and if its first group of settlers was at least two-thirds male, that would call for 146 muskets, a lot of guns and a big investment by any contemporary standard.

Smith's pricing of a suit of armor at seventeen shillings suggests that just as nineteenth-century Britons heading for colonial service bought their outfits at the Army and Navy Stores, so in the early seventeenth century Thomas Stevens of Buttolph Lane was the man to see for armor. A surviving invoice shows that in 1620 he supplied Virginia planter Francis(?) Middleton with "23 Armo^{rs} att 17^{s}p peece, 2 Armo^{rs} better then ordinary for Mr. Middleton & his Sone at 25^s p peece."[9] Thus, John Smith may well have obtained his seventeen shillings per suit price from Thomas Stevens. More important is the question of the degree to which such suits differed from the twenty-five-shilling variety. The answer to that came eight years later, from another Thomas Stevens invoice, this one dated March 6, 1628/9, when he sold to the Massachusetts Bay colony "20 armes, viz: coslett, brest, back, culet [a rump protector], gorgett, tases [thigh defenses], & hed peece to ech, varnished all black, wth lethers & buckles, at 17 ^{s} ech armour, excepting 4, wch are to bee wth close head peeces, & theis 4 armours at 24, a peece, to bee [delivered] all by the 20th of this monthe; w^r of 1 left noew for a sample."[10] It is a safe bet that the two suits provided for the Middletons at twenty-five shillings apiece had close helmets—which brings us right back to Martin's Hundred and the vexing question of why anyone would throw away two close helmets.

The second, or "potter's pond" helmet proved to be more badly crushed than we had at first supposed, but since all the damage was to the side uppermost in the ground, I could not be sure whether it was caused by earth pressure or by a deliberate effort to render the armor useless. Such helmets certainly were inappropriate headgear for warring in the wilderness with an elusive, unorthodox, and, to the European mind, unsporting enemy. One's head movement was severely restricted, hearing reduced, and vision narrowed. In a Virginia summer, wearing a close helmet would have been akin to sticking your head in a portable oven. Were they, we may wonder, more ceremonial than practical, and as such a potential trophy of sufficient psychological value to the Indians to promote even greater boldness? If so, might not the massacre's survivors have put their officers' helmets out of reach, into water-filled holes, before retreating to Jamestown? The argument is not particularly convincing, for it is evident that the Indians preferred hair to helmets.

The potter's pond in Site C's Company Compound reached to within 15 feet of the Long House's southeast corner, and occupied most of the eastern element of the kidney-shaped, palisaded compound. Despite the pond's large size, we did not doubt that it, the house, and the fence had co-existed. That was not so of another adjacent feature—a rectangular soil stain only 10 feet from what I believed to have been the location of a doorway leading into the easterly element of the Long House. We had found this 6-foot, 5-inch-by-3-foot patch of black soil during our preliminary scraping, but I had decided to leave it alone until we had a better understanding of what the larger patch (the potter's pond) was all about.

Left to themselves, archaeologists take their work pretty much as it comes, drawing and photographing as they go along. In our case, I usually did whatever color photography was needed, while Ruth Anne Clarke handled the black-and-white pictures. But with the *National Geographic* having assigned its own photographer to the project, we had a new problem. Dave Brill was available on call should anything photogenic turn up—on call 470 miles away in Atlanta. Time and again, therefore, an artifact would be found, and we would have to decide whether to leave it in the ground until we could find Dave (and he could find a plane reservation) or to go ahead without him. I thought I knew what we would find in the long pit beside the house, and so took a chance and asked Dave to be there for the great uncovering. On Monday, May 22, Eric Klingelhofer made the following notation in the day book: "INH said he will take out Pit 3092 in front of cameras on Thursday. He believes it's a grave. I doubt it." Eric argued that there was too much loam and trash in the top fill for it to be anything but a rubbish pit. I, on the other hand, contended that the hole was of the right proportions for a grave and too close to the house doorway to be a repository solely for trash. As for the nails and bits of pottery visible in the fill, they could have been scattered around the yard as the result of two or three years' domestic occupation, and have been shoveled in when the hole was filled. We agreed to differ.

Sitting on the spoil-heap on Thursday morning I explained my reasoning to the motion-picture camera. If I was right, and we were about to excavate a human grave, its placement so close to the Long House doorway suggested that the building had ceased to be inhabited. We might also assume that if the person's death occurred inside or close by the house, digging the hole there might be a logical proposition. If the buildings really were part of Wolstenholme Towne and were destroyed by the Indians, the grave's occupant might well have been a victim of the massacre, and so been buried by survivors close to where the body was found. But that would be hard to prove (Fig. 10–11).

We needed to find four things: Any artifacts in the fill had to date before 1622; we needed a skeleton showing signs of hasty, coffinless burial, and underneath it some evidence of the wind-blown ashes that should have settled into any hole within 10 feet of a recently burned wood-framed building. Lastly, and the most difficult thing to prove, we needed evidence of violent death. A cut throat, a knife between the ribs, death from loss of blood or even by choking could be impossible to detect on a skeleton buried for more than three centuries. Even heavy, bone-damaging blows would be hard to identify when the ground's own weight can crush a skull and shatter the largest bones.

With the criteria spelled out, foreman Nate Smith and I began to dig, with assistant Mary Ryder on hand to record and draw whatever we might find. Artifacts from the top fill proved to be fewer than we had at first supposed—several nails, a few fragments of tobacco-pipe stems, and a large iron fish hook, almost four inches long and of

10–11. Engraved by Theodore de Bry for his *Historiae Americanae* (1634), this is the only relatively contemporary depiction of the great Indian uprising of 1622. The picture purports to show the assault on an unsuspecting Jamestown. In reality the town was prepared, and for that reason the attack was called off.

the size that must have been used to land the great sturgeons that were so plentiful in the James River in the seventeenth century (Fig. 10–12). Below what seemed to be a deliberate leveling of ashy soil, the fill tipped sharply downward and varied from heavy clay to gray loam.

Evidently the hole had been back-filled by two people, both shoveling from the west side but from different heaps of dirt. I reminded Mary that when you dig a hole and back-fill it, the last soil dug out will be the first to go back, and therefore we should expect to find clean yellow clay toward the bottom.

After a day of careful scraping and sectioning of the fill, the sequence seemed to be following the expected chronology. Out of the clay came the smallest tobacco-pipe bowl we had found on any of the Martin's Hundred sites. Its size and shape put it as early as 1600 to 1620, certainly to the first days of Wolstenholme Towne. Here was just the kind of dating I had been hoping to find—providing we were willing to accept the pipe pundits' conventional wisdom. The small pipe was not alone, however; we found three more, all larger and less closely datable.

10–12. A large iron fishhook from the top filling of the grave in the Company Compound. Deposited ca. 1622.

They *could* have been made as early as 1620, but then again they could have been made ten or twenty years later.

The second day's digging was slow, and the photographers' initial interest began to wane. For hours we found nothing but barren clay fill, and then, to my dismay, we hit bottom—clean yellow clay with not so much as the stain of a bone to support my massacre grave theory. Few human traits are nobler than being a good loser, but being a restrained winner is one of them. Eric was content to express regret that so much hard and careful digging had yielded so little. The film crew checked its log and estimated the footage it had wasted.

I again studied the hole and its relationship to the Long House, and to me it still looked like a grave, albeit empty. It was, I had to admit, unusually wide: broad enough to have taken two bodies. Checking Mary Ryder's drawing, the sectional view showed that the kind of filling looked exactly like that which one expects to see in a hole quickly dug and plugged with the same soil that came out of it. On a modern military base one might pass this off as the product of exercises in the digging and filling of foxholes. Certainly, in the seventeenth century, the hard-pressed settlers had better things to do than to dig and back-fill holes just for the hell of it.

Despite the bright sunlight, I had not been wearing sunglasses while working in the "grave." But now, standing beside the hole inspecting our handiwork, I put them on. As has happened so many times in the past, the filtering action of the brown-tinted lenses revealed nuances in ground tones that I would otherwise never have noticed. The east half of the bottom of the hole looked slightly less uniformly yellow than the west, the change occurring along a straight line running down the middle. More scraping showed that although we were at the bottom along the length of the hole's west side, at the east we were not. There, a slot eighteen inches wide went deeper. Because the clay was wet and sticky, and the working space so narrow, progress was slow, and it was not until late in the afternoon of Friday, May 26, that I found anything encouraging. At the extreme north end of the slot two small, yellow objects appeared—two human teeth. Gentle wiping with a cotton swab showed them to be front incisors and still *in situ* in a skull whose mandible had dropped, leaving the mouth wide open. At this stage all we could see was the teeth, but it was too late in the day to do more than photograph them and cover them over again to protect them through the long Memorial Day weekend.

Showers and storms began on the Saturday afternoon and punctuated the rest of the weekend, and when we returned on the following Tuesday, we found our grave to be full of water. *National Geographic* photographer Dave Brill was back, but there could be nothing for him to shoot until the ground dried out. The next day I was able to uncover most of the skull, but careful probing around it revealed no other bones. A test hole dug at the foot of the grave also failed to find anything. The head seemed to be alone, and for a time we speculated that the body had been decapitated and that this was all that was buried. But if so, why was it lying at the end of a grave-long hole exactly where the head of an extended skeleton ought to be? That debate was still going on when the rain began again. The day book for May 31 reads: "Washed out in afternoon. INH drenched!"

In the torrential downpour of that afternoon and evening, the site was flooded, and although new defenses around the grave did their job fairly efficiently, they could not save us from the water that welled up from below. Once again, the grave filled to overflowing, and in spite of our elaborate protection for the skull, two front incisors on the mandible were washed loose. The next day, after bailing the grave dry, I decided that one more drowning might well destroy the skull altogether. I resolved to go on with the excavation in spite of the clay's still spongy condition. The rest of the skeleton was there—crushed flat —but there. The skull proved to be somewhat jacked up, explaining why I had at first been unable to locate any vertebrae or rib cage. As for the test hole at the other end, that had gone down *between* the feet, missing both by barely half an inch—a fresh reminder of the dangers inherent in relying on the evidence of test holes.

With most of the bones uncovered, it was time to call for the expert help that only physical anthropologist Larry Angel could provide. If this really was a victim of the 1622 massacre, we had found the oldest documented white colonial skeleton yet excavated in Virginia—in short, our earliest colonist. Larry agreed to come down from Washington on the following Tuesday.

I had little doubt that the person had been buried in haste. No winding sheet had held the arms in place; instead, the body had been swung into the hole from the west side by two people, one holding it by the shoulders and the other by the feet. The left arm had swung loose, hitting the side of the grave and falling behind the left buttock, which, in turn, was somewhat elevated. This had been no slow and reverent interment, no gentle lowering into the ground while mourners watched and wept. A clay pipe bowl rested on the abdomen and presumably had been thrown in with the first of the fill. More important were fragments of charcoal and small pieces of burned clay under the left leg, arguably the evidence of windblown building debris that I had hoped to find in support of the massacre-victim theory.

In spite of a third inundation by the time Larry Angel arrived, we had uncovered as much of the skeleton as we dared without risking its smaller bones washing loose. Part of the left humerus had already collapsed and had been glued back together. I showed Larry the two dislodged teeth.

"They're not shovel incisors," he said firmly. "So I think we can say right off that this isn't an Indian." He pointed to lateral bands that had developed across the enamel as the teeth grew. "You see those? That's evidence of interrupted growth; some kind of childhood disease or perhaps malnutrition."

Then Larry turned to the skeleton itself (Fig. 10–13). One by one he measured the long bones, working down from shoulder to heel. He pointed to arthritic fusion of the fourth and fifth lumbar vertebrae, a clue that the individual had been of mature years—though the teeth (with only two large cavities) exhibited no more than slight to medium wear. Brow ridges on the skull, the mastoid processes, and details of the pelvis identified the individual as male, and the large size of the long bones indicated that this 5 foot, 9 inch man was heavy-set and strong—but not strong enough to have survived a massive blow to the right side of his head.

Studying the crushed skull as it lay still partially bedded in clay, Larry agreed that the damage was lateral and not downward, as could result from earth pressure after burial. As the skeleton was lying in what amounted to a subgrave only eighteen inches wide, there also was no likelihood that the extensive damage to the right side of the

10–13. Physical anthropologist Dr. Lawrence Angel examined the skeleton in the Company Compound grave. A broken clay tobacco pipe can be seen resting on the lower rib cage.

skull could have been caused by lateral earth pressure. More paring away of the wet clay exposed what seemed to be a lesser degree of damage to the head's left side. I asked whether, if the man was lying on the ground, a heavy blow to one side could be reflected at the other.

Larry nodded. "I've never seen anyone who's been hit in that way," he said. "But I guess that would do it."

Bedded in the sticky, wet clay, and in a grave so narrow that the sides and back of the skull could not properly be studied, the head gave Larry little help in drawing definitive conclusions. To make matters worse, the bones were as soft as wet pie crust. The skull's frontal element had split above the right side of the nasal aperture. Part of the parietal section of the cranium had broken along what appeared to be the natural suture line, and projected forward like a cap. Determining the damage sequence would be a slow job and could not be done to Larry Angel's satisfaction until the bone fragments were dried, stabilized, and the skull restored. And Larry had a plane to catch.

I decided that in spite of my long-held credo that moving human bones can lead to social and legal problems, and that they should therefore be studied *in situ,* this was a discovery of such importance that moving the skull to the laboratory was the only sensible course. We would use the plaster mushroom technique and move the head in its entirety so that the clay could be pared away from all around the bone fragments. With more rain threatening, the lifting job would have to be done before nightfall.

The problems that can burgeon from the uncovering and moving of human remains have been summarized as follows:

Descendants and relatives are apt to spring from nowhere claiming that their family graves are being most foully and sacrilegiously robbed. Patriotic societies may claim that the honor of a generation or a class is being defiled: the Civil Rights groups may be expected to take an equally gloomy view of disturbing a slave; and furthermore (and it is quite a furthermore), there may be a section in the state's penal code providing unattractive penalties for the desecration of human remains. In short, therefore, it is advisable to weigh the advantages and disadvantages of excavating human remains with considerable care. Unless the circumstances are very special, I would advise quickly covering them over and forgetting that you ever saw them. But if you decide to go ahead, be sure that you first have legal clearance. Do not rely on doing the job quickly and hoping that no one will notice . . . Before you know it, a volunteer will mention it to a friend who happens to know either a cleric or a newspaper reporter, and either way you are sunk.[11]

The advice was my own—and I had not taken it.

Just as lucky accidents have played major roles in my archaeological career, so a series of apparently unrelated events were shaping what was about to happen. One stemmed from a problem that besets all archaeological directors, that of keeping work going forward in a dull and unrewarding area while something of great interest is happening in another. All the people doing the dull work want to stop and watch. When the labor force is provided by unpaid volunteers, letting them do so loses nothing but time, and helps sustain morale. But when the excavators are paid by the hour, you cannot afford to let some stand around while others work, no matter how interesting that work may be. Consequently, an undercurrent of dissension may bestir itself among some crew members.

Finding the possible massacre victim was just such an incident. Only three people could work on it; the rest had to keep on scraping.

Discovery of the bones coincided with a visit from the National Geographic Society's science writer Donald Frederick, who had been assigned to drafting a news release about the progress of our work. The artifacts coming out of the potter's pond had brought him down, but I knew that the finding of what was likely to be hailed as colonial America's oldest homicide victim would be far more newsworthy than a collection of broken pots or even a second helmet. I had visions of pictures of our open-mouthed (screaming?) skull being front and center in newspapers from coast to coast.

I telephoned Williamsburg's Commonwealth Attorney and told him what I had done and why. He was cordially understanding, but that did not prevent him from reading me the section of the Virginia Code that deals with the moving of human remains. It made no provision for scientific studies; on the contrary, it unequivocally stated that any disturbance without a court order was a class-four felony. "You'd better get yourself a court order, right quickly," was the attorney's advice.

I did not doubt that he was right; but Colonial Williamsburg's legal officer had gone on vacation, and I had no experience of applying for court orders. I called our old colleague, and then Virginia Commissioner of Archaeology, Dr. William Kelso, and asked him how he was dealing with problems of moving human remains from highway construction sites. He answered that he had contacted the Attorney General's office in Richmond and had been advised that the Code might not apply to the *accidental* disturbance of human remains, but that in questionable or potentially controversial instances it would be desirable to obtain a court order. I could see that a road-builder's uncovering a grave could be construed as accidental, but an archaeologist's deliberately looking for the remains of anything could hardly be put in the same category. Next I explained our problem to Circuit Court Judge Russell M. Carneal, who agreed to issue the order if I could have the application properly drawn up—something that took several days to accomplish.

As soon as we knew that a court order was needed, Eric and I called the crew together to explain where we stood and to ask that until we had the order in hand, they should keep the discovery of the skeleton to themselves. The next day, however, a reporter telephoned Bill Kelso, asking for information confirming a tip from an anonymous source claiming that I was involved in the illegal disinterment of human remains and was deliberately attempting a cover-up—magic words in the lexicon of any keen, investigative reporter.

"Have you talked to Noël Hume?" Bill asked the reporter. She had not, and did not intend to until the following Monday when her story would be complete and ready for press. Then she would invite me to comment on it. This, of course, is a classic, if unsportsmanlike ploy. If the victim declines to comment, the reporter says so, and readers assume that there is something to hide. On the other hand, a denial can be equally damaging when tossed in at the end of a titillating tale of mouth-watering malefaction.

In reality, there was nothing to cover up. The legal machinery was moving, and on Friday, June 30, the court order was issued. But Monday came and went without any word from the reporter. Had she talked to me, I could have told her that far from being secretive, we had approved Don Frederick's news release featuring both the Company Compound and the "massacre victim," and that it would be on the wire services and on the desks of more than a hundred editors the following morning, making nonsense of any allegedly secretive misconduct on my part.

I can only conclude that the lady's own editor received the National Geographic Society's story in time to scrap hers, for all that appeared was a brief statement of the discovery written as though Eric and I had just announced it. Few of the nation's papers were as reserved. As I had expected, Wednesday morning found our skull, mouth wide open, on breakfast tables from D.C. to California.

Spadework

11

A BURIED TOWN FOUND IN VIRGINIA announced the *New York Times* on July 9, 1978. Three days earlier, and closer to home, the Newport News *Daily Press* had told its readers in a four-column headline: ARTIFACTS BEING UNEARTHED DAILY—which was true, though as much can be said of almost any dig anywhere. The nation-wide newspaper coverage generated by the National Geographic Society's press release also spawned a burst of television interest and a site invaded by microphone-waving reporters and camera crews wanting to film something—anything—being found. The quality of their broadcasts ran the gamut from the relatively accurate and thoroughly professional to an appallingly hammed up "instant replay" commentary on the 1622 massacre from a reporter who, without our knowledge, went into his solo act out of sight behind the spoil heap.

Our own reactions to all this ranged from red-faced embarrassment to satisfaction that news of our work was reaching the public—and that the public was interested. The National Geographic Society had about ten million members and Colonial Williamsburg about one million annual visitors, and responsible press coverage is therefore of value to both. I had once written, however, that I could "think of no strictly archaeological reason for telling the press anything,"[1] a comment that won few friends among journalists. I should have added that my cynicism stemmed more from early encounters with the British press than with the American. In any case, the words were published long before anyone had heard of Martin's Hundred, where the coverage (with a few nightmare exceptions) stuck pretty well to the script. Nevertheless, I had broken my eleventh commandment that "Even if [an archaeologist's] museum or sponsors require publicity, it is imperative that nothing be released until the excavation is virtually completed."[2] Not only was time wasted, but the ever-delicate relationship between leaders and led was unnecessarily strained. For one thing, the always detested additional housekeeping needed when shooting our own film had to be extended to keep us clean and decent on a much broader scale, for although I could put limits on what showed in the viewfinders of our own cameras, I could do little to restrict the freedom of the television press to film whatever and wherever it chose. Furthermore, although those crew members who saw themselves on television felt compensated, those who got "shot" (and told their friends to watch for them) only to be axed on the editor's bench became corrosively unhappy. Then, too, there was my own concern that senior archaeologist Eric Klingelhofer and his top assistant should be interviewed, for it was they and not I who had supervised most of the work. Reaction from reporters to that proposal was always the same; they wanted to interview the director and would not be satisfied with what they unfairly considered second best.

For a young archaeologist needing to make a name for himself, press attention can be the measure of his success—though not always; in England it nearly sank my career before it got launched. The press thrives on superlatives: the biggest, the smallest, the longest, the tallest. Archaeologists, on the other hand, hide behind a palisado of weasel words: "perhaps," "maybe," "possibly," "conceivably," and when we get unbearably pretentious we are liable to "postulate"—an inadequate synonym for conjecture. The press hates every one of them and can be expected to leave them out. Consequently we found ourselves in print as claiming, unequivocally, to have found Wolstenholme Towne. Gone were our escape words; instead we found ourselves out on a limb, and beneath it stood Audrey, ax in hand.

"You've got one long building, another smaller one, and something inside the fort that you can't yet define. That's not exactly a town," she said. "It doesn't even add up to George Sandys's one large fort, one dwelling house and four other houses." She was right; Sandys's plantation contained more than we had yet found. I remained convinced, nevertheless, that our site could not be that. Even so, I wished most fervently that the media had quoted only from the cautiously worded press release.

The excavation of the "potter's pond," and our arrival at the conclusion that this was what it was, developed less briskly than my previous description might suggest. The affair of the "massacre victim's" bones came to a head when work on the pond was still in a relatively early stage, and it would be mid-July before most of the major finds were extracted and safely in the lab. By then, most of the crew had moved on from the Company Compound, scraping north and west toward the fort—which turned out not to be triangular, and certainly not large enough to contain Wolstenholme Towne (Fig. 11–1). Four-sided and with no two angles alike, it was trapezoidal, laid out, I suggested, by someone trained in the "Why-don't-we-stop-about-here?" school of military engineering.

The fort's greatest width and length measured 93 by 130 feet, and the clearly defined watchtower we had found at the southeast corner was duplicated at no other. We had known since the autumn of 1977 that no bastion projected from the northeast corner, but for several weeks I remained convinced that another had stood at the northwest. Eventually, however, I was wooed to Eric Klingelhofer's argument that the very irregular and shallow holes at that corner were really no more than the ghosts of fortuitously located roots. I have never been happy about my capitulation, for the "roots" created a projecting box measuring 7 feet, 6 inches square—more or less what was needed to protect the fort's vulnerable north wall (Fig. 11–2). Being closest to the nearest tree-flanked ravine, this was the direction from which any Indian attack was likely to come. Furthermore, although we were finding traces of slots parallel to the four interior sides of the palisades of the fort, and were reading them as evidence of a parapet step or platform on which musketeers could stand to fire over the walls, muskets (as previously noted) could not be fired at an angle below the horizontal without the ball rolling out. Thus an area extend-

11-1. The fort after excavation, as seen from the southeast with its watchtower in the foreground.

ing at least 20 feet from the palisades was safe from musketry unless, at a minimum of two corners—of which the northwest corner could have been one—there were projecting flankers enabling enfilade fire to rake the walls from the outside.

A flanker or bastion at the southwest corner of the fort was undisputed. The holes there were clearly left by posts and not by roots, but unlike the big watchtower at the southeast corner (or my imagined flanker at the northwest), this one tapered from an interior width of 7 feet, 6 inches to an exterior dimension 2 feet narrower. Much of the inside was occupied by a shallow, loam-filled trough nestling in the subsoil, which we believed to be the remains of a large piece of wood 4 feet, 4 inches long, 1 foot, 6 inches wide, and of unknown thickness. We interpreted it as a block to support and carry the downward thrust of a large post reinforcing the floor of the flanker. If this interpretation was correct, it could have had but one purpose—to help support the weight of a cannon.

Standing on a pair of tall steps and sighting along the lines suggested by the tapering structure, I could see that the gun must have been mounted to fire downriver, narrowly missing the corner of the Company Compound storehouse. To reach any effective distance out into the river, the cannon had to be large, and we had a single clue that in Martin's Hundred there had been such a weapon. The cannonball found on Site A, which we had associated with Governor Harwood and his "Peece of Ordnance," now assumed new importance. The ball, as previously noted, weighed 6 3/4 lbs., and had a diameter of 3 3/4 inches. Standard wisdom has it that shot 3 1/2 to 4 inches in diameter were fired from two types of cannon, sakers and demi-culverins. They were heavy guns, ranging in weight from 1,500 to 3,000 pounds, and at a 10-degree elevation a saker had a useful range of 2,170 yards and a demi-culverin of up to 2,400 yards, an ample distance to hit shipping in a river whose channel sweeps relatively close to shore as it passes Carter's Grove. Clearly, the gun platform was not built to defend against the Indians but against England's long-time bogeyman, the Spaniard.

The big gun interpretation had its problems. Unless the platform extended inside the fort in some manner not revealed by the archaeological evidence, it had a floor length of only 6 feet, 6 inches; yet a saker (the smaller of the two guns) had an average barrel length of 8 feet and required a run-back or recoil distance of about half its barrel length. Mounted on a four-wheeled naval carriage, and with its muzzle assumedly projecting out from the flanker as far as the front wheels would allow, the gun's crew barely had room to draw it back far enough for loading (Fig. 11–3). On the other hand, if the gun was of a size to fit comfortably on the platform, its ball size and range would have been insufficient to keep enemy ships at bay. We were left to draw what comfort we could from the Tower of London's ordnance expert, Howard Blackmore, who admitted that the documents hint at greater variations in barrel lengths to bore measurements than surviving seventeenth-century guns suggest. Thus, we cannot discount the argument that guns of saker bore and shorter length were made, but have not survived.

As noted earlier, we had fewer problems with the evidence provided by our fort's palisade post-holes than we did with its cannon; they equated well with Strachey's description of Jamestown's "Planckes and strong Posts," and with Ralph Hamor's portrayal of Henrico, the new town further up the James River, as being defended by a palisade of "pales posts and railes."[3] The character of the pales was revealed in a 1613 intelligence report smuggled out of Virginia in a shoe, and sent to the Spanish ambassador in London. The British defenses were described as being "of boards and so weak that a kick would break them down."[4] Although the pales may have rotted and been parting company from their rails, it is hard to believe that the supporting posts were ready to fall. Strachey had told us that those at Jamestown were set 4 feet into the ground. Our fort's post-holes were nowhere near as deep, and even allowing for loss of depth through subsequent erosion and land use, the evidence clearly pointed to a lighter and therefore less tall defensework. But how much lighter, and to what degree less tall?

The Jamestown palisades were said to be 14 feet high, but there was no mention of any platform inside for musketeers to fire over the top. Protection must have been provided by enfilade fire from the large bastions at each of the three corners. I felt certain that we should be thinking of palings only tall enough to prevent an enemy from scaling them and to provide chest-high protection for defenders standing on our parapet step. We knew that instructions issued in London to the settlers of Berkeley Plantation (another, Martin's Hundred–like venture further upriver) called on them to build a palisade 7 feet, 6 inches high around their 400 acres. No mention was made of whether this wall was to give protection from an enemy or was merely a deterrent to wild animals; but

38.

N

Root holes
or northwest
flanker

Post &
rail fence?

38.36'

from much further away, at Ferryland on the Newfoundland coast, came more specific information. There, that colony's governor, Captain Edward Wynne, wrote to his employer Sir George Calvert in July 1622, reporting that:

> We got home as much or as many trees as served us to palizado into the Plantation about foure Acres of ground, for the keeping off of both man & beast, with post and rayle seven foot high, sharpened in the toppe, the trees being pitched upright and fastened with spikes and nayles.[5]

11–2. The fort and its principal internal features.

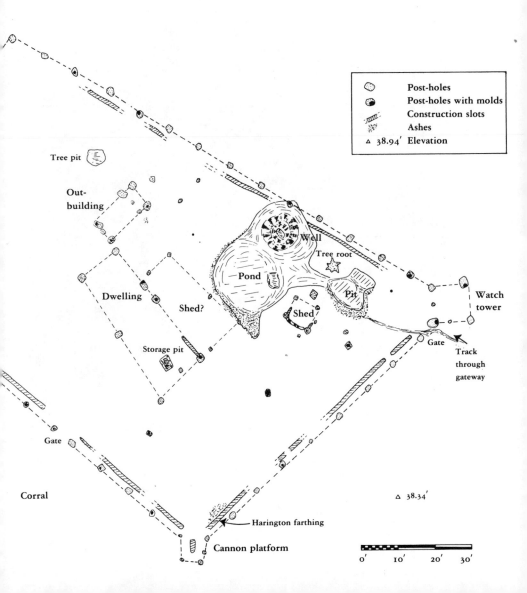

11–3. The *National Geographic*'s reconstruction of the fort's gun platform and flanking parapet steps.

At Ferryland, therefore, the pales were 7 feet high, and pointed. Taken at face value, Captain Wynne's description suggests that his pales were made from tree trunks fastened to the rails; but that is difficult to do if the trees have not first been split to provide one flat face. Even then the "spikes and nayles" needed to secure half a tree to a rail would have to be long enough to pass through both and still project far enough to be clenched—very large nails. So far, we had found relatively few of any size along our palisade lines.

Remembering that John Smith's list of equipment needed by an emigrant family included "2 frowes to cleave pale,"[6] I concluded that even the Ferryland "trees" would have been split, and that the Virginia evidence was sufficient to justify interpreting our pales as flat surfaced. We had no justification, however, for our parapet step, though logic dictated that if the pales were tall enough to keep attackers out, defenders would have to stand on something to see and shoot over the top. I estimated the height of my step as being close to 3 feet. Taking an average male height from the skeletons on Site A as being about 5 feet, 6 inches, I asked artist Pat Kidd to be a musketeer and stand with a matchlock musket in the firing position. Measuring down from the underside of the gun to her feet gave us an estimated distance from the top of a 7-foot, 6-inch pale ("sharpened in the toppe" a distance of 6 inches) to the top of the parapet step (Fig. 11–4). I deduced that the back of the step was supported by vertical timbers and that it had been filled with dirt. The only problem was that when standing to fire, Pat needed a width of 2 feet, 5 inches, and the platform would have given a maximum of 2 feet, 9 inches—no room for stepping back to reload. That flaw in my interpretation bothered me for several years, just as did the lack of depth to the gun platform. A published report of a surviving parapet platform in a ruined village fort in Northern Ireland led us to Dungiven in County Londonderry, but when we got there the platform had been torn down to enlarge a parking lot. Eventually the evidence I was seeking came to light closer to home, on Southampton Island at Bermuda. Protecting one side of the entrance to the harbor stands a small stone fort reputedly built in 1620 by Governor Nathaniel Butler (the man whose uncharitable report hastened the demise of the Virginia Company), and having a parapet step edged with stone and filled behind with rubble. Tidewater Virginia has no natural stone, while Bermuda has virtually nothing else. I had little doubt therefore that the Southampton Fort construction (though probably an eighteenth-century addition) was the stone-built version of our wood-supported step. It was only 2 feet wide.

The loam filling the slot of our parapet step was mixed at the northwest and southwest corners with quantities of wood ash, but whether this came from the destruction of the fort itself or from the burning of adjacent buildings we never were able to ascertain. On June 15, while we were still debating the meaning of the slots, Eric Klingelhofer found their only spectacular contribution. Standing beside the southwesterly gun platform, he noticed a tiny silvery disc lying on the surface of the slot fill. About the diameter of a little finger nail, the disc was so thin that, put in the palm of a hand, a sneeze would blow it away.

I noted earlier that I knew of only one English coin that had been issued and so quickly withdrawn that its presence on a site would give a date after which it was unlikely to have been lost—a coin of such rarity that unearthing one even on an English site was so improbable

11–4. A conjectural section through the fort's palisade showing how the parapet step may have been built.

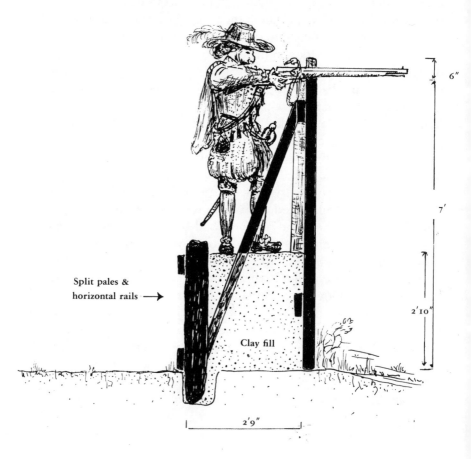

Split pales & horizontal rails ⟶

Clay fill

6"

7'

2'10"

2'9"

as to be discounted. This was the coin that Eric had now found (Fig. 11–5).

In Elizabethan England virtually all coins were of gold or silver, and worth their weight in one or the other metal. The lowest denomination being a halfpenny, it followed that halfpence were very thin and very small (about a centimeter in diameter), and also very frequently lost. James I had issued an equally small silver halfpenny, but what had really been needed was a coin to equate with the theoretical half a halfpenny, the farthing. Queen Elizabeth had tried to tackle the problem by issuing a coin slightly larger than a halfpenny and valued at three farthings—but it was still the one-farthing coin that the poorer folks needed. However, a silver coin worth half a halfpenny would have been half the size of the latter, and so small that it could only have been handled with tweezers.

James solved the apparently insoluble by resorting to the same technique that he was using to advance his expansionist aims in Virginia and Ireland: he sold patents to what we today call the private sector. Business entrepreneurs were given patents to pay for the privilege of doing the nation's work and, in large measure, for taking the blame and paying the freight if it turned sour.

On May 19, 1613, John, Lord Harington of Exton, obtained a three-year patent to solve the public's small-change problem, authorizing him to mint farthing tokens made of copper. Because small-denomination coins had been of silver, Lord Harington, in order to promote confidence in the new tokens, coated his copper with tin to give it a silvery appearance. The tokens were supposed to be worth their weight in copper, no less than six grains' value; but it turned out

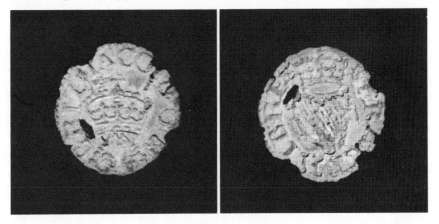

11–5. Obverse and reverse of the tinned-copper Harington Type 1 farthing token of 1613 found in the fort.

that Harington's first issue included many that were underweight. The public rejected them, and less than three months later, Harington recalled his farthings and substituted a larger and heavier version. C. Wilson Peck, in his definitive work on English copper coinage, wrote that "As the period of issue of types 1 and 2 together amounted to barely fourteen months, it is probable that type 1, which is by far the rarer, was limited to two or possibly three months at most."[7] Our coin belonged to Lord Harington's type 1.

Corrosion of the copper had reduced the farthing to a weight of only 2.7 grains; indeed, it largely was the thin, tin surface that held it together. That in itself was strange, because Peck had written that one of the coin's problems was that the tinning easily wore off, a conclusion supported by the numismatic firm of B. A. Seaby, whose catalogue of British copper coins declined even to price still-tinned examples. Its compiler was content to add a footnote stating that "The small size Harrington [sic] which still retain their tinned surface are worth more than the prices quoted."[8]

We were getting used to anomalies and enigmas among our finds, but this was one of the most puzzling. In the construction trench of a fort built no earlier than 1619 we had a coin issued and allegedly withdrawn in the spring of 1613, a coin which should have lost its tinning after only brief circulation, yet which had survived the centuries solely because that had not happened. We had two possible explanations. The first, and to me the least persuasive, was the proposition that the fort was built, not in 1619, but in 1613 by the Virginia Company, and stood on land later granted to a private individual—such as George Sandys. This was a thesis fostered by only one member of the team.

Audrey notwithstanding, I preferred the second possibility, that Lord Harington's faulty farthings were not melted down, but were stored for a few years and then shipped to Virginia to help satisfy the colony's need for small change. There is, I confess, no Wolstenholme period documentation to show that such a need existed—nevertheless it did fourteen years later when Governor Sir John Harvey wrote to the Secretary of State complaining that there was little or no money in the colony, and petitioned the king that "some farthing tokens may be sent over and made current."[9]

I was convinced that the Harington farthing's minting date was a red herring—not so two iron fireback fragments found protruding from a pit outside the fort gate. They were similar to the pieces we had found in 1977. These, however, bore raised letters reading EVET, and by no stroke of Holmesian brilliance could I find a place for them in HONI SOIT QUI MAL Y PENSE. I knew that the British royal arms also bear another motto: DIEU ET MON DROIT—God and my right; but I could not make our letters fit that either—which was singularly blind of me. They prompted me to send drawings of all our fragments to the curator of the Sussex county museum at Lewes, in England, which possesses the largest collection of seventeenth-century firebacks. She gently pointed out that, run together and the U changed to a V (as was common in the period), the letters read: [DI]EVET [MONDROIT]. When asked whether there was any way in which we could tell whether the arms on our plate were those of James I or his son Charles I, she replied that we had one small but potentially crucial clue.

A corroded lump beside the 1977 fragments' [. . . MA]L:Y: PEN[SE] was really the right front hoof of the supporting unicorn. On most Stuart firebacks the animal's left leg covers these letters, while the right is in a quite different position. The hoof location of our unicorn is paralleled, however, not on a surviving original fireback, but on a reproduction of one whose whereabouts are no longer known (Fig. 11–6). The original had been damaged before the Kingsworthy Foundry of Hampshire cast its first mold. The first two digits from this dated fireback had been lost, but the last, reading . . . 21, had survived, to give us 1621 and to identify the Kingsworthy fireback as bearing the arms of James I, who did not die until four years later. When the reproduction and our fragments were compared by A.V.B. Norman, Master of the Tower of London Armouries, he concluded that the original, wooden molding blocks for both designs were the work of the same craftsman—even though the treatment of the DIEV ET MON DROIT differed. Here, then, was convincing evidence that someone of consequence had brought his armorial fireback with him from England prior to 1625, and had used it in his house inside the fort. Once again the evidence pointed to William Harwood.

Scraping every inch of the fort's interior, looking for traces of buildings, proved a long and backbreaking process. But regardless of the persistently frying temperatures and high humidity, the work could not be delayed until the cooler autumn months. By August we were into the hurricane season and the ever-present danger of the site's total ruination. Protective plastic sheeting and tents, no matter how well anchored, are no defense against sustained high winds—as we remembered from April's freak gale, which had picked up our aluminum-and-wood-framed tent and carried it bodily away across the site. I knew that once the acres of clay were exposed to prolonged torrential rain, little would be left of the fort and Company Compound to provide the final, overall photographs needed by us for our records and by the *National Geographic* for its article.

The magazine's photographer, David Brill, looked at our fort and, indeed, at the entire site with a wry smile that seemed rooted in some inner pain. Although he manfully groped for encouraging words, I suspected that he was comparing our bleak post-hole patterns with the photographic opportunities offered by previous archaeological assignments. I had seen and admired Dave's work, and quickly found him to be marvelously inventive; while he, equally quickly,

11–6. A modern English iron foundry's reproduction of a fireback dated 1621 and decorated with the arms of James I. The design details closely parallel those of the fragments found in the fort (see Fig. 9–2).

found me more concerned about the safety of the artifacts and the impact that their portrayal might have on my peers, than about creating pictorial images to excite the *National Geographic*'s readers.

Faced with a visually uninteresting site and with quantities of less than eye-catching artifacts, Dave knew that if life was to be breathed into any of this, it would have to come from people doing things. At the end of his first inspection of the artifacts, he took a deep breath and said, "Just so I understand how far I can go to make this stuff exciting, tell me how you'd react to something like this. We set up the gun parts on some kind of table, outdoors somewhere. Then we dress someone in seventeenth-century costume, and stand him in the background firing an antique musket that matches the fragments. Maybe we could set it up with magnolia trees behind to symbolize Virginia and the South."

My answer held no surprises. First I would be unwilling for the fragile, laboratory-treated artifacts to be displayed in an outdoor setting, and thus give critics an opportunity to charge us with mishandling them. "That's point number one," I said. "Next, we know so little about who wore what in early seventeenth-century Virginia, that I doubt whether we could make or rent a costume that we could say was totally accurate. Then again, we wouldn't risk firing one of our original matchlock muskets any more than we would want to be on photographic record as appearing to risk the safety of the excavated artifacts. And finally," I added, "the magnolia wasn't indigenous to Virginia and wouldn't have been here in the early seventeenth century."

Fortunately, Dave Brill's anthropological schooling and his past experience of working with archaeologists made him more sympathetic than many another photographer might have been. For me, nothing is more distasteful than having to say "no" to people to whom I would much rather say "yes." I was just as eager for Dave's pictures to be as evocative as was he, but my responsibilities to the site had to come first. We did have one practical problem in common: We both needed a single photograph that would encompass the fort and the Company Compound. As each was visible only as rows of small holes in the ground, when one got far enough back to get both in the same picture, many of the holes were so distant as to be out of sight. Concluding that it simply couldn't be done, I was ready to settle for separate shots of the two areas, and leave it to a *National Geographic* artist to draw a conjectural elevation that would bring them together. For photographer Brill, that smacked of failure.

"Have you ever seen painting with light?" he asked.

"You mean when you open the shutter at night and take a flash-light to outline people and objects?"

"Right. Maybe we could do that on the site, outlining all the palisades and buildings—but doing it with fireworks. We could lay them in strips in whatever colors you like. Somebody lights one end at a corner of the fort and someone else sets off the compound series, and we take one long exposure."

It was an ingenious idea and fun to try, but in my bones I knew that I would not be happy with the result. Turning the site into a giant pyrotechnical set-piece would be no substitute for a picture showing what we really had found. Having said "no" to Dave so often, I could not bring myself to refuse again. Nevertheless, I was vastly relieved when, after a few nocturnal experiments, he abandoned the idea.

For our part, we still had pictures to take, and spurred by the hurricane danger, I urged Eric Klingelhofer to be ready for a final fort photo in the first week of August. The day book entries show to what extent the heavens were inclined to bless our endeavors:

July	25.	Rain at night, but tried to clean up and make deadline.
	26.	Site ruined by rain, but we struggle onward.
	27.	Continued clearing fort.
	28.	Rain in a.m., sent crew home at 9:30.
	31.	Pumping out after last night's heavy rain. Pump broke after lunch.
August	1.	Heavy rains again last night; pumped again, photo postponed. Site a disaster, losing post-holes and post-molds.
	2.	Heavy rains again last night; pumped site again.
	3.	Heavy rain in evening [of the 2nd]; pumped site again. Rain expected again today.
	4.	Rain again last night.
	7.	Monday. Very heavy rain over weekend. Big Top [potter's pond] completely filled; site a mess.
	8.	Clear finally, no rain last night. [Forecast] looks good. Big push for photos Thursday or Friday.

The daily pumping and scraping of mud from the same holes, time after time, had taken its toll on the crew's morale. The summer season was drawing to an end, and (as happens every year) some of the student labor was contemplating quitting to take a break before the fall semester. We needed no professional psychic to predict that the rest of August only offered more of the same—eight-hour days of scraping, without much hope of finding many more artifacts to vary the pace. Bill Henry's day book notes for August 8 went on: "Tempers short, crew on each other; everyone says everyone else isn't working."

The next day continued fair, and after Eric took the crew to task, tension eased. Bill Henry called it "a difficult situation handled well." Again everyone scraped and cleaned throughout the day to be ready for photography the following afternoon. But in the morning it rained, and the picture-taking was postponed. Thereafter the gods were kind, and the week ended with the fort securely on film of every kind.

It makes little difference how many sites you have excavated, there is always something magical about standing in the cherry-picker's bucket as it starts to rise and the site unfolds beneath you. All those post-holes, over which so many people have toiled for so long, cease to be isolated pieces in a boxed jigsaw puzzle. Now they fit together, and the higher the bucket rises, the clearer becomes the picture. We had all studied the fort on the plans pinned to the drafting-room wall, but that gave us little idea of how it had fitted into the Martin's Hundred landscape.

Draftswoman Ruth Anne Clarke's master plan of the fort recorded every post-hole and slot, but it also included natural root holes, ditch lines, and even the planting holes for a later orchard. Before shooting our elevated pictures of the fort, all of these irrelevant features had been back-filled and sprinkled with finely ground, dry clay to eliminate them from the photographs. I hoped that when we studied the prints we would, by some miracle, see things that hitherto had escaped us. The palisade lines had always spoken for themselves (with the possible exception of the disputed northwest corner), but the buildings inside the fort remained disturbingly indistinct.

The supposed east and west sides of what we assumed to be the settlement leader's house were not parallel, and none of the corners were right angles. Furthermore, the spacing of the post-holes was far from uniform, and there were too few of them. This was in marked contrast to the clearly defined house and outbuildings on Site A, and to the store and Long House in the Company Compound. Of all the buildings we had found, the "governor's house" inside the fort should have been the most substantial and best defined—and it wasn't. It came as no surprise, therefore, that the photographs had nothing new to offer; but the disappointment was no less intense.

"How are we going to tell the *National Geographic* what buildings to show inside the fort when they come to drawing their reconstructions?" Eric wanted to know.

I told him that we would have to choose an angle that would allow smoke from the Long House chimney to rise in front of the fort and hide any details. That was no spur-of-the-moment answer. I had already made several sketches of my own in an effort to grapple with the problem. When I had agreed to write an article for the magazine, I had sought and been given an assurance that no "artist's reconstructions" would be used to illustrate it. Ideally, reconstructions, be they on the ground or on paper, demand that you know the correct answer to every engineering and architectural question, that every man, woman, and child be correctly dressed, and be known to have existed. If we showed house interiors, they should contain furniture that we could prove had existed in early seventeenth-century Virginia; yet we knew very little about any of the colonists' wooden objects, having found no trace of them in the ground. For these and a multitude of similar reasons, I opposed any kind of pictorial interpretation. But as soon as I began to write and to consider how best the article could be illustrated, I realized that despite all our photographs of what *we* had been finding, the real story—the drama of what had happened in the settlement's short and tumultuous life—was all happening off stage. Shamefacedly I went back to the *National Geographic*'s editors, admitting that an archaeologist (and a writer *about* archaeology) has a responsibility not only to do justice to the past, but also to help the general reader by putting living flesh back on the bones of history. We would be short-changing the public if we did not risk an attempt to capture the pictures that were already half formed in our relatively educated imaginations.

"We thought that sooner or later you'd get around to that conclusion," one editor told me with a smile. "We've got a good man in mind." And they had. Richard Schlecht was not only a fine artist and already conversant with the period, but had patience of Biblical longevity. For months he uncomplainingly put up with my interminable fussing over details: the shape of a knife blade, the construction of a wheelbarrow, whether shutters should open in or out, and didn't those cats look too well fed, and wouldn't one be better than two?

Whenever possible we tried to document our criticism. Artifact artist Pat Kidd provided drawings of our excavated knives, and Audrey came up with seventeenth-century sketches of English wheelbarrows and Dutch shutters; but Dick had to settle for our unsupported view that well-fed cats seemed inappropriate at a time and place where food was often in short supply.

"They could have gotten fat from eating rats," he explained.

"Perhaps. But fat cats in hard times don't look right to me," I told him. Dick could have argued that this was an undocumented opinion that conflicted with his artistic judgment. But he did not do so, then or at any time throughout our association. Instead, he killed one cat and starved the other.

Although we were able to tell Dick how to interpret the Company Compound's store and Long House with far more confidence than we could the supposed "governor's house" in the fort, we still had one major problem: five post-holes in the Company Compound that seemed to belong to an extraordinarily skinny structure measuring 8 feet, 6 inches by 30 feet. Represented by only five holes (instead of the expected six or eight), the shed-like unit stood south of the Long House and 20 feet west of the potter's pond. Unable to explain its purpose, we had taken the coward's route and had ignored it—until Dick Schlecht wanted to know what to put there. As I sat staring at the plan and wondering whether the shed had something to do with the potting operation, it dawned on me that I had been through this exercise before—on Site B. There we had found another skinny, shed-like structure apparently supported on only five posts, and because we did not know how to interpret it we had simply recorded the post-holes on the plan and had said nothing about them (see Fig. 7–3). In addition to the similarities in the shape and construction of the two sheds (and my chicken-hearted reaction to them), they had another factor in common: Both stood on sites that yielded artifacts associated with pottery manufacture. I was convinced that both sheds were either built by the same man (or someone apprenticed to him), or were structures of a standard type used by potters.

Throughout the time that the crew had been working on the fort, most of the Company Compound had been covered by sheets of black plastic (held down by scores of old automobile tires)—black because it was supposed to prevent green weeds from growing under it. Now, with the fort photographed, it was time to uncover the Compound and to do what little scraping still had to be done to prepare it for the final pictures. I assured Eric that the task should be simple, since he had left the site so clean when he stretched the plastic over it.

The covers had indeed protected the site from green weeds—but not from white ones. As the sheets rolled back we were appalled to see the ground bursting with strange white and pale yellow shoots, some 8 or 9 inches long and uncoiling in the sunlight like albino worms—plants hitherto unable to make up their minds what to become as they sweltered in the hot, damp darkness beneath the plastic. The scraping and cleaning had to begin all over again.

Previous scraping had established that the fort and Company Compound were linked to each other by an umbilical fenceline, and Eric had deduced that both areas had been laid out on a plan measured out from a single large tree, which had been subsequently cut down and its stump incorporated into the fence (see Fig. 10–4). If true, this pointed to a planned community—although its shape and extent still eluded us. Assuming an erosion rate of a foot or more a year, the fort must have stood at least 600 feet back from the 1619 river's edge. Although at first glance that might seem an impractical location for a fort intended to defend a settlement lying close to the river, it makes better sense on further reflection. If attacked by Spaniards from the river, the settlers would have a place into which to retreat in order to regroup, and since any Indian assault would almost certainly come out of the ravines and woods behind the settlement, the palisades would provide defenders with a broad field of fire.

While still debating the meaning of what we had found, Audrey and I left for Northern Ireland to accept an invitation to help Magee College develop a program for the archaeological study of seventeenth-century Londonderry. Although the strife that had torn Ulster for nearly a decade seemed to have quieted down, we set out asking ourselves whether we were out of our minds to agree to go there.

In 1607, the same year that Britain's first settlers landed at the site they would call James Towne, a rebellion in Ireland led by the Earl of Tyrone was crushed, and the six counties held by him and his allies were seized by the British. After two years of planning, James I authorized the establishment of a new British colony in the counties of Armagh, Cavan, Donegal, Fermanagh, Londonderry, and Tyrone, the Derry lands being divided between wealthy London mercantile guilds such as the Goldsmiths, Salters, Merchant Tailors, and Ironmongers, which put up the money and sent out the settlers, the first of whom reached Ulster in the second half of the year 1610. Many key backers of the Irish enterprise were also members of the Virginia Company of London, and later investors in such secondary joint-stock companies as the Society of Martin's Hundred. It was this thread that led us to Londonderry in 1978.

Because James I was a Scotsman, it should have surprised no one that Lowland Calvinist Scots were given some of the new Irish lands, and that they and the new English (as opposed to the "Old English" Catholic families resident for centuries in Ireland) were there to subjugate or oust the native population, just as their compatriots were doing in Virginia. From their counting houses in London, English merchant adventurers thought of their colonial investments in Ireland and America in the same breath. So widely shared was this attitude that in 1617, the English traveler Fynes Moryson described Ireland as "This famous Island in the Virginian Sea."[10] Then, too, several key English settlers and administrators in Virginia had gained their military experience fighting the Irish lords in the reign of Elizabeth, and thus in their reports they frequently compared the tactics, habits, and even the clothing of Indian "salvages" to those of the "wild Irish." That long-persisting British attitude toward colonial natives was no better designed to win friends among the Indians than to woo the hearts of Irish Catholics—a thought still much in mind as Audrey and I landed at Belfast airport more than 350 years later.

The digging in Derry proved to have little relevance to our studies, virtually all of the artifacts being much more recent than ours. Nevertheless, two important pluses resulted from our few days in Ulster. The first was meeting Robert J. Hunter, professor of history at the New University of Ulster, much of whose career had been devoted to what is known in Ireland as the Plantation Period (1600 to 1641). When I told him that I was having trouble locating evidence for the construction of our fort's palisades, he delved into his files and came up with a 1641 agreement between the Duke of Ormond and carpenters Edmond O'Magher and Mortegh O'Connor to build a palisade around the towns and lands of Kilbride, Kilgerny, and Kilkely.

The contract spelled out precisely how the palisade was to be built. The pales were to be 7 feet long (like those around Lord Baltimore's Newfoundland settlement), and the two carpenters were to "fell, cut, lop, cleave and make up" the necessary number. Evidently, therefore, the pales were to be split and not sawn, though sawn lumber was specified for making the gates. The palings were to be supported on a frame of posts and rails, both 9 feet long, the posts set 7 feet apart (ours were 9), and seated 3 feet into the ground, the holes back-filled with rammed stones and earth. The rails were to be mortised into the posts, and set "one over another in and throughout the mortices." Thus, with the posts set 7 feet apart, the 9-foot rails should have passed through the posts and protruded at least 9 inches at either side. They were to be secured with treenails, defined as pins sloping downward and "made of dry timber and strongly fastened in setting." The equally securely anchored pales were to be closely mounted "and the two next pales to every post [were] to be cut at the top and laid over the heads or tops of every post."[11] Because no reference was made to pointing the tops of the pales, we must assume that they were flat and intended only as a wall to keep animals in or out.

Bob Hunter's document alone had made the Ulster visit worthwhile, for it contributed most of the information needed to help Dick Schlecht draw his reconstruction of our Martin's Hundred fort (Fig. 11–7). Ulster's second contribution, though less tangible, was no less valuable. It provided us with an increased awareness of the close relationship that had existed between the British colonizing efforts in Ireland and Virginia. Several American historians (notably Anthony Garvan in 1951 and John W. Reps in 1972) have pointed to the potential value of Irish sources in interpreting the development of English settlement and town planning in seventeenth-century America.[12] I had read these studies with abstract interest, but now it dawned on me that the "Irish Connection" was valid not only in terms of village design, but throughout every facet of contemporary colonial life. Promoters of Ulster-American cooperation in matters historical

11–7. A *National Geographic* magazine reconstruction of the fort and Company Compound.

have begun to foster the notion that Irish developments were passed on like later Potato Famine emigrants to America; but that is not strictly true.

Lessons learned in Ireland during the Elizabethan years were learned and digested by British settlement planners in London, and along with a lesser degree of American experience, were packaged in London into colonizing kits. Similar instructions and supplies were given to would-be colonists before they got on the boat. It made no difference where they got off; what they did, and what they had to do it with, remained the same.

In Ireland the British settlements were of two kinds, the larger being walled towns, just as in Virginia, Jamestown was built within its triangular palisade. The smaller Irish villages, on the other hand, were less well protected, relying instead on a fortified enclosure that contained only the home of the settlement's leader. Instructions published in London in 1610 outlined the "Conditions to be observed by the *Brittish* Undertakers of the Escheated Lands in Ulster," requiring that within three years each major landholder should "build thereupon a stone house, with a strong court or bawne about it." Undertakers with smaller parcels of land could build their houses of brick, while those with the least land were required to "make thereupon a strong Court or bawne at least."[13]

The Gaelic word "bawne" originally meant an enclosure for cattle, but in its seventeenth-century context it clearly meant a defensive structure. Its original role was not entirely forgotten, however, there being evidence that in some villages (if not in all), the tenants were allowed to drive their livestock into the bawnes at night.

In 1622, Sir Thomas Phillips, a critic of the way the Ulster colony was being run, submitted a lengthy report to King James, illustrating it with maps and plans drawn by surveyor Thomas Raven. The latter, in the tradition of Elizabethan cartographers, combined mapping with picture painting, drawing and coloring each house and bawne, even showing such details as the pointed palings on a bawne's palisade and the framing of unfinished houses. Because no comparable renderings survive to show us what an English village in America looked like, the Raven drawings are of great interest and importance. They leave little doubt that most of the settlements built in County Londonderry by the major London mercantile companies followed the same basic plan. The bawne was located at one end of a broad avenue whose center line extended from its gateway—regardless of whether or not that gate was centered in the wall. On either side of the avenue ran single rows of dwellings occupied by tenants and undertenants. Each settlement had its Anglican church, but because these were often converted Catholic churches, the newcomers took them where they found them; consequently there is no evidence that their locations fitted any previously prescribed place in the design. At the Merchant Tailors' settlement at Macosquin, however, the village seems to have been planned to locate the existing church at the end of one side of the avenue.

That village was of particular interest to us because the Merchant Tailors Company records in London include a plan showing what the settlers were supposed to build, giving house and lot sizes, and even showing the layout of a formal garden behind the mansion inside the bawne.[14] Thomas Raven's drawing, on the other hand, shows how Macosquin actually turned out—a small village of only six houses (two of them marked "void"), and the bawne walls unfinished.[15] The London plan had not been drawn in a vacuum, for it showed the church askew to the street and the bawne on a knoll at the other end, both of which features persist in modern Macosquin. The plan also showed, projecting from the bawne, a fence that turned at a right angle and ran away toward the nearby river (Fig. 11–8). It reminded me of our umbilical fence between the fort and the Company Compound. For months that fence had been the source of extended argument. Although it ran as far as the Compound's palisade line, it did not abut the latter. Instead, the fence skirted around the impaled

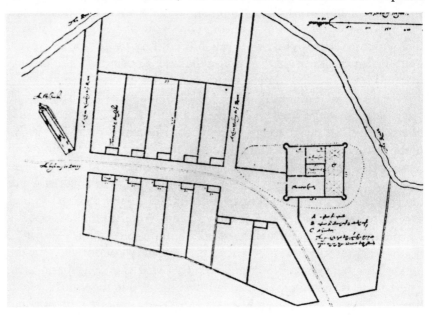

11–8. Plan of the proposed Anglo-Irish settlement of Macosquin in Ulster's County Londonderry. Ca. 1610.

potter's pond, tied into the benchmark tree, turned south for 45 feet, and then disappeared. I had no explanation for this—until I learned that in Ireland, tenants' livestock was driven into the bawne at night for safety. If the Martin's Hundred cattle were put to graze south of the fort, it would make sense that a fence might be erected to corral the animals being driven back into the fort; otherwise they would charge past it, damaging adjacent plantings.

That reasoning contained within it the ultimate conclusion derived from our Ulster expedition. I returned convinced that what we had found was the Wolstenholme Towne bawne, and that the compound to the south represented part of one side of the town's broad avenue. I knew, however, that I would have difficulty getting others to believe us unless we could find at least one more house extending the Long House-compound line into a clear row of separate structures and properties.

As soon as I got back, I explained all this to Eric. He smiled his cream-fed-cat smile. "You mean, like that?" he asked, pointing to the Site plan (Fig. 11–9).

In my absence the crew had carried their scraping to the cliff edge, and had defined a post-built dwelling measuring 15 by 20 feet and having a projecting shed or porch facing onto the avenue. Behind the house they had found an oval, fenced yard, oval because it apparently had been laid out around the periphery of a shade tree whose root hole survived. The fence-post holes were small, and because of their curving line, I concluded that the fence had been built of flexible wattles rather than the more rigid posts and rails we had become accustomed to interpreting on other Martin's Hundred sites.

Beyond the little house (which we named the Domestic Unit) were fourteen more graves, arranged in two rows, as though the occupants had been decanted from a cart standing on a roadway and buried in holes dug on either side of it. The bones proved to be in dreadful condition, several skeletons barely more than brown stains in the ground. In some cases only the enamel of the teeth survived, and in others there was nothing at all. One of the latter group offered us something else instead: the ghost image of a horizontal timber, a loam-filled slot sunk into the grave floor, running the full length of it and in section measuring 6 inches by 6 inches (Fig. 11–10). Although no wood fibers survived in the slot, nails driven into the original timber from three sides remained in position, indicating that the wood had been used for some other purpose before being laid on the bottom of the grave and subsequently pushed down into the wet clay by overlying ground pressure. But why had it been put there?

Audrey suggested that the grave was waterlogged before the corpse arrived for burial, and that some considerate soul thought it would be respectful to lay a timber on the floor to keep the body out of the wet. I found that hard to swallow for all sorts of reasons, not the least of them the fact that the timber was too narrow for the corpse to have been balanced on top of it. Besides, the early Virginia colonists

11–9. Plan of the excavated remains of Wolstenholme Towne showing the key measurements and angles that provided clues to the formality of the design and the extent of the settlement.

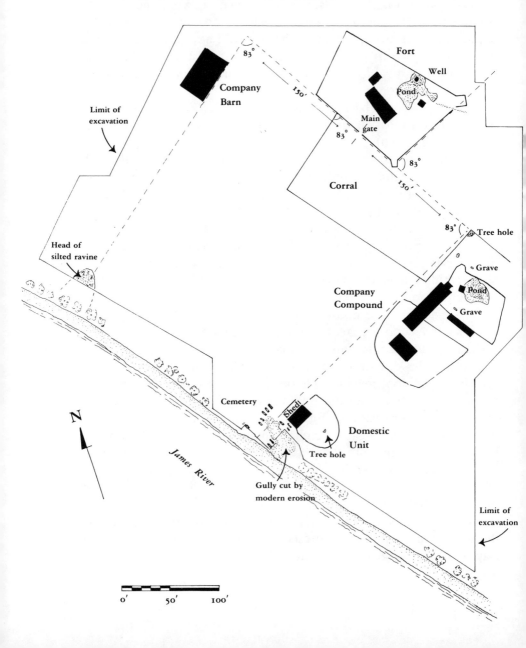

not only took death in their stride, those doing the sexton's work would have known that once they began shoveling dirt into the hole they would displace the water and the loved one would get wet anyway.

My explanation was more dramatic. Audrey called it melodramatic and would have none of it.

We knew from the report of the massacre published in London in 1622 that survivors charged the Indians with the most heinous atrocities. The more I thought about it, the more reasonable I thought it that our buried timber had been a product of the massacre's aftermath. The grave lay only 2 feet from the southwest corner of the Domestic Unit—much too close, if the house was inhabited. I argued that it was not, and that ashes in some of the post-holes pointed to its having burned in the Indian attack (Fig. 11–11). Afterwards, according to the official account, they "fell againe upon the dead, making as well as they could, a fresh murder, defacing, dragging, and mangling the dead carkasses into many pieces, and carrying some parts away in derision, with base and bruitish triumph."[16]

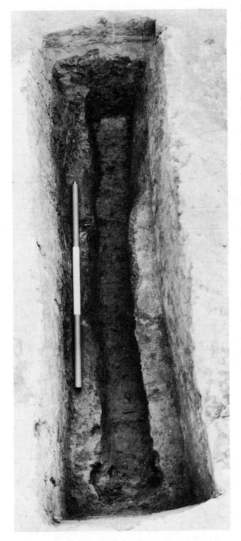

11–10. A grave found beside the Site C Domestic Unit. No evidence of bones survived, only the ghost image of a squared post occupied the hole.

Suppose, I argued, that the main posts of the little house still stood when the Indians returned to finish their work. The body of a colonist found nearby was scalped, dismembered, and then tied to one of the posts and left there to be found by returning survivors. Rather than trying to untie the rotting cadaver, the survivors cut down the post and buried them as one.

Although we had the English charges of mutilation, as well as a De Bry engraving of one Florida tribe dismembering captives from another and a Dutch account of the Iroquois flaying prisoners tied to stakes, Audrey insisted that to raise such a specter would be seen as irresponsible sensationalism—unless I could find documentary proof that such things were done in Virginia. The Algonquians of the Powhatan Confederacy, she rightly pointed out, were neither Iroquois nor Seminole, and it would be unscholarly to tar the Virginia Indians with their brushes.

Audrey was dead right, both academically and from a public relations point of view. More blood-and-guts publicity would not benefit the project. Consequently, we kept quiet about these new graves and my grim interpretation of them—even though the supporting evidence *did* exist. It told a tale infinitely more gruesome than anything I had imagined. Describing Chief Powhatan's own treatment of prisoners, John Smith wrote this:

> He caused certaine malefactors to be bound hand and foot, then having of many fires gathered great store of burning coales, they rake these coales round in the form of a cock-pit, and in the midst they cast the offenders to broil to death. Sometimes he causeth the heads of them that offend him, to be laid upon the altar or sacrificing stone, and one with clubbes beates out their brains. When he would punish any notorious enemy or malefactor, he causeth him to be tyed to a tree, and with Mussell shels or reeds, the executioner cutteth off his ioynts one after another, ever casting what they cut of[f] into the fire; then doth he proceed with shels and reeds to case the skinne from his head and face; then doe they rip his belly and so burne him with the tree and all. Thus themselves reported they executed *George Cassen.*[17]

Cassen had been one of twelve laborers who arrived in Virginia with the first settlers, and had made the mistake of going off on his own in defiance of Smith's orders.

While I had been away in Ireland, conservator Gary McQuillen continued the slow and difficult job of reassembling our supposed massacre victim's skull. Soon after he began, it became clear that we had been wrong in concluding that the man had been killed by a blow to the side of the head. The skull had suffered another even more massive blow to the back which had driven fragments of its occipital bone forward almost into the eye sockets. There also was a short, sharp, and wide fracture just above the right eye beside the nose. I had seen this while the skull lay in the ground and had supposed that it was another of the many breaks caused by the blow to the right side of the head. I was wrong.

Virginia's chief medical examiner, Dr. David K. Wiecking, and his deputy, Dr. Marcella F. Fierro, joined Larry Angel in a collective examination and interpretation of what we had found. All three felt certain that the first blow had been a hard slicing one to the forehead, and that the other, crushing blow or blows followed after the victim had fallen to the ground. Only with blows struck in that order could the natural pressure within have been released to allow the cranial fragments to be driven inside the skull. That explanation posed a question for which no one had a truly convincing answer. Since virtually all the skull fragments survived, we wondered how so monstrously damaged a head could have remained together while the man was being moved from the murder scene to the grave. We had two suggestions: Either the broken head had dried and congealed before the burial party moved the corpse, or the man was wearing a stocking-type Monmouth cap that held his skull together.

Countering the latter argument was the evidence of a narrow scratch in the bone, running from a point close to the left ear and extending up across the brow on a line 1 3/4 inches above the left eye as far as the nose. Larry Angel agreed that this might have been

11–11. A *National Geographic* reconstruction of the Domestic Unit as it may have looked in the midst of the 1622 Indian attack.

caused by a right-handed assailant beginning the scalping process from behind, and added that the scar was consistent with later scalping evidence from Georgia. But our man could hardly have been scalped while wearing a hat; furthermore, it would almost certainly have been done before the skull was battered to pieces.

We were left with other loose ends, not the least of them being the type of weapon used to strike the first blow. The cut was too short for an iron ax (unless the attacker badly misjudged his range), and too sharp to have been caused by an Indian's stone or wooden tomahawk. Remembering that according to survivors' testimony, the Indians "in some places, sate downe at Breakfast with our people at their tables, whom immediately with their owne tooles and weapons, eyther laid downe, or standing in their houses, they basely and barbarously murthered,"[18] I deduced that the weapon was indeed a European's tool—specifically, a garden spade.

Most seventeenth-century spades were of wood shod at the blade edge with a sandwiching strip of tempered iron. We had found such a spade shoe in the nearby potter's pond, and its corner neatly fitted the gash in the skull (Fig. 11–12). Once again the gap between conjecture and proof seemed impossible to bridge. Drs. Angel, Wiecking, and Fierro all agreed that the damage might have been caused by such a weapon; but although they had examined scores of homicide victims, none had been killed with a garden spade. Thus I was left with that always unsatisfactory Scottish verdict of "not proven."

While we were still debating how our man was killed, Margaret Chapman, across the Atlantic at Letchworth, in England, was finding it hard to ignore her ex-guardsman husband's penchant for female clothes—or so she told her lover. Four months later, Mrs. Chapman's solution to her problem would contribute to solving ours.

Lest it be thought that death holds an unhealthy fascination for us, I must make it clear that establishing beyond reasonable doubt that the man behind the Long House had died in the massacre was crucial to arriving at a terminal date for the life of the settlement itself. Again playing devil's advocate, Audrey first argued that even if it was true that our man died as the result of damage to his head and that he was buried in haste, how were we to prove that he was not a Saturday-night drunk run over by a cart or killed in a fight with a friend. In short, evidence of one violent death did not make a massacre.

If my explanation for the presence of the post in the grave beside the Domestic Unit was correct, we would have not one but two unnatural deaths. Admittedly we would be better off with more; but just as my hunch that the rectangular hole behind the Long House

contained a human burial had proved correct, so now I had an unshak-
able conviction that we really did have evidence of the massacre. I was
equally convinced that we were in the midst of Wolstenholme Towne,
and no less firm in believing that what we had found owed its genesis
to the same planning that gave Ulster the British bawne village. To
prove this, however, we would have to find traces of the other, upstream side of our settlement.

Assuming that the Irish villages were laid out along a line extending from the bawne's gate, Eric Klingelhofer measured the distance
from our fort gate to the Long House compound and found it to be
approximately 150 feet. In theory, therefore, a like distance in the
opposite direction should put us on the line of Wolstenholme's matching row of buildings. If we could find even the smallest trace of such
a line before winter set in, we would be home and happy.

In some years we are able to keep digging as late as the second
week in January before frost stiffens the ground. In 1978, the elements and the terrain joined in a conspiracy against us. Heavy rain in
the second week of November left the low-lying Wolstenholme site
waterlogged—but not before we had cut several more trenches
through the plow zone across the northerly 150-foot line. At 13 feet,
6 inches beyond that conjectural line, Eric uncovered three massive
post-holes and two smaller, intermediary holes on a line 45 feet in

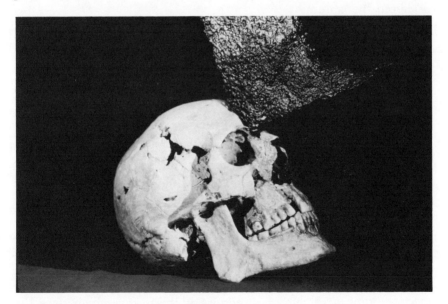

11–12. The Company Compound's "massacre" victim's skull after
reconstruction, showing how an iron spade shoe fits the
gash in the forehead.

length. So big were the major holes that I felt sure they were part of the church. Eric disagreed, believing that the fourteen graves beside the Domestic Unit on the other side of the "avenue" lay at the landward end of a churchyard, the rest of which (and the church) had been lost to the river.

Although we could not agree on the purpose of the building whose post-holes we had found, there seemed little doubt that we had found the other side of our settlement, even though it seemed to belie my centered-gate theory, the distance being 150 feet in one direction and 164 feet, 6 inches in the other.

Colonial Williamsburg's trustees were to visit the site on November 11; but by that time the fort and our other compounds and buildings had been back-filled to protect the subsoil from further erosion. First, however, the crew had set standard-length fenceposts in each of the post-holes, so that outlines of the structures remained visible above ground. By stretching colored plastic tapes from post to post (different colors for each type of enclosure), we were able to create a three-dimensional plan through which our distinguished visitors could walk. But true to form, the weather turned on us. In the night of November 10, high winds ripped the tapes to tatters, and the loosely back-filled soil over the site absorbed the heavy rain like a sponge. We could replace the tapes, but there was nothing we could do about the water.

Somewhat (but not quite) in the mold of the National Geographic Society's intrepid research committee, the trustees showed up, and stood in a cheerless drizzle on the crest of the hill overlooking the site while I tried to recapture the excitement of what we had found. Eric, in a gesture far exceeding the call of duty, volunteered to flounder through the mud, wading in and out of doorways and gates while I explained where he was. Garbed in a bright yellow raincoat, he slid, sank, and staggered like a drunken canary from fort to Company Compound and on to the Domestic Unit at the cliff's edge. It was a performance that drew cheers from the damp trustees and a round of well-earned applause on his return. But that was our last hurrah.

The bad weather which began with the trustees' visit continued off and on throughout the month. Previous high hopes that we might yet be able to uncover the rest of our newly found building were washed away. Instead we faced another winter of waiting and wondering. Were the big post-holes really part of the church? Would we find more buildings stretching between it and the river, and what was the meaning of a triangular patch of dark loam that had shown up close to the building line at the edge of the cliff?

Burning Questions

12

On February 5, 1979, while the remains of Wolstenholme Towne lay frozen and silent, in England the children of Frederick and Margaret Chapman played downstairs in their living room, as upstairs their mother and her lover made their contribution to our research. Having stripped her murdered husband to his corselet and pantyhose, they dressed him in male outer garments and dumped his body from a bridge onto the fast lane of the A1 motorway at Letchworth. It would be November before we could benefit from this odd behavior. In the meantime, while the culprits languished in custody awaiting trial, we marshaled our forces for one more season.

Rain and melted snow lay in pools across the Wolstenholme site well through April, and not until the twenty-fourth could the crew even begin to clear the winter's mess and re-erect our tents. That, however, had not prevented us from investigating another site on a well-drained crest northeast of the settlement. It was yet one more of those locations where 1970 to 1971 testing had revealed evidence of early occupation. The recovered artifacts had come from a single rubbish pit, but they included half a large cream-pan of local manufacture, and several other equally provocative bits of pot. Six weeks of digging revealed a single, post-built house measuring approximately 15 by 20 feet, the same size as Wolstenholme's Domestic Unit.

We were still very unsure of ourselves when it came to interpreting social standing on the basis of house dimensions. The newly found dwelling, on what we called Site E, was much smaller than the house on Site B, the only previous instance wherein we had found the remains of but one residence. Our sole documented measurement for a house in Martin's Hundred came from an instruction to provide a newly arrived servant with a dwelling measuring 14 feet by only 12 feet, barely more than a hut.[1] The 15-foot width, which seemed common to all our identifiable structures in the Wolstenholme settlement, could perhaps be seen as an early standard, and, since the little house at Site E apparently had been destroyed by fire, it was tempting to see it as another victim of the 1622 Indian uprising.

Our Irish sources were not of much help. The London-drawn plan for Macosquin was the only one to give house and lot measurements, but its tenant houses were all a standard 32 by 17 feet, smaller than our 37-by-19-foot house on Site B, and the even larger 40-by-18-foot "Harwood" home on Site A.[2] On the other hand, our 20-by-15-foot units were larger than the tenement houses built by the English in Ireland at Coleraine. The latter were multiple units (long houses) with common framing, each with a single story under an attic, and measuring only 12 by 18 feet.[3] From this, and from more, equally conflicting evidence, we can deduce that in the early seventeenth century, living in small quarters was less claustrophobic than it would be to us.

In the first years of settlement in Martin's Hundred, many colonists (with or without families) no doubt built relatively small houses, walled them with wattle and daub, and roofed them with highly combustible thatch or bark. Lacking protective palisades or sufficient men per unit to defend them, the settlers' future depended in part on faith—faith that the "salvages" would remain friendly in the face of English ambivalence. But, as has so often been demonstrated, the only faith that could not provenly be misplaced was the conviction that even the worst was for the best.

The March 1622 death roll in Martin's Hundred was initially put at about half its population. In the early stages of reviewing the historical evidence, we thought it safe to assume that in the uprising, most of the losses occurred among the vulnerable and isolated farmsteads, and that those residents of Wolstenholme Towne who were not already killed in their houses by Indians would have been able to escape to the safety of the bawne. If, however, the fourteen graves beside the cliff held massacre victims, the in-town slaughter must have been greater than we had supposed. New and grisly discoveries to be made later in 1979 would further contribute to that reassessment.

Determining how long an archaeological site was occupied has always been a difficult, and sometimes an impossible task. Rarely have people's possessions or ways of doing things changed so distinctively at any given moment that we can say that the life and appearance of a site looked one way between the years F and K, and that from L to P it changed to another. To effect such a change, it generally takes a cataclysmic event in the year K—something like a silt-spreading flood or a holocaustic fire—to put an indelible marker between the end of one era and the beginning of the next.

I had hoped that if and when we found the remains of Wolstenholme Towne we would find the ground scorched and strewn with the debris of burned buildings. If no later post-holes or trenches cut through that sealing layer, we could confidently say that the site was never reoccupied, and that everything we found there was part of a three-year time capsule—ca. 1619 to March 1622. Unfortunately, Site C (our assumed Wolstenholme Towne) offered no mantle of destruction. The question of just how much subsoil burning we reasonably might have expected was one we had been debating ever since the excavations began. On none of our sites had we found a clearly outlined rectangle of burned clay subsoil that could be identified as the Hiroshima-like shadow of a torched building. We had found burned posts in some of the holes, but never all those of any one structure. Here and there we had found a scattering of red-baked clay daub from walls or chimneys, but not enough to represent the whole of either.

To try to learn how (or if) the total destruction of a building could leave such haphazard and inconsistent traces, I proposed to buy an abandoned clapboard house of comparable size to one of the Wolstenholme buildings, take it down to the site, set it on top of the plow zone, and burn it. Because the only available houses would be of running sill construction (having been removed from a brick foundation), I intended to set posts in holes dug at appropriate spacings inside the wall lines to simulate those that would have existed had the house been erected in the Wolstenholme manner. The difficulty of finding the right house—and convincing our sponsors that we were not insane—caused this research project to be deferred until the excavations were complete, which was just as well.

While we were still planning, Dr. H. A. Bankoff, assistant professor of anthropology at Brooklyn College, New York, was actually at work. Trying to answer questions similar to ours, but relating them to prehistoric buildings, he found an abandoned, nineteenth-century wattle-and-daub cottage in Serbia, measured and recorded every detail, put representative domestic objects inside, and then set it afire. Within twenty minutes the thatched roof was consumed and the ceiling collapsed, but the fire had died down sufficiently for someone to enter the building and douse whatever flames were still burning. Because heat rises and thatch burns so fast, very little damage had been done to the walls. Clay covering the main posts and wattles had prevented either from catching. Dr. Bankoff and his assistants did not douse the still smoldering roof trusses and ceiling joists; instead, they left them to burn themselves out, a process that took another six hours. The results were dramatic. Roof members burned through and collapsed, rekindling themselves and burning along their lengths to their junction with vertical construction posts within the clay-covered walls, whereupon a few (but by no means all) of those posts ignited and slowly consumed themselves, setting fire to wattles on either side as they burned downward to the ground.

The result of all this was a very localized baking of the wall clay, and the destruction of one post here and another there. Damage to the dirt floor of the cottage was negligible, while the quantity of ash was small and limited to those beams that happened to fall on it. As Dr. Bankoff pointed out, the fragments of burned daub found on the ground (and which archaeologists so often identify as the remains of walls) came exclusively from the ceiling, for that alone was subjected to intense heat for a significant length of time.[4]

My own plan to burn a building made exclusively of wood inevitably would have given us a very different and, as far as wattle-and-daub structures are concerned, entirely wrong interpretation. The fire would have been much hotter, longer sustained, and all-consuming. The Serbian experiment, however, convincingly explained why, among our Martin's Hundred buildings, we found so little evidence of fire, and why what little we did see was so erratic in its distribution. Not only had the heat swept quickly upward away from the ground, but the potentially scorchable clay subsoil must have been buried under four or five inches of loam which, in March, was likely to have been wet or frozen. As an independent experiment of my own, I had taken the white wood ashes and charcoal from my living-room fireplace and had spread them over the natural clay in a prepared, 3-foot-square area of my garden. After photographing them and plotting the positions of the charcoal, I covered the 2-inch ash stratum with 3 inches of loam—and left it for two years. By then a thick mantle of vines, some with stems half an inch thick, covered the area and had to be cleared with shears and an axe. Beneath lay thick-rooted grasses and weeds, bonding the loam into a mat. When that was removed and the natural clay revealed, I could find no trace of the white ash, and only one small fragment from the dozen large pieces of charcoal I had put down. For all practical archaeological purposes, the ash bed might never have existed—yet the ashes had been carefully "preserved" under a protective layer of earth. If they were spread on the land surface, as would have been the case had they come from a burning building, wind and rain would have scattered and destroyed their testimony even sooner. In short, our hopes for finding extensive evidence of Indians having burned the Martin's Hundred dwellings stemmed from an improper understanding of how such houses burn and of what can happen to their ashes in hungry-rooted ground. Measured against those yardsticks, our cumulative evidence of destruction by fire was both substantial and convincing.

The lack of any mantle of destruction at Wolstenholme Towne denied us the stratigraphic punctuation we had hoped to find. Consequently we had no way of knowing with complete assurance whether some of the post-holes and slots cut into the subsoil might not date from a reconstruction period after the 1622 massacre. We could say only that since none of the post-hole lines overlapped or crossed one another, any changes or additions were to standing structures and were not independent of them—with the exception of two rows of post-holes that crossed the fort and the Company Compound, several ditches, and a pattern of large round holes that dotted the northern half of the site. All of these proved to belong either to fences associated with the eighteenth-century Carter's Grove plantation, or to an orchard laid out either in the later seventeenth century or shortly thereafter.

The Carter's Grove mansion was not completed until 1755, and only on Site A had we found evidence of occupation past the early 1640s—and that no later than 1650. Consequently, the archaeological history of the Martin's Hundred and Carter's Grove tract was left with a century-long hole in it. We knew that part of the old Society's holdings became Martin's Hundred parish, and that one or more churches served it through the rest of the seventeenth century; but there is no record of when the name became corrupted into Merchant's Hundred, or from whom Robert Carter bought his acres early in the eighteenth century. Land records do give us the names of several people who owned property in the parish in the second half of the seventeenth century. We know, too, that in 1657 the widow Amy Barnehouse of Martin's Hundred signed a deed of manumission for a Negro named Mihill Gowen (and his son William)—almost certainly the same Mihill Gowree who in 1666 secured a patent for more than thirty acres in Martin's Hundred, putting him among America's earliest free, land-owning blacks.[5]

The apparent absence of any archaeological evidence for the century beginning around 1650 was disappointing in that it divorced the Martin's Hundred saga from the later Carter's Grove story and made it difficult to interpret them to the mansion's visitors. We were overjoyed, therefore, when on April 3, 1979, assistant archaeologist Bill Henry found what promised to be our missing link. While walking the last half mile of a new road being cut to connect restored Williamsburg to Carter's Grove, he found that the road-builders had sliced through a rubbish pit, half of which survived in the adjacent bank. Fragments of brick protruded from it, as did pieces of window glass and the lead used to hold it in place. More important, however, were several broken tobacco pipes, two of them bearing the maker's name, WILL EVANS. William Evans worked in Bristol, England, in the last quarter of the seventeenth century. Lying in the roadside ditch (where it must have fallen from the pit), was a severely worn, tinned-brass spoon of a type popularly known as "Puritan," and therefore attributable to the mid-seventeenth century. Together, the spoon and the marked pipes pointed to occupation in the second half of the century, perhaps around 1680, while the bricks and window remains indicated the nearby presence of a dwelling of more substance than we had become accustomed to in the heyday of Martin's Hundred.

In the spring of 1979 we had no evidence that the newly discovered Site J had its origins in the Wolstenholme period, and so, lacking either funds or time to investigate it further, we were content to mark the spot and add it to the inventory of sites left to be explored at some future time. Newspaper reporters who heard about the discovery of Site J expressed surprise that we had no plans to open it up; one even hinted that we were shirking our duty to history. But important though it might be to the evolution of the Carter's Grove acres, and delighted as we were to locate it, the fact remained that a 1680 site had no obvious place in the story of Wolstenholme Towne and the Martin's Hundred Society.

Although the cultural jump from the 1630s to the 1680s was less breathtaking than, say, the fifty years from 1900 to 1950, fundamental changes were occurring that left Wolstenholme in the shadow of the Elizabethan Age of Exploration. While someone was smoking Will Evans's pipes on Site J, Isaac Newton was working on his *Philosophiae naturalis principia mathematica* and ushering in the Age of Enlightenment. Much had happened in the intervening years. The once awesome power of Spain had declined; the Dutch had emerged as a major colonial nation and as Europe's carriers; England had beheaded her king, flirted with religious republicanism, and crowned a Protestant monarch with catholic ideas. British policy and British thought had traveled many miles from the essentially Elizabethan sense of nationalism that persisted throughout the life of the Virginia Company. Thus, the Martin's Hundred story belonged to the social era of Marlowe and

Shakespeare, and to an England not far removed from the late Middle Ages. The Wolstenholme years were part of the great adventure, when the New World was still seen as an oyster waiting only for Englishmen tough enough to break it open; but by 1680 the adventure was over, and the serious business of colonial commerce had made the New World old hat. It was to this quite different chapter that Site J seemed to belong.

Although Eric Klingelhofer was able to move part of the field crew from the relatively unimportant Site E back to Wolstenholme Towne on April 24, 1979, it was not until May 4 that Bill Henry finished at Site E and the combined crew could set to work to answer the question that had been frustrating us all winter: What was the meaning of the row of large holes north of the fort, which seemed to be part of the missing "other side" to our Irish-type village?

Within five days Eric had found another row of holes parallel to the first and about 14 feet further north. In contrast to the three massive holes he had found in November, these were puny, some barely reaching a couple of inches into the clay. Together, the two rows gave us a very improbable, shed-like structure, 45 feet long and only 14 feet, 6 inches wide. The true dimensions took several more days to reveal themselves. The three large holes turned out not to be the front of the building, but its center line, and to have carried massive posts supporting the roof of a barn or warehouse measuring 45 by 29 feet, the largest structure encountered on any of our sites (Fig. 12–1). Equally gratifying was the realization that the third set of holes, 14 feet, 6 inches south of the central row, put Wolstenholme's north building line 150 feet from the fort gate—exactly where we needed it to be to support the bawne village theory.

That discovery did much to offset my disappointment that our newly found building could not be the church. Intermediate posts between the three roof-bearing supports indicated a central division running the length of the structure, something totally out of character for a place of worship. The plan resembled nothing so much as a tobacco barn, and so we named it the Company Barn or warehouse, the place where Martin's Hundred's produce could be stored under the protection of the fort until it was ready to be shipped to England.

Although the Company Barn stood just where we wanted it in relation to the fort gate, it proved not to be parallel to the other side of our town, or, indeed, to the fort itself. The latter was of a distinctly eccentric shape, but although the Londonderry drawings demonstrated that bawnes came in many shapes and sizes, and were not always at right angles to the village, the same drawings invariably showed the houses parallel to each other on either side of the street or avenue: yet ours were not. We first tried to explain the discrepancy by pointing out that our broad avenue was actually a hundred yards wide in front of the fort, really more of a green than a street or avenue. That being so, there was no need for the sides to be exactly parallel. Then why bother to so carefully center them on the fort gate, somebody asked?

It was Eric who discovered that the lack of right angles was not the result of having no professional surveyor, but rather a deliberate design element. The buildings on both sides of the green stretched along lines set at 83-degree angles to the west wall of the fort—the same angle adopted by the fence linking the latter to the Company Compound, as well as that described by the junction of the fort's west

12–1. The post-hole pattern of the Company Barn, the largest building found at Martin's Hundred. Most of the weight of its 29-foot-wide roof was carried on three center-line posts.

and south walls; altogether too many 83-degree angles to be mere coincidences. But why, we asked ourselves, would the settlement leaders have made laying out their town so inordinately difficult? As late as 1621, Virginia's governor Sir George Yeardley had complained that "we have never a surveyour in the lande and by that meanes cannot performe suche a service to any purpose," and that the people in Martin's Hundred needed him to "be sett on worke to divide their groundes"[6]; but it is hard to believe that the first Martin's Hundred settlers did not have someone trained in surveying to establish all those 83-degree angles—someone, perhaps, who returned to England or was among the hundred or more who died during the pre-massacre years.

This convenient explanation did nothing to account for the settlement's atypical shape. Our clue to that mystery was provided by a triangular patch of loam 25 feet wide and extending inland from the cliff edge to a distance of close on 55 feet. Found at the end of the 1978 season, this proved to be the tail of a ravine or gulley that once sloped down to the river, and which probably gave the settlement its access to the beach. When drawn on our plan and projected out into the river for the distance of about 400 feet believed lost to erosion since 1619, the ravine caused the upstream side of the settlement-supporting plateau to taper. The tail of another ravine survives 500 feet downstream from the Company Compound, and it needs no heroic stretch of imagination to believe that it widened or angled in such a way as to narrow the Wolstenholme plateau to a tapering promontory, thus explaining why the sides of the settlement were not parallel to each other.

Finding the upstream ravine head gave us a logical solution to another of our problems—namely that we had been unable to find traces of any more buildings along our north construction line. If the ravine had indeed provided the settlers with their primary access to the river, it seemed likely that at least a two-lot gap would have been left between the warehouse and the nearest tenant's house.

From the moment that most of us became convinced that we had found Wolstenholme Towne, we began asking how big it could have been. Remembering that the erosion rate could have varied from less than a foot to a yard a year (depending on the height and vulnerability of the bank at different times), an 18-inch average could have resulted in a land loss of up to 540 feet since the town was built. Regardless of whether that figure or our more conservative 400 feet was the more accurate assessment, it meant that at least half the settlement's land had been lost to the river. That conclusion was supported by the following exercise: Recalling that several of the Londonderry bawne village plans showed that their avenues were no narrower than the width of the fort, and knowing this to be true of the landward end of our 300-foot-wide village green, I argued that the converging lines of the flanking building lots would not have run any closer together than the width of our fort. Projected on paper, the point of unacceptable convergence occurred about 300 feet out in the river, giving the settlement a total estimated length of some 700 feet (Fig. 12–2).

On the basis of the width of the Domestic Unit, the space between it and the Company Compound, and the length of the compound itself, Eric deduced that our lots were approximately 45 feet wide. Using that figure, and taking the Domestic Unit as an average Wolstenholme dwelling, I concluded that the "Towne" would really have been no more than a village of perhaps a dozen houses—providing that it had no side streets that we knew nothing about. Using Irish census evidence to suggest the number of people likely to occupy a tenant's cottage, and assuming that there had been no more anomalously large "company" dwellings, the total in-town population may have been no more than fifty or sixty people. If this was true, more than three-quarters of Martin's Hundred's documented maximum population would have been distributed over the Society's 21,500 acres. Such a scattering of the settlers would have been consistent with the pattern already developing at Jamestown, creating a degree of independence that was frowned upon in London. Considering that the backbone of the Martin's Hundred Society's venture lay in selling shares in exchange for acres to be populated and developed by the investors, the wide scattering of settlers was inevitable. It is true that most of the shareholders had no more than two or three shares (300 acres), but farmers and families on holdings of that size could hardly be described as pigging it cheek by jowl. Only four investors, one of them Sir John Wolstenholme, had as many as six shares, and one, John Barnard (about whom we know nothing), capped them all with thirteen.

The question of how many people lived in Martin's Hundred at any one time prior to the Indian uprising can never be answered. Most of what we know comes from a summary contained in the Society's revised patent of 1622, which puts the total it sent out at 280, names the ships, their year of departure, and gives the number of Martin's Hundred settlers aboard all but two.[7] Unfortunately, in addition to the missing figures, lines are duplicated, and in one instance two different numbers are cited; but sorted out, and after we have converted

Conjectural 1619 shoreline

the dates to the new style calendar and added the *Jonathan*'s passenger figure from another source, the tabulation (assuming 10 aboard the *Warwicke*) is as follows:[7]

SHIP	DATE	SETTLERS
Guift of God	1618	220
Jonathan	1620	[6]
ffrancis Bonaventure	"	2
Marmaduke	"	12
Warwicke	1621	10/28
Tiger	"	12
Bona Nova	"	? (18)
		280 Total

12–2. To estimate how much of the Wolstenholme settlement had been lost to erosion since 1622, the archaeologists reasoned that the north and south building lines converged at 83-degree angles and that these lines would not have come so close together as to interrupt the fort's view of the river. Thus, by theoretically moving the fort westward until it collided with the building lines, one arrived at a point beyond which those lines were unlikely to have projected. While the absence of buildings west of the barn might be explained in part by a lack of people to live in them, the space between the Company Compound and the Domestic Unit seems to meet the need to maintain a down-river field of fire for the fort's single cannon.

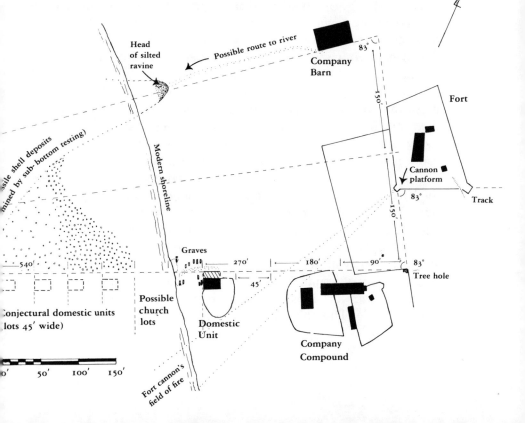

The 280 total includes only those who were on the Society's record as having been sent out from England. We have no knowledge of how many died at sea, ran away upon arrival, or died soon after they got settled. As for the long-term stability of the group, we have to rely on the rather unreliable testimony of William Harwood's servant Richard Frethorne, who wrote that immediately after the 1622 massacre "att our Plantacon of seavenscore [140], there was butt 22 lefte alive."[8] In a subsequent letter Frethorne told his parents that "wee are but 32 to fight against 3000 if they should Come, and the nighest helpe that Wee have is ten miles of us, and when the rogues ov[er]came this place last, they slew 80 Persons . . ."[9] Something, clearly, is adrift in Frethorne's arithmetic, for seven-score minus eighty is sixty, and not twenty-two. Nevertheless, Frethorne's total of eighty slain differs only by two from the official list of seventy-eight sent back to London. Among those named are several who later turned out to be prisoners. Adding to the confusion is the fact that Frethorne knew about the hostages. On March 5, 1623, he reported the capture of two Indians who revealed "that the Indians have 15 alive."[10]

My wife Audrey's final estimate, based on all the surviving scraps of evidence, is that as many as twenty prisoners were taken by the Indians in Martin's Hundred, most of them women, and that the death toll was closer to fifty-eight than to seventy-eight. From what remained of the town, we had so far found sixteen graves, only one occupant offering us physical evidence of violent death. But if the fourteen graves close to the cliff edge were indeed those of massacre victims, we would have to conclude that 29 percent of the fifty-eight died in the village—too high a percentage considering the vulnerability of the outlying farms and the protection offered by the fort. On the other hand, we might argue that if our estimate of the town as being home to about a quarter of the Hundred's total population is valid, it may also have absorbed about a quarter of the casualties.

Seeking confirmation for our estimated town size, I persuaded the Virginia Research Center for Archaeology's underwater archaeologist, John Broadwater, to mount a river-bottom investigation extending a distance of 600 feet out from the present shore, this in the hope of finding the remains of revetments seated in the river's clay bed along the 1619 shoreline. We both knew that it was the longest of longshots, for although timbers bedded in the clay could be expected to survive, we were looking for a ribbon of wood no more than 6 or 8 inches wide. The only sure way to find it (if it existed) was to dig an underwater trench through the centuries' accumulated silt all the way out to the 600-foot mark, a project for which John lacked the time and we the funds. The best we could manage was a series of short test holes and trenches every 10 feet out along the town's projected south property line. I had so little faith in the success of this enterprise that I explained it to the equally dubious National Geographic Society's research committee as primarily something that had to be done to silence critics who inevitably would ask: Why didn't you look in the river?

The diving team was led by the Research Center's David K. Hazzard, who in 1970 and 1971 had been Bill Kelso's principal assistant in digging all of the trenches and test holes that eventually would lead us to Martin's Hundred and to Wolstenholme Towne. Now, eight years later, Dave again came up with the unexpected. Although failing to find any seventeenth-century pilings, his test cuts revealed a bed of redeposited fossil shell, thick inshore but tapering to nothing about 400 feet out in the river. These shells came from the Miocene marl beds underlying the natural clay along the Carter's Grove shoreline, and are common through much of Tidewater Virginia, recalling a time around ten million years ago when the entire region lay beneath the ocean. Today the marl deposits are exposed only in areas of high ground when Nature or Man slices through them. Where there are swamps and low-lying clay areas (as is the case at Jamestown Island) the shells are nowhere to be seen. Thus, when they disappeared, at about the 400-foot mark out from the Carter's Grove cliff line, we could cautiously deduce that at some point close to that distance from shore, the natural contours of the Wolstenholme headland sloped away into an older river bed. A shell loss at about 400 feet suggested that the actual bed had terminated or dipped downward somewhat closer inshore, and that some of the eroded marl was carried further out across the seventeenth-century river bed. Estimating that carry-out distance to be about 50 feet, one can state a case for an old shoreline about 350 feet out. Although we cannot put a date to this estimated shoreline, the underwater evidence, coupled with the land-based deductions, can be used to suggest that the eroded settlement did not extend more than about 250 feet beyond the 1979 cliff edge (see Fig. 12–2).

To test the shell-loss thesis, I asked Dave Hazzard to dig another series of holes upstream from the first and parallel to the shore. If we were right in identifying the triangular patch of loam on the cliff top as the silted head of an old ravine, then—as it became wider and deeper into what has since become part of the James River bed—it should have caused the Wolstenholme headland's underlying shell print to disappear in a northerly direction. It did. Geologists at the Virginia Institute of Marine Science advised against putting too much store by this evidence, although they agreed that there might well be something to it. What was needed, they said (and as we well knew) was a much more thorough program of underwater testing, not only upstream from the town site but downstream to try to locate the extremity of the shell print in that direction. But John Broadwater's divers had other commitments, and we had no more money in the budget.

Inconclusive though the underwater evidence proved to be, the up-stream edge of the shell distribution pattern suggested that the ravine whose head we had found close to the existing cliff edge may have widened abruptly, drastically narrowing the headland on which Wolstenholme Towne stood (see Fig. 12-2). Indeed, such an interpretation could argue that no buildings had been lost to the river on the north side of the green. If that was so, our estimated in-town population could drop to as few as thirty to forty people.

The rest of our 1979 survey funds were allocated to yet another project to be undertaken for us by the Virginia Research Center for Archaeology. Bill Kelso's 1971 testing had located an Indian cemetery on the ridge immediately northwest of the Wolstenholme fort, as well as traces of Indian occupation scattered both along the ridge and down toward the rear of the Company Barn. The question we had to have answered was: How long and how recently had Indians lived in the Wolstenholme area? We had found a few quartzite points in the topsoil overlying the town site, and these belonged to the Late Woodland period. To historical archaeologists agonizing over dates within a decade, the prehistorians' time brackets can be frustratingly loose. The Late Woodland period in Virginia embraces everything from about A.D. 1000 to A.D. 1600. Consequently, an arrow fired in the Late Woodland Period might have missed a colonist in the early seventeenth century or dropped a deer in the same year that King Harold got one in the eye at Hastings.

A burned-out tree root system found southeast of the fort had contained several fragments of Late Woodland pottery, suggesting that the Indians had cleared the land for their own use. If that clearance had immediately preceded, or persisted until, the arrival of the English, it might explain why the Martin's Hundred settlers chose that spot to build their town. Even if the land had been vacated for ten or twenty years, reclearing it of relatively young trees would have been far less backbreaking and time-consuming than cutting a plantation out of primeval forest. We hoped, therefore, that testing by qualified prehistorians might yield stratified Indian organic artifacts and food waste that would lend themselves to dating by the carbon-14 process.

Most laymen can readily appreciate that diving archaeologists need specialized training not possessed or needed by those who dig on land—like avoiding drowning. Fewer people (and some archaeologists are among them) recognize that terrestrial sites of different time periods and cultures call for their own corpora of specialized knowledge, without which they cannot properly be interpreted. Careful and revealing digging is journeyman's work; only the correct interpretation of what one finds turns a digger into an archaeologist. Similarly, any relatively sober fellow can turn the pages of a book without tearing them, but reading and understanding the words written on them calls for something more than sobriety. Thus, when it came to excavating a prehistoric Indian site, we could assemble a yeoman group of page turners, but no readers. For that reason I contracted with the Virginia Research Center for Archaeology, whose prehistorian Keith Eggloff would undertake a new survey of the Indian acres.

The results were inconclusive. Occupation went all the way back to the Archaic Period, which began around 3500 B.C., although some of the sherds found in the plow zone ran into the Late Woodland centuries. Unfortunately, the only undisturbed rubbish deposit from this, to us, critical period, failed to provide an adequate carbon-14 sample. Consequently, the Indian Connection, like the offshore geological evidence, remained tentative and unproven.

Although May 1979 was a month of intense archaeological activity in and around the Wolstenholme site, little was being found to excite anyone but an archaeologist. This was a pity, because the June issue of the *National Geographic* was on its way to Society members around the world, and a May 22 press conference was scheduled to take place at the Society's Washington headquarters to promote the lead article. Titled "First Look at a Lost Virginia Settlement," it provided the first relatively authoritative summary of our efforts through the previous three years. Dick Schlecht's paintings glowed from the pages, as did photographer Ira Block's photographs of the artifacts, and we were all satisfied that we had made the article as "popular" as we dared without making fools of ourselves. However, the National Geographic Society's science writer, Donald Frederick, who was charged with luring Washington's jaded reporters to the conference, was only marginally ecstatic.

"So what's new?" he wanted to know.

"We've found the warehouse and the other side of the town," I told him.

Don looked glum. "More holes in the ground?"

"Well, yes." We really had nothing newly newsworthy to report. The "massacre victim" story had run its course a year ago; so had the discovery of what we thought to be the town. Finding the second helmet had not been widely reported, but we both knew that the press has little interest in "another" anything. Don, nevertheless, had to write a provocative yet accurate press release, and to assemble a group of eye-catching photographs that had not previously been published. All I could supply was sympathy, and a reminder that he had only to write his piece and sit back and hope the papers used it—whereas I had to stand in front of the reporters (always supposing they showed up) and hold their attention for half an hour, while concealing the fact that most of what I would be telling them had been in their papers before, even twice before.

My approach to the press conference was to try to cover the paucity of new information by turning it into a show-and-tell session —with emphasis heavily on the show. To that end we carried some of the least fragile artifacts to Washington, including the restored skull and the spade blade of the type I believed to have cut it. I also took along an antique musket of the same kind as those used in Martin's Hundred, and told Audrey that if the worst came to the worst, I would try to hold the reporters' waning attention by demonstrating how to fire it, complete with burning fuse and flashing powder.

"That's pandering," she said.

"Which is exactly what we're there for," I added. To minimize the chance of laying an egg, the conference was rehearsed the day before, beginning with film clips made for television stations, following with a twenty-minute slide presentation, and ending with a question-and-answer period using the artifacts as catalysts and props. Although giving press interviews was not new to me, I had never before had to handle a full-blown press conference. Thoughtlessly adding to my apprehension, someone pointed out that I was about to stand where some of the century's foremost anthropologists and explorers had stood to bring to an astonished world several of the great scientific revelations of their times.

"Don't you feel honored to be following in such distinguished footsteps?"

The thought hadn't crossed my mind, but, yes, I suppose I did feel honored.

"Isn't it remarkable that an archaeological site less than four centuries old, should be given the treatment hitherto reserved for discoveries thousands, even millions of years older?"

That too. So now I had the burden of awe to add to my fear that the press would quickly discover that I had nothing fresh to say. Together they sent me scurrying to the men's room moments before I was due to go on. It was there that a miracle occurred. All fear suddenly was swept away as I was reminded that even the mighty National Geographic Society is peopled with people. Inscribed on the back of the lavatory door I found a three-verse graffito penned in red, green, and blue—a scatological creation of such calligraphic beauty that it could only be found within portals dedicated to a publication as elegantly colorful as the *National Geographic*. Buoyed by that discovery, I returned to a packed hall, gave my lecture, answered the questions (and "fired" the gun), and apparently satisfied the reporters.

Appearances, however, are notoriously deceptive. For reasons of its own, *The Washington Post* elected to bypass the substance of the conference (perhaps deducing that there was none) and instead featured the still-to-be-excavated 1680 site. Overcoming the absence of pictures to illustrate it, someone resourcefully removed the caption from a shot of pottery being unearthed in the pre-1622 Company Compound and wrote another shifting the location to the new site and updating the artifacts to 1680.

"Wouldn't it be nice," said Audrey, "if we could solve *our* problems that easily."

Driving back to Williamsburg we heard on the car radio that we had found evidence of the oldest Indian massacre in the New World.

Granny in the Ground

13

The price of free publicity can be high, and throughout the summer of 1979 mail trickled in from around the world, largely from people tracing Wolstenholme and Harwood ancestors, but also from gun collectors, students of fortifications, and from a man in Pakistan studying distilling; others from England, Ireland, Holland, and Sweden; and one from an American Indian in New Jersey looking for a fight. He objected to our describing the Indians' surprise attack on the colonists as a massacre, arguing that when whites massacred Indians, historians call it a battle. I tried to explain that although I had great sympathy for the Virginia Indians' feelings toward the English, I could think of no more accurate term to describe what they did in 1622. My point, nevertheless, was not well taken.

Meanwhile, back on the site, it was obvious to us that Wolstenholme's archaeological potential was exhausted. With no more buildings to be found along the north side of the settlement, we were soon out of work. There remained only the task of devising yet another ending for our TV film. The previous year's tilt-up shot from the fort toward Jamestown was not only pictorially dull, it also would have left an audience assuming that we considered the fort to be our big payoff. Now we knew that it was not; the town was what mattered. Beginning with Dave Hazzard and his divers at work in the river, I wrote a new closing sequence that zoomed toward the shore and the eroding cliff, while a voice-over narration declared that although the underwater evidence had yet to be found, we could say with assurance that beyond the tree-lined cliff lay the site of one of Britain's oldest American settlements. In the midst of this wrap-up speech I planned to dissolve through the trees to a new painting by Dick Schlecht showing the town as it might have been seen by a bird approaching from the river. When told what I had in mind, Dick rightly observed that the view would have been right up the middle of the village green, a large expanse of nothing.

In the midst of the summer's digging, and with the crew needing to know what to do next, there was no time to solve the film's problems. Knowing (and having frequently demonstrated) that archaeological sites rarely turn out as we expect, I had written a back-up proposal into our National Geographic Society grant request: If Wolstenholme Towne's "other side" failed to materialize, we would move to another site several hundred yards downriver, one formally identified as Site D, but generally known as "Audrey's Choice." It was another of those located during the 1970 to 1971 survey, and one that had yielded the best-quality English ceramic fragments from any of the Martin's Hundred sites—hence my wife's enthusiasm for it.

Among the pottery items found at Site D was the base of that English delftware salt bowl decorated with stippled manganese whose discovery had hinted at the importance of the seventeenth-century remains lying buried at Carter's Grove (see Fig. 1–11). It was an object without any known parallel in British museum collections. Because decorative salts were luxury rather than essential household items, Audrey argued (and I agreed with her) that the site where it was found must have been occupied by a relatively well-off family, perhaps someone with a plantation as extensive as the supposed Harwood spread at Site A. Such reasoning is only valid if we are sure what we mean by *quality, luxury,* and *well off,* all terms imprecisely pinned to the sliding scale of wealth.

Although the salt seemed to be of a shape unparalleled in delftware, it clearly copied a silver form and was, therefore, inferior to the latter—and we know that several people in Virginia did own vessels of silver. Thus, for example, in March 1623, when the colony was at its lowest ebb, Peter Arundle of Buckrow wrote that "I have ben forced to buy a hogshead of Meale w^{c}h cost me xij^{li} sterl: [12 pounds sterling] A faire guilt silv^r bowle w^{t}h a Cover payed for part of it."[1] Silver gilt looked like gold and was more costly than plain silver. We can conclude, therefore, that the owner of a delftware salt copying a silver or silver gilt form was not at the top of Virginia's social or economic tree—but then neither was Peter Arundle. Nevertheless, a delftware salt was more grand than one of locally made earthenware, and a lot better than none at all. In the virtual absence of any household inventories for the 1620s, we have no way of knowing who, in which economic brackets, owned what.

Ignoring these uncertainties, we looked to Site D with Dickensian expectations. For Eric Klingelhofer, in charge of logistical problems posed by packing up on one site and moving to another, the immediate concern was not status symbols in seventeenth-century Virginia, but his water supply. Without water to hose down the sun-baked clay, the ground could neither be scraped nor its post-holes found. We had solved the problem on the Wolstenholme site by running several hundred feet of plastic hose from the Carter's Grove mansion, hose that had to be buried in a trench to protect it from vehicles and to deter it from bursting in the heat. Despite these precautions, pressure on the pipe often caused it to rupture, geysers bursting from the ground to the amazement—and moistening—of passing tourists. Faced with the major task of digging up all the hoses and laying them over again in a new trench extending to Site D, Eric reminded me that we had one more site close to Wolstenholme that ought to be looked at before we pulled up our pipe.

The site to which Eric referred was low on our list of interesting places to dig. Found in 1971, it was represented only by a rectangular hole in the clay, from which Bill Kelso's survey crew had extracted a few small sherds of pottery and a couple of musket balls. Notes taken at the time recorded that on the flat floor of the hole were several brown, organic stains which the excavators took to be the remains of tree branches. On the evidence of those and of the musket balls, they concluded that the hole could possibly have served as a hide or blind for seventeenth-century hunters shooting game flying in from the river. It was located on the downriver side of the ravine that flanked the Wolstenholme site on the south, and in a field that had been almost totally stripped by Bill Kelso while uncovering the extensive remains of brick clamps (above-ground brick kilns) used during the construction of the eighteenth-century mansion. Our own testing along the ravine had been unproductive. All in all, therefore, I had little enthusiasm for relocating a half-excavated hunting blind.

"But can we be sure it was a hunting blind?" Eric persisted. "There were seventeenth-century potsherds in the fill. How did they get there if nobody lived on the site?"

I had no answer, and so reluctantly agreed to take another look —if only to be able to say that we had left no stone unturned. It meant splitting the crew, keeping a few under Eric's direction looking for the hole we labeled Site H (after all, it was his idea), and sending the rest, led by artifact officer John Hamant, to set up shop on Site D, while maintaining contact between the two groups by short-wave radio. Those left behind with Eric felt discriminated against, until they realized that they would be working in the shade of the ravine-flanking trees and cooled by breezes off the river, while their colleagues on Site D could hope neither for shade nor zephyrs.

Days of machine trenching and then total stripping of Site D's plow zone yielded virtually nothing. Work had begun on June 25, but it was July 26 before we relocated the pit from which the delftware salt base and other tempting artifacts had come. Although the 1971 notes showed that the hole had only been partially excavated, what was left proved to contain few artifacts of interest, other than the previously mentioned earthenware cup with pieces of lead shot trapped in its glaze. The single structure found in the vicinity of the pit was represented by only six post-holes, and measured 15 by 25 feet, the two sets of three post-holes being at the narrow sides or ends of the building (Fig. 13–1). No sill-slots survived, no recognizable doorway, and no chimney, yet the post-holes and molds were large.

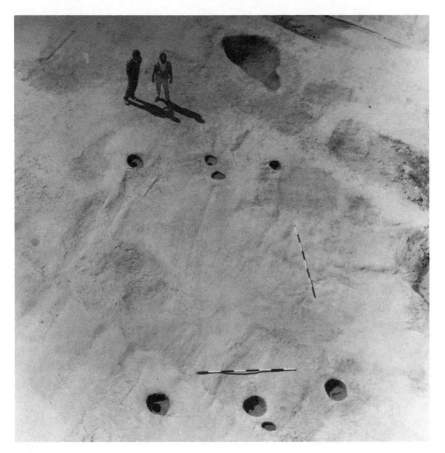

13–1. All that Site D had to offer, one pit and the posts for a structure that no one could convincingly interpret.

Several conjectural interpretations were offered: a blockhouse, a massive tower, a cattle shed—anything but a straightforward dwelling. At the same time, however, the 15-foot width measurement of the building was the same as that for most of the Wolstenholme houses, while both measurements matched the store in the Company Compound. In short, "Audrey's Choice," the site in which we had put such store, turned out to be singularly uninformative. But back at the supposedly no-account Site H, Eric Klingelhofer was turning up artifacts wherever he dug.

Like the armor-rich Site B, Site H lay largely on the edge of a wooded ravine that offered so little arable land that the trees had not been cleared in at least a hundred years. Consequently, much of the site had suffered little from recent and even colonial agriculture. Unlike the open field immediately to the south, on whose edge Bill Kelso's team had found the supposed hunting blind pit, and which now yielded little or nothing from its plow zone, the wooded area was giving up artifacts as soon as the surface loam was breached.

Lead shot of several sizes were scattered through the soil; so were several pewter lids from bandolier powder flasks. Other finds included parts from snaphaunce-type muskets, and from one large pit came a complete armor plate for covering the left thigh, an element called a tasset. These were usually made in one of two ways: The earliest and best were made up from six or more narrow iron plates called lames, each overlapping and anchored to one another by leather straps. The other variety was fashioned from a single plate, hammered into horizontal ridges to resemble the separate components of multiple-lame tassets. These one-piece plates were worn by pikemen, and generally date from the seventeenth century (Fig. 13–2). The tasset we had found matched neither variety; instead, it seemed to be a cross between the two, a single plate hammered to represent only three lames and with rivets along its lower edge, indicating that it had been anchored by leather straps to another plate of the same size—in short, a pikeman's-style tasset but articulated in the middle (Fig. 13–3).

Just as our close helmets from Wolstenholme Towne had no exact parallels in any British or American museum we had contacted, so did the newly found tasset generate curatorial disbelief. Our initial interpretation had to be wrong, or, alternatively, the type was quite common—until the requested parallel could not be found. I remained convinced, in the face of expert opinions to the contrary, that our tasset was a transitional type between the multi-lamed units of the sixteenth century and the single-plate versions common in the seventeenth century. The more I studied the ordinary arms and armor of the early seventeenth century, the less I found to be known about them.

Each time I had told the armor experts that we were finding the scale-like plates from brigandine vests, I had been asked whether I was sure they were not from jacks. Brigandines, they insisted, were obsolete in the sixteenth century. Made (as I have previously noted) from overlapping iron plates riveted to a fabric that could be anything from canvas to velvet, brigandines were light and flexible, but relatively difficult to make. Jacks were a later, more easily made version of the same idea, but one in which the metal plates were sewn rather than riveted, between two layers of canvas, creating an externally quilted appearance (Fig. 13–4). In 1575, during the reign of Elizabeth I, the master of the Tower of London's armories received orders to chop up enough old plate armor to make a sufficient number of pieces to be sewn into 1,500 jacks for use by troops at sea.[2] Nevertheless, a small supply remained in the Tower's reserves, and in 1622 was shipped to Virginia to offset armor lost to the Indians. Although the records are contradictory, it seems that about 115 brigandines were sent over, as well as 40 vests described as "Plate Coats." The latter probably were jacks, though one list lumps them with 100 brigandines and then puzzlingly adds "Iacks of Male . . . 40." The next entry was for 400 "Ierkins or Shirts of Male." To add a little extra confusion, a subse-

13–2. Early seventeenth-century pikemen's armors in the collection of the Tower of London. Their tassets are of one-piece construction.

quent and more complete listing of the armor to be sent to Virginia omits any reference to jacks but does identify 40 "Plate cotes" and 400 "Shirts and cotes of male." Reporting to the Virginia Company that by the generous authority of the king these contributions were ready for shipment, the Commissioner of Ordinance added that the armor was "not only old and much decayed but with their age growne also altogether unfit and of no use for moderne service."[3]

Scattered through the filling of the same pit that contained our anomalous tasset were our first jack plates, 28 of them. Other pits and layers would raise the total to 82, although as many as 1,164 were needed for a complete jack coat (Fig. 13–5). Careful cleaning and X-ray studies of the plates supported the 1575 evidence that old armor was cut up to make jacks. According to the Tower of London's keeper of armor, one of our plates had started life in the fifteenth century as a brigandine. Several more retained the shanks of brass rivets, indicating that they had once been part of more elaborate armor. The Virginia muster of 1624 to 1625 showed that in Martin's Hundred, William Harwood then possessed "Armours 8; Coats of Male, 10; Coats of Steele, 3."[4] Two other residents had either a "Coate of Steele" or a "Coat of Plate,"[5] but whether these were brigandines or jacks—or one of each—we have no way of knowing.

Each of our sites had given us artifacts different from those found on any other, and Site H was no exception, being unique in yielding jack plates and the unparalleled tasset. It also provided an iron tool that screwed to the end of a musketeer's ramrod and was used to clean scale from inside his gun's barrel—which was why, in the seventeenth century, a ramrod was called a scourer or scouring stick. Although

13–3. An incomplete tassett found at Site H. Three rivets close to the top anchored buckles used in attaching it to the breastplate. Ca. 1620–1622.

contemporary engravings of this tool survive, the Tower of London's firearms expert, Deputy Master of the Armouries Howard Blackmore, could not direct me to an original scourer—other than the one we had found (Fig. 13–6). The more mundane the object, the less likely it is to survive. When scourers were damaged, or when cleaner-burning gunpowder rendered them obsolete, they were thrown away in Virginia just as they were tossed out of the armories at the Tower of London.

Some of the objects from Site H quite clearly had not been ready to be thrown out —like a group of ten small buttons, each decorated in relief with a Tudor rose. Most of the buttons surviving from the early seventeenth century are of brass, silver, or gold; these are of an iron-nickel alloy with brass wire loops pressed into their backs when the metal was still molten. Dr. Jan Baart, archaeologist for the city of Amsterdam, had published an important paper on buttons found there, among them several examples rather similar to ours. Like me, he considered them to come from men's doublets.[6] Dr. Baart's buttons, however, are a little larger than ours, and it was the small size of the

13–4. An Elizabethan jackcoat in the Tower of London collection.

13–5. Examples of iron jack plates from Site H. The top left example retains the stub of a brass rivet, evidence that the plate had been cut out of old plate armor. Discarded ca. 1619–1622.

271

latter that prompted a London costume expert to state that in her opinion ours are so small that they probably come from a woman's dress.

The buttons were by no means our only problem artifacts; a relatively ordinary ax added its own small mystery. Marked with the initials of its maker (P.P.), the blade was found in a pit at one edge of the site, while the poll (the socket into which the handle fitted) turned up in another pit thirty yards away. Clearly, therefore, both pits must have been open at the same time, but that provides no explanation for two pieces of the same ax being discarded into holes at opposite ends of the site—unless a perverse settler simply wanted to make life difficult for future archaeologists.

Artifacts that did have a clear message for us were three incomplete lead bale seals, each bearing either the now familiar Gothic A or the pine-cone emblem of Augsburg, seals identical to the five we had found in the potter's pond in Wolstenholme Towne's Company Compound (see Fig. 10–3). This evident link between the two sites prompted us to call Site H the Wolstenholme Suburb.

Just as no two sites yielded exactly the same range of artifacts, so no two offered identical patterns of holes in the ground. Site A had been relatively simple to interpret, its buildings defined by large and uniformly spaced post-holes, and its many fences equally clearly delineated. Site B, on the other hand, was singularly short of post-holes, yet those we did find outlined an easily recognizable house. The various elements of Wolstenholme Towne—note how easily one

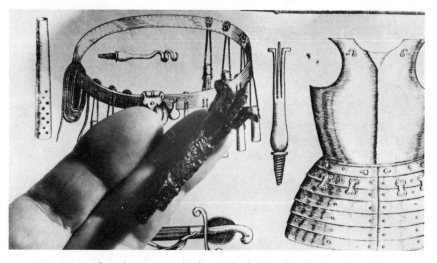

13–6. A scourer for cleaning scale from the bore of a musket barrel, seen here against a contemporary engraving of a musketeer's equipment. Found at Site H and discarded ca. 1620–1622.

sheds the qualifiers—though dramatically different from each other, were readily readable. Even the disappointing Site D was unequivocal in its post-hole pattern, unique and uninterpretable though it was. Our suburb, on the other hand, differed from all of them. It provided the greatest concentration of post-holes we had encountered anywhere. Although we could find no definable lines cutting through one another to suggest a changing sequence of construction, every attempt to fit them into a single scheme of house- and fence-building left us with too many unexplained, leftover holes. The best we could make of the puzzle was a central dwelling measuring 12 by 26 feet within a basically triangular fence or palisade, most of whose post-holes were 12 feet apart (Fig. 13–7).

Although the width of the house matched the only documentary reference to dwelling sizes in Martin's Hundred, namely the 12-by-14-foot house ordered to be built for Sir Lawrence Hyde's servant Richard Chelsey,[7] it had no parallel among any of the structures we had found on our sites, all of whose widths measured no less than 15 feet. The 12-foot spacing for the fencing posts was equally anomalous. Two of the corners terminated in boxlike projections, one of them looking very much like the watchtower at the fort. Both projecting elements suggested that they had been built as flankers to provide musket fire along the outsides of the enclosure, and we therefore had to conclude that the barrier defined by the fencing posts had been a protective palisade and not a post-and-rail fence. On the other hand, our experience at the fort and Company Compound had been that palisade posts were set no more than 9 feet apart, while the Duke of Ormond's Irish contract called for them to be on 7-foot centers; ours, however, were 12 feet from post to post. The only reasonable explanation seemed to be that these palings were shorter and therefore lighter than those at our other sites or around the Irish villages. There being no evidence of a parapet step behind the Site H fence, we could hesitantly conclude that the palisade would have been short enough for a 5 foot, 6 inch settler to fire over the top. If that was true, the two flankers probably were of comparable height and served, not as observation towers, but merely as projections from which to provide enfilade fire along the outside of the low palisade.

Any attempt to reconstruct the appearance of an archaeological site before it *became* an archaeological site is inextricably linked to the question of who built, lived, and worked there. In the absence of documents, we must seek answers from the artifacts that the people left behind—and from their bones.

The alleged "hunting blind" that had brought us to Site H

proved not to be that at all, but rather a multiple grave—the first to be found on a seventeenth-century site in Virginia. It was not hard to see how the brown stains found in 1971 could have been mistaken for rotted tree branches; in reality, however, they were the remains of four people. At first I could make little of what we were seeing. It is not every day that you encounter a skeleton with what appears to be its feet tucked into the back of its neck. It took me a while to realize that the feet belonged to somebody else.

Although half the contents of the grave had not survived the 1971 survey, photographs and careful sketches made at that time enabled us to reconstruct what was now missing. Two of the people had been put into the grave with their heads toward the river, while the others were laid between them with their heads at the landward end, explaining why Number One had his feet behind the head of Number Two. I have used the male pronoun, not because the bones had anything to tell us about sex, age, or race (they were too decayed to do that), but because slender traces of clothing pointed to Number One being a male and probably of the laboring class. Around his right foot I could see a thin, dark line in the soil, suggesting that this might be the remains of a leather shoe. Knowing that the bones could

13–7. Seen from above, Site H has the look of a model. The four post-holes for a flanker are visible in the left foreground. Three kneeling figures in the middle distance mark corners of the dwelling, while another kneeling excavator at the right works on a female skeleton. The woman known as Granny still lies in her pit at the end of the long tree shadow in the left background.

never tell us whether these people were colonists or Indians, I hoped that the shoe might provide the answer. The heels of colonial shoes were built up from several layers of leather and so should leave a thicker black stain than the soles or uppers. Indian moccasins, on the other hand, had no separately built heel and so would leave a sole-line of uniform thickness. Faced with the unsympathetic weather and the flooding that seemed to bedevil us whenever we were in the midst of a delicate task, I decided that the feet should be excavated in the laboratory rather than in the ground. To that end, we again used the plaster mushroom technique I had employed to lift the second helmet and the skull of the "massacre victim," and again the lifting process went without a hitch.

I explained to conservator Gary McQuillen what we were looking for, and hoped that if the shoe was of European construction he might be able to salvage some of the fibers of the leather heel. After paring away the clay around the feet down to within half a centimeter of the dark stains, tiny spots of rust began to appear around the sole of the right foot. These were totally unexpected. I had excavated many medieval and Tudor shoes in England, all of them held together with cobbler's thread and wooden pegs—but no nails. As Gary continued to narrow the distance between the clay and the dark line around the feet, he took a series of X-ray pictures, and each more clearly than the last showed a pattern of half-inch nails clustered at the heel and outlining the rest of the right foot (Fig. 13–8).

I thought at first that they might be hobnails reinforcing the sole of a boot, but the heads were too small, and the nails—being confined to the sole or welt—evidently were part of the shoe's construction. Puzzled though we were, two facts had emerged: The shoe was not Indian, and there was only one. When Gary reached the left foot, the X-rays showed nothing, and there was no surrounding black stain. The man or boy had gone to his grave inadequately shod.

The clue to the shoe's strange construction was to be found in a manuscript in the British Museum's Harleian Collection. Among notes and sketches assembled by the seventeenth-century heraldic painter and genealogist Randle Holme for his book *The Academy of Armory* are several drawings of footwear. One of them shows what can only be interpreted as a thick wooden sole attached to a leather upper (presumably by nails), and there described as "a clogg or countrey mans shooe."[8] I could not doubt that this was what we had found, or that our man had been carried to his grave with so little ceremony that the other clog had fallen off en route.

The "countryman's" companion, skeleton Number Two, also

exhibited traces of leather, this time at the waist and presumably the remains of a belt, though no buckle was found. The assumption that all four people were buried clothed prompted me to consider more carefully the placement of the two musket balls as recorded in Bill Kelso's 1971 notes. Neither ball appeared to have been fired, and as they had been found side by side, we concluded that no one had been shot. Although the "countryman" was represented only by his legs (the faint traces of his head and torso having been destroyed by the previous digging), it was evident that the bullets had been at his waist, probably hung from it in some kind of bag or pouch.

This, then, was the sum of the evidence before us: Four people, one of them a European male of the laboring class, and at least two buried still-dressed in a communal grave, but a grave that had been carefully and relatively deeply dug, and contrasting with the suggestion of haste in the actual interment. It all pointed to someone's desire to handle the corpses as little as possible while still affording them decent burial; in short, it pointed to death by contagious disease rather than at the hands of Indians. Documentary support for this was provided by a contemporary illustration of the Great Plague of London in 1665, showing cartloads of dead beside a mass grave in which the corpses were laid head to toe.[9] The remaining question was the date at which our "plague" occurred, and an answer to that was dependent

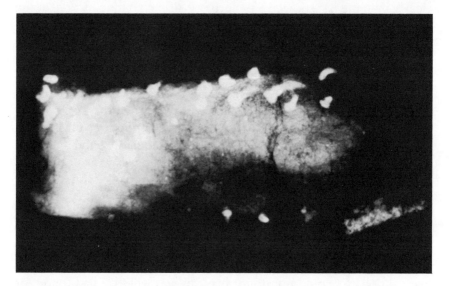

13–8. An X-rayed foot from the multiple grave on Site H, showing the pattern of nails indicating that the man had been buried wearing a workshoe having a leather upper and a wooden sole. Date of interment ca. 1619–1622.

on our establishing the date brackets for Site H as a whole. The remains of burned posts in the post-holes for the house indicated that it had been destroyed by fire; but tempting though it was to blame that on the Indians, we had to remember that accidental blazes were commonplace when houses were roofed with thatch and partitioned with highly combustible Indian mats. Indeed, in 1609, the whole of Jamestown had been gutted by one accidentally ignited dwelling. If, however, Site H had been razed by the Indians—and since we had found no evidence of rebuilding after the fire—logic would put the deaths of our contagion victims prior to March 1622, and before the great outbreak in the winter of 1622–23 that carried off more people than the Indians had killed.

Despite finding numerous graves on Site A, the infant burial on Site B, and sixteen more interments on Site C (Wolstenholme), our lasting impression of those sites was of life and vigorous activity. Site H spoke to us only of death. Three more skeletons remained to be found, all of them the bones of adult women, all lying outside the paled enclosure. The first was identified by Larry Angel as being about twenty years old, and was found in a grave so shallow that it cut only three to four inches into the clay subsoil. To properly cover her body, the back-filled loam would almost certainly have been mounded above the land surface. Although the bones gave no hint as to how she had died, the shallowness of the ground spoke of burial in haste. So, too, did the second grave. Located on the sloping edge of the ravine, this one apparently had paid the price for its lack of depth. Only the bones of the legs survived, and we deduced that the rest of the body had been uncovered and carried off by animals. Indeed, three articulated vertebrae, found in a ditch a few feet away, may have come from this skeleton.

Few physical anthropologists will identify the sex of a skeleton on the evidence of leg bones alone, and Larry Angel could say only that the bones were sufficiently robust to have been of either sex. It was the artifacts that told the tale.

Here was another feature unique to Site H. On all the other sites the only artifacts found in graves were either pins and points used to secure shrouds or headcloths, or were inadvertently shoveled into the filling—like the pipes and fish hook in the grave of Wolstenholme Towne's "massacre victim." In the suburb, however, we first had the clog and musket balls to identify a man, and now a key and a thimble to speak for a woman (Fig. 13–9). The thimble lay close to the top of the left femur, while the key was found 7 1/2 inches lower and between the legs. X-ray pictures showed that the badly rusted key had possessed a complicated web, indicating that it came from a better-than-average lock, perhaps from a casket or spice cupboard.

The thimble was as close to being a symbol of female domesticity as any archaeologist can hope to find, and its presence in the grave alongside the right leg of the skeleton is readily explained. Housewives and maidservants often carried such things in a small, cloth bag called a pocket, suspended from a girdle at their waists. Thus, for example, in William Congreve's play *The Way of the World* (1700), Lady Wishfort chided her maid Peg for having brought her a bottle of wine, but only a china cup out of which to drink it, saying: "Dost thou take me for a fairy, to drink out of an acorn? Why didst thou not bring thy thim-

13–9. An iron key and a brass thimble from a grave at Site H. Ca. 1622.

ble? Hast thou ne'er a brass thimble clinking in thy pocket . . . ?"[10] Thus, the finding of a thimble would by itself suggest that the legs were those of a woman, be she maid or mistress. Add the clue of the key, and we have responsibility, and that points to a housekeeper or a housewife. Either could be expected to keep the key to the household's valuables on a string hanging from her waist. In his famous painting *The Peasant Dance* (1568), the Flemish artist Pieter Bruegel shows a woman being towed along behind her cavorting partner, a key such as ours hanging from a string attached to her purse or pocket, both on a cord reaching to within a foot of the ground.[11]

If my interpretation was correct, neither the hanging key nor the pocketed thimble could have remained with the corpse unless the woman went clothed into her grave. Later, as the fabric rotted, the key would have dropped between her legs. A shallow grave and a clothed occupant pointed to a hasty burial—and there was more. The left femur, though protected by a shallow wall of clay and safe from disturbance by later plowing, was broken about four inches from the top in a remarkably clean break that had moved the shaft laterally more than half an inch. The two fragments had also parted by about the same amount. We lifted the bone in another of our plaster mushrooms and took it to the laboratory in the hope that our pathologist and orthopedic friends would be able to determine whether this was a pre- or postmortem fracture. One said it was consistent with a heavy blow from a blunt instrument; but two said it was not. Few people died quickly from broken legs, and so, either way, we had to assume that the "key lady" had suffered other injuries. Once again we turned to the obvious culprits, and once again Audrey urged caution and posed her now familiar run-over-by-a-cart scenario. I, in turn, argued that by her own reckoning we had documentation for the slaughter of at least fifty-eight settlers in 1622, but none to prove that Martin's Hundred was a hotbed of dangerous drivers.

Neither of the barely buried women lay in coffins; indeed, if they had, my assumption that they had been interred in haste would have dissolved like ice cream in the Carter's Grove sun—rather like my carefully constructed theory of the A-roofed or gable-lidded coffin was threatening to do. After the fiasco of the 1979 vault opening at Clifton I had placed a letter in the correspondence pages of the magazine *Country Life* explaining what we were looking for and hoping that someone who owned a family vault would write to say that he or she had had an appropriately boxed ancestor. But nobody did. At the suggestion of the Bishop of London I wrote to the Council for Places of Worship in the hope that an organization devoted to ecclesiastical architecture would also have a list of Tudor and Stuart vaults. It did not; but it passed the inquiry on to an authority on church history, whose response can best be described as blunt: "I can tell you at once that there is no hope of Mr. Hume finding an A-lidded coffin in any vault in England."[12]

Gable-lidded coffins had never existed in England. My illustrations could not show plague victims being prepared for burial in coffins of any sort, for none was used. Those pictures that might seem to show gable-lidded coffins really showed frames called "herses" used to cover flat-topped coffins and intended to enable the pall to be well displayed. Furthermore, said the ecclesiastical scholar, neither the lower nor middle classes of the sixteenth century were buried in coffins. In short, I was wrong on every count, though he did admit that he had no explanation for the row of large nails down the centers of the skeletons that had led me to develop the gable-lidded coffin thesis. Upon reexamining my pictorial evidence, and in the light of documentary proof that by 1614 middle- to lower-class people were being coffined, I came to the conclusion that the ecclesiastical expert's torpedo was unarmed. He had cited not a single document to support his negative assessment. Nevertheless, even missiles without explosives can do damage, and by having made my research efforts sound ill-conceived and frivolous, I knew that I could expect no further help from the Council for Places of Worship, and that without it, hopes of finding a clergyman willing to open his vaults for us were rendered more slender. I was not yet completely out of business, however. In the course of her historical research, Audrey had discovered that two members of the Sackville family had been buried in the early seventeenth century, and that the Sackville family vault in the little Sussex village of Withyham was designed to house its occupants on shelves, meaning that the coffins were not stacked as they normally would be if they were flat-lidded. The present Lord Sackville agreed to allow the vault to be opened when I made my annual visit to England in September 1980.

It is difficult to look at any skeleton without asking: Who were you? What did you look like? Would we have liked each other? I am well aware that many of my colleagues would consider such questions unprofessional and hopelessly steeped in Victorian romanticism. It will come as no surprise for them to be told that I do not agree. Having been disappointed by the extent to which a preliminary artist's concept of the Company Compound's "massacre victim" differed from Larry Angel's North European interpretation, I was delighted when, as a result of the summer's publicity, we received an unexpected offer to make a scientifically arrived-at reconstruction of the head. It came from Betty Pat Gatliff, a well-known and widely respected medical illustrator then on the staff of the Federal Aviation Administration's Civil Aeromedical Institute at Oklahoma City. Working in close collaboration with Dr. Clyde C. Snow, chief of the Institute's physical anthropology unit, she had developed a technique that combines the skills of the sculptress with pathological knowledge to reconstruct in clay the facial features that once covered a skull.

Used primarily as an aid to the identification of belatedly discovered homicide victims, the technique has proven itself in the field. Of the more than forty reconstructions made between 1967 and 1979, 70 percent of the victims had been recognized by relatives or witnesses. That impressive batting average, plus the intriguing prospect of applying this new development in forensic anthropology to what could claim to be European America's oldest known homicide victim, made Betty Pat Gatliff's offer irresistible. On October 22, she arrived in Williamsburg ready not only to make the reconstruction but also to demonstrate how it was done, for the benefit of our future film and television audiences.

All Betty Pat's previous reconstructions had been built over the victim's actual skull (with the exception of her work for the U.S. House of Representatives Select Committee on Assassinations when she rebuilt the features of President Kennedy using another skull adapted to conform to his measurements); but in our case we could not risk any pressure being applied to the "massacre victim's" extremely fragile remains. First, therefore, a cast accurate to the millimeter had to be made, and it was on this that she worked. Her technique's scientific base was by no means new; it rested on tissue measurements taken from the faces of forty-five male and eight female cadavers recorded in Austria and published as long ago as 1898. As Betty Pat was quick to point out, the sample was too small, and is immediately open to criticism when applied to Mongoloid and Negroid skulls. But since we were presenting her with a Caucasian male, we could be confident that the forty-five Austrians were sufficient for our needs.

Starting at the hair line and ending at the heel of the mandible, Betty Pat began by gluing pieces of pencil eraser, cut to match the average tissue measurements, to each of twenty-six locations. With those secured, she next connected them with a spiderweb network of modeling clay strips (Fig. 13–10). That done, and using other standard measurements based on such details as the orbit of the eye, the barrel of the mouth, and the width of the nasal opening, she filled in the gaps using her sculptor's skills to make the features come alive.

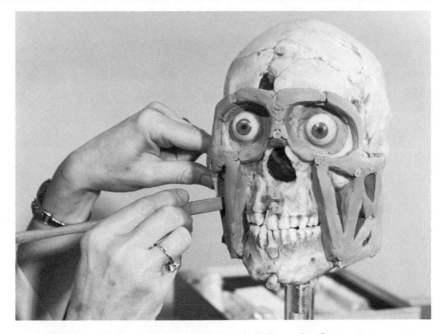

13–10. Putting "flesh" over a cast of the skull from the Company Compound grave. Using numbered rubber depth markers, Betty Pat Gatliff reconstructs average tissue thickness in modelling clay.

In her forensic work, Betty Pat sometimes had surviving hairs to provide clues to its color and length, and so for the purposes of police recognition photographs she would add an appropriate wig. If the remains were those of a middle-aged or elderly person, she would also take pictures of the face with and without glasses. But, as she explained to us at the end of her demonstration, as far as the tissue-related features are concerned, "I only do what the skull tells me to do, and no more."

That was all we expected of her; indeed, had she gone one whit further, we immediately would have had reason to doubt the validity of the end product (Fig. 13–11). At the same time, however, Betty Pat's very proper refusal to use her imagination left us with a sense of frustration. She had rebuilt our "massacre victim's" face with all its natural proportions skillfully rendered—on the evidence of tissue-thickness averages. Inevitably, therefore, we would wind up with an *average* face, perhaps distinctive enough for the victim's mother or even his murderer to recognize, but still the face of a mannequin untouched by life.

If our man had spent most of his adult years working the land, marching with armies in Ireland or the Netherlands, or sailing the high seas, his face would have been weatherbeaten. He almost certainly would have been bearded, but whether he kept that beard neatly trimmed like that of a gentleman, or just scissored it now and then to get rid of the knots, we can never know. His features could have grown bloated with drink, been pitted by smallpox, or wasted away through starvation and dysentery. A skull provides none of that information, yet without it we see no more than the shadow of the man.

There being no relatives to come forward crying "That's my boy!", critics may question the purpose of attempting the reconstruction. Was it, in reality, a mere exercise in morbid curiosity?

I would have to answer: curiosity, yes; morbid, no. The rationale for all archaeology is curiosity. In the eighteenth century, to be described as a "curious gentleman" was considered a compliment. The adjective did not imply that he might have two heads, but rather that he was a person possessing a scholarly and inquiring mind. It was in that spirit of curiosity that we wanted to see for ourselves whether or not we agreed with Larry Angel in his interpretation of the skull as being the bone behind the face of a northern European. By the time Betty Pat was through, I had no doubts on that score; the finished features would have looked good on a Viking. I had another less scholarly motive for being delighted to accept Betty Pat's help: for popular exhibition purposes I wanted a visual interpretation of the archaeologist's goal—that of trying to breathe life into the past by putting flesh on its bones.

Three weeks after the sculpture was completed, in England the eccentricities of the late Frederick Chapman brought his wife and her lover into the dock at St. Albans Crown Court charged with his murder. On November 27, *The Daily Telegraph* ran the headline LOVERS KILLED DOPED HUSBAND WITH SHOVEL, thus bringing the Chapman case into the orbit of our interest. If we could find no American forensic evidence to support my belief that our "massacre victim" had been felled with the corner of a spade, perhaps the pathologist's report of this British murder would help. Remembering the old English adage about calling a spade a spade and not a bleeding

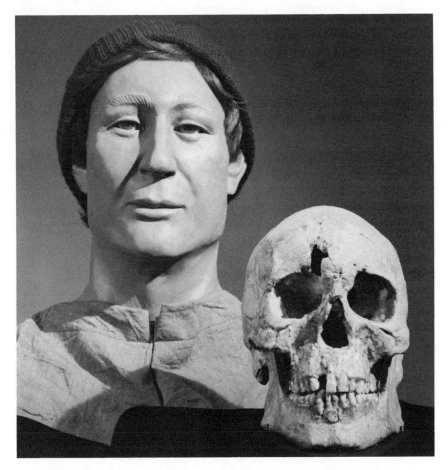

13-11. The Company Compound's "massacre" victim's restored skull, and beside it Betty Pat Gatliff's reconstruction of his features.

shovel, I knew that a blow from a flat-bladed spade would make a short, sharp cut, but that a shovel's turned up edge would produce broad, crushing damage. The question, therefore, was whether the court and the newspaper reporters were making the same distinction. Apparently not; for on December 1, the *Telegraph* announced, "Wife admits killing sleeping husband with garden spade." When shown photographs of the gash in our man's skull, Dr. P. G. Jerreat, the pathologist who performed the Chapman autopsy, wrote that he considered the damage to be "perfectly consistent with the corner of a spade."[13] At the same time, he noted that the spade blows that killed Frederick Chapman were to the side of the head and not to the brow, and that their damage had been somewhat obscured by the victim's having been thrown onto the motorway.

In trying to reconstruct the circumstances of our "massacre victim's" death and burial, I had been worrying not only about the kind of weapon that had been used, but also how the body could have been moved from the murder scene to his grave without his head falling apart—unless he lay unburied sufficiently long for the blood to congeal. The Chapman case showed that my concern was well founded. In her statement to the police, Mrs. Chapman had admitted that she struck her husband twice with the spade and then pulled a plastic bag over his head to catch the blood and stifle him if he was not already dead.[14] In our case, Virginia State Medical Examiner Dr. David Wiecking had said that although the single, sharp blow to the forehead would have rendered the victim insensible, he doubted whether it would have caused immediate death.

I recall chiding myself for being so ungrateful as to be pleased that on December 5, 1979, Margaret Chapman and Peter West, her accomplice, were sentenced to life imprisonment. Without their help we never would have found Dr. Jerreat.

In spite of the wealth of artifacts coming from our continuing work on Site H, the Wolstenholme Suburb, its dead were providing both its most substantive clues and its most puzzling enigmas. That a building within the compound had burned, we had no doubt. Ashes and scraps of red-baked daub came from several of the post molds, one of them a classic of the genre. There the post had slowly consumed itself, filling the mold with tightly compacted ash while scorching the clay under and around it to a bright orange. Destruction by fire was not in itself evidence of an Indian attack. The strongest evidence that our fire was no accident was found northwest of the impaled area, where, in a large rubbish pit, lay what at first appeared to be an isolated, yet articulated, human left leg.

I remembered the graphic, survivors' description of the Indians returning after the massacre "and mangling the dead carkasses into many pieces, and carrying some parts away in derision, with base and bruitish triumph."[15] Was our leg such a trophy? We knew that the Indians of Florida were attracted to legs, and remembered the Theodore de Bry engraving based on a lost drawing, that showed how the dismembering was done.[16] There, however, the cutting was performed at mid-thigh. Ours was different, the bone being intact almost to the pelvis—or so it seemed. A little more thought rendered the trophy theory less convincing, for no souvenir-happy Indian would have gone to all that trouble and then have left his prize behind. The real explanation lay deeper in the pit, where foreman Nate Smith and excavator Dennis Pogue found the rest of the body. The cadaver was lying on its side and had settled into the wet, clay silt leaving its left leg higher than the rest of the skeleton. It proved to be that of a woman who had lost all her lower molars, and although we knew that such tooth loss is not necessarily evidence of advanced age, we called her Granny. Larry Angel later put her age at about forty, and found her pelvis too decayed to tell whether or not she had borne children. But Granny we had called her, and Granny she remained. She lay on her right side, her left arm across her chest and its hand clenched, her right hand up to her head, and her legs parted due to the right having settled deeper into the mud than the left (Fig. 13–12). This, clearly, had been no way to treat a lady.

I at first supposed that she had been thrown into the pit, possibly after being killed in the 1622 uprising; but that ignored the vitiating evidence of the other two women, whom we also believed to be massacre victims, but whose bodies had been properly, if shallowly buried. If returning survivors had returned to dig graves for two, why not for three?

Although artifact officer William Myzk did a remarkable job of casing the skeleton in plaster mushrooms so that the original placement of the bones could be retained for laboratory study, neither we nor Larry Angel could spot any obvious evidence of foul play. The skull proved to be in far worse shape than that of the man from the Company Compound. It was surprisingly small, very square at the back, and extremely thin and fragile, so delicate, in fact, that it was not until some weeks after Larry's visit that conservator McQuillen was able to piece it partially together. The job took longer than expected, owing to our finding that a narrow, iron band extended from a point above the left ear, down around the nape of the neck, up over the right ear, and finally down to a blob of pewter or lead close to the heel of the right mandible. I first suggested that it might have been some kind of surgical strap to secure a broken jaw, but X-ray pictures gave no credence to that idea (Fig. 13–13). The iron was`so badly decayed that the pictures even failed to show how the strap was twisted or folded over the right ear, something difficult to

13–12. Crew foreman Nathaniel Smith gets Granny ready for photography.

do to a flat, spring-like piece of metal. Although the right end was lying flat against the skull, the left end (which we had first seen in the field and had thought to be an unrelated nail) was projecting out from the head at a seemingly crazy angle. Since Granny was lying on her right side, the bending had occurred before she was thrown into the pit.

My failure to correctly identify the band's purpose resulted from my ignorance of ladies' hairdressing in the period 1590 to 1615—or in any other, for that matter. Costume authorities C. Willett and Phillis Cunnington were better educated, and wrote that in the late Elizabethan and early Stuart periods, women wore their hair "brushed up high from the forehead and temples over a pad called a 'roll,' or over an arched wire support producing a knife-edge curve [whose] height decreased towards 1608 [when] the roll pads became more usual."[17] So early a terminal date was not without exceptions, however. As late as May 1617, Lady Anne Clifford, wife of Richard Sackville, third Earl of Dorset, wrote in her diary: "The 12th I began to dress my head with a roll without wire."[18] The Countess was then twenty-seven, several years younger than Granny and more closely in touch with changing taste in English fashions. I was convinced, nevertheless, that the wife of one of England's most prominent men and the lost lady of Wolstenholme Towne had a hair roll in common (Fig. 13–14). Tiny traces of brass wire pins showed up between the iron band and the back of Granny's head, suggesting that they had helped secure fabric wrapped around a springy, metal core.

Many archaeologists seem to have an almost universal dislike for writing things down, and efforts to get them to keep a daily record of their thinking and half-formed conclusions are seen as an eccentricity to be humored to a degree short of actual lucubration. For my part, however, "putting it on paper" not only helps me to hang onto useful thoughts that might otherwise slip away, but also to anatomize conclusions in search of their flaws. Thus, while Granny's skull still nestled in its plaster mushroom, I wrote "There is no likelihood that our lady had been scalped." After all, I reasoned, if she was still wearing her hair roll, she must also have kept her hair. No sooner did I see that conclusion staring back at me from the typewriter than I knew it to be wrong.

Granny's iron-cored hair roll had originally framed the crown of her head from ear to ear, and the only way that it could have remained in its correct position in front of the right ear, while being bent back away from the left, was by force. I recalled, too, that the roll had been wrenched back from the same brow region that bore the supposed scalping scar on the skull of our Wolstenholme Towne "massacre victim." If a souvenir-hunting Indian had treated Granny in the same way, he would quickly have found progress arrested by the roll. If he intended to take only a scalp lock rather than the entire head of hair, he might very well have wrenched the encumbrance out of the way, leaving it still gripped by the hair at the right side. What we needed was corroborating evidence in the form of a scalping scar along the left brow line; but for the time being Granny was lying on it.

While all this remained unresolved, I succumbed to the flu germ that methodically had been working its way through our staff, and so retired to bed. Twice I awoke to find myself in a position almost identical to that assumed by Granny in her pit. Lying on my right side, my right hand was up by my head while my left arm crossed my chest and lay somewhat extended, the hand's fingers bent under and folded into the palm—the same hand position which, in Granny's case, I had defined as "clenched," and attributed either to rigor mortis or to pain. Although in my sick bed I was feeling tiresomely sorry for myself, I could not be said to be either in pain or in rigor mortis. My fingers were bent for the very simple reason that my hand was relaxed and yet braced enough to prevent me from rolling on my face, which I would have done had not the hand and arm served as a prop. I was convinced that Granny's left arm had assumed the same position while she still lived. Her right arm, too, was in a lifelike, albeit sleeping position; indeed, her entire posture was akin to that of a "sleeping"

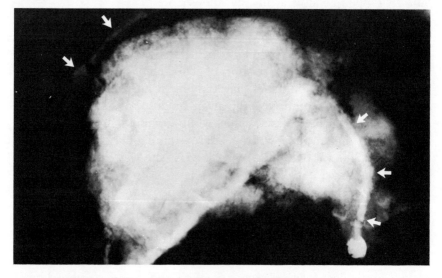

13–13. An X-ray of Granny's skull showing the flat iron wire of her hair roll.

model in a well-known magazine advertisement for mattresses. Was it possible that Granny had hidden in the hole and had died there of exposure?

The idea seemed to have little to commend it. My sick-bed experiments to determine how I would lie were I freezing to death led me to conclude that my arms would have ended up wrapped tightly round my chest. Instead, Granny's posture seemed to be one of contented relaxation. I would later discover that my knowledge of how to freeze to death was no better than my familiarity with Elizabethan ladies' hair styles. Our pathologist consultant, Marcella Fierro, explained that in the last hours before death, exposure victims often pass into a state of hallucinatory well-being and warmth, and have been known to shed clothing in the belief that they were too hot. Marcella therefore concluded that Granny could indeed have died of exposure.

That possibility gained more credence when Dr. Samuel V. Dunkell, Director of the Insomnia Clinic at the New York Hospital's Payne Whitney Institute, examined photographs of Granny's *in situ* bones. "The position of the skeleton closely resembles the most com-

mon sleep position," he wrote. "In this side position the trunk is somewhat curved to conserve heat and protect the vital internal organs. The arms are flexed moderately and extended away from the body, and the knees are drawn up slightly." Dr. Dunkell characterized people who sleep in this semi-fetal posture as "middle of the roaders who go along with the opinions and intermediate positions of their group culture." When I countered that I could interpret Granny's elaborate if old-fashioned hair style as evidence of a stubborn insistence on maintaining the standards of her youth, Dr. Dunkell disagreed. He insisted that "this personality type is norm seek-

13–14. A Flemish engraving by Crispin van de Passe (ca. 1610) showing the use of a hair roll and above it a second ornamental wire, a device more elaborate than that worn by Granny, but supporting a comparable hair style.

ing" and rather than seeing Granny's refusal to let her hair down as an act of defiance, he interpreted it as "seeking to hang on to a known structure in an uncertain world."[19]

Marcella Fierro had pointed out that exposure deaths are often related to alcohol poisoning, but despite there being more broken bottle glass in the pits around our suburb than we had found on most of the Martin's Hundred sites, I was reluctant to dismiss Granny as an amiable drunk who couldn't make it home. I was equally unwilling to believe that her arms and legs had accidentally assumed their sleeping posture when she was thrown into the hole. I was convinced either that she had died there, or that her limbs were in that position when she died elsewhere, and were locked in rigor mortis at the time she was dumped into the pit. That still left the unanswered questions: Why, and by whom?

If we accepted the rigor mortis theory, that condition imposed relatively narrow time brackets for Granny's unceremonious interment. Beginning about six hours after death and continuing for around forty-eight more, the muscular stiffening dictated that she had to have been tossed into the pit within three days of death. That factor brought us back to another still open question: Why were the other two women placed in graves while this one was thrown into a hole? Why, too, if Granny was in an awkward, rigor mortis–arrested posture, were the other women able to be laid out to fit in narrow graves? If all three died on the same day and were found by returning survivors at the same time, then all three should have presented the burial party with similar problems to be solved in the same way.

The only explanation that did not pose as many questions as it answered was that Granny took herself into the pit and died there, out of sight of her neighbors, who expected to find her body inside the compound. When they could not find her, they assumed that she had either burned to death in the house or had been carried off by Indians, and so never thought to search beyond the fences. This scenario still was not problem-free. If Granny was the kind of woman to maintain standards and do her hair in her old-fashioned way while living on the edge of Western civilization, she should also have worn clothing of better-than-average quality—clothing that would have left buttons, hooks and eyes, even gold or silver threads, for us to find. Yet there was nothing. I remembered the rose-decorated buttons that archaeologist Nicholas Luccketti and his excavators had found scattered through the soil beside the burned house, buttons which a British costume expert had believed to come from a woman's dress, and I was tempted to reconstruct the circumstances of Granny's death in the following manner: On the morning of March 22, 1622, she was up, dressed, and her hair carefully done before the Indians struck. Her husband and any male servants were already out in the fields, too far away to help or to survive. Fleeing from the house Granny was caught, her dress stripped from her and her hair roll wrenched back as an Indian hacked at her scalp. Left for dead, and amid the confusion and the smoke from her burning home, Granny crawled away through the palisade gate that led to the nearby ravine. Perhaps she intended to escape down it to the beach and to a boat, but changed her mind when she found that other Indians were already at the river's edge, cutting off her escape. Instead, she huddled down in the open pit, hoping to join up with survivors from neighboring farms after the Indians had had their fun and gone home; but shock, loss of blood, and a cold March night were too much for her. And there she died. Spring rains caused silt from the pit's side to slide over her, and before long, Virginia's fast-growing weeds mantled the hole. Months later, when a clean-up squad swept building debris into the pit, nobody could have guessed that Granny was there.

Such a reconstruction is the stuff of melodrama—and suspect for that reason. We were never able to prove that Granny had been scalped. When the left side of her skull was freed from its plaster bed, we found it to be in such poor condition that no shallow cuts could have survived. Then, too, the ten buttons considered to come from a woman's dress were later paralleled on a man's doublet. That contradictory evidence came to us from Dutch button expert Dr. Jan Baart. Furthermore, he did not see our buttons as coming from a quality garment. Once again we were faced with the problem of assessing quality and taste at a distance of three and a half centuries. If I was wrong about the buttons, perhaps I was also in error in interpreting Granny's hair roll as evidence of high social status. Perhaps the woman with the key and the thimble was really the mistress of Site H.

Even after robbing Granny of her place at the foot of the table, we were still left with three women in that household, two of them buried in haste and one dead under mysterious circumstances. We knew that the house burned, and there is no denying that Martin's Hundred lost half its population to the Indians. Thus, it remains reasonable, and indeed mandatory, that we should try to identify this three-woman household from among the massacre's listed dead. Out of the seventy-eight "Persons slaine at Martins-Hundred some seaven miles from James-Citie," only two groups seem to be possible candidates, the households of Thomas Boise and Richard Staples. The list reads as follows:

> Master Tho: Boise, & Mistris
> Boise his wife, & a sucking Childe.
> 4 of his men.
> A Maide.
> 2 Children.
> Nathanael Jefferies wife.
> Margaret Davies.
> Richard Staples, his wife, and Childe.
> 2 Maides.
> 6 Men and Boyes.[20]

The problem here is to determine where the dead from one household end and those of another begin. If Thomas Boise's list ends with "4 of his men," the "Maide" belonged to someone else. Then, too, if Nathanael Jefferies's wife was killed in her husband's house (as seems likely), the Boise household did not lose three women. To add to the possible permutations, we know that settlers often stayed overnight in each others' houses, and in the grisly aftermath of the massacre might well have been buried where they were found—yet listed under their own households. Richard Staples lost his wife and two maids (along with his own life)—the only man in the list with whom three women are unequivocally associated. But even here we have problems. The documentary evidence, inconclusive though it is, shows that Staples owned land at the north end of Martin's Hundred, and if he lived there, his family could not have died five miles away in our Wolstenholme Towne suburb. Then, too, there is the question of what was meant by "Maides."

The term could mean a serving girl or an unmarried woman of any age. In 1621, the ship *Tiger,* one of those carrying settlers to Martin's Hundred, had aboard "as many maids & yong weomen as will make upp the number of fiftie,"[21] sent over to provide wives for tenants. In that context, and as stated, "maids" might mean women who were no longer young—but still virgins. There is no knowing whether any of the fifty wound up in Martin's Hundred, though the *Marmaduke,* which sailed with twelve passengers for Martin's Hundred earlier in the year, is also recorded as carrying a dozen similarly described women. None too surprisingly, the quality of some of this human merchandise was disappointing, and in a long list of complaints against the Virginia Company treasurership of Sir Thomas Smythe (from which he resigned in 1620), he was accused of sending out "but few women & those corrupt." To this his spokesman gallantly countered that "He sent a great many & those of the best hee could gett & some such whose Husband since hath ben knighted & made Governo^r of Virg."[22]

Playing numbers games with the list of the massacre dead, and trying to equate that with the other scraps of information, leads only to chronic frustration. With sixteen women catalogued as killed in Martin's Hundred, identifying the bodies of three found on Site H should be relatively simple—until one remembers that in March 1623 William Harwood's servant, Richard Frethorne, wrote that the Indians were still holding fifteen hostages of unspecified sex. On April 1, Christopher Best (of whom nothing else is known) wrote that "There are none but women in Captivitie wth th'Indians for the men that they tooke they putt them to death."[23] If, as has been suggested, the fifteen people held by the Indians were from Martin's Hundred, and if those fifteen were women, it follows that out of the official tally of seventy-eight persons killed there in the massacre, all but one of the women were carried off—making the presence of three murdered women on one site hard to explain.

Archaeological reasoning is akin to trying to reassemble a watch that has lost half its parts. When you are through, it may look all right, but it still won't tick. Furthermore, if you do not fully understand the mechanism, there is always the chance of fitting the wrong cog in the wrong hole. In trying to reconstruct what happened and to whom on Site H, we had only to misread one clue to throw our reasoning hopelessly awry. Everything hinged on *three* women having died there in the massacre; but if one of the skeletons was that of a man, or if two of the women had died of sickness and not savagery, all bets would be off.

That Granny was a lady there could be no doubt, and Larry Angel was equally confident that one of the two shallow graves contained a female; but the "key lady" was represented only by legs whose bones were sufficiently robust to be of either sex. In this case, Larry bowed to the artifactual evidence and to the documentable fact that women carried keys on strings and thimbles in pockets—but so, perhaps, might a tailor.

The pit that came to be known as Granny's Grave had first been a repository for domestic ashes, ashes always tipped from the same position, so that the pile rose to a peak against the pit's wall—a gray arrow, pointing toward the gate in the compound through which I surmised Granny had escaped. Many small animal and fish bones were scattered through the ashes, which were taken back to the laboratory to be screened under running water. Among the artifacts recovered were tiny brass tacks, the hook from a hook-and-eye of the size used on women's clothes today, and part of a cob of Indian corn, the oldest example of a British colonial maize core yet known to us, and a reminder of the settlers' debt to the Indians in happier days. The ashes also gave up five L-shaped iron nails which turned out to be tenter-hooks, and came, as the name suggests, from a tenter, a wooden frame having sharp, angular hooks at each end over which newly woven fabric was stretched and dried (Fig. 13-15). As two of the hooks had

been so tempered in a fire that they had escaped oxidation in the ground, we could deduce that part, if not all, of a tenter had served as fuel in the kitchen fireplace. We could also conclude that someone versed in the weaving or fulling trade had lived in the Wolstenholme suburb. Thus the tenter-hooks (and a heavy iron thimble found elsewhere in the site) could be placed in evidence to argue that the leggy lady with the key and thimble—was a man.

Dating evidence for Granny's Grave came, as usual, from the broken tobacco pipes, most of whose bowl shapes and sizes matched examples which pipe expert Adrian Oswald placed in the first quarter of the seventeenth century. Although previous experience in Martin's Hundred had destroyed our faith in formulae

13-15. Tenter-hooks from Site H, discarded into Granny's pit prior to 1622.

for dating the pipes by their stem-hole diameters, Oswald's bowl-shape charts, that showed the smallest as the oldest, had still made sense. Now, however, from the kitchen ashes came fragments of three of the smallest pipe bowls I had ever seen. The type seemed to belong right at the head of Oswald's series, and into his rather broad time bracket of 1580–1620. Since Martin's Hundred was not settled until 1619, and since the three bowls were accompanied by eleven others of similar shape but conventional size, I deduced that these were not miraculously surviving antiques from Elizabeth's reign, but miniatures for people who took their tobacco in small puffs; in short: Pipes for children.

Recalling several references to children smoking, and Hendrick Terbrugghen's 1623 painting *Boy Lighting a Pipe,* [24] I wrote to Adrian Oswald seeking his reaction to my juvenile pipe-smoker thesis. In the meantime, we looked again at the list of massacre dead, this time for families with children. In addition to their own "sucking Childe" the Boise household had two, while Richard Staples's group included his own child and "6 Men and Boyes." This was not a particularly productive line of research, for there was no archaeological evidence that children had died in the massacre on Site H. It was almost a relief, therefore, to get Adrian Oswald's answer rejecting my pipes-for-kids theory. He agreed that the bowls were miniature versions of contemporary pipes, but they were made, he said, not for children but for women.

Back we came to Granny in the ground and to her better-buried companions. Perhaps our mistake was not in wrongly sexing the "key lady," but in assuming that the shallowness of both graves was evidence of fear-tempered haste in the aftermath of the massacre. Suppose, like our four-man mass burial, the two women had died of contagious disease, but in the depths of winter, when weakened survivors found the clay too hard to dig. Countering the argument that no matter how disinclined the buriers were to handle the still-clothed body, they would first have retrieved her key, we can answer that it might have been carried beneath her apron or even hidden inside her skirt, and so never found. Less easy to swallow is the idea of a woman sufficiently in command of affairs to be carrying her key and her thimble one minute, and dropping dead the next. Nevertheless, the man with the clog and the bullets in the mass grave had apparently done the same. Although there is no evidence that contagious diseases in Virginia included the bubonic plague that swept London three times in the seventeenth century, some strains of it took their toll in as little as two hours. Indeed, it was the suddenness of death, preceded by sneezing, that gave life to the nursery rhyme that so many happy children have sung without having the first idea of what it meant.

> Ring-a-ring o' roses,
> A pocket full of posies
> A-tishoo! A-tishoo!
> We all fall down.

For a few blissful moments early in the excavation of Site H, I truly believed that we were within inches of associating it with an identifiable family that met its end in a definable, if grisly manner. But ironically, the more we found, the further we drifted away from that possibility. Our only hope was to find an artifact with a person's initials scratched on it, initials matching those of someone in the list of massacre dead or in those of the dead and living in 1623. Finding such an artifact was by no means impossible. At Site B, for example, we had found a pipe bowl with the initials IR scratched on its heel. It was just bad luck that no one with those initials figured in any of the list of Martin's Hundred settlers! Rare on pipes, scratched initials are much more common on pewter, and we had a pewter spoon handle from Granny's Grave. Alas, no one had had the foresight to mark it.

From another pit came what should have been a clue of unquestionable clarity—a brass seal for embossing wax on documents and closing letters, a signet. Had the engraved matrix exhibited a shield of arms or even a family crest, we might well have been able to pin it down; instead, the device was simply a swan-like bird, the kind of mass-produced trinket used by people whose lineage did not rate crests or shields of arms (Fig. 13–16). English families who did use the swan as a crest were numerous, but none of their names rang bells for us in Martin's Hundred. The shape of the bird's body and the placement of its feet, however, did remind me of something I had seen before, namely the incomplete, slip-painted design on the 1631 dish from Site B (see Fig. 6–1). A closer look at it left me prepared to believe that the potter's bird could have had a swan-like neck. Was it possible, we wondered, that a swan was the emblem of Martin's Hundred?

On December 20—a day so cold that up in the cherry-picker the film froze in the camera—the movie crew assembled on Site H to shoot yet another ending. My previous wrap-up (the third) had carried the viewer ashore from divers searching in the river, dissolving through the trees to Dick Schlecht's view of Wolstenholme Towne in its brief heyday. But that was before we found the suburb—and

Granny. Although the new ending only called for a brief summary of what we had found, while the camera focused on work in progress here and there on the site, deteriorating weather closed us down before the sequence was complete. Plans to resume after the Christmas and New Year's holidays failed to foresee eighteen inches of snow on January 5, the century's heaviest single fall in Tidewater Virginia. As it melted, the site slowly dissolved into a sea of mud. Pits and post-holes eroded and were no longer well-enough defined to be shown in the film, and several familiar faces were now missing from the archaeological crew, the team having been severely cut back before Christmas in the expectation that the dig would have been com-

13–16. A brass signet found at Site H. The swan-like bird of its matrix is reminiscent of birds depicted on the Martin's Hundred slipware and sgraffito dishes. Discarded ca. 1620–1622.

pleted in December. Had the weather held, it might have been; instead, the small, permanent crew toiled on into 1980. Not until January 25 could senior archaeologist Nick Luccketti assure me that he had cleaned out the last post-hole and that nothing remained to be found within the suburb's paled enclosure.

Of the field crew who had been with us when we began in 1976, only foreman Nate Smith was there to the end. Eric Klingelhofer and his assistant Bill Henry, both of whom had worked so hard, and contributed so much for so long, had left in the autumn to seek higher academic laurels. Indoors, however, most of the team with which we had begun was still intact—four years older and infinitely wiser in matters seventeenth century. Laboratory techniques for treating fragile and decayed metal artifacts had advanced so far that we could claim with confidence that if the excavators could see it, we could save it, be it a crushed helmet, a "sleeping" human skeleton, or just a dirty mark in the ground.

Although we knew full well that the Carter's Grove acres contained several more unexcavated seventeenth-century sites that might have more to tell us about the history of Martin's Hundred, we also knew that if we did not stop, analyze, and publish the mass of artifacts and information already in hand, the sheer size of the task might prevent us from ever completing it. So, on March 11, 1980, almost 358 years after the massacre, three years and eleven months after excavations began, and four movie endings later, we were back at Site H to film the last scene. In a biting wind off the river, and against a bleak background of leafless trees, I told the camera through chattering teeth that the ground of Wolstenholme Towne had surrendered its last secret and that Dick Schlecht's painted reconstructions were as close as we could get to seeing the settlement through a colonist's eyes.

But we were not done yet. Colleagues who were asked to comment on the film's rough-cut ending called it abrupt, drab, downbeat, a whimper instead of a roar. Granny had been short-changed, they said, and worse still, my narration had left the audience thinking that the Indian attack marked the end for Martin's Hundred. Back I went to the typewriter.

And the Gods Looked Down

14

$\overline{A}$n old archaeological adage has it that three months of digging on a major classical or historical site generates nine months of artifact processing and data analysis. Few of us are that lucky, for there is an almost universal assumption that unless dirt is seen to be flying, archaeologists are malingering. Although both Colonial Williamsburg and the National Geographic Society recognized that research would have to follow the discoveries at Martin's Hundred, the three-to-one ratio was too daunting to be countenanced. At that rate, the four years' digging that had ended in January 1980 would send us into laboratory seclusion until 1992!

That three-to-one division of effort was conceived in the days when the expedition leader shipped all the artifacts home from foreign parts (ignoring the proprietary rights of the natives) after doing little during the digging season but map, catalogue, and curse the quality of the local labor. The Martin's Hundred "expedition" was different. A fully equipped and manned laboratory awaited our artifacts only seven miles up the road, where treatment and study could begin within hours of their excavation. Artifact artist Pat Kidd was drawing the finds from one site while the next was being dug; archaeologists Eric Klingelhofer and Bill Henry took turns, one writing while the other dug, and throughout it all, Audrey was analyzing and annotating the historical record. Thus it remained only to weave all the accumulated archaeological and historical information into a final report which, in all probability, not even scholars would have the fortitude to read. In an age that puts little more academic store by simple, snappy sentences, it is mandatory that archaeological reports be excruciatingly dull, often uninterpretable, and laced with sufficient jargon (never say "farming" when you mean "the exploitation of the environment") to earn the plaudits of one's peers. Crawling to the tyranny of sociology, one writes about "lifeways" and "interpersonal relationships" while reducing exciting conclusions to depersonalized (there's another dreadful word!) flow charts and statistics.

We, fortunately, were not limited to that audience. Favorable reader response to the first *National Geographic* article (June 1979) spawned a second, focusing in part on discoveries made since the winter of 1978, but also on ideas and information that had reached us from National Geographic Society members. First, however, that had to be checked—beginning in Bermuda, where Allan Wingood's excavations on the wreck of the alleged *Sea Venture* (1609) had yielded the West of England storage jars matching examples from Wolstenholme Towne (see Fig. 10-7). Here was proof that such jars were in use prior to our terminal date of 1622. No other examples could safely be dated as early.

Potentially more significant were discoveries being made by Bermuda's best-known diver, Edward "Teddy" Tucker. He had found a wreck in Castle Harbour that he believed to be the *Warwick* (apparently a predecessor to the *Warwicke* which took settlers to Martin's Hundred in 1621) and that had been dashed against a cliff in a November 1619 hurricane. This was the ship that had brought Captain Nathaniel Butler to be Bermuda's new governor—the same Captain Butler who three years later visited Virginia and wrote his devastating "Unmasking" that contributed to the demise of the Virginia Company and to the reshaping of British America's embryonic history. It was not the beastly Butler who interested us, however, but rather the broken tobacco pipes that Tucker was finding in the wreck of his ship. Their bowl sizes closely paralleled several from the Wolstenholme fort, all of whose bowls could only otherwise be dated within the brackets 1600 to 1620, 1610 to 1630, or 1600 to 1640, depending on which expert you asked. If, therefore, Tucker's ship really was the *Warwick*, it would provide us with the first truly reliable anchor to identify pipes that were leaving England at a specific date, 1619—the same year that the first Martin's Hundred colonists reached Virginia.

The location of the wreck fitted the written description of the *Warwick*'s destruction, and most of the recovered artifacts seemed to fit comfortably between 1612 (when Bermuda was first settled) and about 1630—with the exception of a pewter spoon bearing the same maker's mark as on another almost identical spoon that Teddy Tucker found aboard the 1659 wreck of the *Eagle*, several miles away on the island's outer reef. Surprisingly, several of the recovered potsherds seemed more likely to have come from vessels made in the Low Countries and Spain than from England. Particularly disturbing were fragments of crude, Hispanic maiolica akin to many pieces Teddy had found aboard the 1621 wreck of the Spanish *San Antonio.* That such wretched earthenware should have been aboard a ship straight from England, where much better maiolica (delftware) was readily available, was puzzling, even suspicious. On the other hand, fragments of pewter flagons were identifiable as Tudor English types, and a lead weight stamped with the crowned "J" of James I, as well as the City of London's dagger of St. Paul and the St. Michael emblem of the London Plumbers' Company, was as avowedly English as one can get.

The Castle Harbour wreck's greatest surprise proved to be a small fragment of red-gloss pottery made in France, not in the seventeenth century but in the first century A.D., when France was Roman Gaul. After telling Teddy what it was, and between my first and second visits, he found two more pieces, one no bigger than a little-finger nail (Fig. 14–1). Two gray earthenware sherds could also belong to the Roman period, as could a fragment from a glass bowl. I could think of only one explanation for the presence of these Roman relics—they had come aboard in ballast.

14–1. Sherds of Romano-Gaulish Terra Sigillata pottery of the 1st and 2nd centuries A.D., found aboard a wreck in Castle Harbour, Bermuda, and believed to be that of the *Warwick* which sank in 1619.

I knew from my years as archaeologist for London's Guildhall Museum that the bed of the river Thames has not only been a source of gravel ballast, but that in the vicinity of London Bridge, dredgers often pull up Roman and even older artifacts mixed in the Thames Valley gravel. Indeed, I well recall standing aboard one such dredger on a wet Saturday afternoon and finding a coin of the emperor Vespasian shining like a new penny amid the black flint pebbles.

All around and between the timbers of the alleged *Warwick* lay quantities of black and white pebbles, perhaps several tons of them, and evidently part of her ballast (Fig. 14–2). I brought up as large a sample as would fit into the pocket of my swimming trunks and sent it to the Geological Museum in London to have my identification confirmed. By the time the stones reached London, their blackness had faded, and although the museum's geologists could not be sure of their source, they could say with confidence that this was *not* Thames gravel. More than half the pebbles were limestone, and there is none in the Thames Valley. We would have to find another river or harbor, one from which limestone pebble ballast came garnished with Roman potsherds—a tall order yet to be filled.

Only three weeks after sitting on the midships timbers of the Castle Harbour wreck's hold, I found myself standing in more or less the same spot aboard the *Vasa*—Sweden's 1628 forerunner of the

14–2. Teddy Tucker and the author inspecting a castiron cauldron found on the Castle Harbour wreck.

Titanic. Looking up from the hold past three decks, it was hard to remember why I had been so awed by my first encounter with the relatively slender remains of the Bermudian wreck, and yet there had been a magic about it that was absent here. Sunlight shafting down through a green sea, and inquisitive fishes that peer into your mask and seem to be mouthing presumptuous questions, have an unmatched appeal that readily explains Teddy Tucker's ever-boyish enthusiasm for jumping over the side of a boat. The *Vasa,* on the other hand, works its wonder at a different and more pragmatic level, first awe at its relatively vast size (actually 200 feet long and 1,300 tons), then confidence that one would gladly sail anywhere through any sea in such a ship, and finally admiration for the Swedish engineers and archaeologists who, in 1961, had brought the *Vasa* up from her grave in Stockholm harbor, where she had lain since her 1,500-yard maiden voyage (Fig. 14–3). We had gone to Stockholm pursuing a *National Geographic* reader's tip that a German stoneware jug found in the wreck matched the one recovered from our pit on Site B. The premise seemed likely enough, for our jug was found with the 1631 dish, and the *Vasa* had gone down only three years before.

The jugs turned out to be of different sizes, but they certainly belonged to the same class. However, a square glass bottle with a pewter cap found aboard the *Vasa* turned out to be a close parallel

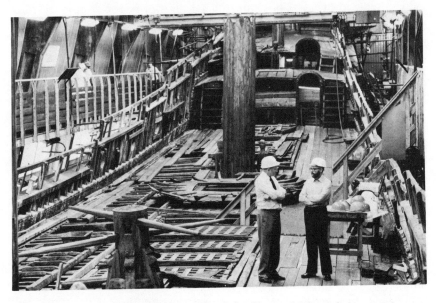

14–3. The raised and restored wreck of the *Vasa* which sank in 1628 in Stockholm harbor. Her contents provided parallels for several artifact types from Martin's Hundred.

for many found both in the Wolstenholme suburb and on the supposed Harwood home site. Figure-eight-shaped brass buckles from the latter site were also matched among the *Vasa*'s artifacts, as was a thimble from the fort. I had hoped for more, but it turned out that relatively few artifacts were found aboard the ship itself, and that many of the small objects in the *Vasa* collection were salvaged from the harbor floor after she had been raised, and so cannot be proved to have come from the wreck.

If the quantity of domestic and military artifacts from the *Vasa* was less than I had expected, we were to have no complaints on that score when we reached our next stop. At Graz in the Austrian province of Styria stands the Landeszeughaus. Built in 1642 to house arms and armor needed to equip mercenary armies in the Holy Roman Empire's prolonged wars with the invading Turks, the arsenal at Graz still stands ready—the only appreciable change being that the supplies are kept in good order by conservators rather than armorers, and that curator Peter Krenn substitutes for the master of ordnance. Hundreds of matchlock muskets in immaculate order wait in their racks, as does a forest of pikes and halberds. Powder flasks matching a nozzle found in our Company Compound hang from the rafters like bats in a cave; so, too, do pikemen's helmets. Their body armor lines the walls, glinting in sunlight that shines like theatrical spots through the arsenal's small windows. The building's four floors reportedly contain somewhere between 29,000 and 33,000 pieces of military equipment, ranged and looking as must the Tower of London's supplies warehoused in the nearby Minnories when King James authorized the shipment of old arms and armor to offset Virginia's losses to the Indians in 1622 (Fig. 14–4).

Although the Sword of Islam continued to whack away at Europe's eastern flank until 1700, most of the Landeszeughaus's armor is older than the building, having been assembled in the second half of the sixteenth and in the early seventeenth century. When, in the eighteenth century, Austria's mercenaries were replaced by a standing army headquartered in Vienna, Styria no longer bore the responsibility of protecting the eastern frontier. In response to instructions from the capital that any of the old arsenal's still-useful equipment should be turned over to the army and the rest discarded, the Graz city fathers petitioned Empress Maria Theresa to allow the collection to be retained in the Landeszeughaus as a monument to Styrian bravery in defending against the "sworn enemy of Christendom." The Empress agreed, and so by royal decree it remained, escaping the ravages of two World Wars, to become the world's only fully equipped seventeenth-century arsenal.

Among the smallest of our military artifacts from the Wolstenholme suburb was the previously mentioned scourer for cleaning scale from musket barrels (see Fig. 13–6). We knew of an engraving showing such a tool, but the Tower of London had none, and our efforts to find parallels in other museum collections had been unsuccessful. But when I showed a drawing of our scourer to Landeszeughaus curator Peter Krenn, his conservator promptly produced half a dozen in assorted sizes—one an exact parallel for ours. "How many do you have in all?" I asked.

"More than eight hundred," he replied.

It had been a dumb question. In an arsenal possessing 7,800 small arms, there should be a scourer for each musket. There also were matchlocks having parallels to all the parts we had found, including one mechanism plate whose shape had hitherto eluded us. The most important discovery, however, was a group of cavalry armors bought in 1601 and having one-piece visors strikingly like those on our Wolstenholme helmets—the type of construction that some of our advisors had insisted did not exist. These visors differed only in having

14–4. For students of seventeenth-century arms and armor, the arsenal at Graz, Austria, provides an unparalleled research resource. The armors in the foreground date from 1601 and may closely match those worn with the Wolstenholme Towne helmets.

a small, mouth-shaped opening, and their separated eye-slots (more properly called sights) have no bill or peak above them (Fig. 14–5). Here, nevertheless, was convincing evidence that the kinds of munition armor (that made for the rank and file) worn in Europe in the first decades of the seventeenth century were closely paralleled in Virginia, and therefore must also have been common to England.

Being right without saying "I told you so" is one of Civilized Man's more difficult accomplishments, and our successes at Graz sent us on to London in a condition of mild euphoria. But being a born pessimist (which makes it so nice to be wrong), I quickly began wondering how long it would be before some reporter put me on record as claiming that the armor found in Martin's Hundred had been manufactured in Austria. "Nonsense," said Audrey, "all you have to do is explain. . . . Well, on second thought," she added, "why don't you just say nothing."

She was right. But a chance remark at an only marginally related news conference provoked a question about the Austrian armor, and only three days after I got back to the office, I read in the morning paper that we had "traced the origin of two closed helmets unearthed at the seventeenth-century Wolstenholme Towne site to Austria"!

Our premier reason for going to England was to try to lay to rest the last of our ghosts—the ones inhabiting our still elusive, gable-lidded coffins. When we had approached Lord Sackville for permission to enter his family vault at Withyham, I had no idea that the church was on the estate of the Earl De La Warr and that it was he who had the key. I should have remembered that the De La Warr family name is West, but not (I submit) that the Fifth Earl married Elizabeth Sackville, and that it was through this couple, in 1843, that the united family name of Sackville-West was created by royal license. The Lady Elizabeth became the First Baroness Buckhurst, and the village of Withyham was once in the Manor of Buckhurst. I mention this connection solely to explain (after a fashion) how the present Lord De La Warr became custodian of the key to the Sackville vault. Granting permission through his agent, Lord Sackville did not mention this small but pertinent complication, but only told me to contact the vicar of Withyham. When we got no reply, the National Geographic Society's representative in England took charge of the quest, and learned that Lord De La Warr was away in Europe and that nothing could be done until he got back—date uncertain.

Time was running short, and after being doused with cold water by the Council of Places of Worship's consultant, I was sure we stood

14–5. Landeszeughaus conservater August Gschiel servicing a close helmet having a single visor unit similar to that of the Company Compound example (see Fig. 10–10). The Austrian helmet was purchased for the Styrian army in 1601.

no chance of finding another potentially helpful vault before leaving for Europe. Then came both good and bad news from London: The vicar had obtained the key; he had been down in the vault but could find no gable-lidded wooden coffins. So that seemed to be that—until it occurred to me that the coffins could have fallen apart and, to someone unfamiliar with their supposed construction, might now be indistinguishable from collapsed, flat-lidded examples. Then, too, if the seventeenth-century Sackvilles lay in flat-topped coffins, that in itself would be evidence, albeit of the negative variety.

Three days before we were due to leave, Audrey and I were invited to dine with two distinguished but unscheduled visitors to Williamsburg—the Earl and Countess De La Warr. They knew nothing of us or our request; they had *not* been in Europe; but they would be delighted to help, and personally would open the vault for us. Better still, they would permit *National Geographic* photographer Ira Block to take pictures.

Driving home after the dinner party, I told Audrey, "This has to be an omen. The odds against trying to reach someone you don't know who is believed to be in an unspecified somewhere in Europe, and then finding yourself sitting next to them at a dinner in America, are such that not even a computer would want to figure them out. It can't be just a coincidence," I insisted. "It can't, can it?"

"It can't what?" she answered, stumbling back from the edge of sleep.

"Never mind."

In spite of the apparent evidence to the contrary, the Williamsburg meeting had convinced me that the Withyham vault held something we needed to know. But now, as we followed Lord De La Warr up the churchyard path, my confidence ebbed away. The De La Warrs had come down from London at some personal inconvenience, solely to open the door for us. The *National Geographic* had sent Ira Block over to be on hand at the moment of discovery—and the vicar had told us that we would not find what we were seeking. Even my hopes that fragments of decayed coffins might be lying unrecognized on the shelves had been dashed when Lady De La Warr explained that her mother-in-law, in a burst of spring cleaning earlier in the century, had had the tomb swept out and everybody tidied up.

The vault lies beneath the Sackville Chapel and is reached down a steep flight of stone steps. At the bottom there are both a heavy wooden door and an iron gate. While Lord De La Warr struggled to turn the key, I recalled Lord Carnarvon standing behind Howard

Carter at the entrance to Tutankhamen's tomb and asking that breathless, deathless question "Can you see anything?" But when the door to the Sackville tomb swung open, the only "wonderful things" in sight were the red-velvet-covered coffins of several eighteenth- and nineteenth-century Dukes of Dorset and their wives, the gilded brass escutcheons, handles, and sheet-brass coronets resting on top, the closest we were to get to the splendor of King Tut. Neatly shelved, more than seventy Sackvilles and Sackville-Wests silently await the last trump—with the possible exception of a few who, in the cleanup process, had been reduced to a collection of loose parts tucked away in a corner. Beside the doorway, a massive, brown-velvet-covered wooden coffin was succumbing to the damp, its side yawning outward, not to reveal a sleeping duke but to expose an inner coffin of lead. Sealed within that there may yet be another wooden box, for like the multiple sarcophagi of Ancient Egypt, the wealthy English of the eighteenth century went to their reward in a trinity of boxes.

Many of the Sackvilles lay stripped to their lead liners, and one close to the door bore an inscription in high relief on its *flat* lid, telling us that inside lay the body of Lady Margaret Howard, daughter of Thomas, Duke of Norfolk, and wife to Robert Sackville, Earl of Dorset. She had died on August 19, 1591—right in the period wherein I thought coffins should have been A-lidded. I had said that I would settle for negative evidence, and here it was.

So crowded is the vault that each shelf is shared between two and even three occupants. Directing a flashlight beam into the darkness at the back I spotted a liner whose roof was not flat. For a moment I thought my eyes and the yellow light were playing tricks, but on raking the coffin from end to end, I was left with no doubt; this lead lining was gabled. I reached in to touch the metal just to be certain. Never before had it occurred to me that lead liners inside gable-lidded coffins might be of the same shape; but that clearly had been so—at least in this instance. Of course the occupants of our Martin's Hundred coffins had not aspired to liners, every ounce of lead being needed by the living. I felt all over the Sackville lid in the hope of locating an inscription that would name and date its occupant, but, disappointingly, there was nothing. Unlike Lady Margaret Howard's liner, the identifying plaque must have been attached only to the wood, and now was lost.

Even as I exalted in my modified success, Audrey went one better. "There's another over here," she called, "and it's dated!"

By the light of one of those ridiculously small flashlights that prudent women carry in their purses, she began to read the Latin inscription incised into a rectangular panel soldered to a steeply gabled coffin only three feet long:

Anna

c. Liberis

Dom · Richardi Fil: Unici

Honorat Edoardi

Com · Dorset

Vixit Trien · Menses Dvos

Obit · Solstit: Brvmali

1649 ·

Anne, the three-year-old daughter of Richard, fifth Earl of Dorset, was telling us that gable-lidded coffins *had* existed in England in the first half of the seventeenth century; and that, I am convinced, was the message that destiny (or whatever one calls it) insisted we should receive—regardless of discouragements that might so easily have caused us to abandon the search (Fig. 14–6).

It is true that we still had no information on precisely how the wooden coffins were built, but from Aphrodisias in Turkey, the distinguished archaeologist Kenan Erim wrote that he had studied our interpretation and found it to be consistent with the construction of A-lidded coffins being made in the Islamic world today. He

14–6. The Earl De La Warr examining the gable-lidded lead coffinliner of an infant ancestor in the Sackville family vault at Withyham in Sussex.

sent us photographs of an Ankara coffin builder at work—hammering in nails down the center line of the lid—just where we expected them to be (Fig. 14–7). A later research trip to England discovered a gable-lidded mortuary chest that had survived not in a burial vault, but perched atop a stone screen in Winchester Cathedral. The coffin-shaped wooden box was made around 1525 to house the bones of early English kings whose graves had been disturbed during improvements to the building. Although broken into during the civil war by treasure-seeking Parliamentary troops, the damaged chest still exhibited its original lid construction, the two boards secured along the ridge by seven large nails. The Winchester mortuary chest is almost certainly the work of a common coffin-maker and provides valuable joinery details not found in the Withyham vault.

Still unexplained, however, was the problem of why, in the Sackville vault, Lady Margaret Howard's lead liner was flat and the little girl's gabled. I believe that the answer was being given to us by

14–7. A modern gable-lidded-coffin builder at work in Ankara, Turkey.

the brass coronets resting on the lids of the later Dukes of Dorset, and which supported observations by the Librarian at Westminister Abbey, who noted that the nobility's coffins had to be flat-lidded so that funerary effigies could be carried on top. What the admittedly incomplete Sackville evidence seemed to be saying was that first-line peers and royalty rated ornamental toppings and that those further down the social slide did not. Thus, if one had no effigy or coronet to adorn the coffin, a gabled lid served to show off that more universal coffin cover, the pall. If that conclusion has a familiar ring it is because this is the same one we had reached before our quest for supportive English evidence began.

We said goodbye to Lord and Lady De La Warr and drove back to London wearing smiles worthy of a Cheshire cat, our triumph only slightly tarnished by the awareness that this had been Ira Block's last day with us—the end of a mini-odyssey that had begun aboard the *Vasa* and had gone from success to success, culminating in the "wonderful things" of Withyham. Over a farewell dinner at a celebrated Soho seafood restaurant (where Colchester oysters are priced on a par with Tut's gold), we counted our chickens. Among them was a potsherd, about the size of a postage stamp, that I had picked up from the foreshore of the river Thames. Ira and I had gone down there at low tide to photograph the place where, thirty years earlier, I had found the Augsburg lead bale seal whose design paralleled the examples we had discovered in the Wolstenholme potter's pond and in Granny's grave. Squatting by the water's edge

with the seal in my hand as Ira took shot after shot, my eyes wandered to the fragments of Tudor and Stuart pottery that lay scattered all around. Most of the sherds were of well-known types, but one green-glazed piece almost leaped up pleading "Here, don't miss me!" It came from a fuming pot having a rim form unparalleled in any collection known to me—except the one from the disappointing Site D ("Audrey's Choice") in Martin's Hundred (Fig. 14–8). This chance discovery was proof that although no pots of this shape survive in Lon-

14–8. The Thames foreshore provides archaeologists with an unrivaled source of potsherds testifying to the kinds of ceramics used in London in the seventeenth and other centuries. The arrowed fragment (opposite), provided the only known parallel for a fuming-pot type discovered at Site D in Martin's Hundred.

don museums, it was known and used in the city before being reproduced in Virginia. Once again the odds against finding that sherd
were too long to calculate.

Although my archaeological lares had guided us with seemingly
unerring precision, even gods must sleep, and my hopes of learning
more about the buttons from Site H were not realized (Fig. 14–9).
The only clue was provided by a man's leather doublet in the collection of the Museum of London, whose buttons were of the same small
size as ours. This did nothing to support the previous expert opinion
that our buttons' diminutive size pointed to their having been lost
from a woman's dress—a supposition that very conveniently fitted my
scenario for the murder of Granny in the 1622 massacre. Instead, the
London doublet reinforced Dutch button expert Jan Baart's masculine
evidence.

Baart had sent me a photograph of the doublet or jacket in
Rotterdam's Historical Museum, on which are buttons of even smaller
size than ours but decorated with very similar roses (Fig. 14–10). The
garment, he wrote, had belonged to a bricklayer. I, however, had
imagined such attractively decorative buttons as belonging to someone of greater wealth. I confess, too, that I had been encouraged to
look higher up the social skirts by my English correspondent, who had
drawn my attention to the decorative use of small buttons on dresses

14–9. Nickel alloy buttons found within the Site H compound and likely to
have been scattered at the time of the Indian attack on March 22, 1622.

worn by Queen Elizabeth. If our buttons did come from female apparel, I concluded that they, too, were more ornamental than functional, and would have been worn by the kind of woman who would have dressed her hair over a roll—namely Granny. I was not at all anxious for Jan Baart to be right.

Even if he was correct in claiming that the rose-decorated buttons came from male clothing, they had to have belonged to someone more important than a bricklayer. Besides, after 350 years, how could

14–10. The doublet worn by Hugo Grotius in his escape from prison on March 22, 1621, its buttons closely paralleling those from Site H.

Baart know that the Rotterdam doublet had belonged to a bricklayer? Before leaving for Europe I wrote and asked him that question. When I got back, the answer was on my desk.

The garment had been given to the museum by descendants of a man remembered by most of the world's law students as one of the architects of international law and father of the concept of freedom of the seas. Hugo Grotius was born Huig van Groot in 1583, the son of Jan de Groot, a burgomaster of Delft. In keeping with the time wherein he lived, Hugo grew up fast. He attended the University of Leiden at the age of twelve, and took the oath of advocacy at The Hague in 1599 when he was only sixteen. By the time he was thirty, Grotius had a national, even an international reputation as a "classical scholar, theologian, historian, and lawyer."[1] Five years later this reputation landed him in jail. Arrested in 1618, tried, and condemned to life imprisonment in March 1619, he began serving his sentence in June at the fortress of Loevestein near the town of Gorcum on the river Waal.

The Dutch were a civilized people and respecters of intellect; it was not long, therefore, before Grotius's jailers permitted him to resume his writing, and through the next two years he worked on one of the books on which his reputation rests, *The Jurisprudence of Holland.* But only novelists and poets can write books without the help of other books, and to this end, friends at the University of Leiden sent him whatever he needed, the volumes brought in and out of the castle in a large wooden box that also transported his laundry. Captivity for Hugo Grotius was not of the dank, dark, dungeon variety. His wife was allowed to live with him, and her coming and going became as familiar to the guards as the arrival and departure of the book box. Familiarity sired neglect, and in time the jailers no longer bothered to examine the books or poke through the dirty laundry. One day the books stayed and Grotius went. His wife had the box carried to the home of a friend at Gorcum, where Grotius hurriedly exchanged his clothes for those of a brickmason. Looking at the doublet today, one can well imagine the fugitive feverishly fumbling with the long row of tiny buttons. Once into his shabby disguise, and carrying a brickmason's hod, Hugo Grotius boarded a ferry, crossed the Waal river, and escaped to Antwerp. The date was March 22, 1621—a year to the day before the Indians struck at Martin's Hundred perhaps causing buttons like his to be scattered about the Site H yard.

Grotius's borrowed doublet provided us with unequivocal proof that iron-alloy buttons decorated with molded roses were in use in

Europe by 1621, and can therefore safely be dated prior to the Indian uprising in Virginia. It says, too, that such buttons were worn on male clothing (without precluding their also being worn by women), although it does not necessarily prove that buttons of this type were to be found only on clothing worn by the lower classes. Shiny, steel-like, and rose-decorated buttons certainly are of better quality than many of the plain brass examples that turn up on Tudor and Stuart sites. Be that as it may, the Dutch evidence suggests that on the day of her death, Granny had a male companion—whose buttons, and not his bones, have survived.

Small as the buttons but much larger in potential significance had been the Harington farthing from the fort. The notion that a coin issued for only two months in 1613 should turn up in Virginia in almost mint condition more than five years later still made no sense. As noted earlier, my only rational explanation was that after the coins were withdrawn, the unissued stock was stored and later released for use in the plantations, where the shortage of small change might make even the meanest coins acceptable. Unfortunately, I could find no documentation and no numismatic historian willing to support that thesis. By this time, however, I had become accustomed to sitting alone on creaking limbs.

High on the list of an archaeologist's least pleasurable tasks is cataloguing his artifacts, particularly when he is faced with tens of thousands of them. That, nevertheless, is an essential first step toward studying those artifacts in relation to each other, and this in turn leads to their becoming clues to the evolution of the site whereon they were found. Not until these steps have been taken can we begin to piece together the history of a site into a final report. In Martin's Hundred we were dealing with several sites, and although interim field reports had been written on each, they had to be reevaluated in the light of the continuing artifact research. Eventually all of this material will be woven together into a broader history of the settlement as a whole. Not until that is done can we hope to be ready to examine Martin's Hundred in the context, first of colonial Virginia and then of British colonial cultural and political history. Indeed, regardless of early calls for such cosmic conclusions, I am of the opinion that they should be avoided until both archaeologists and historians know more about the period than we do today.

In the autumn of 1980 I was still at the cataloguing stage, and as part of it I asked an assistant to assemble all the mathematical counters from Martin's Hundred sites. It was not a big job; there were only four

—plus a small copper disk about a centimeter in diameter that clearly did not belong with them. One side of the disk had corroded away into a microscopic moonscape of peaks and craters, but the other retained traces of a design: a crown and a pair of crossed scepters. Nothing of the legend survived, but the disk's size and central decoration left little doubt that this was no counter, but was instead an example of Lord Harington's second token farthing issued between 1613 and 1614.

Found at the edge of the potter's pond within the Company Compound (and unrecognized for two years after it was unearthed), this second Harington farthing neatly put to rest the theory that a single example might miraculously have survived since 1613, lurking in the lining of someone's clothing until it fell out after the stitching gave way in the exertion of fort building. We now had three coins from Wolstenholme Towne: One cut-down Spanish piece, and two Harington token farthings, or, to put it another way—66.6 percent of the coins found in Martin's Hundred are of the Harington type. Even setting aside so grossly misleading a statistic, we are left with the inescapable conclusion that Harington farthings served as currency in Martin's Hundred, and that at least some of them had seen little or no prior circulation—hence the survival of the tin coating on the first example (see Fig. 11-5).

Even though the Martin's Hundred excavations ceased early in 1980 with the completion of work on the suburban Site H, the plantation's archaeological resources were far from exhausted. Some sites, like those in the woods to the east, seemed to promise only more of the same—more homesteads of the 1630 to 1640 period, and whose excavation is unlikely to change our interpretation of Wolstenholme Towne or of the supposed Harwood home site. But then there was Site J, the one we had found in the winter of 1979, which seemed to date to the 1680s, close to the midpoint of the century-long gap between the abandonment of Site A in the 1640s and the completion of Carter Burwell's brick mansion in 1755. This was the site on which *The Washington Post* had lighted, claiming expectations that it would "provide new insights about living conditions and habits of colonists between the founding of Jamestown in 1607 and Carter's Grove plantation, built in 1740."[2]

According to the *Post*'s headline, the outrageously magnified discoveries "May Shed Light on Va. 'Dark Ages' "; but while that was our hope for Wolstenholme Towne, our expectations for Site J were more modest. We hoped for no more than a slender thread to span

Carter's Grove's silent century. When the Site J field was again plowed in the spring of 1980, archaeologist Luccketti and several of his assistants walked the area picking up artifacts scattered over the furrowed surface. Among them were a few more potsherds of the 1680 to 1700 period; but more importantly, about 50 yards to the south, the searchers came upon a concentration of sherds and pipe fragments dating at least as far back as the 1640s, indicating that Site J may have picked up where Site A left off—thus representing a potentially tougher thread than we had supposed.

Among the pottery fragments was part of the foot from an unusual maiolica vessel, its pale-blue and orange bands of decoration certainly not English and hardly likely to be Dutch. My best guess was that the vessel was Italian, probably from Montelupo near Florence. The sherd was too small to be firmly identified, and although I deduced that it came from a fairly elaborate vase, I could find no published parallel; so the fragment went into a box and its shape into the back of my mind.

Our 1980 research trip to Europe had provided enough high points to keep us levitated for several months, but one saddening experience had injected a sobering counterpoint. A career-long friend had unexpectedly been relieved of the chairmanship of one of London's most prestigious companies. We found him clearing out the office that he had occupied for more than thirty years. In the process he came upon a large and tattered envelope containing potsherds he had collected during rebuilding on one of his firm's properties in Southwark. "Here," he said, "you'd better take these. They're more use to you than they are to me." I accepted the envelope without more than a glance at its contents, put it into a parcel, and mailed it home to Williamsburg. Five weeks later, the package arrived. Still caked with the dirt that had been on them since they were dug up in the 1950s, the potsherds proved to range from Tudor earthenware to eighteenth-century Chinese porcelain—plus four fragments from a maiolica vase whose chinoiserie decoration terminated above its lost foot in bands of pale blue and orange, the same Montelupo colors that decorated the foot fragment from Site J. Both foot and bowl sherds are from vessels of the same type and began their life in the same factory (Fig. 14–11). Together they reveal a vase of captivating quality, something that I, for one, would never have expected to find in far-flung Virginia in the mid-seventeenth century.

Might this yet-to-be-explored Martin's Hundred site hold secrets that one day will eclipse those already revealed? Was it possible that my household gods had leaked their message to *The Washington Post* before giving it to me?

Surely not?

14-11. Fragments from similar Montelupo faience vases. The foot sherd found at Site J in Martin's Hundred, and the polichrome-decorated body pieces unearthed in London. Ca. 1650-1675.

Terminus Interruptus

15

Rarely will an archaeologist risk claiming the last word, for his evidence by its very nature is incomplete, always vulnerable to new interpretation, always fair game for the young Turk with the new and shiny trowel, anxious to make his mark by thrusting it between the shoulders of his predecessors' sacred cows. Alas, conclusions reached in Martin's Hundred are no less fragile. No plaque was found to prove that we were standing on the village green of Wolstenholme Towne; no timber-built wharves were discovered beneath the waters of the James River to pinpoint the 1619 shoreline and enable us to measure the yardage subsequently lost to erosion. We could not prove beyond the shadow of a lawyer's doubt that William Harwood had lived on Site A, or that Indians had stripped "Granny" naked and taken her hair before she lay down and died in her pit at Site H. The mute evidence of bones and potsherds can satisfy those who *want* to believe, yet remains easy prey to the cow-slayers—until documentation proves it right or wrong.

Without contemporary words to tell us that the Society of Martin's Hundred was formed, that Wolstenholme Towne was built, and that the settlement was almost totally destroyed in the Indian attack of 1622, the archaeological testimony could have said only that the acres that became Carter's Grove in the eighteenth century had been extensively occupied in the first half of the preceding century, when at least forty-nine now nameless men, women, and children had died there, twelve of them under abnormal circumstances. Even, however, if our conclusions had been no more precise than that, the Martin's Hundred discoveries would still rank as a major contribution to our knowledge of life and death in the teething years of American colonial history, and, by extension, to a richer understanding of British material culture in the early Stuart period.

Because nothing has yet been found of early, fortified James-

321

town, the discoveries at Carter's Grove provide the oldest complete ground plan for a British timber-built fort yet found in America, and the excavated military artifacts offer information about British munition armor and weaponry hitherto available from no other source. Were it not for questions raised by the excavations, Dr. Stephen Clement might never have embarked on his comparative analysis of potting clays, which eventually may open a new avenue for tracing the sources of pottery of any period. Then, too, the great coffin-lid enigma would never have been posed or solved.

"Who cares?" cynics may ask.

To answer: "Me—and maybe seven others," wins few points. Knowing whether seventeenth-century coffins were flat- or gable-lidded certainly does nothing to help us better grapple with an apocalyptic future—but neither does most of the knowledge that makes life bearable and pleasurable. I am well aware that such a defense is akin to throwing several damaged pirates into a sea of sharks, grist to critics who argue that public money spent on archaeology all too often benefits no one but the archaeologists, who like to amuse themselves digging holes and thinking abstruse thoughts about them. Indeed, there is truth in this, sometimes because the work is never finished or the results published; but more often because nothing is found that has any application or interest beyond learning about a place where nothing historically important happened to insignificant people.

Had the Carter's Grove tract been chopped up into housing developments and parking lots once Mary McCrea died, and had the information derived from our excavations been solely archaeological, one might justifiably have asked whether they had been worth the four years and half a million dollars invested. Instead, however, the felicitous circumstances that enabled the excavations to go on from discovery to discovery also gave us a protected locale, its noble eighteenth-century mansion already preserved and open to the public. Even so, a preserved site with no story to tell would have availed us little. The people of today are far more interested in the people of the past than they are in the inanimate artifacts that history left behind. Then, too, they are drawn to places where something important or dramatic occurred. They derive vicarious satisfaction from standing at "the place where . . ." and imagining themselves being there when whatever happened, happened.

At Carter's Grove (Martin's Hundred) all these requirements have been met, woven one into another through the archaeology—and the historical evidence. Although most of the Martin's Hundred Society's records must either have been discarded when the company folded or have burned when the City of London was consumed in the Great Fire of 1666, and regardless of the loss of the county court records in Richmond two centuries later, enough evidence has survived to place Martin's Hundred and Wolstenholme Town squarely on the map of American history. It merits its place in part, as I have noted, by default, an archaeological surrogate for early Jamestown, but also in its own right as the place where the real Americans, the Indians, were most successful in their 1622 attempt to destroy Britian's still shaky foothold.

Because these chapters have been shaped by the sometimes eccentric progress of an excavation rather than by an historical chronology, there has been no place here for most of the documentary evidence that either could not be linked to the archaeology or was not pieced together before the digging ended. Thus, for example, the impact of the contagion brought to Virginia aboard the relief ship *Abigail* in the winter of 1622 has barely been touched on, any more than has the fate of the female hostages and the cynical negotiations on the part of both English and Indians that eventually secured their release. Then, too, there was no recognizable archaeological evidence of the starving time in the late winter of 1623, when Governor Harwood was forced to tell his surviving servants that within two weeks the last of the food would be gone and they would then have to go out into the woods and eat roots. No artifacts recall that at that time the handful of Martin's Hundred survivors, like the rest of Virginia's sick and starving colonists, were pinning their hopes on the arrival of the corn-laden supply ship *Sea Flower*—which blew up in Bermuda's Castle Harbour and sank not far from Teddy Tucker's *Warwick*.

The high drama of the Indian attack and the visual impact of the scorched earth and hastily buried dead paints a terminating picture, and tends to leave an impression of a failed venture and wasted lives. In reality, it was only a beginning. Those who survived, along with the few new families who had faith enough to throw in their lot with the Society and who arrived in 1623, put down fresh roots from which grew the farms that would eventually become Merchant's Hundred parish and Carter's Grove plantation. All this, and more, is part of the history of Martin's Hundred.

Archaeology has been described as a handmaiden to history. Its products offer, at worst, an inadequate substitute for lost documents, and at best they provide dull historians and intimidating words with an added dimension to help them reach out to a broader public. As a rule, it is history that provides archaeologists with a reason to dig, but in Martin's Hundred it was the other way around.

The continuing research extends also to the artifacts, a trove from which both archaeologists and social historians will continue to draw for decades to come. If proof be needed, it was provided by conservator Hans Barlow even as this book was on its way to the press. While cleaning small strips of lead from lattice windows unearthed five years earlier on the supposed Harwood plantation (Site A)—hitherto thought to have nothing more to tell us—Hans discovered words and a date molded in relief and hidden within the leaden fold that had gripped the glass. The message read : IOHN : BYSHOPP OF EXCETER GONNER 1625—the earliest dated artifact from Martin's Hundred.

Although convincing proof that the filling of the "cave" house pit, where some of the lead was found, could not have occurred before 1625 and that leaded windows had been installed in a Site A house after that date, the inscription raised many more questions than it answered: Who was John Byshopp? Certainly he was not John, Bishop of Exeter. A "Gonner" sometimes was a varient of "Gunner," and a gunner occasionally was a synonym for gunsmith, but the word on the lead could be read as "Conner," and a conner was an inspector, usually of ale. Does "Exceter" mean Exeter in Devonshire, and is it thus supporting evidence for the presence on Site A of the Devon man, William Harwood? Or could "Conner" be a misspelling of "Corner"? There was a prominent corner in London's Strand where one of the city's great houses jutted into the street. Was it just a coincidence that the house belonged to the Earl of Exeter? Then, too, if Byshopp lived in London and not in Devon, would he not have described his place of business as being "at" rather than "of Exceter Corner"?

Given enough time and tenacity, we can expect to run John Byshopp to earth. When we find out who he was and what he did, we also may learn why he wanted his name and address hidden in tiny letters where no one would read them—until an eagle-eyed archaeological conservator opened the folded lead three hundred and fifty-six years later.

A View from
the Square
16

In the classical era of movie editing, the transition from the last chapter to this would have been marked by the blowing away of calendar pages or by accelerated seasonal changes in a tree's foliage. Lacking any such artistry, I can say only that having turned the page you find us nine years older, still hard at work on the products of the Martin's Hundred excavations, but pausing now and then to wipe the egg of error from our faces.

After 1979's annual *National Geographic* readers' poll had placed the "Lost Settlement" article fourth in a field of more than sixty, the editors somewhat reluctantly agreed to run another carrying the story beyond the completion of work at Wolstenholme Towne on to the discovery of Site H and the luckless Granny. My first suggestion that such an article might be in order had been received with shaking heads and the comment that "We rarely, if ever, run a follow-up archaeology piece," But they did, and in January 1982 "New Clues to an Old Mystery" landed in several million mailboxes. Asked by the picture editors to recreate the death of Granny, our by then good friend Richard Schlecht outdid himself (Figs. 16–1 and 16–2). Stripped to the waist and in the clutches of bad-intentioned Indians, Granny became the article's controversial frontispiece—and thus, albeit indirectly, the catalyst to turn all our thinking upside down. She also earned the article first place in that year's readers' poll.

In April 1980 Granny's story had gone to Washington as part of the National Geographic Society's exhibition titled "Searching for Another Century in Explorers Hall"—the hall being the society's headquarters exhibition area (Fig. 16–3). The show ran for nine months and reportedly drew close to three quarters of a million visitors. At the same time our completed film "Search for a Century" was aired on public television stations across the country, win-

16–1. Richard Schlecht's hair-raising interpretation of Granny's scalping as published in the *National Geographic* magazine.

16–2. Richard Schlecht's less controversial reconstruction of Granny's burial, a painting commissioned for inclusion in the archæological museum at Carter's Grove.

ning a Cine Golden Eagle and the New York Film Society's best documentary award. A somewhat shortened and improved version was reedited for use in England by the BBC, and that, coupled with the publication of this book in Britain, generated new interest on both sides of the Atlantic. There was no denying that although nobody had ever heard of Martin or knew what a hundred was (most called it Martin's One Hundred), the name had come to stay—which was more than could be said for the site.

The posts we had installed two years earlier in the holes at Wolstenholme Towne were still there, though their ribbons had been replaced by colored nylon ropes to differentiate more permanently between palisades, fences, and buildings (Fig. 16–4). At least they did so for us; the public, on the other hand, was less entranced yet still kept coming, drawn there by the magazine articles and television programs. Had it not been for that visitor interest, Colonial Williamsburg would have ordered the Wolstenholme site backfilled and returned to the plow. Instead, the word "reconstruction" began to be whispered on the wind, and I shuddered. Harrington had wisely deterred the National Park Service from rebuilding at Jamestown, and we certainly had no better evidence on which to do so at Wolstenholme Towne. My posts-in-the-holes solution, therefore, was as far as I thought we dared go before plunging over the cliff of speculation. If you knew what you were supposed to be looking at, the posts and their ropes made sense; but if you didn't, they didn't. And the public, by and large, didn't.

The single most important requirement for understanding how the people of past ages lived is to visualize the space in which they did it, space both horizontal and vertical. How big was the fort, how small the houses? Because one could see under the ropes and between our posts, no spaces could be defined. Indeed, from a distance, the several hundred posts resembled a forest of toothpicks. Not until I met a puzzled and obviously disgruntled visitor coming up the hill away from the site did I realize how uninformative they really were.

"Good morning," I said

"Grunt," came the reply.

"I hope you enjoyed your visit."

"Enjoyed?" huffed the grunter. "Let me tell you something. The Park Service did a pretty lousy job on that place."

"Is that so?" I mumbled, and Judas-like hastened on my way.

Shortly thereafter, Colonial Williamsburg's Carter's Grove development committee came to much the same conclusion and called for the reconstruction of part of the fort—as an experiment, they said, to see how visitors would react. Why not, they went on, whey not rebuild the flanker with its cannon platform?

My reactions to that were twofold. First, when we put money into building anything that substantial, experimental or not, it acquires a permanency that would be hard to eradicate. Second, of

16-3. This National Geographic Society's 1980–81 exhibition of the Martin's Hundred discoveries would lead to the funding of a permanent, on-site musuem.

16-4. Wolstenholme Towne in its "post and ropes" phase of reconstruction, visited by Sir Gordon and Lady Wolstenholme, descendants of Sir John Wolstenholme.

any structure we could choose to rebuild, the cannon platform was far and away the most problem fraught. Once it was up, the next requirement would be to find a cannon to mount on it—and it wouldn't take an ex-artilleryman to notice that if fired it would recoil off the back of the platform. However, I had been around long enough to know that in dealing with management committees, an unequivocal no is perceived as quirky negativism and quickly overruled. The only successful ploy is to warmly embrace the concept but to change the detail by offering a "better" alternative. Although one may not be wild about the substitute, it offers half a loaf and puts the committee in the negative role if it rejects it.

My proposal to reconstruct the fort's watchtower was accepted without objection, as was my suggestion that because the original fort would have been built from green, that is, unseasoned wood, we should do the same—to see how long such a structure would survive. I figured that if it was not an interpretive success, it could be relied on to rot and fall down quicker than a committee would agree to destroy it. Then, too, building the tower presented far fewer architectural and interpretive problems than would the gun platform. So up it went.

Built by Colonial Williamsburg's housewright, Roy Underhill, and a crew using colonial tools, the tower proved to be an impressively stable structure (Fig. 16–5). Measurements and other construction details for the flanking palisade sections came from the Duke of Ormond's contract (see p. 235) and from descriptions of Ferryland in Newfoundland and of Plymouth in Massachusetts. The

16–5. The fort's watchtower reconstructed but contrasting uneasily with the "post and ropes" demarcation.

placing and number of treenails used to hold the boards in place were taken from fifteenth-century illustrations to *Froissart's Chronicle,* while the treatment of the slotted musket ports came from a mid-sixteenth-century French woodcut of a wooden-walled tanklike vehicle. Hinges for the adjacent postern gate were copied from an example excavated at Jamestown (nothing that big having been found on the Wolstenholme site), while the padlock on the watchtower's door was copied by blacksmith Peter Ross from one found at Site A (Fig. 16–6). All in all, we had done as good a job of authenticating our tower as was possible short of having a drawing or a written description of the original. It remained to be seen what the public would make of it.

Roy Underhill had done a fine job; but to my eye the thing looked very odd, for with the rest of the fort and all the other Wolstenholme structures still defined by short posts and ropes, the tower stuck up in the middle of the field like a giant French privy. I secretly hoped that the public would hate it and that termites were already lunching on its posts. Architectural historian colleagues had made much of the fact that Wolstenholme-style post-in-the-ground structures could be regarded as impermanent architecture and would soon have been replaced by something much better.

The public, it turned out, loved the structure; agile kids could climb up its ladder to look for Indians from its platform, others could hide from their parents, and old men taken short could find surreptitious solace inside. I could only hope that collapse would

16–6. Attention to detail: an excavated padlock provided precedent for the reproduction used on the watchtower's door.

not long be delayed. Although a 1986 lightning strike blew a dramatic hole in the bark roof and split a corner post (surprisingly without igniting anything), our experimental green-wood watchtower stands today as solidly as ever. The posts and ropes, on the other hand, are gone, doomed not by some modern, high-tech inspiration but by the legacy of an Egyptian temple built in the first century A.D.

While standing on the roof of the temple at Dendera photographing graffiti left there by Napoleon's troops, I noticed how the low, early-morning sun cast heavy shadows along the ruined outer walls. These walls, built from mud brick, in some places had eroded away from their original sixteen-foot height down to a mere two or·three, yet the space they enclosed remained sharply defined. At each side, however, the great gates, being built of granite, had defied the centuries of windblown sand and survived to their original heights (Fig. 16–7). Could we not create a similar relationship for the palisade walls at the Wolstenholme fort, I asked myself? We had already raised the watchtower and its adjacent gate to something approximating their original height. We needed only to do the same for the river-facing main gate and to raise the connecting palisade walls to a height of eighteen inches or two feet, just high enough to create the necessary shadows.

With the help of a talented neighborhood builder and carpenter, Woodrow Abbott, that's what we did—and dubbed it the Dendera Solution. We treated the Company Compound palisade in the same way; but having gone that far, we could no longer leave the buildings to be marked only by the short posts and ropes. Instead, we replaced them with hewn pasts of sizes representing the average widths of those whose stains had been measured during the excavations. Between them we laid interrupted sills, filling the area contained within the resulting rectangles with heavy gravel to more graphically define the lived-in spaces—and to keep down the weeds (Fig. 16–8). Where the architectural geometry permitted it, we also reconstructed the framing for one end of each structure, thus to define their vertical as well as their horizontal space. The same technique was employed to interpret the Company Barn.

The barn had been a curious structure in that it had such massive roof-bearing post-holes down its center but only the lightest post evidences at its corner where much of the weight should have been carried (see p. 254). In the midst of the excavation, we had no time to pursue structural nuances, and as the *National Geographic* needed an interim interpretation from the brushes of Richard

16–7. The view from the roof of the Ptolemaic temple at Dendera in Egypt that provided inspiration for the final Wolstenholme Towne reconstruction.

16–8. Wolstenholme Towne reconstructed, with the Company Compound in the foreground and the fort beyond it. The intrusive visitor-orientation shed on the ridge behind would be replaced by the buried museum.

Schlecht, I had decided to reconstruct the building in the centuries-old European style: short side walls barely head high under vast roofs covering upper-floor storage spaces. But when it came to carrying our interpretation beyond the printed page to actually set timbers in the ground, the question, "Why no corner posts?" had to be answered.

A careful study of the small holes' profiles showed that some at the west tilted east while some at the east tipped west. It was belatedly clear that the rafters had not rested on low walls but reached right to the ground, creating a triangular-ended, tentlike structure known in its smaller versions in the seventeenth century as a cabin. In short, it had been an aboveground version of the cellared structure we had found at Site A (see p. 56).

Because the surviving traces of Wolstenholme Towne represented something akin to two and a half sides of a square, we could see at a glance that from the visitors' point of view we had a problem. We wanted them to visit the fort, the Company Compound to its left, *and* the barn a hundred yards to the right. But more than that, we wanted them to walk round the remaining side and a half of the square that represents what is left of the village green. With no archaeological attraction at the riverside corner, there was nothing to incite visitors to continue in that direction—except the river, the atomic power station on the opposite bank, and the navy's reserve fleet of transport ships farther downstream. So why not encourage the tourists to look at those through a boardwalk-style telescope while telling them about sailing the river in the seventeenth century?

Telling was to be an integral element of the Dendera Solution. I had proposed installing taped explanations at each stopping point along the route, concealing the speakers in wooden barrels.

"Barrels!" exclaimed one committee member. "Why barrels, for God's sake?"

"Why not regular brick pillars like the Park Service uses?" asked another. "Why try to be cute?"

I wasn't trying to be cute. Because our reconstructions were to be entirely of wood, it seemed inappropriate to impose anachronistic brick pillars into a setting which otherwise was representative of place and period. As a photographer myself, I had grown to curse exhibit designers who allowed such intrusions to spoil my pictures. Barrels, I explained, were used in the seventeenth century to carry anything from apples to yard goods. If they had had audio equipment in the seventeenth century, they would have transported it in barrels. The logic of this argument had weaknesses, but delivered with sufficient fervor it baffled the critics. So barrels there would be—and a buried spider's web of wires spread across the ground of Wolstenholme Towne, all leading up to a phalanx of tape players housed in the Carter's Grove mansion.

Within a week of their installation, lightning from an over-the river thunderstorm shot an electrical jolt into the ground, sending it surging through our wires up the hill and into the mansion, there surprising the tape players to the point of self-destruction. The damage was estimated at close on twenty thousand uninsured dollars. "No," said the suppliers, "acts of God are not included under the warranty."

A system of breakers was quickly installed, and while that reduced the impact of lightning strikes, lesser damage has occurred several times over the years, the wires under Wolstenholme remaining a vast antenna attracting surges even when the strike is far out in the river. Curiously, however, until 1990 neither the barrels nor their speakers had ever been damaged.

Winning the battle of the barrels was gratifying; but what they had to say, and how they'd say it, would be the key to ultimate success or failure. Armed with a stopwatch, I had listened to what I called "guff boxes" at several outdoor museums and parks, to find out how long visitors would stand and listen. Four minutes was the maximum, so we kept ours to an average of two and a half. More importantly (and I had not seen this at any of the examples I had visited), our push-button labels identified the duration of each talk. Thus, before pressing the button the visitor knew how long he or she might expect to stand there. We found that while visitors would stand contentedly through the first two or three barrels' worth, at the next points on the route many would be shifting from one foot to the other after about ninety seconds and would walk away before the lecturette ended. There are now seventeenth-century-style benches beside those later barrels.

Most audio programs we had listened to at Jamestown and elsewhere were either roundly enunciated by a professional voice or radio-style conversations read by actors speaking eccentric and sometimes unintelligible olde English dialects derisively known to thespians as Mummersetshire. Neither reached out to involve the listener, and consequently he remained an outsider. There being nothing to involve his eyes, he was likely soon to be asking himself "Why am I standing here listening to this stuff? What's in it for me?" I decided, therefore, that if the visitors could know that they were being talked to, not by a hired mouth, but by the project director; and if they could be challenged to help solve outstanding problems, they would feel sufficiently involved to stay with us. To that end, each barrel's segment would conclude with a segue to the next: "If you want to know why the village green is tapering toward the river, I'll tell you about it when we get there." And by and large, they *do* get there.

Not everyone gets the message, however. When I proposed raising the palisade paling just high enough to cast the necessary shadows, I jokingly hoped that no one would assume that this was a full reconstruction. The hope went unrealized. On opening day, an enthusiastic visitor came up to me and assured me that this was as exciting a historical experience as she could remember. "But fancy," she said, "fancy those poor colonists having to lie down behind such little walls."

In spite of our far-reaching documentary research, none could deny that it was all secondary material, for not one word survives to tell us that there was a fort at Wolstenholme Towne, let alone describe its construction. Once we cut boards of undocumented width and secured them with treenails of conjectured sizes, we were sliding down the slippery path of speculation toward the netherworld of fantasy. It is true that few if any restoration or reconstructive projects avoid it, and Williamsburg is certainly no exception. Nevertheless, when presenting a period about whose military domestic architecture we know all too little, the need for integrity is even greater.

At least one of my professional peers persuasively takes an opposing view. If nobody can prove you wrong, go ahead and do it, he says. You can always fix it later, when somebody comes up with proof that you erred. I should add that my colleague is capable of charming students into thinking that he and they can walk on water.

Isn't it better, he argues, to give people an impression of the past, even if it's false, than to give them nothing at all? Then with a disarming smile, he adds: "I'm just being the devil's advocate, you understand." On the contrary, he is the real Beelzebub, for such a rationale in the wrong ear can appear to justify even the most blatant and irresponsible exploitation.

At Wolstenholme Towne the barrels were to be our crutch and our salvation. With them we could do anything we liked—providing we explained what we had done and why. Thus at the fort we used sawn planks, though we could not be sure whether the originals would have been sawn or riven. And we say so. And at the Company Compound we used split boards without knowing whether they were riven or sawn. Again we say so. Thus the visitor has an opportunity to inspect the very different-looking products of each method, while knowing that they may not have been used where he sees them.

Marking graves posed another problem. No evidences of post-holes for wooden crosses were found, nor were slots for standing head-stones for flat gravestones. That was hardly surprising, for such iden-tification was rare even in English churchyards before the late seventeenth century, most earlier memorials to wealthy individuals below the level of the nobility being limited to ledgers set in the church floors. In Virginia, one of the earliest surviving gravestones whose date is still legible is also the only artifact bearing the name of Martin's Hundred. Discovered on the site of the second Martin's Hun-dred parish church, some three miles from Wolstenholme Towne, it reads:

> Here Lieth in hope of joyfull
> Resvrrection the body of
> SAMVELL POND of Martins
> Hundred parish in james
> City covnty in the Dominio^n
> of Virginia Physician whoe
> DeparteD this Life the 26 of
> october in the year of ovr
> Lord 1694 aged 48

A landscape architect hired as a consultant suggested using similar flat slabs to mark the Wolstenholme Towne graves, inscribing each with what little we think we know about their occupants. My objections were threefold: Such stones were not used in the Wolstenholme period, visitors would not see them unless they were standing right beside them, and grass mowing would damage both stones and blades. In-stead, I proposed a gabled wooden marker, the shape reminiscent both of our gable-lidded coffins and of the long mounds of displaced dirt that would have covered the back filled graves (Fig. 16–9). Painted green, inscribed with their occupants' sex and estimated ages, and elevated sufficiently high for weed-eaters to cut beneath their edges, the markers provided a dignified, easily recognizable, yet unobtrusive memorial to the dead of Wolstenholme Towne. But where, visitors wanted to know, was the grave of Granny?

That became the most frequently asked question. Thanks to the *National Geographic* article, she had come to epitomize both the pioneering spirit and the violent deaths of all the Martin's Hundred settlers. For reasons buried deep in the human psyche (where they are best left undisturbed), countless serious and respectable visitors felt cheated by being denied the opportunity to stand at the place where Granny's lifeblood had ebbed away. A marker telling them that she had died beyond the next tree-line at the so-called Wolstenholme Suburb, which had not been reconstructed, drew the response, "Well, why not?"

Why not, indeed?

After considerable debate, Colonial Williamsburg decided to bow to Granny's constituents and agreed that we should treat the suburb in the same way that we had Wolstenholme proper. You will recall that we had found Site H after the work at Wolstenholme Towne was completed. Being no more than a single house surrounded by a palisade, it was much smaller than, say, the Company Compound, and being some four hundred feet east of the compound and located beyond a separating ravine, it had to be an afterthought, an extension, thus a suburb of the town. Besides, we had found it second—which had absolutely no legitimate bearing on anything beyond the fact that it had cemented the word "secondary" firmly into my mind.

16–9. Gabled grave markers beside the reconstructed Domestic Unit at Wolstenholme Towne.

Located partly on the edge of a much-plowed field and partly in a densely wooded strip flanking the ravine, Site H had not been easy to excavate. The ground was pocked by numerous root holes as well as by a miscellany of legitimate post-holes far more difficult to untangle and interpret than had been anything at Wolstenholme Towne or, indeed, at any other previously explored Martin's Hundred site. Now, however, if our contractor Woody Abbott was to have our suburb up and ready for the 1985 season, the post-hole patterns had to be untangled in a hurry. Furthermore, if my new barrels were to have anything intelligent to say, we would have to decide just when the suburb was added and who lived there.

Sorting out the post-holes and making rough reconstructive sketches were my responsibility; Audrey's was to establish the who and the when. We had initially concluded that Granny had to be the lady of the house, on the evidence of her superior hairdo. You may recall, too, that we also had the evidence of the four servants lying in their single grave—two invaluable clues to be correlated with the published listings of the massacred dead. But they also raised disturbing questions. Why would survivors take the trouble to dig a neat grave for the four servants while leaving their mistress amid the ashes and mud of a household refuse pit?

Remembering that in addition to the mistress and four servants, we had found the graves of two more women, we had come up with only two family groups that seemed to fit the cast list, those of Nathanael Jefferies and of "Master Tho: Boise, & Mistris Boise his wife" (see p. 292). A visiting scholar just returned from working in Holland pointed out that what I had been calling a hair wire could equally well have been a spring used to secure a lace or linen cap—caps worn not only by people of consequence but also by their servants (Fig. 16–10). By this time we had discovered a brass-wired grip in the collection of the Museum of London, one terminating at both ends in beads of pewter or lead. Our iron wire had just such a bead at one end. But Granny's head was small, and the band had been shortened at the other end, its lead bead replaced by a simple twist of the metal. In short, it was a hand-me-down kind of head spring, the kind of thing less likely to have been worn by a mistress than a maid—a maid who when found in a trash pit could have been left where she conveniently lay and covered only with enough dirt dug from the side to conceal her from hungry animals.

With Granny downgraded from mistress to maid, another household became eligible for consideration, that of John Boise (possibly a brother to Thomas), whose listing read

Master Iohn Boise his
Wife.
A Maide.
4 Men-seruants

There being no comma after Boise, the citation is read, not as John Boise and his wife, but as Boise's wife alone. Subsequent events were to prove that either interpretation would have been wrong. Mistress Boise did not die in the attack; she was carried off as hostage by the Indians and would not be released until April of the next year, by

16–10. Portrait of an unidentified seventy-four-year-old Dutch woman, dated 1654. Her cap is secured by a spring visible as a light line between the fold and the frill.

which time her husband may have returned to England. Thus, with Sarah Boise off the list, her husband's losses were reduced to the maid and four male servants. There remained in addition, however, the skeletons of one young female and the woman we called "The Key Lady"; and so to make any of our interpretations work, we had to accept either that they had died at some other time (see p. 295) or that they were visitors to the Boise homestead who were listed among the dead of other plantations. I cannot deny that this out comes perilously close to brushing contrary evidence under the rug, but I am emboldened to do so because so much else falls neatly into place.

As we played and replayed the childhood game of connecting the dots (post-holes) on our plans of Site H, two features showed up time and again, namely the previously discussed pair of flankers—far larger than was necessary to provide mere enfilading musket defense for so small a compound (Fig. 16–11). The smaller of the two faced east across the adjacent field, but the larger projected alongside the ravine and pointed toward the river, seemingly defending the compound from any attempt to land an enemy onto the beach at the mouth of the access route to the settled high ground. The upstream side of the flanker exhibited a curious jog created by an intermediate post absent from the opposite side. If a cannon had been mounted on the platform (if, indeed, it had one), the jog would have provided the gunners with

16–11. The Boise Site partially reconstructed; its palisade pierced by musket ports, no traces of a firing step having been found.

space to change the angle of fire toward ships approaching from down-river. The flaw in that argument, of course, was that we only knew of Martin's Hundred possessing one cannon and that, we contended, would have been mounted in the undersized flanker in the fort and not at the suburb.

But what about John Boise (or Boys as his name was most often spelled), what role did he play in the Wolstenholme scenario?

Audrey's historical research had led her to conclude that the Martin's Hundred settlers who came over on the *Gift of God* were actually Puritans who, like the later Massachusetts "pilgrims," had settled at Leiden in the Netherlands before leaving to seek religious freedom in the New World. Their ship, Audrey reasoned, was a now-unidentified vessel carrying the Separatists under the leadership of a man named Blackwell, which reached Virginia at about the same time as the *Gift of God,* after having lost a major proportion of her passengers on the way over. If, as Audrey supposed, Blackwell's vessel and the *Gift of God* were one and the same, then the 220 settlers sent over the by the Society of Martin's Hundred in 1619 had been whittled away to a desperate few by the time they reached Jamestown. This could explain why Virginia's governor, Sir Francis Wyatt, rather than sending them down to take up the 20,000 acres due to them, instead put them to work on his own property on the Maine adjacent to Jamestown. With their leadership dead (if such was the case), the governor could legitimately keep them under his protection and control until the society sent out new leaders and fresh instructions. This interpretation could also explain the belated arrival in 1620 of Martin's Hundred's governor, William Harwood. We know, however, that John Boise represented the hundred at Virginia's first general Assembly in July 1619, at which time he was identified as the plantation's warden.

The term has several meanings, but in this case it would seem to represent a viceroy or regent appointed to rule in the absence of a superior. That the title was not appended to his name after Harwood arrived is supportive of that interpretation. Previously, however, Warden Boise had much to do. Because the lands assigned to each of the Virginia Company's subsidiaries were dependent not on the number of settlers but on the number of shareholders, and because it had been ordained that no settlement could be located within five miles of another, it was imperative that the Society of Martin's Hundred's 20,000 acres be secured while there was still prime real estate for the asking.

Once the application for acreage had been made to the governor and it had been assigned, somebody had to take possession. Otherwise, newly arriving applicants could argue that unoccupied lands were fair game. No document says that in so many words, but the opportunities for confusion and intrusion are clear enough. It seems safe to argue, therefore, that to secure the society's claim, Warden Boise moved with his wife and servants onto the land while the rest of the settlers, most of whom were employees of the shareholders, remained at Jamestown—where Governor Wyatt was glad of the labor.

Pursuing this scenario, John Boise selects a strategic location on high ground wide enough and flat enough to later build a town. He finds a draw leading up to that high ground and in it a freshwater spring. Recognizing that by establishing himself on the bluff immediately downstream from the draw will protect both the water supply and access to the town from the beach, he builds a small fort whose palisades project into a flanker capable of supporting Martin's Hundred's one big gun (Fig. 16–12). Keeping the fort small but strong would make it possible for Boise's four male servants to defend the enclosure with their muskets as well as to service and fire the cannon should a Spaniard lie off and try to lighter troops ashore for an assault up the draw.

Intending that the town should be built on the flat acreage on the upstream side of the draw, Boise concludes that while his first small fort will remain his well-defended home, it will continue to be of service to the main settlement by providing both an early warning station and its first line of defense (Fig. 16–13).

Our Wolstenholme Suburb thesis proved to be a classic example of thinking that merited what military correspondent David Evans has defined as the pyramid perspective. To most people a pyramid is a triangle; but from below it is a square, while from above it becomes an X within a square. We had been content to see only the triangle; now we were seeing the square, if not the X inside it. From this fresh perspective, other problems resolved themselves, not the least of them the need to explain why Wolstenholme Towne's fort lay at the back of the town and not at the cliff edge where it could defend against shipborne Spaniards.

John Boise's palisaded homestead was the settlement's front line. The fort protected the rear, and by being so placed it gave settlers both time to retreat and a place to regroup. As for the nagging problem of the big gun on a ludicrously tiny platform, that, too, disappeared. The saker was never there. Instead, the small flanker almost certainly supported a much smaller swivel gun, probably of the kind defined as a falconet or murderer. Able to fire nails, small rocks, and miscellaneous sharp trash at an enemy advancing up the green, it could also swing around to enfilade attackers trying to breach the fort's

16–12. The Boise Site's cannon platform. The saker's tube has been cast from a 1601 example in the Tower of London, and its carriage copied in part from those found aboard the 1628 wreck of the *Wasa*.

16–13. Central detail from Richard Schlecht's painting of the Boise Site, commissioned for use in the Martin's Hundred museum at Carter's Grove.

main gate. This interpretation readily explained the presence of the large log of wood beneath the platform which hitherto had been thought to carry a vertical post used to reinforce the floor to carry the big gun's weight. Instead, it seated the post into which the swivel gun was mounted.

Thanks, therefore, to the public's interest in Granny, the freshly written history of Martin's Hundred was turned on its ear, demonstrating the fallibility of one-dimensional archaeological conclusions. That, however, was not to be the limit of Granny's influence, nor was it the end of her story.

Umbrellas and Chain Saws

17

With excavations at the Boise Site ended, it had been time to return once again to eighteenth-century Williamsburg, specifically to renewing excavations on the site of the Public Hospital for the Insane, then to be rebuilt as part of Colonial Williamsburg's multi million-dollar decorative arts museum. But although fieldwork had ceased at Martin's Hundred, the processing, conservation, and analysis of its extensive artifact collections went on—though steadily losing space to the stream of eighteenth- and nineteenth-century material flowing into the laboratory from the Public Hospital site. Archaeology, particularly *historical* archaeology, is a space-hungry activity, and Williamsburg's archaeological plant had been neither enlarged nor significantly improved in more than fifteen years of almost round-the-calendar digging.

The growing logistical crisis took on a new dimension when in the spring of 1982 Colonial Williamsburg decided to go forward with its long-resolved intent to build a new visitor center at Carter's Grove. The access road to the chosen site threatened to slice through the middle of the unexcavated Site J—the one the *Washington Post* had declared "May Shed Light on Va. 'Dark Ages.'" Although that claim was specious, there was no denying the site's importance to the history of Martin's Hundred and Carter's Grove. Something had to be done, and done quickly, before the Site J field became not only the visitor center's access road but also its parking lot.

Under the immediate supervision of old Martin's Hundred hand John Hamant, a new crew assembled to try to find a road route that would not adversely impact on the archaeological site. Because all that we knew of it had been concentrated toward the middle of the field, I decided that our safest bet would be to cut a thirty-foot-wide swath through the plow zone hugging the tree line at its westerly edge. As a demonstration of intuitive decision making, mine ranked very low indeed. The entire strip was riddled with seventeenth-century post-holes, pits, ditches, and two graves (Fig. 17–1). Although most dated from about 1640 to 1655, there were hints that part of the site had included a fortification dating as early as the 1620s. This clearly was not the place to put a road.

It is (or it should be) an old archaeological adage that an absentee director is no director at all. As he or she is ultimately responsible for a site's interpretation, it follows that what he does not see, he cannot verify. Nevertheless, it a fact of life in most professionals that people at the top no longer do what once they did best. Throughout the first decade of my work in Williamsburg I had been in the field controlling and checking every inch of progress; but now I was trying to direct excavations both in town and at Carter's Grove and supervise operations in an increasingly clogged workplace, while sitting on committees focusing more on business than research and attending management classes on how to be nice to naughty employees. It was enough to promote a heart attack. So it did.

Six weeks after bypass surgery, I was back trying to pick up the pieces at Site J, this time with a cut down the opposite side

17–1. A plethora of post-holes at Site J made this an unpromising location for a visitor-center road.

of the field. Though less scarred by seventeenth-century occupation, the new clearance exposed the remains of two post-built houses of the 1680s as well as the opposite ends of several ditches and fence lines previously revealed in the first cut. By this time the visitor center planners were losing patience with archaeology. A road there would be whether archaeologists liked it or not. But the only remaining alternative route lay down the middle of the field where we believed lay the heart of the colonial site. It made compromising sense, therefore, to release the eastern route and agree that the road should go over the late seventeenth-century house sites.

Testing in the woods where the visitor center was to be located had yielded slender traces of Indian occupation—a few scattered potsherds of the quantity and kind one finds throughout most of tidewater Virginia. Nevertheless, it was mandatory once the building site had been defined that we should go in and convert the test holes into area excavations, if only to be sure that there was nothing there. The hit-or-miss character of test-hole surveys and their quite remarkable propensity for missing what matters had been graphically demonstrated at the Boise Site. Nevertheless, the dearth of Indian artifacts in the visitor center area had convinced us that this was to be an exercise in necessary futility. Wrong again.

Once the standard ten-foot squares were opened, most of them exposed a four- to five-inch layer of Indian occupation comprising thousands of oyster shells and hundreds of potsherds dating from the Early Woodland period (Ca. A.D. 200–800). That the occupation may, in reality, have been concentrated not in centuries but in months would later be revealed when the pottery was mended and found to represent pieces of the same vessels scattered widely across the site. This was the most artifact-rich Indian site found at Carter's grove. But the ground was extremely sandy and unstable, therefore calling for very slow and careful digging—too slow for the construction engineers to countenance. So, as at any building site, we archaeologists outstayed our welcome (as well as our budget) and had to abandon the dig long before it had yielded all that it might.

Disappointment is archaeology's rule rather than its exception, and more often than not it is the prospect of what *might* be, rather than what is, that keeps archaeologists from seeking more gainful employment. For us, the quest for a surviving gable-lidded coffin continued through these early years of the 1980s. By then, however, a onetime London skeptic had now become our most important ally. A respected student of funerary art, Julian Litten, deputy curator in the Victoria and Albert Museum's department of prints and drawings, had grown as anxious to locate a surviving coffin as were we. Having accepted that our Martin's Hundred evidence, supported by the corpus of contemporary illustrations, left little doubt that gabled coffins had been common in the early seventeenth century, Julian wanted to carry them back even further—specifically to 1545.

That was the year in which the *Mary Rose,* Henry VIII's famed flagship, sank at the entrance to Portsmouth harbor. There she lay until October 11, 1982, when she emerged from the stormy water to bring to its triumphal end one of the world's most spectacular archaeological salvage exploits. Perhaps fearing the wrong kind of publicity, the Mary Rose Trust had been reticent about the number of drowned crewmen and soldiers its divers had found aboard the wreck. Nevertheless, the ship had gone down with the loss of about 660 lives, and it was inevitable that many would be recovered. Once studied, the bones of all but one were returned to the sea. In Portsmouth Cathedral on July 19, 1984, that remaining unknown sailor soldier was to be buried as representative of all. It therefore fell to Julian Litten to provide drawings for the coffin, whose lid, thanks to a seventeenth-century carpenter working three thousand miles away in Martin's Hundred, would be gabled (Fig. 17–2).

In 1983 Julian wrote to say that at Steane Park in Northamptonshire he had found a 1634 memorial to one Temperance Browne whose monument showed her sitting bolt upright in her gable-ended coffin (Fig. 17–3). Julian felt sure that an excavation below the monument would find Temperance not upright, but certainly in her gabled coffin. Preliminary magnetometer testing by specialists from the Department of the Environment had assured him that the grave had not been disturbed by later burials.

Permission to dig up the floor of Christian churches, no matter how scholarly the purpose, is not easily obtained, and the final authority from the diocese was not nailed to the church door (as the law required) until hours before we were due to begin. It was not a good omen. My hopes that we would be gently troweling down through easily worked loam were promptly dashed when the floor slabs came up to reveal more compacted rocks than soil (Fig. 17–4). Local workmen who had been hired to shift the dirt for us smiled and shook their heads at the peculiar behavior of these city folks. Meanwhile, adding a Hogarthian touch to the affair, Steane Park's elderly and mildly inebriated owner made amorous advances to Audrey betwixt the pews. As we dug slowly down, hoping at

17–2. Craftsman Michael Spreadborough made this Martin's Hundred—derived coffin for a representative casualty of the 1545 *Mary Rose* tragedy in Portsmouth harbor.

17–3. A "resurrection tomb": this 1634 monument to Temperance Browne at Steane Park in England suggested that she had been buried in a gabled coffin. The trick was finding it.

any moment to find the dark line of the coffin's ridge, the foundations of the church wall stepped ever farther out into our trench, until eventually they filled the entire space. Behind us stood the brick wall of an eighteenth-century family vault whose construction had almost certainly reduced Temperance Browne and her coffin to little more than we found—one corner reinforcement and a single finger bone.

A year later we were back to follow another promising Julian Litten lead, this time at the stunningly beautiful Wiltshire church at Lydiard Tregoze (Fig. 17–5). Among its several treasures is a magnificent triptych painted in 1615 and depicting Sir John St.

17–4. Excavating under Temperance Browne's monument left everyone in the dark.

John and his family—and in the foreground the gabled ends of three coffins (Fig. 17–6). Julian's research indicated that the family's vault had been built in the fifteenth century, but when it was remodeled in 1748 all the earlier St. Johns were sealed behind a rubble wall. Wrote Julian, "Should we peer behind this rubble wall or would we be on a hiding for nothing?"

17–5. The simplicity of the church at Lydiard Tregoze in Wiltshire belied the splendor of the seventeenth-century monuments inside it, not the least of them the tantalizing coffin-depicting triptych of Sir John St. John and his family.

17–6. A detail from the 1615 St. John triptych showing the three gabled coffins that prompted yet another ecclesiastical debacle.

It was a good question that could be answered in only one way. With research funding almost depleted, in September 1984 the team reassembled for what we all agreed would have to be our last attempt.

The entrance to the St. John tomb was covered by a massive stone slab set in the church floor, beneath which a flight of narrow brick steps led down into a vaulted chamber containing several sagging, late eighteenth- and nineteenth-century coffins. Several of their corroded brass fittings had fallen off and lay on the floor as fanciful green shapes amid the remains of moldering wood. The smell was noticeably unattractive. Beyond the main chamber where the few coffins rested relatively neatly was a narrow doorway, and beyond it another chamber containing a jumble of lead coffins, the weight of those on top flattening the ones beneath into unrecognizable shapes. Were these, we asked ourselves, the remains of those early St. Johns who had supposedly been sealed away in 1748?

One thing was certain: If any of the lower and earlier lead coffins had been gabled like those at Withyham, there was no way that we could get to them. Besides, what we needed was a surviving *wooden* coffin. But then again, here was no rubble wall. If such a wall lay beyond the stacked coffins it would place the family far distant from the chapel containing their monuments. It seemed more likely, in Julian's view, that the medieval burial place lay in the other direction, beyond the first vault's west end, a wall apparently constructed entirely of rough stone. We therefore instructed the mason who had been hired to open and reseal the vault to chip a hole through it just large enough to determine whether Julian was right (Fig. 17–7).

The instruction was easily given, but the chipping was something else again. If this was a wall to close another vault, its builder evidently intended that no one should ever reenter it. Inch by inch, and through two hours, the mason pecked away the mortar around the rocks, creating a ragged and tapering hole, its shape dictated by such stones as reluctantly consented to be pried loose. Watching and waiting, we compared ourselves to Howard Carter and Lord Carnarvon as their Egyptian workmen removed the sealing stones from the entrance to Tutankhamen's tomb. But where they broke through into stygian darkness, we got a trickle of sand and black dirt. We had chippy-chip-chipped our way through a three-foot-thick foundation of the church and into the backfilled builder's trench beyond.

The great gabled-coffin caper was over. Although Julian knew of other churches where we could expect better luck, I was certain that with the last of our National Geographic Society grant funding exhausted, nobody would be fool enough to underwrite another expedition. Indeed, I had by then convinced myself that while we might find more gabled lead liners, our chances were nil that we would ever find a tomb whose seventeenth-century wooden coffins had not be moved and damaged beyond recognition in the eighteenth or nineteenth century.

Several weeks later, while repairing Exton church in Somersetshire, surveyor François Jones saw its nineteenth-century floor collapse into an unfilled grave. In it, partially obscured by fallen debris, lay the occupant in the remains of his wooden gabled coffin (Fig. 17–8). A scarcely readable ledger stone nearby put its date at 1608. Although François Jones preserved samples of the wood and measured and photographed what he saw, he did not immediately recognize its significance. Consequently, by the time Julian Litten heard of the breakthrough (in all senses of the term), the floor had already been replaced.

17–7. Penetrating the "rubble wall" at Lydiard Tregoze.

17–8. The history of archaeology is replete with accidental great discoveries. Here was another: the remains of a 1608 gabled coffin found at Exton church in Somerset.

Although the gabled character of the Exton coffin was unde-
niable, the photographs clearly showed that nothing of the lid had
survived in situ. There was no point, therefore, in applying for the
grave to be reopened—a request which, with the new floor just
laid, would have been received by the vestry with minimal joy.

If the point still needed to be made (and some doubted that it
did), the Exton evidence laid to rest the claim by the historian
spokesman for the British Council for Places of Worship who had
insisted that "there is no hope of Mr. Hume finding an A-lidded
coffin in any vault in England." There was no denying a modicum
of satisfaction from proving that I was right and he wasn't, but that
was not the object of the exercise. The quest's purpose was to find
a coffin whose construction could be studied and its nail placement
compared to the positioning of those found in the Martin's Hundred graves. At that level, therefore, our efforts and even our luck
had availed us naught.

Six thousand miles away on the coast of southwest Africa, Rutgers University professor Carmel Shrire was excavating on the site
of a Dutch fort built in the 1660s and known as Oudepost I, when
she found the grave of a middle-aged man. His grave had been dug
through and backfilled with beach sand, which had filtered into the
coffin as its wood slowly rotted away. Carmel had read about our
Martin's Hundred research and knew at once what she was looking
at when she saw a row of nails running down the centerline of the
grave (Fig. 17–9). At Martin's Hundred the weight of clay over the
decaying lids had caused them to collapse onto the skeleton, dis-
placing the nails. At Oudepost I the running sand had prevented
the ridge nails from dropping, leaving them suspended in the sand
where, by dint of brilliant excavating, Carmel and her team were
able to provide the evidence that had so long eluded us.

This unexpected conclusion came at a propitious moment. We
were about to order the building of two reproduction coffins, one for
exhibition use and the other as Granny's final (we hoped) resting place.
Lifted from her pit in December 1980, her bones had allegedly been
in the course of study for close on nine years. I use the word "allegedly" because in reality the level of study was akin to the kind of
claims Hollywood producers used to trumpet their epic movies:
"Three years in the making!"—meaning four months shooting in '34,
six months firing and hiring directors in '35, and so on. Granny had
taken a prolonged trip to the Smithsonian and had been subjected to
several specialized bone analyses over the years, but most of the time
had been spent on a storeroom shelf while we put off deciding what to

do with her. The court order authorizing her exhumation required that once she had served her scientific purposes, she (and all other human remains) should be returned to the place whence they came.

Returning bones to their graves made perfect sense, but Granny had not been in a grave. Putting her back into the trash pit that could not have been her burial place of choice seemed less then considerate. Surely she would have wished for a dignified interment. But what constituted dignity by seventeenth-century colonial standards, and how would they correspond with burial practices today? Should we be replicating those of her time or conforming to ours? Should there be a graveside service, and if so for what denomination? Was she a Puritan as Audrey believes most of the *Gift of God's* Martin's Hundred passengers to have been, or was she just a standard, God-fearing servant hired in London whose religious beliefs were governed by whatever her master thought best?

These debates surfaced whenever the question "What are we to do with Granny?" was asked, but like bubbles in a soufrière they rose,

17–9. From a small Dutch fort in southwest Africa came the ultimate archaeological evidence, a gabled coffin buried in sand which suspended its roof nails in more or less their original locations.

burst, and vanished until the question came up again. In 1989, however, it became more than academic. As part of the reorganization of
Colonial Williamsburg's archaeological collections, the newly appointed collections managers saw Granny in terms of coveted linear
shelf space—and wished her gone.

I had insisted that regardless of the fact that to our knowledge
no victim of the 1622 Indian attack had been buried in a coffin,
Granny could not go back as a collection of loose bones. She should
be allowed the luxury of a coffin—and nobody doubted what kind I
had in mind. Ever conscious of the image-tattering winds of public
opinion, Colonial Williamsburg's public relations chiefs ordained that
there should be simple Anglican prayers, but that there should be no
hint of exploitation, no leakage to the press, no invitations to local
dignitaries. So tight was the security that even the Foundation's own
photographer assigned to record the burial was not to be told what he
was to shoot until hours before the interment was to take place. But
successful secrecy requires that everyone in on the secret knows that it
is a secret, and in this instance they didn't. Gardeners had to be scheduled to dig the grave, coffin-lowerers had to be invited, equipment
borrowed from a local funeral director, and transportation organized,
not to mention arranging photo opportunities for the National Geographic Society's contracted photographer. Then, too, someone
thought it appropriate to invite people involved both in the original
excavation and with the bones' subsequent conservation.

The coffin had been constructed by the rebuilder of Wolstenholme Towne, Woodrow Abbott, and to it was nailed a plaque engraved by Colonial Williamsburg's silversmith, summarizing what we
knew about Granny and noting that she had been reburied on November 8, 1989. It did not specify, however, that it was to have taken
place at 3:00 p.m. as the invited attendees were advised. Inside the
coffin, in a sealed plastic tube designed and made by National Geographic Society technicians (and expected to survive until and beyond
the last trump), was a copy of the January 1982 issue of the magazine
that told and illustrated Granny's story, albeit, as we now knew, somewhat incorrectly.

The weather forecast for November 8 prophesied several shades
of doom, and for once it was right. Rain showers began around 1:30
p.m., and by two o'clock it had settled into a bone-chilling downpour.
Several frantic phone calls elicited the command decision that come
hell or high water (and possibly both), Granny would be buried at
3:00 p.m.

I had asked that the coffin be on site beside the newly dug grave no later than 2:15, and that for the benefit of the photographers the lowerers would be there by 2:30. These were to be coffin-builder Woody Abbott, John Hamant representing the original archaeological supervisors, foreman Nate Smith who had actually excavated the skeleton, and myself. The prayers were to be read by the vicar of Bruton Parish, the Reverend Richard May, who arrived on the increasingly muddy site shortly after 2:30, where he changed into his vestments under a dripping umbrella in the gateway of the reconstructed Boise pallisade. Rivulets of rain trickled into the open grave and down the necks of the waiting burial detail, while a biting wind off the river turned soaked faces various shades of pink and blue. In spite of well-meaning but competing umbrellas, the Reverend Mr. May was becoming significantly sodden.

"I think maybe we'd better get on with it," said a senior vice president. And so we did (Fig. 17–10).

17–10. In a somber and sodden ceremony delayed by 367 years, Granny's formal funeral took place on November 8, 1989.

Ten minutes and more after Granny's gabled coffin had disappeared beneath the backfilled dirt, dripping invitees were completing the quarter-mile walk to attend the three o'clock ceremony. Their comments are not recorded.

Along with those of us who had waited in the rain to send Granny on her last journey were a couple whom none of us had ever seen before. "We hope you don't mind," said the man, "but we heard about the burial up at the visitor center."''

"We've known about Granny ever since we read about her in the *National Geographic,*" added his wife. "We couldn't miss this chance to be part of history."

And so this ordinary American couple, whose names (to my shame) we did not obtain, stood in the rain for more than half an hour to pay tribute to an equally anonymous woman who 367 years earlier had contributed her thread to the fabric of the nation. For me, that couple's presence meant more than the satisfaction of seeing Granny finally at rest.

If my claim for Granny's contribution appears overblown, consider the second coffin. It had been made as an exhibit for use in an archaeological museum which, even as we dripped, was under construction within the hill behind Wolstenholme Towne. Without the *National Geographic* article featuring Granny's death, it is unlikely that public interest would have been sufficient to keep the Martin's Hundred story alive. Instead, continuing visitation at the partially reconstructed sites and the frequently asked question "Where do we go to see the artifacts?" prompted Colonial Williamsburg to designate three million dollars of a Winthrop Rockefeller Charitable Trust grant to its answer. That, plus a three-quarter-million-dollar grant from the National Endowment for the Humanities, was enough to build the museum.

Few sites are as lucky. I had long contended that no archaeological project fulfills its public responsibility unless it has an educational end product, one that transcends an unpublished report and boxes of artifacts stored unseen and eventually forgotten in a university basement. Not all excavations, indeed, not *many* excavations, merit a museum to themselves, but few fail to generate either facts or artifacts that deserve to be put on public view—somewhere. But very few ever are.

The ideal, of course, is to preserve the site for public visitation, for that is the ultimate interpretive artifact. Alas, most historical sites lie in the path of progress and cannot be protected. Those fortunate enough to have been preserved as national or state parks (and few new ones have been so designated in recent years) may also sport a visitor center which, in addition to centering visitors, exhibits a selection of pertinent things. Rarely, if ever, are the exhibits treated as an integrated, educational prologue to the site visit. The museum for Martin's Hundred is designed to do precisely that. Through its artifacts, art, and language, it tells both the history of the site and the process of its discovery and interpretation. Knowledge gained from one display is augmented by another, until by the time the visitors emerge from the subterranean museum onto the site, they have seen and learned all that the archaeologists and historians have to show and teach them. That, at least, is the theory. The practice, of course, depends on anything from belligerent apathy to unfit feet.

Looking back across the years of excavation and, indeed, through the pages of this book, one is forever reminded of the frailty of archaeological reasoning and of the dangers of elevating what *might* have happened into what did. How wrong we would have been about the dating of Site B had we not found the 1631 dish and instead had accepted the conventional wisdom of the tobacco-pipe stem dating! What might we still be saying of Site H if Granny had been laid to rest in a grave rather than being left in a trash pit? When archaeo-anthropologists rashly apply the always debatable testimony from a mere handful of such sites to draw broad cultural conclusions, I cannot help wondering whether, by such uncritical yet thesis-biased use, our modest individual contributions may have done more harm than good.

At times of such glum introspection, theoretical comfort can be drawn from remembering that we had deliberately left several known sites unexcavated so that they might be available to future archaeologists whose advanced techniques and accumulated knowledge may enable them to extract levels of information far beyond our imagining. To that end, the sites found by Bill Henry's survey team in the winter of 1976–77 were explored no further. After the sampling described on pages 111–13 was completed, the tested features were sealed under thick black plastic and covered with four inches of loam. Triangulated coordinates taken from a carefully marked tree stump were placed in the record, and with that done we left the sites to the honeysuckle and to the ages. I confess to having enjoyed a moment of unbecoming smugness. We had resisted the urge to dig and had made a gift to archaeologists yet unborn.

The emotion was not only unworthy, it was dumb. And if you have not realized why, it is spelled out on page 112.

Placing one's surveying apples in the stump-basket of an already dead tree was monumentally shortsighted. I like to think that we had intended to return to reset the base marker in concrete, and maybe we had. But we didn't. In our defense, we could insist that although it was inevitable that the marker stump would eventually crumble away, everyone knew that the sites were there. Their information was on file. They were undeniably safe.

But people come and people go. They move to different jobs, they leave, and like me, they retire. Pretty soon there are new land managers with new goals and no knowledge of what pertinent information may lie deep in the archives. Thus it came to pass that in the winter of 1988–89 the screech of chain saws, the roar of bulldozers, and the thud of falling trees were loud in the woods. They had been leased for clear cut logging.

By the time a chance comment from a colleague in the landscape department alerted archaeologists to what was happening, Matilda Jones's gravestone lay smashed in the dirt, one site had been obliterated, and the tested seventeenth-century sites at Grice's Run had been rutted by heavy machinery, their protective plastic ripped up and the survey stump uprooted (Fig. 17–11). Mercifully, however, the clear-cutting that had turned several acres into something akin to the Somme in '17 had yet to reach the key sites; and once Colonial Williamsburg's management was informed of the danger, the work was stopped and the sites were saved.

17–11. The past's future can be brief when historic sites are "harvested" by loggers.

The moral to this tale has nothing to do with assigning blame; the lesson, instead, is one of warning—a warning that today's absolutes are tomorrow's maybes. In a world wherein nobody stays anywhere for any length of time, and wherein entrenched and seemingly invulnerable policies can disappear with the switch of a job title or a management planner, heritage watchdogs must never sleep.

Whereas thirty years ago—even a decade ago—much of Martin's Hundred's 20,000 and more acres were still in woods and farmland, by 1990 the price of land had become so attractive to owners and the acres so desirable to buyers that little remains beyond Colonial Williamsburg's protected holdings that is neither sold nor coveted. The same is true the length of James City County and to a greater and lesser extent up and down the James River from Richmond to the ocean. It may not be overstating the case to foretell that within thirty years (i.e., one generation of archaeologists) the last of Virginia's yet-to-be-excavated early seventeenth-century sites will be gone. One must fervently hope, therefore, that Granny's grave and the restored Wolstenholme Towne will survive amid the industrial parks, shopping centers, asphalt parking lots, and tract condos to remind caring and perhaps rain-soaked couples that once, many centuries ago, American history was made in dozens of places very much like Martin's Hundred.

While the first *Martin's Hundred* edition was on its way to the press, the discovery of a message from "Gonner" John Byshopp of Exeter hidden in Site A's window lead left us with a tantalizing question: Who was this John Byshopp? Now, as this new edition is halfway to the printer, a letter from Mark Charles Fissel, associate professor of history at Ball State University, offers a convincing answer. In January 1631/32 Charles I appointed one John Bishopp to be the royal "hand-gunmaker" (see Fissel, "The Identity of John Bishop, Gunner," *Journal of the Society for Army Historical Research* 68, no. 274 [London: National Army Museum, 1990]: 138–39). Although there is no evidence that King Charles's John Bishopp came from Exeter, it is not at all unlikely that at some time between 1625 and 1631 he moved to London where his skills would be better appreciated. Be that as it may, Professor Fissel has demonstrated that in archaeology the last word is rarely, if ever, written.

Notes

A Proclamation

1. Susan Myra Kingsbury, ed., *The Records of the Virginia Company of London* (Washington, D.C.: Library of Congress, 1906–1935), 4: 40. A warrant for keeping holy the 22nd of March. This work is hereafter referred to in the notes as *Kingsbury*. Here, and throughout, the original spelling is retained, except in those instances where abbreviating ciphers were used and where a "v" substituted for a "u." The printed date of 1622 refers to the Old Style calendar which, until 1751, began the new year on March 25. In the New Style, therefore, the date would read "the 4th day of March 1623."

Chapter 1

1. W. Duncan Lee, "The Renascence of Carter's Grove," *Architecture* (April 1933), reprint, n.p.
2. *Virginia Magazine of History and Biography* (Richmond, 1897), 5: 416. Will of Robert Carter of Lancaster County, Virginia.
3. *Ibid.*, p. 415.
4. Mary A. Stephenson, *Carter's Grove Plantation, A History* (Colonial Williamsburg, 1964), p. I, fn. I.

Chapter 2

1. Henry Chandlee Forman, *Jamestown and St. Mary's, Buried Cities of Romance* (Baltimore: The Johns Hopkins Press, 1938), pp. ix, 81, 82.
2. H. Summerfield Day, "Preliminary Archeological Report of Excavations at Jamestown, Virginia," July 1, 1935, p. 8. Ms. copy on file among U.S. National Park Service records at Jamestown.
3. John L. Cotter, *Archeological Excavations at Jamestown Colonial National Historical Park and Jamestown National Historic Site Virginia* (Washington, D.C.: U.S. De; partment of the Interior, 1958), Archeological Research Series Number Four, p. 163.

Chapter 3

1. Beatrix G.E. Hooke, "A Third Study of the English Skull with Special Reference to the Farringdon Street Crania," *Biometrika* (London, July 1926), 18 (Pts. 1 & 2): 1–16.
2. David Pietersz de Vries, "Short Historical and Journal Notes," *Collections of the New-York Historical Society,* 2nd Series (New York, 1857), 3: 35.
3. "Information Respecting Land in New Netherland," *Pennsylvania Archives,* 2nd Series (Philadelphia, 1876), 5: 182–3.
4. *Virginia Magazine of History and Biography* (Richmond, 1908), 4:31.

Chapter 4

1. *Kingsbury*, 1: 5.
2. Annie L. Jester, *Adventurers of Purse and Person, Virginia 1607–1625* (Richmond: First Families of Virginia, 1956), p. 43. This work is hereafter referred to in the notes as *Jester*.
3. *Kingsbury*, 3: 651. Letter to the Governor and Council in Virginia from the Virginia Company's Council in London, June 10, 1622.
4. *Kingsbury*, 3: 646. Letter as above.
5. *Kingsbury*, 3: 610. Commission to Capt. Ralph Hamor, April 15, 1622.
6. *Kingsbury*, 4: 41. Letter from Richard Frethorne to Mr. Bateman, March 5, 1623.
7. *Kingsbury*, 4: 556. List of titles and estates of land sent to England by Sir Francis Wyatt, May 1625. The obviously mistaken Martin's Hundred reference reads "Martins hundred Contayning as is alledged 800000: Acres: part planted."
8. H. R. McIlwaine, ed., *Minutes of the Council and General Court of Colonial Virginia*, 2nd edition (Richmond: Virginia State Library, 1979), pp. 132, 135–6. Court proceedings at James City, January 11–13, 1627. This work is hereafter referred to in the notes as *McIlwaine*.
9. *Kingsbury*, 2: 382. Minutes of a court held on April 25, 1623.
10. *Ibid.*
11. John Brand, *Observations on the Popular Antiquities of Great Britain*, ed. Sir Henry Ellis (London: Henry G. Bohn, 1849), 2: 284.
12. Howard M. Nixon, F.S.A., personal communication, Sept. 3, 1979.

Chapter 5

1. Nathaniel Bailey, *An Universal Etymological English Dictionary* (London, 1749), n.p.

Chapter 6

1. Virginia Land Office, *Patent Book*, No. 2, p. 362.
2. "Lord Sackville's Papers Respecting Virginia, 1615–1631," *The American Historical Review*, 27 (No. 3, April 1922): 504. Lord Treasurer's Warrant Respecting Arms, July 29, 1622.

Chapter 7

1. Myra Stanbury, *Batavia Catalogue* (Perth, W.A.: Western Australian Museum, n.d.), p. 23.
2. C. Willett Cunnington and Phillis Cunnington, *Handbook of English Costume in the Seventeenth Century* (London: Faber and Faber, 1963), p. 73.
3. *McIlwaine*, p. 194. Testimony before acting Governor John Pott, March 25, 1629.
4. *Ibid.*
5. *Ibid.*, p. 195.
6. *Jester*, p. 44.

Chapter 8

1. *Kingsbury*, 3: 309. A Declaration of the State of the Colony and Affaires in Virginia, June 22, 1620.
2. *Kingsbury*, 4: 283–84. Governor's proclamation, September 21, 1623.
3. *Jester*, p. 43.
4. Samuel Purchas, *Hakluytus Postumus, or Purchas His Pilgrimes, contayning a*

History of the World in Sea Voyages and Lande Travells by Englishmen and Others, Bk. 10 (London, 1625), p. 1753.

5. *Ibid.,* p. 1752.

6. *Ibid.,* p. 1753.

7. Ivor Noël Hume, "Survey Report on Excavations on Seventeenth-Century Sites at Carter's Grove, July–September 1977," Ms., p. 6.

8. *Acts of the Privy Council of England,* Colonial Series Vol. 1, 1613–1680 (London: H.M. Stationery Office, 1908), reprinted by Kraus Reprint Company (1966), p. 72. October 24, 1623.

9. Nathaniel Bailey, *An Universal Etymological English Dictionary* (London, 1749 edition), n.p.

10. *Jester,* p. 46.

11. *Ibid.,* p. 40.

12. *Kingsbury,* 3: 594–5. Martin's Hundred repatent, January 30, 1622.

Chapter 10

1. Stanbury Thompson, ed., *The Journal of John Gabriel Stedman 1744–1797* (London: The Mitre Press, 1962), p. 364.

2. Cynthia Gaskell Brown, ed., *Castle Street, The Pottery,* Plymouth Museum Archaeological Series, Number 1 (Plymouth: City Museum and Art Gallery, 1979), pp. 17, 59, and figs. 38–9.

3. Ian D. Eaves to author, personal communication.

4. Howard L. Blackmore, *British Military Firearms 1650–1850* (London: Herbert Jenkins, 1961), p. 17.

5. Jacob de Gheyn II, *The Exercise of Arms for Calivres, Muskettes and Pikes . . . &c.* (The Hague, 1607).

6. George B. Cheever, ed., *The Journal of the Pilgrims at Plymouth in New England in 1620* (New York: John Wiley, 1898), p. 40. First published in London in 1622.

7. John Smith, *Travels and Works of Captain John Smith,* ed. Edward Arbor, Pt. 2 (Edinburgh: John Grant, 1910), p. 608.

8. *Ibid.,* p. 609.

9. *Kingsbury,* 3: 262. A bill submitted by James Berblocke to John Ferrar listing purchases from Thomas Stevens on behalf of Smith's Hundred, February 25, 1619/20.

10. Nathaniel B. Shurtleff, ed., *Records of the Governor and Company of the Massachusetts Bay in New England,* Vol. 1, 1628–1641 (Boston: William White, 1853), p. 31.

11. Ivor Noël Hume, *Historical Archaeology* (New York: Alfred A. Knopf, 1969), pp. 159–60.

Chapter 11

1. Ivor Noël Hume, *Historical Archaeology* (New York: Alfred A. Knopf, 1969), p. 249.

2. *Ibid.,* p. 250.

3. Ralph Hamor, *A True Discourse of the Present State of Virginia* (Richmond: Virginia State Library, 1957), p. 28.

4. Lyon G. Tyler, *Narratives of Early Virginia, 1606–1625* (New York: Barnes and Noble, 1952 edition), p. 221. Letter from Diégo de Molina to Ambassador Don Alonzo de Velasco, May 28, 1613.

5. D. W. Prowse, *A History of Newfoundland* (London and New York: Macmillan and Co., 1895), p. 129.

6. John Smith, *Travels and Works of Captain John Smith,* ed. Edward Arbor, Pt. 2 (Edinburgh: John Grant, 1910), p. 608.

7. C. Wilson Peck, *English Copper, Tin and Bronze Coins in the British Museum 1558–1958* (London: The Trustees of of the British Museum, 1970), p. 26.

8. P. J. Seaby and Monica Bussell, *British Copper Coins and Their Values* (London: B. A. Seaby Ltd., 1969/70 edition), p. 13.

9. W. Noël Sainsbury, ed., *Calendar of State Papers, Colonial Series, 1574–1660* (London: Longman, Green, Longman, & Roberts, 1860), p. 239. Sir John Harvey to Secretary of State Sir Francis Windebank, June 26, 1636.

10. Fynes Moryson, *An Itinerary,* Bk. 3 (London, 1617), Chap. 3, p. 156. Quoted by David Beers Quinn, *The Elizabethans and the Irish* (Ithaca, N.Y.: Cornell University Press, 1966), p. 122.

11. Article of agreement between James Earl of Ormond and Edmond O'Maghea and Mortagh O'Knoghea, August 26, 1641. Bodleian Library, Oxford. Ms.Carte 176, ff. 170–71v.

12. Anthony Garvan, *Architecture and Town Planning in Colonial Connecticut* (New Haven: Yale University Press, 1951). John W. Reps, *Tidewater Towns, City Planning in Colonial Virginia and Maryland* (Williamsburg: Colonial Williamsburg Foundation, 1972).

13. Revised articles of the Ulster plantation (London: Robert Baker, Printer to the King, 1610), pp. 4–5. Bodleian Library, Lansdowne Ms. 159, ff. 219–21. Reproduced in Robert J. Hunter, *Education Facsimiles 161–180: Plantations in Ulster, c. 1600–41* (Belfast: Public Record Office of Northern Ireland, 1975), Facsimile 163.

14. Garvan, *op.cit.,* p. 36.

15. Sir Thomas Phillips, *Londonderry and the London Companies 1609–1629* (Belfast: H.M. Stationery Office, 1928), p. 156, pl. 19.

16. *Kingsbury,* 3: 551.

17. John Smith, *Travels and Works of Captain John Smith,* Pt. 1, ed. Edward Arbor (Edinburgh: John Grant, 1910), p. 377.

18. *Kingsbury,* 3: 551.

Chapter 12

1. *Kingsbury,* 3: 451. Sir George Yeardley to Sir Edwin Sandys, May 16, 1621, attachment regarding Sir Lawrence Hyde's servant, Richard Chelsey.

2. Anthony Garvan, *Architecture and Town Planning in Colonial Connecticut* (New Haven: Yale University Press, 1951), p. 36.

3. Philip Robinson, "Vernacular Housing in Ulster in the Seventeenth Century," *Ulster Folklife* (Ulster Folk and Transport Museum publication, 1979), 25: 20.

4. H. Arthur Bankoff and Frederick A. Winter, "A House-Burning in Serbia," *Archaeology,* 32(No.5, September–October, 1979): 8–14.

5. Warren M. Billings, ed., *The Old Dominion in the Seventeenth Century* (Chapel Hill: University of North Carolina Press, 1975), p. 164. York County Order Book, 1657–1662.

6. *Kingsbury,* 3: 451. Sir George Yeardley to Sir Edwin Sandys, May 16, 1621.

7. *Kingsbury,* 3: 594.

8. *Kingsbury,* 4: 41. Richard Frethorne to Mr. Bateman, March 5, 1623.

9. *Kingsbury,* 4: 58. Richard Frethorne to his parents, March 20, 1623.

10. *Kingsbury,* 4: 41. Richard Frethorne to Mr. Bateman, March 5, 1623.

Chapter 13

1. *Kingsbury*, 4:231. Notes taken from Letters which came from Virginia in the 'Abigail,'" June 19, 1623; Peter Arundle to Mr. Caning, March 25, 1623.

2. Arthur Richard Dufty, *European Armour in the Tower of London* (London: H.M. Stationery Office, 1968), p. 8.

3. "Lord Sackville's Papers Respecting Virginia, 1615–1631" *The American Historical Review*, 27 (No. 3, April 1922): 503–5. *Kingsbury*, 2: 96. Minutes of the Court of the Virginia Company of London, July 17, 1622.

4. *Jester*, p. 43.

5. *Ibid.*, pp. 43–44.

6. Jan Baart et al., *Opgravingen in Amsterdam* (Amsterdam, 1977), No. 287, pp. 190–191.

7. *Kingsbury*, 3:451. Sir George Yeardley to Sir Edwin Sandys, May 16, 1621.

8. British Museum manuscript collection, Harleian 2027, folio 319.

9. William L. Langer, ed., *The New Illustrated Encyclopedia of World History* (New York: Harry N. Abrams, 1975), 1:451. No picture source cited.

10. William Congreve, *The Way of the World,* Act 3, Scene 3.

11. Timothy Foote, *The World of Bruegel c. 1525–1569* (New York: Time-Life Books, 1968), p. 137.

12. Quoted by Donald I. Findlay to author, personal communication, August 12, 1980.

13. Peter Graham Jerreat, M.D., to author, personal communication, March 28, 1980.

14. *The Daily Telegraph* (London), November 27, 1979, p. 3.

15. *Kingsbury*, 3: 551. Edward Waterhouse's account, quoting a letter from Sir Francis Wyatt received in London at the end of May 1622.

16. W. P. Cumming et al., *The Discovery of North America* (London: Elek Books, 1971), p. 189, fig. 217.

17. C. Willett Cunnington and Phillis Cunnington, *Handbook of English Costume in the Seventeenth Century* (London: Faber and Faber, 1963), p. 117.

18. *The Diary of the Lady Anne Clifford,* introduction by V. Sackville-West (London: George H. Doran Company, 1923), p. 67.

19. Samuel V. Dunkell, M.D., personal communications, April 2 and April 20, 1981.

20. *Kingsbury*, 3:570. A "true list of the names of all those that were massacred by the treachery of the savages in Virginia, the 22 March last," 1622.

21. *Kingsbury*, 3:505. Virginia Council and Company to Governor and Council in Virginia, September 11, 1621.

22. *Kingsbury*, 4:82. Captain John Bargrave's charges against Sir Thomas Smyth, with answers by Sir Nathaniel Rich, April 1623.

23. *Kingsbury*, 4:238. Christopher Best to Jo: Woodall, April 1, 1623.

24. Moklós Mojzer, *Dutch Genre Paintings* (Budapest: Corvina Press, 1967), pl. 1, n.p.

Chapter 14

1. Pieter Geyl, *The Netherlands in the Seventeenth Century 1609–1648* (New York: Barnes and Noble, Inc., 1961), p. 53.

2. Ron White, "Archeologists' Find May Shed Light on Va. 'Dark Ages,'" *The Washington Post,* May 23, 1979, p. B7.

Appendix:
Artifact Dimensions

Rather than cluttering the illustrations with unsightly scales whose placement rarely ensures accurate interpretation, or encumbering the captions with measurements of no interest to the general reader, I have elected to list a single measurement for one item in each of those pictures wherein artifacts are illustrated. The measurements are given in inches rather than in centimeters, for it was in inches that their original makers and owners measured them.

1–2. Width: 3 1/2 inches
1–10. Surviving diameter: 3/4 inch
1–11. Base width: 3 3/4 inches
2–1. Bevor length, ear to chin:
  8 3/4 inches
3–4. Height: 11 3/16 inches
3–5. Height 8 1/4 inches
3–10. Fragment height: 2 5/8 inches
3–11. Surviving length: 21 1/4 inches
3–12. Height: 7 13/16 inches
3–13. Height: 4 15/16 inches
3–15. Knife length: 22 1/16 inches
3–18. Point length: 1 3/8 inches
5–1. Center hook length: 1 1/4 inches
5–6. Height: 5 3/4 inches
5–8. Intact bottle height: 11 1/8 inches
5–9. Plate diameter: 8 7/16 inches
5–10. Alembic height: 13 3/16 inches
5–13. Pipkin height: 7 1/16 inches
6–1. Diameter: 16 1/4 inches
6–2. Guard height: 5 inches
6–3. Bottom right bowl length:
  1 1/4 inches
6–4. Top plate length: 2 5/8 inches
6–5. Width: 7 3/16 inches
6–6. Diameter: 10 7/8 inches
7–1. Left width: 2 1/16; Right width:
  2 3/4 inches
7–4. Height: 13 9/16 inches

8–2. Height: 6 9/16 inches
8–3. Length: 6 3/16 inches
8–6. Barrel length: 3 1/2 inches
8–8. Height: 4 3/16 inches
8–11. Height: 16 1/2 inches
9–1. Approximate combined height:
  7 7/16 inches
9–2. Length of corner fragment:
  7 1/2 inches
9–5. Height: 13 3/8 inches
10–3. Center seal diameter: 13/16 inch
10–6. Rim diameter; 7 1/8 inch
10–8. Length: 18 5/8 inches
10–10. Height of right helmet:
  11 inches
10–12. Length: 3 7/8 inches
11–5. Surviving diameter: 7/16 inch
11–6. Height: 26 3/8 inches
13–3. Width: 12 1/4 inches
13–5. Width of top left plate:
  1 1/2 inches
13–6. Length: 2 3/16 inches
13–9. Surviving length of key:
  2 7/16 inches
13–15. Length of top hook: 1 1/2 inches
13–16. Matrix diameter; 1/2 inch
14–1. Held sherd length: 1 3/8 inches
14–9. Average diameter: 3/8 inch
14–11. Base diameter: 4 1/8 inches

Bibliography

Bankoff, H. Arthur, and Frederick A. Winter. "A House-Burning in Serbia." *Archaeology* 32 (No.5, September–October 1979): 8–14.

Billings, Warren M., ed. *The Old Dominion in the Seventeenth Century.* Chapel Hill: University of North Carolina Press, 1975.

Blackmore, Howard L. *British Military Firearms 1650–1850.* London: Herbert Jenkins, 1961.

Cheever, George B., ed. *The Journal of the Pilgrims at Plymouth in New England in 1620.* New York: John Wiley, 1898.

Cotter, John L. *Archeological Excavations at Jamestown Colonial National Historical Park and Jamestown National Historic Site Virginia.* Washington D.C.: United States Department of the Interior, 1958.

Cuming, W. P., R. A. Skelton and D. B. Quinn. *The Discovery of North America.* London: Elek Books, 1971.

Cunnington, C. Willett and Phillis Cunnington. *Handbook of English Costume in the Seventeenth Century.* London: Faber and Faber, 1963.

Dufty, Arthur Richard. *European Armour in the Tower of London.* London: Her Majesty's Stationery Office, 1968.

Forman, Henry Chandlee. *Jamestown and St. Mary's, Buried Cities of Romance.* Baltimore: The Johns Hopkins Press, 1938.

Garvan, Anthony. *Architecture and Town Planning in Colonial Connecticut.* New Haven: Yale University Press, 1951.

Geyl, Pieter. *The Netherlands in the Seventeenth Century 1609–1648.* New York: Barnes and Noble, Inc., 1961.

Hamor, Ralph. *A True Discourse of the Present State of Virginia.* Richmond: Virginia State Library, 1957.

Hunter, Robert J. *Education Facsimiles 161–180: Plantations in Ulster c. 1600–41.* Belfast: Public Record Office of Northern Ireland, 1975.

Jester, Annie L. *Adventurers of Purse and Person, Virginia 1607–1625.* Richmond: First Families of Virginia, 1964.

Kingsbury, Susan Myra, ed. *The Records of the Virginia Company of London.* 4 Vols. Washington D.C.: Library of Congress, 1906, 1933, 1935.

Lee, W. Duncan "The Renascence of Carter's Grove," *Architecture,* April 1933. Reprint, n.p.

McIlwaine, H.R., ed. *Minutes of the Council and General Court of Colonial Virginia.* 2nd edition. Richmond: Virginia State Library, 1979.

Morton, Richard L. *Colonial Virginia.* 2 Vols. Chapel Hill, N.C.: North Carolina Press, 1960.

Noël Hume, Audrey. "Clay Tobacco Pipes Excavated at Martin's Hundred, Virginia, 1976–1978." *The Archaeology of the Clay Tobacco Pipe.* British Archaeological Reports (1979): 3–36.

Noël Hume, Ivor: *Historical Archaeology.* New York: Alfred A. Knopf, 1969.

Nugent, Nell Marion. *Cavaliers and Pioneers, Abstracts of Virginia Land Patents and Grants 1623–1666.* Vol. 1. Baltimore: Genealogical Publishing Co., 1974. Originally published Richmond, 1934.

Peck, G. Wilson. *English Copper, Tin and Bronze Coins in the British Museum 1558–1958.* London: The Trustees of the British Museum, 1970.

Peterson, Harold L. *Arms and Armor in Colonial America.* New York: Bramhill House, 1956.

Phillips, Sir Thomas. *Londonderry and the London Companies 1609–1629.* Belfast: His Majesty's Stationery Office, 1928.

Prowse, D. W. *A History of Newfoundland.* London and New York: Macmillan and Co., 1895.

Purchas, Samuel. *Hakluytus Postumus, or Purchas His Pilgrimes, contayning a History of the World in Sea Voyages and Lande Travells by Englishmen and Others.* London, 1625.

Quinn, David Beers. *The Elizabethans and the Irish.* Ithaca, N.Y.: Cornell University Press, 1966.

Robinson, Philip. "Vernacular Housing in Ulster in the Seventeenth Century." *Ulster Folklife* 25 (1979): 1–28.

Reps, John W. *Tidewater Towns, City Planning in Colonial Virginia and Maryland.* Williamsburg, Va.: Colonial Williamsburg Foundation, 1972.

Sainsbury, W. Noël, ed. *Calendar of State Papers, Colonial Series, 1574–1660.* London: Longman, Green, Longman, & Roberts, 1860.

Smith, John. *Travels and Works of Captain John Smith,* ed. Edward Arbor. Edinburgh: John Grant, 1910.

Stephenson, Mary A. *Carter's Grove Plantation, A History.* Williamsburg, Va.: Colonial Williamsburg, 1964.

Tyler, Lyon G. *The Cradle of the Republic, Jamestown and James River.* Richmond: The Hermitage Press, 1906.

Index

Illustration Sources

The author gratefully acknowledges the following for their
kind permission to reproduce photographs and other illustrations.

A Note On The Type

The text of this book was set in a film rendering of
Garamond, a type first cut by Claude Garamond
(1510–1561). Garamond was a pupil of Geoffroy Troy and
is believed to have based his letters on Venetian models,
although he introduced a number of important differences.
It is to him we owe the letter that we know as "old style."
He gave to his type a certain elegance and a
feeling of movement that won for him an immediate
reputation and the patronage of Francis I. of France.

Designed by Al Chiang